Ten Problems in Christian Thought and Belief

A Minister-Turned-Atheist Shows Why You Should Ditch the Faith

David Madison

Tellectual Press
tellectual.com

Tellectual Press

tellectual.com

Valley, WA

Print ISBN: 978-1-942897-12-5

Tellectual Press is an imprint of Tellectual LLC.

Many thanks to Bruce Gerencser for his Foreword, and to Hector Avalos, Linda LaScola, and David Mills for their kind words about the book.

Cover design by Michael Trollan, adapted by Edwin A. Suominen. Pictured is *The Incredulity of Saint Thomas* by Caravaggio (1571-1610).

Author photo by Andrea Reese.

Unless otherwise indicated, Scripture quotations are from the NRSV: New Revised Standard Version Bible, copyright 1989, Division of Christian Education of the National Council of the Churches of Christ in the United States of America. Used by permission. All rights reserved.

For the RSV: Revised Standard Version of the Bible, Apocrypha, copyright 1957; The Third and Fourth Books of the Maccabees and Psalm 151, copyright 1977 by the Division of Christian Education of the National Council of the Churches of Christ in the United States of America. Used by permission. All rights reserved.

For the NASB: Scripture quotations taken from the New American Standard Bible® (NASB), Copyright © 1960, 1962, 1963, 1968, 1971, 1972, 1973, 1975, 1977, 1995 by The Lockman Foundation Used by permission. www.Lockman.org.

In some Scripture quotations, paragraph breaks have been inserted for clarity of dialogue or lyrical formatting has been added.

Table of Contents

To my husband of 38 years,
David Thomas Pandozzi,
who is the wind beneath my wings.

"Paris est toujours une bonne idée."
–Sabrina Fairchild, *Sabrina*

"We'll always have Paris."
–Rick Blaine, *Casablanca*

Foreword

by Bruce Gerencser

I WAS BORN AND RAISED in the Evangelical Christian church. At the age of fifteen, I made a public profession of faith in Jesus and two weeks later informed my Baptist church that I believed God was calling me to preach. In the mid-1970s, I attended a small Independent Fundamentalist Baptist Bible college. It was there I met my beautiful wife, and we hand-in-hand spent the next twenty-five years pastoring Evangelical churches in Ohio, Texas, and Michigan.

Armed with certainty, I believed God had called me to evangelize the world and win as many souls as possible for Jesus. I preached over four thousand sermons from an ancient book I believed was the inspired, inerrant, infallible Word of God. Hundreds of people were converted through my preaching.

Yet, today, I am a card-carrying atheist who spends his days examining and critiquing Evangelical beliefs and practices. Those who once called me Pastor Bruce find it difficult to accept that I am now playing for the A-team. Concerned former parishioners continue to ask me, "Why?" The *why* is actually quite simple. I came to understand that the claims Evangelicals make for the Bible and Christianity are not true. I tried to hang on to some sort of nominal Christian faith, but in the end, I concluded that a rational argument could not be made for the existence of Gods– particularly the God of the Christian Bible. In November of 2008, I attended church for the last time. From that moment forward, I have been an enemy of Christianity.

Christianity is a big tent. I belonged to its Evangelical wing, whereas David Madison belonged to what we Evangelicals derisively considered the liberal, apostate wing of Christianity. David's theological training and voracious reading habit exposed him to evidence that led him to conclude that Christian orthodoxy could not be intellectually or rationally sustained. Despite increasing doubts about the veracity of Christianity, David remained in the ministry. He would have been a perfect candidate for the Clergy Project had it existed in the 1970s. Instead, he attempted to balance his increasing doubts with the responsibilities of being a parish minister. I can only imagine how difficult it must have been to stand before congregants preaching the unsearchable riches of Jesus Christ while believing, at the same time, that those riches were as fake as a Zirconium diamond.

If David Madison and I had met in the 1970s, I suspect that I would have branded him an apostate and shaken the dust off my feet, never to be in his company again. In the 1980s and 1990s, I pastored an Independent Fundamentalist Baptist church in the hills of Southeast Ohio. One day, I received a letter from the head of the local ministerial association inviting me to its monthly meeting. I tersely replied and let them know that I would never join their group. And besides, they met at a local restaurant that served alcohol. How dare they meet in a place that serves the devil's brew! In response to my letter, the local Lutheran minister sent me a kind letter, reminding me that even Jesus ate with sinners! As I read David's story, I couldn't help but smile and think that he could have been that Lutheran minister.

Despite wildly different religious, theological, and social experiences, David Madison and I now find ourselves part of an exclusive club made up of men and women who were once pastors and church leaders and who are now atheists. Madison is older than I am by a decade or so, but both of us are now entering the home stretch for this race we call life. Knowing that the only thing that awaits us after death is a six-foot hole in the ground or the fire of a crematorium, Madison and I spend our days making a case for atheism, secularism, and humanism. Each of us runs in his own lane. My upbringing, education, and ministerial experiences are vastly different from his, yet we are both on the same track running towards the finish line. Both of us have stories to tell, and with what strength and breath we have left, we intend to promote a worldview *sans* God.

In his Introduction, here's how David answers the question about whether there is a need for yet another atheist book by yet another former Christian pastor or theologian:

> We keep writing and speaking because—well, because we each have something to say *in our own way*. The next atheist author could be a perfect match—the very voice, just the right message—for folks who are at the tipping point, who won't take much nudging to walk away from Christian silliness.

The more people tell their deconversion stories, the more likely it is that such stories will find a hearing. The Internet, along with affordable book publishing, gives atheists a golden opportunity to shout their stories from the rooftops. No longer is the public space a monotone cacophony of religious voices. Christian preachers and theologians no longer have the cultural stage to themselves. An increasing number of vocal ex-Christians are entering the public sphere, ready and willing to play an apostate David up against a Christian Goliath, to borrow a metaphor from the Bible story. David Madison is one such David.

He puts his doctoral-level theological training to good use as he challenges cherished Christian beliefs. Starting with the problem "Evil and Suffering," he works his way through ten challenges to Christian belief. Using personal anecdotes, along with astute—dare I say *unassailable*—intellectual arguments, he sets fire to Christian orthodoxy and burns it to the ground. Much like Bart Ehrman and his books on the text of New Testament, Madison presents arguments which, if believed, must, at the very least, require readers to abandon organized Western Christianity.

While some readers might be able to fashion some sort of non-involved deistic God out of the ashes, the only way for them to hang on to any semblance of orthodoxy is to choose, for whatever reason, to live with massive levels of cognitive dissonance. Such readers remind me of a ministerial colleague of mine who, when confronted by me with numerous errors in the King James Bible, replied, "I don't care if you can show me errors in the Bible. By faith, I am going to believe that the Bible is the perfect Word of God." People such as that colleague will likely not be swayed by *Ten Tough Problems in Christian Thought and Belief*, but others, those who harbor doubts and questions will certainly find answers to their uncertainty.

Some readers might be put off by Madison's snark and comedic storytelling, but I see his gleeful interludes much the same way as I see preachers and their sermon illustrations. Let's face it, theology without a bit of levity is boring, and David does a wonderful job breathing life into a critique of the old faith once delivered to the saints. Diehard Evangelicals will likely not appreciate his snarkiness, but I suspect most other readers will enjoy the way he weaves his life experiences in and out of his arguments against Christianity.

While David doesn't necessarily make any new arguments against Christian belief, he does provide a new voice from the liberal end of Christianity, one that is woefully underrepresented today. Most books on the atheist shelf are written by authors from conservative or Evangelical backgrounds. Liberal and Progressive Christians—who often have a hard time understanding Evangelical craziness—will be forced to wrestle with arguments from one of their own. And *Ten Tough Problems in Christian Thought and Belief* is not just for mainline Christians.

Madison writes about theological and textual problems that are common knowledge among seminary-trained clergy. They know that what most parishioners believe about Christianity and the Bible is not true. These facts remain hidden out of fear of job loss or causing church unrest. Sunday after Sunday, millions of people file into America's 300,000 Christian churches, hoping to be inspired and blessed. Above all, these worshipers want to know that what they believe is true. While many Evangelical pastors are as ignorant as a grade-school-educated hillbillies, others know that Evangelicalism is a house built on sand. Kick out the support beams of Biblical inerrancy and the house will come tumbling down. Left in a heap of construction debris lie unsupportable historical narratives, theological contradictions, and outright absurdities.

It is for this reason that *Ten Tough Problems in Christian Thought and Belief* should be widely read by Evangelicals. I envision numbers of fuming Evangelicals lining up at the doors of pastors' studies once they have finished it, wanting to know why they have never been told about the theological issues raised in Madison's book. No longer will claims of "faith-it" suffice. The proverbial horse is out of the barn, and he ain't coming back.

In many ways, we are still in the infancy of the atheist movement. Standing on ground tilled by intellectual giants such as Robert Ingersoll and Henry Mencken, atheists such as Madison and I have the privilege and honor of playing a small part in an ever-growing post-God world.

Fifty years ago, *Time* magazine asked the question, *Is God Dead?* In 1963, Madalyn Murray O'Hair successfully challenged the constitutionality of Bible reading in public schools. In an 8-1 ruling, the U.S. Supreme Court ruled that school-sponsored Bible readings in public schools were unconstitutional. In 1962, the Supreme Court ruled 6-1 that public school prayers were a violation of the U.S. Constitution and the Establishment clause of the first amendment. These two monumental court decisions gave birth to the modern atheist movement in America. For the first time, atheists and non-Christians were successful in challenging the Christian status quo. A decade later, the Supreme Court, in its 7-2 *Roe v. Wade* decision would legalize abortion. Christians, alarmed by what they believed were frontal assaults on Christianity, established groups such as The Moral Majority, the American Family Association, and Focus on the Family. Atheists and agnostics banded together, establishing American Atheists and the Freedom From Religion Foundation.

Fast forward to 2016, and the number of Americans who are no longer a part of a religious sect is at an all-time high. These unbelievers have been labeled *Nones*–those who are atheists, agnostics, humanists, or are indifferent to organized religion. Among Millennials–those born between roughly 1982-2004–one in three people consider themselves Nones. The twenty-first century has also brought to the forefront bestselling books by atheist writers such as Richard Dawkins, Sam Harris, Daniel Dennett, and Christopher Hitchens. Evangelical-turned-atheist authors such as Bart Ehrman, Robert M. Price, and John Loftus have penned books attacking the very foundation of Christianity: the authority of the Bible.

God still exists in countless human expressions of faith, but he is showing signs of old age. The advent of the Internet, for the first time, has allowed non-Christian voices a forum to tell their stories and present arguments against the theological, cultural, and sociological claims of Christianity. Former pastors, myself included, now use their theological training to systematically dismantle cherished Christian beliefs. Countless doubting Thomases frequent atheist websites, often finding answers to the questions and uncertainties that have plagued them for years.

In 2011, the Clergy Project was established to help clerics who were atheists or agnostics extricate themselves from the ministry. As of today, the Clergy Project has over 700 members, many of whom are still pastors and priests. Having sent numerous prospective candidates to the Clergy Project, I can say with great certainty that an increasing number of clergy are having serious doubts about Christian beliefs and practices. Currently, I correspond with six pastors and church leaders who are still actively involved in Evangelical ministry. While not all of these doubters are atheists, all of them have serious doubts about the existence of the Christian God.

I doubt that either David Madison or I will witness the death of God, but we can hope we will live long enough to see Christianity's iron grip removed from its hold on American society. Perhaps we may even dare to hope that future generations will come to love curiosity, scientific inquiry, and reason, driving a stake into the heart of religious faux-certainty and ignorance. While I suspect there will always be people who will need to worship something or someone, I do think there is coming a day when Christianity is driven to the backwaters of America, found only in the homes of those who think their God wrote the English Bible and the U.S. Constitution, and Duck Dynasty is must-see T.V. That David Madison's book will prove to be helpful in slaying the Christian Goliath I have no doubt.

I heartily recommend *Ten Tough Problems in Christian Thought and Belief* to atheists and Christians alike. Atheists will find Madison's book an excellent, well-argued counter-apologetic. Christians, however, will find much to keep them up at night. Here's to sleepless nights, until a new day dawns with Americans putting a premium on skepticism, reason, and humanism. When that day arrives, American Christianity can finally be relegated to the dustbin of human history.

–Bruce Gerencser
August 1, 2016

Prologue

> The thoughts of man, in order to be of any real worth, must be free. Under the influence of fear the brain is paralyzed, and instead of bravely solving a problem for itself, tremblingly adopts the solution of another.
>
> —Robert Green Ingersoll, *Lecture on Gods*

My Journey Into, Through and Out of Faith

ON THE NORTHERN Indiana prairie where I was raised in the 1940s and 1950s, two religions commanded the loyalty of the locals: basketball and conservative Christianity—and in that order. The energy and devotion lavished on basketball far outpaced unflustered adherence to the obligations of faith. No one would have *said* that basketball was more important, but the imbalance of emotional investment was obvious. Even today, a drive through Hoosier suburbia reveals this priority. In almost every driveway there is a basketball backboard and hoop. Future archaeologists will be convinced that these were the implements of the dominant cult.

When I was growing up and coming of age, I had zero interest in basketball. I did run the popcorn machine at the basketball games, but the closest I came to playing the game was in high school gym class. I resented this enforced athleticism, and protested by simply standing at one corner of the court while everyone else ran back and forth. A basketball is a hard object, and I was alarmed to have one thrown at me, being a 90-pound weakling. I even detested the sounds: the squeaking of shoes on the floor and the awful *twang* of the ball hitting it.

The runner-up cult, however, was the one for me.

A Kinder, Gentler Approach

Christianity received the full measure of my devotion, largely under the influence of my mother. My oldest brother once said of her, long after we had both walked away from Christianity, that she was the most Christian woman he had ever known. By this he meant that she was guided by compassion and generosity. She really did try to live her faith. When we were growing up, giving children "a faith to live by" was considered an element of good parenting, and my mother was equal to the task.

I don't say this uncharitably, because I was not subjected to a hard-nosed fundamentalist version of Christianity. I recall no emphasis on guilt, damnation, and hell. There was no trauma in my mother's version of the faith. Nor was there anything cloying about it.

A young friend of mine who was raised in an evangelical family in Tennessee says that a common question that family and friends ask each other is, "How is your walk with the Lord going today?" The companionship of the Lord, it seems, is felt throughout every waking hour, and many people excel at this "God is your pal" brand of Christianity. I never once heard my mother ask anyone the "walk with the Lord" question. Such smarmy piety was alien to me, even though religion was part of the fabric of our life with mandatory Sunday church attendance, grace at meals, and Bible reading. My mother and I read the Bible together.

The Billy Graham Crusades were on TV in my teen years, but my mother found him irritating. She had no use for his theatrics, waving the Bible above his head and coaxing tearful conversions to Christ from his listeners. She disdained emotionally charged religion and found "getting carried away with it" unseemly. My mother prayed, she studied the Bible more deeply than most laypeople do, and if she ever doubted the existence of God, I saw no hint of it. Her faith ran deep, and she got on with life, mindful that God was *there* and mattered. But she was not checking in with the Lord on an hourly basis.

My mother was no fundamentalist, though it's a mystery to me how she avoided that, having been born in Terre Haute, Indiana in 1905. She believed in evolution and in a non-literal reading of the Bible. She could say of this or that in the Bible, "Well, you can't take that literally." She had a good laugh when I asked if Hell was at the fiery center of the earth.

Immersion in Books

My mother never attended college, but she probably attained the equivalent of a degree by being a voracious reader, until Alzheimer's wiped her memory clean. She loved biography and history, and assumed that the Bible should be studied as well as read. When I was in high school—and this is crucial to my story—she purchased *The Interpreter's Bible*. This was a hefty, 12-volume commentary on the entire Bible, which included, in adjoining columns, the traditional King James translation (1611) and the recently released Revised Standard Version (1947 & 1952). On every page, accompanying these texts, were two other sections aimed at explaining the texts: the exegesis and the exposition. These books were for ministers, for those who were seriously into Bible study.

The **exposition** was usually written by preachers, who explained the spiritual lessons of every Bible chapter. More often than not, these lessons were unctuous drivel, and even at that early age I could spot at least some of the drivel. The **exegesis**, however, had substance. This was the science, the research-based analysis of the texts. It was written by scholars and critical issues were tackled: where the texts came from, who wrote them, the meaning of words in the original Hebrew and Greek. It discussed translation problems, contexts and challenges. For the most part, *The Interpreter's Bible* was the product of liberal Protestant scholarship, which meant that it was not fundamentalist propaganda about the Bible. The Bible's flaws, fault lines and contradictions were acknowledged and analyzed candidly, usually without resort to *ad hoc* arguments to prop up the Bible as God's infallible word.

Mother was the only person in town other than the pastor, possibly, who owned *The Interpreter's Bible*. Not long after a new pastor was appointed to our church, mother asked him a question about something she had read in the commentary. He was surprised: "*You have The Interpreter's Bible?*"

Those twelve volumes were at my disposal. I was an enthusiastic teenage Christian, gifted with mother's curiosity, love of reading, and thirst for knowledge. I was drawn to the exegesis, and had no trouble cozying up to liberal Protestant scholarship and adopting a critical attitude toward the Bible. And since my father's first career had been teaching high school science, we grew up with respect for science; questioning evolution would have been considered eccentric. At that point, belief in God was fairly secure; there may have been a few cracks in my faith, but not many. When I went off to college I was a liberal Christian soldier. Well, I was a priggish liberal. I believed fervently, as my mother did, that swearing, smoking, drinking and sex (outside of marriage) were *verboten*.

Living Under the Canopy of Stars

In my teenage years, I developed a strong interest in another of God's handiworks, if you count the Bible as one. Living on the prairie, some 80 miles south of Chicago, with the land completely flat to the horizon in all directions and minimal light pollution, our view of the night sky was spectacular. My curiosity kicked in here too: What is out there? How does it all relate to God? Late at night I would lie on the grass, looking up at the sky with binoculars. My parents bought me a telescope, about the size of a baseball bat, large enough to require a tripod mount. The rotation of the Earth was a dramatic reality as I had to move the telescope to keep up with a Moon that advanced steadily out of view. My triumph was locating Saturn, and my mother's response, when she peered through the eyepiece, was to marvel at God's beautiful creation. But even then I may have had suspicions.

About that time I wrote a letter to the science columnist for the *Chicago Tribune*, curious about God and science. Did they go together? I received a one-sentence response, "I am a believer," which came as a relief. Maybe I needed reassurance.

During my first year of college, I took an astronomy course. Alas, one of my weakest academic subjects had always been math, and I soon discovered that mathematics was a core competency for astronomers. Any hopes I might have had for an astronomy career came to an end. But my fascination with the night sky would come back later to haunt me, or at least my theology, as the years went by. It was less than twenty years before my birth that Edwin Hubble had discovered that the universe is expanding, and that the Milky Way is not the entire universe, that there are countless other galaxies. That discovery, which I found out about only later, would have profound impact on my assessment of theology and its claims to legitimacy.

An Undergraduate Scholar

Although most of the 26 kids in my high school class didn't go on to higher education, there was no question that I was destined for college. My father had established the family tradition. He was born in 1904 on a farm in Clay County, Indiana and didn't set foot outside of the county until he went away to college. Yet somehow he had envisioned a life beyond farming, as had his farmer father, who was willing to loan money for college to his sons. My father was the only one who took him up on the offer, studying to become a schoolteacher and later a doctor.

For many years, he was a family practitioner in a small town on the prairie. When I was born, he'd been a doctor for several years already. His charge was $2.00 for a visit to his office and $5.00 when he made a house call in the country. Since the closest hospital for most of my youth was 45 miles away, his office served as the town's emergency room.

My two older brothers had gone to Bloomington after high school, and there was never any doubt that I would follow. *The Interpreter's Bible* went with me to my college dorm room, and I established myself as the resident Christian enthusiast, but again with a twist. While I was a prude when it came to swearing, smoking, drinking and sex (that was out of the question completely, for reasons that I will discuss later), I never was an obnoxious evangelical asking people if they had been saved, or if they knew Jesus. It would never have occurred to me to ask anyone, "How is your walk with the Lord going today?" My approach to Christianity was more cerebral. Having been schooled in religion by my mother, and after soaking up the scholarship of *The Interpreter's Bible*, I knew better than to take the Bible literally or to be swayed by religious sentimentality.

Oddly enough, in retrospect, it was only when I arrived at college that I came up against unbending fundamentalists, those who were dead serious that the Bible had to be taken as God's truth, word for word. And they were well represented and well organized on campus. The Intervarsity Christian Fellowship, which, sad to say, is alive and thriving to this day, attracted the Bible fanatics who had their heels dug in against a liberal arts education. They studied the Bible fervently to prove that it was infallible. There could not be even one error.

It was a bit of a stunner for me that people my age could be so misguided and trapped in backward thinking."Surely, once they study the Bible the right way," I thought, "they'll grow out of it." I soon discovered that my assumption was naïve. After just a few encounters, I realized that there was no point in discussing the Bible with these folks. Present-day atheist activist Al Stefanelli has said that arguing with a Christian is "like trying to teach calculus to a toaster." There is no way to penetrate their worldview and the fear of an indifferent universe that lurks behind it.

I was committed to studying the Bible because I was genuinely curious about how it had been cobbled together, and how it is then possible to glean God's message from its imperfect pages. And surely, if anywhere, God's message should reside in the words of Jesus. The hunt had been on for more than a century to retrieve the *real* words of Jesus from all of the words attributed to him in the Gospels. In liberal Protestant scholarship, it just wouldn't do to accept the simplistic view that all of the words of Jesus in the gospels are authentic. Scholars, even devout ones, were honest enough to admit that it was a real challenge to isolate the words that could realistically be traced back to Jesus.

Not the Normal Teenage Preoccupation

Now bear with me as we detour briefly to demonstrate just how much I qualified as a teenage nerd, if you have not figured that out already. This challenge, to identify the genuine remembrances of Jesus, appealed to me. In *The Interpreter's Bible*, I'd read about the Four-Document Hypothesis, which scholars used as a template to understand the creation of the first three gospels. Liberal Protestant scholars placed very little stock on any literal understanding that the Bible was "inspired."

If you believe that an angel sat next to Matthew, for example, and whispered the gospel in his ear as he wrote (per Rembrandt's somber rendering of the scene), all of the challenge is taken from Bible scholarship. There's nothing left to study if scripture was created by dictation. If you take the texts at face value, you are on a make-believe adventure, ignoring the obvious problems that exist. Curiosity has no foothold to stand on. I found it much more interesting to look at gospels as a puzzle to be solved.

Sorry, not how it happened.[1]

Nerd that I was, I wanted to get a good grasp of the Four-Document Hypothesis, which can be stated simply: Mark wrote his gospel first (document one), which was copied by Matthew and Luke, who in turn both used a hypothetical document commonly known as **Q** (from the German word for "source," *Quelle*, and hypothetical because it has never been found). Because so many of the sayings of Jesus in Matthew and Luke are almost identical, they must have copied from the **Q** source (document two). And both Matthew and Luke each have stories that are found nowhere else, meaning that they each had a source as well (documents three and four). Hence, the four-document hypothesis.[2]

John's gospel doesn't figure in this formula because he borrowed very little verbatim from the first three gospels. He seems to have looked at them from afar, with contempt. His goal was to set the record straight by conjuring a strikingly different hero. What he ended up with, though, was an alarmingly egomaniacal Jesus.

Now, I wasn't obsessed with bringing people to Jesus, but I was obsessed with learning how the Bible had been created, and how to find nuggets of history. This was clever detective work, supposedly, digging for the real Jesus, but it's turned out to be a fool's errand. Jesus studies have proliferated in recent decades, and dozens of versions of "the real Jesus" have been proposed, because it is virtually impossible to determine which texts are authentic. Scholars are inescapably influenced by their own biases and hunches. But the four-document hypothesis had been a useful thought experiment to explain how the gospels are layered. I posted a diagram of it on the dormitory bulletin board. What further proof is needed that I was a nerd? Within a day or two it got torn down.

I attended church in Bloomington, after allowing myself a few months of remaining in bed on Sunday mornings. I became active in the Wesley Foundation for

Methodist students, where I met the woman who would become my wife, the daughter of Methodist missionaries. Although Indiana University was a secular state institution, there was a department of religious studies, and I fell under the spell of an especially charismatic professor who helped me get more deeply into liberal Protestant biblical scholarship.[3] Although I rubbed shoulders with secular and non-believing students in the dormitory, I crafted a Christian support network and remained an outspoken champion of the liberal faith.

My First Real Stab at Scholarship

Although my major was Political Science (sad to say, being a son of Indiana, I was an over-the-top Republican at the time), the possibility of studying the Bible and teaching it in academia emerged as a career possibility. During my senior year, I demonstrated that I had the makings of a biblical scholar.

One of the topics that had long held my fascination was the virgin birth of Jesus. For a long time I had sensed that religion would always lose when it attempts to knock heads with science, so the virgin birth was off the grid in terms of credibility. It just wasn't worth defending. It even failed theologically, despite fervent Catholic and Evangelical attachment to it. (Liberal Protestant theology has long conceded its mythic antecedents and irrelevance.)

My keen interest probably had deeper roots. I was raised in an intensely Protestant environment, and this identity was felt even more keenly because, in my small town in northern Indiana (Kentland, population 1,600), there was Catholic-Protestant rivalry. There were three Protestant con-gregations in town, and one Catholic parish. Interfaith marriages were usually considered a catastrophe by the families involved, and nothing irked Protestants more than the dreaded pledge that children of such marriages had to be raised Catholic. One Protestant woman refused to attend her niece's wedding at the Catholic church because she could not bring herself to "set foot in that heathen temple."

The author, a lifetime ago.

People could remain very good friends across the religious divide, but there were deep divisions about what was important to believe. If Protestants were suspicious about anything, it was what we regarded as the exaggerated devotion to Mary. So perhaps it was my anti-Catholic bias that fueled my interest in dethroning the virgin birth as a vital Christian belief. In my senior year at Indiana University, I took two courses related to religion, *New Testament* and *The History of Christian Thought*. I somehow talked the two professors into accepting one paper that I could write to fulfill requirements for both courses.

The result was a 55-page essay titled, "The Legend of the Virgin Conception in the New Testament: Its Origin, Formation, and Contemporary Significance." Of course, *I* didn't dethrone the virgin birth. Instead, I pulled together the writings, by theologians and Bible experts, demonstrating that it doesn't have a leg to stand on. I received grade *A* from both teachers, and even today I'm proud of the scholarly instincts shown in it. I was ready for graduate school.

The World of Religious Academia

A career in religious academia generally required a Ph.D. in Biblical studies, as well as ordination as a Methodist minister, so I set my course in that direction. I was accepted at the Boston University School of Theology. BUST is the *alma mater* of Dr. Martin Luther King, and it enjoyed a reputation as one of the most liberal Methodist seminaries. The week that I graduated from IU in 1964, I also got married and we moved to Boston.

My study of the Bible was taken to a whole new level. Reading proficiency was expected in Hebrew and Greek (the languages of the Bible), as well as in French and German (the great centers of liberal biblical scholarship were, and remain, Germany, France, Britain, and the U.S.). German was especially important, since German scholarship has played the leading role in biblical and theological studies for the last 200 years. Preparation for ordination and the ministry also required coursework in church history, preaching, counseling and pastoral skills. Despite my interest in the gospels, I opted to major in Old Testament, primarily because of my aversion to the letters of Paul, which are a large portion of the New Testament. Even as a teenager, I found Paul's dense theological ramblings tedious and off-putting.

Even as I was preparing for this Bible-oriented career, the fundamental concept underlying it all, the concept of God, was eroding, despite a curriculum that was heavily stacked in God's favor. Today I regard seminaries as blights on the academic landscape. They betray the ideal and purpose of academia, namely, the search for truth. Seminaries are devoted to the study of something that has never been proven to exist, which rightly falls under Sam Harris's indictment that "theology is now little more than a branch of human ignorance. Indeed, it is ignorance with wings."[4] Bible scholar Hector Avalos is just as blunt in his stunning critique of the theological-academic complex, saying that "the goal of any university should be to undermine not just orthodox theology but all types of theology."[5]

In any philosophy department at any university, the question of the existence of God is debated, and foregone conclusions are disallowed. But schools of theology are devoted to those foregone conclusions; they exist to defend the faith and to manufacture clergy. The last thing that professors of divinity want to do is damage faith in God. While it may be said that there are "no atheists in foxholes" (which is not true at all), it was certainly true at that time that there were no atheists on seminary faculties (or if there were, they were closeted). Perhaps that has changed, but the *raison d'être* of seminaries is to preserve, protect, and defend the prevailing concepts of God.

As my adventure in graduate academia was beginning, I sensed the lack of objectivity, the illegitimacy of the underlying assumption that there was a category of thought that could or should be walled off from inquiry: The concept of God was the foregone conclusion that could not be touched or tampered with. God was why we were *there*. Indeed, worship of God was considered a part of seminary protocol. I regarded this as a symptom of bad academic methodology and practice. Hence I declined to ever attend daily chapel services, despite having gone to church all my life. Since this was a liberal seminary, I was not forced to go.

I was the contrarian seminarian, the class eccentric. Yet my fascination with Bible study did not diminish. With or without God, I could maintain my focus preparing for a career in academia. The Bible was worth studying, I told myself, because it had been a major influence on Western thought.

Flashes of Heretical Insight

Seminaries do not hire atheist theologians, and aggressive questioning of God is out of bounds. But it's unavoidable—at least it was for me—that flashes of insight do light up the mind, sometimes because of off-hand or even belittling comments made by professors. They can be too candid.

In trying to anchor knowledge of God, for example, the sources of God-knowledge must be defended and justified. All of the usual suspects for God-knowledge—prayer, visions, meditation, sacred texts, a personal relationship with God—are hobbled by problems, not the least of which is that all of these are *unverifiable by outsiders*. Hence professors of theology work hard at making all of these sources appear as respectable and believable as possible. They've written thousands of books in this endeavor, which are read mostly by other professors and preachers. Lay people couldn't care less. They are not bothered in the least by the "unverifiable factor." They want to believe, so they just do.

Sometimes cynicism about this undertaking, this huge outpouring of effort to make God-knowledge respectable, is hard to avoid. One of the giants of Protestant theology of the twentieth century was the Swiss theologian Karl Barth, whose output was prodigious. Between 1932 and 1967 he wrote a 13-volume work entitled *Church Dogmatics*, which is virtually unreadable by anyone outside of the theological academia. Barth's influence was at its peak when I was in seminary. But one of my professors, in a rare moment of candor, said that "no one knows 8,000 pages about God—not even in German."

That provoked a light-bulb moment. The sources of God-knowledge are problematic, and if it is possible to joke that *no one* knows 8,000 pages about God, on what basis do we claim that *anyone* knows *even one page* about God? Don't you have to explain exactly why and how that is possible? Otherwise, isn't it all smoke and mirrors? To this day, I've not found a satisfactory solution to that problem, and, in fact, that is Tough Problem II in this book: "How Do You Find Out About God?"

Jesus Takes a Hit, Too

My belief in the grand centerpiece of Christian theology, the Resurrection of Jesus, eroded as well during my seminary experience. It is indeed crippled by so many problems and inconsistencies, as will be covered in Tough Problem VII.

From a secular, scientific point of view, resurrection is silly and indefensible. A dead body walking around? Why not call it the Halloween Faith instead of the Easter Faith? But to die-hard Christians, Jesus' resurrection is one of those articles of faith that must be *taken on faith*. It is a miracle in defiance of science, we were always told, which enhanced its value. Well, what if it falls apart on *religious* grounds?

What if it just violates intellectual honesty too much? The New Testament reports that the resurrected body of Jesus ascended into heaven, literally, up through the clouds. According to the Book of Acts, this happened forty days after the resurrection. Now we know that heaven is not "up there," a few miles or even thousands of miles above the clouds. So there is no way that the resurrected body of Jesus left planet earth.[6] In other words, *he died again*. And this most obvious of conclusions prompted one of my Bible professors to ask, "So what is the value of a forty-day resurrection?"

That comment wiped out resurrection as an article of faith worth believing, let alone defending. It became crystal clear to me—again, acknowledging the *obvious*—that the New Testament accounts of the resurrection preserve a rumor that got out of hand, a cover-up, a lie, or—more innocently—simply a fantasy, a product of imagination. This meant, furthermore, that resurrection says nothing at all about the power of a god or the "triumph of Jesus over the grave." From either the scientific or theological standpoint, resurrection was worthless. It became even more tempting for me to push the idea of God itself into the realm of fable.

Going Out on a Dangerous Limb

Early in my seminary career, as my belief in God was losing ground, I decided to put some thoughts onto paper. The foregone conclusions were looking less and less secure. The 8-page essay is still in my file, more than 45 years later. This was not required for any course, and as I recall, I worked up the nerve to show it to only one of my classmates, Charlie, whose hand-written comments remain on three pages that are attached to the manuscript. The title of this daring essay is "On the Improbability of God." Atheism was breathing down my neck.

Here are a few of my reckless thoughts from the mid-1960s. I think the first paragraph has stood the test of time, going right to the heart of the matter. How does anyone know *anything* about God?

- How do we know what is revelation and what isn't? Every prayer, every verse of the Bible, every creed, every doctrine, every article of faith, is a product of that organ known as the human brain. Now, if it is going to be insisted that some of the output of this organ has been stimulated by a deity, i.e., that it merely comes *through* the brain from an exterior and superior source, we must have criteria for judging what is of human origin and what is of divine origin. If we do not have these criteria—which we don't—we are in a hopeless situation, for there is no way of determining if there is *any* material of divine origin at all, or whether we are merely deceiving ourselves. We run the risk that a human system expressed with eloquence and wisdom will be mistaken for the word of God.

- Theology has for a long time been threatened by the gnawing evidence as to the size of the universe and relative smallness of the earth: who has not been driven to his most gnawing doubts by continual pondering of the infinity of deep space?

- Christian theology finds itself trying to impute truly universalistic dimensions to a deity previously embodied in terrestrial thought forms, previously described completely anthropomorphically: the Christian deity bears a curious resemblance to a creature that happened to evolve at one drifting point in space.

- But our theological systems have been formulated within the confines of one small planet. Until we have greatly widened our experience of the universe—and this might be centuries away—it would seem to be folly to make pronouncements about the nature of God.

- [There may be people] who are eager to devote their lives in service to others, who find the figure of Jesus winsome and compelling, but for whom theological affirmations are impossible and irrelevant. Hopefully, the church will welcome these people into the company of the committed, and, hopefully, if God (after all) is, he will look with compassion and understanding upon these citizens of the post-Christian era who feel compelled to deny him.

Now *there's* a thought: The church should extend its welcome to those who don't believe in God. That little matter about a deity can be deleted and we'll still get along just fine.

Clearly, I was already a citizen of the post-Christian era, but my friend Charlie was not, and he was not amused. He came back with stinging criticism and theobabble. Well, what did I expect? Charlie retorted that his God was the "high and lofty one who inhabits eternity" (theologians and preachers love to talk like that)."Man, you are really hung up in astronomy aren't you?"

My reaction then, as it remains today, was, "How could he be so obtuse?" I was absolutely not hung up on astronomy. I was hung up on our *isolation* that astronomy so starkly revealed, especially in the wake of Hubble's discovery in 1927.

How can it possibly be—stuck on one planet, not even in the *middle* of nowhere—that we are entitled to make the oh-so-confident claims for which theology is so famous? Why doesn't it bother Christians that their theologians embrace, and are forever polishing and apologizing for Bronze Age ideas about God? Charlie ended with this comment: "Some of your paper is well thought out and concerned, some is sophomoric scientism." It would take a few more years for me to fully appreciate that science is the key to understanding the Cosmos and life itself, and that it is the *rejection* of science that is sophomoric.

Still Out on the Limb

Please Hand Me a Saw

The parish ministry was an unavoidable detour from academia. Until I could find a job as an instructor of biblical studies, I had to support my family; my kids were born in 1968 and 1971. Hence, as my graduate work slowly progressed from 1968 to 1975, I accepted appointments as church pastor, and served almost ten years in two parishes before I finally exited the ministry and gave up my ordination.

I was able to accept the first pastoral appointment because I was on course for ordination, and I was required to write an essay about my beliefs. The essay that I wrote in 1970 to qualify for final ordination was a skillfully crafted, moderately worded, and politically correct document, but an utterly heretical and seditious one. Were the people who read the essay to approve my ordination paying attention? In this 21-page document I rose to the challenge of churning out some of my own theobabble, and I said enough about God loving unconditionally and universally to make the grade. Yet it was all white noise. How much did I realize that I was faking it?

I had the nerve to quote from a book entitled *The Christian Agnostic* by Leslie Weatherhead: "There is no authority for God's existence except the inward conviction that is born of mystical experience."[7] *What?* Most Christian theologians would scream protests at this statement, which leaves God-knowledge on the shakiest of foundations. And, I had the nerve to add, "I have never had such an experience." So much for my having any daily walk with the Lord. I managed to sneak in other zingers—I mean, these are grenades thrown into the chapel—that should have sent me packing by the ordination board:

- The love of God is something which certainly comparatively few men are aware of.

- It makes little sense to speak of Jesus as the Lord of History or the Savior of the World, simply because it is impossible to give such titles and the claims they represent any real meaning. Very little of history gives evidence of being under the lordship of Jesus; very little of the world gives evidence of having been saved by Jesus.

- The idea that, by his suffering, death, and resurrection, Jesus redeemed all men, or that he suffered on behalf of sinful men to appease the anger of God (i.e., Jesus Christ the Ransom), is a concept which means very little to me.

- Certainly it is wrong to claim that God's love for a person depends upon that person "believing in Christ" in any narrow sense.

- I cannot seriously entertain the belief that God is narcissistic, that he desires to be worshipped and praised by men.

So the evidence is right there, of all places, in my ordination essay. Atheism was breathing down my neck.

My Doctoral Dissertation

Perhaps I was trying to divert attention from my diluted version of Christianity by retreating, for my final burst of scholarly glory, into a massive research project. Liberal idealist that I was, my goal was to turn out something that would help the world. Has it turned out that way? My dissertation is enjoying eternal rest in a dusty archive somewhere. I would be surprised if even five people have read it, or even snippets of it, since I finished it in 1975.

I cannot recall a time–maybe I really became aware only in college–when I was not troubled by the human population growth problem. In the liberal environment of Boston University, where (almost) all liberal causes were embraced, overpopulation was on the list. While I was in seminary, Paul Ehrlich's book *The Population Bomb* was published (1968), and I was convinced as I still am today of its dramatic message that humanity was on a collision course with *the numbers*. Ehrlich was accused of sensationalism, but now, 45 years later, the population growth numbers are more alarming than ever. Here was a cause, almost above all others, that could be championed by Christians who cared about the planet and the fate of humanity.

And what better way for me to be a champion than to bring my skills as a biblical scholar to an analysis of the Bible verse that seems to block the way to advocating population control: "Be fruitful and multiply and fill the earth." My doctoral proposal was to research how this verse had been interpreted at various times during the Christian era. One of the guiding principles of sound Biblical interpretation, supposedly, is to listen to what other commentators have said over the centuries. Their insights might be very helpful. Or as the theologians like to position it: "God may still be speaking to us through other people who have studied the texts" (more theobabble). So it is considered good methodology to know what other thinkers have said about any given Bible verse.

My research was summarized in a 212-page work, about the "History of the Interpretation of Genesis 1:28a and Related Texts in Selected Periods." I brought my skills in theological sophistry to the task of showing that this text does *not* stand in the way of advocating population control.

Believe it or not, I got help from those Christian thinkers, usually Catholic, over the ages who had come to believe that celibacy was more favored by God than marriage. Be fruitful and multiply? They argued that this commandment had *already been fulfilled*–hence there was no need for more people."Be fruitful and multiply" could be, and had been, downplayed and qualified. So, ironically enough, it was Catholic tradition in defense of celibacy that could give support to the Protestant and secular endorsement of population control.

Notice that my dissertation was not about God *per se*, nor was it about any of the great theological concepts that are thought to be anchored in the Bible. In this project, as a citizen of the post-Christian world, I had settled for analyzing minutiae—with the best of intentions, of course.

The Crisis of 1975

Escaping the Church

The only time I have envied Catholic priests was when I was slogging along on my PhD. They had been appointed by the Catholic Church to *study*, to work on their PhDs, as well as teach and publish along the way. They became superior scholars.

When I finally received my degree in 1975 and began testing the job market, I realized that I was at a significant disadvantage: I had not taught. I'd been a parish pastor, and I had not published. My busy schedule as a pastor precluded that. If I did manage to get job interviews, with no teaching or publishing on my résumé, it would be virtually impossible to outclass the competition. When I started graduate school in 1968, schools of religion were being established at a brisk rate in the U.S. That trend had stopped by the time I graduated seven years later. I sent out 200 résumés and got not even a nibble.

I'd never intended the parish ministry as a career, and, given the erosion of belief, the sooner I could get out, the better. As my graduate studies dragged on, I had been able to continue my ministerial functions because I had held on for dear life to an esoteric, intellectualized concept of God.

The other theologian who wowed liberal theological students—more than Karl Barth—was Paul Tillich, who was also at the peak of popularity. Tillich's obtuse theology appealed to thinkers who were unnerved by the naïve God-concept imbedded in the Bible. His sophistry reached apogee when he suggested that God could not be said, strictly speaking, to *exist*. No, I'm not kidding. That concept, i.e., *existing*—how's this for obfuscation?—was too limiting for the Power that infuses the Cosmos. Tillich was fine with calling God "the Ground of All Being," which sounds pretty good to someone who is trying to cling to some vestige of Christianity. Of course it was too slick to have staying power.

My parishioners and I were on different planets. The Ground of All Being would not resonate with the folks in the pews. I never really admitted that my theology had drifted that far off into la-la land, and they came to church every Sunday to pray to The Man Upstairs, the kindly father whom they could ask for all manner of favors and forgiveness. They could flatter him earnestly and even sing songs to him: "Hallowed be thy name," as if God needed to be reassured. How many billions of times has God heard The Lord's Prayer and the hymn "How Great Thou Art!" Is the world any better off—is *God* any better off—after centuries of human fawning and babbling?

I came to see the absurdity of people abandoning their mental faculties to religious sentimentality every Sunday morning. In the plush glow of stained glass windows, coddled by organ music and forced congeniality (yes, there are factions), they imagined that they were channeling a god. They seemed confident that this could be achieved by closing their eyes, earnestly thinking pious thoughts and muttering formulas. I wondered, *What do you people think you're doing?* Had they given even one moment of critical thought to such piety and posturing?

And there I was presiding over it all, grinning and bearing it, even as the Ground-of-All-Being nonsense was wearing thin. The weekly worship services were torture, a pathetic blend of banality and silliness. No one from on high is paying attention, ladies and gentlemen, snap out of it.

My salvation, so to speak, came in the form of one of my parishioners, a young gung-ho insurance salesman. He saw my promise and potential as a life insurance salesman. He was dead wrong about that, but I was desperate. My future boss saw dollar signs when he interviewed me, because I knew so many people. My first day on the job I was asked to fill out a form, "Who Do You Know?" with slots for 200 names. I was given a phone and a cubicle, and a crash course in how to sell one of the most unpopular commodities imaginable. Given my level of unhappiness in the parish ministry, it's saying a lot that the year I sold insurance was the worst year of my life."There are worse things in life than death," Woody Allen has said."Have you ever spent an evening with an insurance salesman?" Well, I was that salesman, and I shared the misery. But it was a transition to other opportunities, and I did make the move into a business career. The parish ministry vanished in the rear view mirror.

As much as I hated it, I actually did well selling insurance. My success with that gave me a boost getting into another field. When I bailed from the insurance business, I was hired by a personnel agency to sell job candidates to client companies. I helped people secure employment, and a major component of that was coaching people to find satisfying work. So, in an important sense, I remained in a helping profession. After a couple of decades of solid experience in this role, I was recruited to direct a staff of career coaches, whose main function was to guide people into the most satisfying careers possible.

This dramatically increased the helping-people component of what I was doing for a living. When I was in the parish ministry, helping people was the good part. Encouraging their religious fantasies was the bad part. So I had landed on my feet, a retooling of myself that took many years, but maintained a focus on "doing good," with better pay thrown into the bargain.

Escaping the "Straight" Jacket

And then there was the personal crisis into which I was descending, which I have not touched on yet.

The prairie landscape of northern Indiana where I grew up was very flat. It was very receptive to being laid out as a grid by surveyors and mapmakers. There were no curves or turns in the roads. It was like living on a checkerboard. I've often thought of this as a metaphor for the morality grid that we lived on as well. This was brought to mind when, years later, I read the play *Inherit the Wind*. The defense attorney, modeled on the great Clarence Darrow, makes this declaration:

> I must say that "Right" has no meaning to me whatsoever! *Truth* has meaning—as a direction. But one of the peculiar imbecilities of our time is

the grid of morality we have placed on human behavior: so that every act of man must be measured against an arbitrary latitude of right and longitude of wrong–in exact minutes, seconds, and degrees![8]

On the morality grid of northern Indiana in the 1950s, there was no place whatever for homosexuality. I can recall no time at all that my parents uttered a single word against gay people–and certainly not using that adjective–for the very simple reason that there were none. Well, I'm sure they were there in our small town–how could there not be?–but they were invisible. So there was no reason, therefore, for my mother to dwell on the obscure Bible verses that blasted homosexual acts. Such behavior just wasn't anywhere on the grid. I know now, so many years later, that homosexuality has been assigned a place on the "arbitrary latitude of right and longitude of wrong." I stay away from the Indiana grid.

Somehow, in some way, I absorbed the message that being gay was not an option, and that it was grotesquely off the scale of normal. Yet I knew, from a very early age, to whom I was attracted. Hence I had no interest whatever in dating girls, and it was almost at gunpoint–the pressure was ridiculous–that my parents forced me to get dates for the junior and senior proms.

Now this may seem strange, but I can recall no guilt whatsoever about being attracted to other boys. I did realize that these were feelings that *I had to ignore*. Today, gay role models are everywhere–how wonderful that Doogie Howser[9] is married to another man, and everyone knows about it!–but there were *none at all* at that time.

I did not date girls in college. I felt no compulsion to play that game, although I knew that my attraction to men had to be ignored. Had I not met my future wife at the Wesley foundation, where hanging out together was comfortable–and our pals thought we *ought* to be a couple–marriage probably would not have happened at all. How perfect, after all, that I should marry a daughter of missionaries. Why not go along with it? Marriage was something I was supposed to do, and as a nerd I was lucky to get the chance. It was the classic story of following, by default, a script that I had not written.

But the suppression of sexual orientation comes at a high price. The pressure builds. Sexual attraction is one of the most powerful forces that evolution has built into us, whether it's a matter of the same or opposite sex. I was far more attracted to men than I was to my wife, and it was agony to be in the presence of men–some of my fellow seminarians–for whom that attraction was strong.

On one occasion there was an unexpected invitation to intimacy. Because of a snowstorm, an acquaintance stayed overnight in our apartment in the city. He was getting ready to bed down for the night in my study, and there he was, naked in my bathrobe. He was reclining in my chair, with the robe open, handling his full erection, looking right at me. It was a come-hither stare, but far from sly. Did he really expect us to have sex then and there? My wife was in the other room. Perhaps it was a signal that, at another time and place, we could make it happen. I ignored the overture. It could have been a floodgate moment. I was so ready. But not ready for descent into personal crisis. My marriage had put me into a sealed chamber. *Pressure builds.*

Just as I had felt no teenage guilt about being attracted to other boys, it didn't occur to me that my desire for men was a moral error. How could the desire to be in love with the *right* person possibly be wrong? *Pressure builds.* Marriage to a woman was not natural for me, and in fact, was a moral error. This was not *my* life. My wife was a feminist, by the way, and thus I heard a lot in our home about "being all you can be." She had a phonograph record created by Marlo Thomas, *Free to Be You and Me.* How could I not take these messages to heart myself?

Added to my mix of torment was another dead weight: My wife remained deeply committed to her religious beliefs. After we divorced, she married *another* Methodist minister, and when that marriage ended, too (but not because he was gay), she went to seminary herself and became—you guessed it—a Methodist minister. As I was desperate to get out of religion, she was plunging farther down that rabbit hole. On no level whatever were we a match.

The Cause That Dare Not Speak Its Name

I knew that my career in the ministry was doomed because of this other reality as well. The Methodist church did not accept openly gay pastors. Even then, in the mid 1970s, I had the smarts to realize that hiding who I was would be a devastating burden for my emotional health and well-being. I mentioned earlier that liberal BU embraced *almost* all liberal causes. But gay rights had barely made it to the edge of the radar screen: Homosexuality was immoral. Period. This was, after all, only three or four years after the Stonewall Riots.[10]

Yet there were those who were bold enough to *Just Say No* to homophobia. A very dramatic act of defiance, one that put gay rights in the spotlight, happened while I was nearing the end of my PhD work. It was in April 1973 when Methodist pastor William Alberts performed the marriage of two men at historic Old West Church in Boston. The bishop had ordered him not to do it, and a firestorm ensued. The bishop, a kindly man, was not really opposed to the ceremony; he just didn't want it to be called a marriage. But now gay marriage, not just gay rights, made the headlines. The story, with photos, was carried in the *Boston Globe.* The just-say-no-to-homophobia folks soon realized they would have to steel themselves for the long haul; the outraged good church people in the homosexuality-is-immoral camp were not about to back down.

Was it an act of folly that I got involved? I was in the closet, deeply anguished in my sealed chamber, posing as a straight man. But my liberal instincts kicked in and I wrote a long article in defense of gay rights, including gay marriage, "A Pastor's Viewpoint on Homosexual Marriages." It was published by the newspaper *The Methodist Churchman* in its June-July 1973 issue, and in the magazine *Christian Advocate* that September. Another liberal pastor and I planned and delivered a full day seminar for pastors on religion and homosexuality. My colleague had pulled off the tricky business of being an *openly* gay pastor.

Here I was, advocating, with so much energy and eloquence for a cause that I knew very well applied to me personally. So this too was agony, and it pushed me closer to the edge, hastening the day when I finally had to come out to my wife and family.

I went into therapy to help me deal with the trauma of the ensuing divorce, and to erase the scars caused by all those years of heterosexual pretending. The divorce was a hugely painful experience, because my kids were seven and four. But I'd read enough about family health to know that "staying together for the kids" rarely made anyone happy. Divorce commonly has horrendous fallout as well, and my divorce was no exception, but drastic course corrections in my life were necessary.

Perhaps the ultimate irony in this whole saga is that, up to that time, I had never actually "been with a man." Yet I knew my true orientation as well as I knew anything about my life. I was wired that way. I could have, I would have, if circumstances had been otherwise, seized the moment on that snowy night in Boston with the man in my study.

He was willing to live dangerously, as I was not. But sadly, in the long run he failed to live authentically as a gay man. He never was able to break out of his marriage to an especially shrewish woman. When gay men marry women, it is usually anything but a match made in heaven. How can it be when the motive is not love but subterfuge?

They're not thinking clearly and settle for a greatly reduced quotient of happiness. The soul-mate factor is missing; the love factor is counterfeit and shallow. If there is anything they *should* feel guilt about, it is the straight marriage pretense. This is where I feel guilt, but I never had the least shred of guilt about my orientation, I never tried to pray-away-the-gay, and it never crossed my mind that I should try to change. I made sure to find a therapist who understood that.

If there is anything deeper than the deep blue sea, it is Christian ignorance *about Christianity*. But the general Christian ignorance about homosexuality is down in the abyss, too. There is a powerful incentive for Christians to argue, in the face of all the evidence, that homosexuality is a choice, as opposed to an orientation, something put in place by nature. Only if it's a choice can they still call it a sin. So "choice" remains their argument of choice, despite massive research and personal testimony to the contrary. They are dug in for a long battle.

Of course, in all fairness, there are Christians who support gay rights and marriage equality, and the literature on homosexuality and religion–showing why there is no basis for all the moral outrage–is substantial. But the informed, compassionate Christians seem to be crying in the wilderness. Catholics, Evangelicals and Mormons have been very successful in defining the debate and setting the tone.

I did not leave Christianity because of its imbedded homophobia. My reasons are far more complex and substantial than that. But the arrogant and aggressive ignorance about homosexuality that the majority of Christians display is a scandal. None of the Ten Tough Problems is about the widespread moral obtuseness of Christian leaders and followers–now and throughout the ages–but it can certainly be considered a subset of Tough Problem I, the problem of evil. The church has been one of the primary sources of anti-Semitism throughout Western history, the New

Testament being largely to blame. And there will be a lot of kicking and screaming before the church abandons its willful, enthusiastic embrace of homophobia.

Mom and Dad, Still on the Old Grid

At the time my marriage was crumbling, I was living in Massachusetts and my parents had moved to Florida. I wrote them a long, carefully worded, closely reasoned coming-out letter. Their reaction was ferocious. For a while I thought I might never see them again. I sent them the book *Society and the Healthy Homosexual*,[11] which my mother dismissed as "garbage." My father, in burst of white-hot rage, wrote me a hate letter. I still have it today, but even after all these years, it would be too painful to read.

Over the years I have wondered so often: Where does the hate come from? Why is it so intense? I actually have little patience with those who say that the church is the cause of homophobia. While the church must indeed bear a full measure of responsibility for its role in stoking hatred of gay people, the fact is that homophobia is also deeply rooted in traditional Chinese, Islamic and African cultures.

My brother was proved right about our mother being the most Christian woman he had ever met. After the initial explosion, it was she who began to extend olive branches. About this time, Anita Bryant, the popular singer and orange juice spokesperson, was on her one-woman crusade against gay people. My mother had come for a visit, her first since I had come out, and "the subject" never came up, but she was careful to get in the observation that Anita Bryant was a nutcase. That was her signal that I was okay, after all. My mother loved me, and she could not endure a permanent break. A year or two later when I took my boyfriend (now my husband) home to meet them, within minutes mother was showing him my baby pictures. My dad had calmed down too, and my new marriage (although with no legal status for many years) was accepted as a fact.

Was I Ever Really a Christian?

My church bosses were probably glad to see me go. Divorced pastors are a rare item, and they might have feared that scandal was lurking below the surface. They had no idea of the scandal I *could* have handed them; they probably suspected "another woman." During my exit interview, I deflected probing questions.

It was an enormous relief to be away from Sunday worship and the church culture, but study of the Bible was too deeply embedded for me to abandon it. During the first few years that I pursued a business career, I did walk away from it, but it crept back to grab my attention. And my thoughts on religion kept churning. I began making notes on the things that are wrong with Christianity–it does amaze me that people continue to take it seriously–and three or four years ago the "things that are wrong" coalesced into ten categories, many of which are rooted in the Bible. Thus this book began to take shape.

Not long ago a Christian troll on my Facebook page, which bears the same title as this book, said that he was not awed by my PhD in Biblical Studies. It didn't count for much either that I had been an ordained minister. Ignoring the injunction of Jesus not to judge, he said that my name had never *really* been written in The Book of Life.

What is the rejoinder to that? Of course I had to agree, above all because there is no such thing as The Book of Life. This is Christian code (gleaned from the Book of Revelation) for being in such a special relationship with God–based on believing in Jesus Christ–that you are guaranteed a berth in heaven.

But I could also agree with him, even on his terms. I was never a real Christian if he meant having a daily walk with the Lord, and having a personal relationship with Jesus. I embraced Christianity because it was in the drinking water when I grew up, and I plead guilty that I brought my mind to it more than my heart.

Things have to make sense.

When it comes to loving my husband and children, I am a sentimentalist. But not when it comes to figuring out how the Cosmos works. For that we need hard evidence, not personal feelings and prayer rugs. The Christianity I embraced didn't run deep enough to survive rigorous critical examination. It *doesn't* make sense, and in the chapters that follow I will explain why it is a house of cards.

Was I ever a real Christian? Well, obviously there's a spectrum. I suspect that a good many of the folks in the pews aren't as confident about their walk with the Lord as others are. But the smug Christians have their standards. Because of my failure to launch as a fundamentalist–no matter how pious my mother was–and my cerebral approach, I don't qualify for The Book of Life.

Let's just say that I gave Christianity a good shot. Now I'm firing back.

Notes

1. *St. Matthew and the Angel*, Rembrandt (1661). Public domain image from Wikimedia Commons, post-processed in black & white.

2. I have more to say in Tough Problem VI concerning doubts about the existence of **Q**.

3. His name was Harold Hill. He savored the celebrity that came from sharing his name with the counterfeit professor in the hit movie musical at the time, *The Music Man*.

4. Sam Harris, *The End of Faith* (W.W. Norton, 2005), p.173.

5. Hector Avalos, *The End of Biblical Studies* (Prometheus Books, 2007), p. 298.

6. This is discussed at length in Tough Problem VII concerning the Resurrection of Jesus.

7. Leslie Weatherhead, *The Christian Agnostic* (Abingdon Press, 1990), p. 72.

8. Jerome Lawrence and Robert Edwin Lee, 1955.

9. The role that made Neil Patrick Harris famous, which he played on TV, 1989-1993.

10. In June 1969, in New York City, the Stonewall Inn, a gay bar, was raided by the police. The ensuing riots are widely regarded as a turning point in the modern movement for gay rights.

11. Dr. George Weinberg, 1972.

Introduction

Former Christians leave the faith for a wide variety of reasons since there are so many problems with the Christian faith.

> —John W. Loftus, *Why I Became an Atheist: A Former Preacher Rejects Christianity*

The Atheist Publishing Surge
Its Antecedents and The Need for More

WHEN CHRISTIANS DISCOVER that I am a minister-turned-atheist, they sometimes seem to want to meet me halfway: "I've struggled with doubts too–it's not been easy."

Isn't this a curious confession, that inherited doctrine is, well, hard to swallow? But they've won the battle, and they want to pat themselves on the back for holding on to their faith, although I sense they may not be entirely out of the woods. I can almost hear them say, "What's the point of being so ornery? Why don't *you* just snap out of it too?" Being in the faith is considered the wiser, almost heroic default position.

Of course, others who have been taught the "one true faith" from the cradle don't freak out when doubts encroach. One of my favorite rebels, George Carlin, was raised Catholic, and tried to coax his adult mind to bend to the dogma:

> I tried to believe that there is a God, who created each of us in His own image and likeness, loves us very much, and keeps a close eye on things. I really tried to believe that, but I gotta tell you, the longer you live, the more you look around, the more you realize, something is fucked up.[1]

He figured out that sanctimonious formulas designed to cover the mess don't work: "This is a wonderful fairy tale they have going here, but it's not for me."

Why don't more folks balk like Carlin did? Why do they just assume that there is an obligation to overcome doubts? Is it a duty to which one is bound by parents, ancestors and priests? I want to reply–but usually don't–"Why bother?" Doubts are usually a symptom that something is wrong. The flaws and contradictions weigh too heavily. Doubt, Peter Boghossian has pointed out, "is your intellectual conscience pleading with you to be honest with yourself."[2] After all, doubt is the suspicion that religion has wandered too far into fantasy land–things just don't add up–which prompted Mark Twain's famous jab that "faith is believing in something you know ain't true."

Serious thinkers–by which I mean those who do not adopt a bunker mentality to defend the faith at any cost–have realized that there are too many *this-doesn't-make-sense* moments. They feel as well that it's pointless–and more than a little draining–to devise convoluted arguments to get around the flaws and contradictions, although thousands of Christian apologists have made their livings doing just that. Don't they get *tired*?

Christian author Jack Nelson-Pallmeyer speaks candidly when he notes that there are times when "theology becomes the art of making square pegs fit into round holes."[3] But neither art nor science can actually do that—let alone theology.

Following the Curiosity

It is far better to welcome the doubts."Where do these lead me?" is an honorable question. On the honesty scale, "I want to find out the truth" always beats "My church says that this is a No-No. I should banish the doubts."

Well, doubt—even outright atheism—is probably just as old as the ancient impulse to personalize the powers that reside in the sky. (I suspect that lightening had as much to do with "making believers" as anything else.) An atheist seems to have gotten under the skin of at least one Old Testament holy man. Thus holy folks today like to throw Psalm 14:1 in our faces: "The fool hath said in his heart, there is no God. They are corrupt, they have done abominable works; there is none that doeth good" (KJV). This text demonstrates at least two things:

- *Someone* must have said, "All this bowing and scraping to the sky doesn't make sense."
- And even back then, religious folks resorted to name calling and character assassination, i.e., atheists are fools, they are corrupt, they do abominable things—and not one of them does any good.

Doesn't that sound familiar?[4]

But we also see evidence of doubt in the New Testament. In Mark 9, we read the story of a distraught father who asks Jesus to heal his son, who had been a victim of seizures since childhood."Take pity on us and help us," the father begs, "if you can." Jesus appears to be miffed. He replies, quoting the man, "'If you *can*?'," then adds this bit of dreadful nonsense: "Everything is possible for one who believes." Notice that this undercuts Jesus as a miracle worker. If you want to brag about Jesus as a great healer, isn't it strange that he suggests that healing depends upon a person believing? Does Jesus have the power to heal or doesn't he?

Anyone who knows how the world works knows that Jesus was wrong, as well as insensitive. Tormented by the thought that his own weak belief may be the source of their problem, the man responds, "I believe, help my unbelief" (Mark 9:24). Doubt was a reality even then. How many times had this father wondered, "Is there really a good God?" He had experienced too many this-doesn't-make-sense moments.

British Atheism

No God to Save the Queen

But these doubters mentioned in the Bible were long ago and far away, and modern atheists seem to present a novel threat. Where did they come from all of a sudden?

Some Christians—those few who may be paying attention—have become alarmed and indignant that atheists have been making so much noise for at least the last decade. What a shock that provocative books by Richard Dawkins, Christopher Hitchens, and Sam Harris have survived stubbornly on the bestseller lists. I've sometimes wished that the blockbuster books about atheism had been written fifty years ago. Perhaps then I could have snapped out of religion a lot earlier. But probably not: Christians, especially of the Hoosier variety, assuredly have a long history of not paying attention.

Dawkins-Hitchens-Harris may seem to be all-of-a-sudden, especially since atheism has exploded in high profile on the Internet only in the last few years. But they stand on the broad shoulders of many others.

I mentioned in the Prologue that my mother was a voracious reader. She read widely in history and biography, and the apple didn't fall far from the tree. But no one—neither my mother, nor the librarian in our intellectually quarantined Christian village—thought to introduce me to Bertrand Russell. In 1927—mind you, this was 15 years before I was born—Russell had delivered a lecture at the Battersea, England town hall. The lecture, *Why I Am Not a Christian*, became a popular pamphlet, and later the title of a book of Russell's essays. That's a pretty blunt title. Why aren't Christians everywhere clamoring to get a copy of that lecture? Why aren't they curious to see how their religion might have gone off the rails? Don't they want to find out what one of the smartest guys of the 20th Century had to say about their faith?

It's hard for me to imagine anyone delivering a lecture with that title anywhere in my hometown, let alone the town hall. Russell touched on a few of the more glaring problems of Christianity, but he said little that was new. Atheism had been running parallel to religion for a long time. More than a century before Russell's talk at Battersea, the Christian establishment had not taken kindly to the blatant heresy of the young poet Percy Bysshe Shelley. In 1811, the 19-year old Shelley was kicked out of Oxford for writing an essay, *The Necessity of Atheism*.

Even earlier, Thomas Paine, the great English friend of America during the Revolution, made too many enemies by his blistering criticism of Christianity, and died poor. Paine was a deist; a personal caring deity made little sense to him, and Christianity made no sense at all.

Good Old Fashioned American Atheism

Maybe we could say that the ferment in English thought was just too far away to have much impact in my neck of the woods. But there are American thinkers whose work Christians have crossed off the reading lists—or at least censored—to shelter the faithful. American atheists have been hiding in plain sight.

The preeminent representative of the Golden Age of Freethought in the middle of the 19th Century was probably Robert Green Ingersoll. He lectured widely in the U.S. during the years following the Civil War, and drew large audiences. He was unsparing in his ridicule of Christianity:

> The notion that faith in Christ is to be rewarded by an eternity of bliss, while a dependence upon reason, observation and experience merits

everlasting pain, is too absurd for refutation, and can be relieved only by that unhappy mixture of insanity and ignorance, called "faith."[5]

When I was growing up, Ingersoll had been forgotten, but Mark Twain was a household name. Twain's contempt for religion, however, was never mentioned in the books available to me.

I collected a series of biographies of great figures, aimed at young readers, but these were cleansed of corrupting influences. One of the books was about Thomas Edison, and his genius as an inventor was the theme of the book. There was no mention of a 1910 article in the *New York Times* entitled "No Immortality of the Soul Says Thomas A. Edison," in which Edison was quoted as saying he could not "believe in the immortality of the soul." He called himself "an aggregate of cells, as, for instance, New York City is an aggregate of individuals. Will New York City go to heaven?" No, he said, and "nature made us—nature did it all—not the gods of the religions" (2 October 1910).

"So far as religion of the day is concerned, it is a damned fake," Edison had commented elsewhere."Religion is all bunk."[6]

Ironically, the library in my hometown, presided over by guardians of Christian truth, was a Carnegie library. We thought of Andrew Carnegie as a benevolent man because of his philanthropy; he was noted especially for his generous funding of more than 2,800 libraries. He was not treated kindly in Matthew Josephson's 1938 book *The Robber Barons*, but the critique of wealth accumulated at the expense of exploited labor had not yet reached us.

Little did we know that Carnegie was an atheist, though he did not hide his antagonism toward Christianity. In a 1905 letter he had written:

> The whole scheme of Christian Salvation is diabolical as revealed by the creeds. An angry God, imagine such a creator of the universe. Angry at what he knew was coming and was himself responsible for. Then he sets himself about to beget a son, in order that the child should beg him to forgive the Sinner. This however he cannot or will not do. He must punish somebody—so the son offers himself up & our creator punishes the innocent youth, never heard of before—for the guilty and became reconciled to us . . . I decline to accept Salvation from such a fiend.[7]

And then there was that other giant American literary figure, slightly later than Mark Twain, that my mother and librarian neglected to bring to my attention. They can be forgiven for their failure to notice Bertrand Russell, so far away in England, but H.L. Mencken had flourished at the same time as Russell, and his brilliant commentary on religion, *Treatise on the Gods*, was published just three years after Russell's Battersea lecture. The teenage me would have found it highly accessible."Religion," Mencken wrote,

> is fundamentally opposed to everything I hold in veneration—courage, clear thinking, honesty, fairness, and, above all, love of the truth. In brief, it is a fraud.[8]

And he had very low tolerance for preachers: "Deep within the heart of every evangelist lies the wreck of a car salesman."[9]

H.L. Mencken was the model for one of the characters in the film version of *Inherit the Wind*, played by Gene Kelly. The hero of that film (played by Spencer Tracy) was based on another incendiary American thinker, the attorney Clarence Darrow. Darrow was famous for his agnosticism as well as for his defense of despised criminals. When I was growing up, I learned about the famous Monkey Trial that had put evolution on trial in 1925. My parents would have appreciated the defense of evolution, but Darrow's opinions on religion were kept out of view. Darrow had stated in a speech, "I don't believe in God because I don't believe in Mother Goose."[10] American atheists were hiding in plain sight.

There was another brainy hero as well–although brainy on an entirely different scale in this case. As I mentioned in the preface, my parents had respect for science, so it's no surprise that Albert Einstein was held in awe. I'm pretty sure we didn't understand exactly why, but most people were aware of Einstein's reputation as a profound thinker. And Einstein was candid about his atheism. He wrote in a 1954 letter:

> It was, of course, a lie what you read about my religious convictions, a lie which is being systematically repeated. I do not believe in a personal God and I have never denied this but have expressed it clearly. If something is in me which can be called religious then it is the unbounded admiration for the structure of the world so far as our science can reveal it.[11]

Mad as Hell, and Not Going to Take It Anymore

Eventually, atheism would emerge from hiding in plain sight. After running parallel to religion, it would slowly achieve a higher profile. Perhaps one of the most important trailblazers was George H. Smith. His book *Atheism: The Case Against God* appeared in 1979. Copies disappeared from library shelves because patrons destroyed them–book burning is an honored tradition in Christendom–but it was the best selling book on atheism to date, well before the atheist publishing surge a quarter of a century later.

Then there was a major stealth atheist attack in 1980. We know from a 1996 survey that 93 percent of the members of the National Academy of Sciences were atheists, but that high level had probably been typical in scientific ranks for a long time. And planetary astronomer Carl Sagan turned out to be the right person at the right time to make a compelling pitch for understanding the Cosmos *sans* deity.

His TV series *Cosmos* aired on PBS in September through December 1980. It remains the most watched PBS series ever, having been seen by more than 500 million people in sixty countries. Sagan was everything atheists could want in a spokesman: calm, gentle, eloquent, persuasive, and totally convincing that the universe is the product of natural phenomena. In the broadcasts themselves he was not overtly atheist, but on the lecture circuit and in debates with theologians he was, and he was razor-sharp in his critique of theism and religion. He was an atheist in plain sight. I suspect that Sagan softened up the opposition; he prepared the market and gave heart to atheist writers to say their piece, and momentum gathered.

In 1989, philosopher Michael Martin published *Atheism: A Philosophical Justification,* and this was followed two years later by his book *The Case Against Christianity.* In 1990, the MIT press issued an English translation of *The Atheist and the Holy City: Encounters and Reflections* by Swedish cancer researcher George Klein. In 1994, economist and public policy analyst, Joseph Daleiden, entered the ranks of atheist authors with *The Final Superstition: A Critical Evaluation of the Judeo-Christian Legacy.* Two years later, Robin Le Poidevin, a philosophy professor at the University of Leeds, added his thoughts with *Arguing for Atheism: an Introduction to the Philosophy of Religion.*

And the pace has quickened since the late 1990s. There has been a steady flow of books from serious thinkers critiquing and debunking Christianity and theism in general. Atheism on this scale–unapologetic, in-your-face atheism–had never been seen before. Skepticism came out of the closet and reached center stage in the public discourse.

The Bible Scholar Christians Love to Hate

Bart Ehrman

One of the most startling of these books is Bart Ehrman's *God's Problem: How the Bible Fails to Answer Our Most Important Question–Why We Suffer.*[12] He is one of the preeminent New Testament scholars of our time, known especially for his widely used college textbook on the New Testament. Ehrman was a fundamentalist when he began his career as a biblical scholar, but gave up on the Christian faith and now describes himself as an agnostic.

He's written highly accessible books for the lay reader, several of which have been on the *New York Times* bestseller list. These works expose the flaws and fault lines in the New Testament. Ehrman has had no atheist axe to grind, but has nonetheless–as one of the world's leading specialists on the New Testament–punctured Christianity with devastating clarity and precision: "Jesus was mistaken about that," he writes about Jesus' expectation that the end of the world was near. "He was mistaken about a lot of things. People don't want to hear that, but it's true. Jesus was a man of his own time. And just as all men and women of their own time are wrong about so many things, so too was Jesus."[13]

In *God's Problem,* Ehrman explains why he left the Christian faith: So much evil and suffering in the world cannot be reconciled with the belief that there is a loving all-powerful God. Despite the "agnostic" label he's used for himself, there can be no mistake that he rejects the God of the Bible.

Christian Publishing Has a Head of Steam

Secular consumers have welcomed and savored–after so long a drought–the steady flow of atheist titles in recent years. I confess, however, that there is a touch of bravado in my labeling this modest flow as a "surge," considering how much it is dwarfed by the monumental output of mass-market Christian titles by the likes of Rick Warren, Joel Osteen, Tim Keller, Francis Chan, John Bevere, and Norman Geisler.

There are a few Christian writers—they can be ranked as serious theologians—who probably don't aspire to the mass-market threshold, but who have felt the need to counter the atheist challenge specifically.

- Alister McGrath: *The Twilight of Atheism* (2004); *Dawkins' God*, (2004); *The Dawkins Delusion* (2007).

- John F. Haught: *God and the New Atheism: A Critical Response to Dawkins, Harris, and Hitchens* (2007).

- Keith Ward: *Is Religion Dangerous?* (2006).

- William Lane Craig: *Reasonable Faith: Christian Truth and Apologetics* (2008); *On Guard: Defending Your Faith with Reason and Precision* (2010); *A Reasonable Response: Answers to Tough Questions on God, Christianity and the Bible* (2013).

- Richard Swinburne: *The Existence of God* (2004); *Faith and Reason* (2005); *Is There a God?* (2010).

- Alvin Plantinga: *Where the Conflict Really Lies: Religion, Science and Naturalism* (2011).

The reach of these books has been more limited than the blockbuster Christian titles, with sales far below those of the prominent atheist writers—with the exception of those by William Lane Craig. Even many Christians may be embarrassed by Craig's prominence in the debate since he is firmly anchored in fundamentalism.

Jesus Is My Friend

My hunch is that the majority of the rank and file in the pews have simply ignored the atheist publishing surge. Even if they're not oblivious, *they are just not interested.* Few Christians have bothered to dip into the growing atheist library. I doubt that any of the hundreds of atheist titles are available in Christian bookstores; there are no shelves under a heading "Our Atheist Critics."

Believers are eager to put up a brave front, acting confident that the foundations of their faith are secure. They don't wish to go digging beneath the surface. They remain secure by ignoring the reasons why serious thinkers debunk Christianity. Usually, they aren't able to describe and explain the aspects of the faith that have provoked such vigorous assaults.

If asked to identify a few of the tough problems with Christianity that have brought criticism and ridicule from people like Paine, Shelley, Ingersoll, Twain, Mencken, Russell—as well as from Dawkins, Hitchens, Harris and Ehrman—how many would the average Christian be able to articulate? Would any of them come as a surprise to most Christians? When I told Christians I was writing a book about ten major problems that hobble the Christian faith, I was never asked–literally, not even once–"Gee, really, there are *ten* problems? What are they?"

Most people, it seems to me, settle into a form of Christianity that they have been brought up with; or they find a mild Jesus-is-my-friend version of Christianity, with little regard for, or knowledge of, what Bible-based Christianity is. *That* version of Christianity–truth be told–is pretty hard to stomach. If you don't believe me, read the New Testament carefully, word for word. People are often shocked, puzzled and even alarmed when they read the details of the Jesus story and the hardline severity of Paul's thought. They become very selective about which verses to take seriously, and find clever ways to finesse the embarrassing verses. This way they manage to hold on to what Ehrman has called the Jesus-of-their-imaginations.

Jesus becomes what they want him to be.[14]

Hasn't Christianity Been Roughed Up Enough?

Is there really anything more to be said in the critique of Christianity? Why do atheists keep writing? A critic once whined about the gay rights movement that, while homosexuality was once "the love that dare not speak its name," now it was impossible to get it to shut up. Why don't atheists just shut up already?

The reason that we don't is that there is so much more to be said. We're still flogging the horse because it's not dead. We are up against a major world religion with 2,000 years of momentum behind it–but with plenty of cracks and weaknesses to be exposed and exploited. We're still aiming at those Christians whose minds are not in lockdown mode.

It has been said that you can't talk people out of Christianity because they weren't talked into it. It's an emotional thing, embedded in the earliest years, that can't be dislodged. Well, maybe, but that's too simplistic, and it's not the whole story. Some of our high-profile atheist champions today are ex-pastors, e.g., John Loftus, Dan Barker, Ryan Bell, and Jerry DeWitt; they reasoned their way out of deeply embedded faith, and the same thing happened to scholar Bart Ehrman. There are now more than 700 members of The Clergy Project, the online support group for clergy who have become atheists. They show that even the most committed Christians are not hopeless cases, and almost every escape-from-faith story of the members of The Clergy Project could probably be turned into a book.

And there are no doubt countless others–in the ranks of the laity as well–whose escape stories are worth reading; they have heard too many shallow answers to profound questions or have been slammed by life. While many people rushed to church in the wake of 9/11 for solace (did they really find it?), perhaps just as many wondered where God was that morning. They might feel, deep down inside, that sophomoric Christian formulas such as "everything happens for a reason" just don't ring true.

Most hard core evangelicals *are* probably out of reach; they are the "toasters" whom Al Stefanelli admits can't be taught when he said that "arguing with a Christian is like trying to teach calculus to a toaster."[15] But I suspect that many people feel under no obligation–no matter how many years they've gone to church–to accept the retread answers to many of the objections that have been raised to the Christian faith. Thus atheists should go right on telling and publishing their stories.

The confrontational approaches of Richard Dawkins, Christopher Hitchens, Sam Harris and Greta Christina may not resonate with some people, so maybe they'll be reached by the calmer approaches of Carl Sagan, Bart Ehrman, Guy Harrison, and Nica Lalli. We keep writing and speaking because–well, because we each have something to say *in our own way*. The next atheist author could be a perfect match– the very voice, just the right message–for folks who are at the tipping point, who won't take much nudging to walk away from Christian silliness.

There can never be too many atheist books, given what we're up against. We keep writing and speaking because of the frightening possibility that we may be fighting a losing battle. The world is drowning in religion, and in the fanaticism and aggressive ignorance that it breeds. Christianity may possess unstoppable momentum: its most conservative brands oppose contraception, abortion or anything else that would slow birth rates. Consider this: by one estimate, by 2025 there will be one billion–yes, you read that correctly, billion with a *b*–Pentecostals in the world.[16] That should scare you as much as global warming or rogue nations with nuclear weapons. Do we need a billion people whose conception of the world derives, almost unmodified, from the Bronze Age? These are folks who follow primitive, mind-numbing Christianity, and who are indifferent to democratic values and scientific education.

There is a glimmer of hope, though, in the evidence that secularism is on the rise in the West. We need to do all we can to make sure that this trend continues. A thousand atheist titles would not be enough.

So Many Problems
John Loftus Is Right

The schematic for this book, and even its title, were partly inspired by John Loftus's words that I quoted at the beginning of the Introduction: "Former Christians leave the faith for a wide variety of reasons since there are so many problems with the Christian faith."[17] The problems just pile on top of one another. Indeed, some people have asked me, "Only ten tough problems, aren't there a lot more?" Of course, but ten is an easy number to wrap your mind around. After all, David Letterman found it a winning formula, although I really don't rank the problems.

Any one of the problems is probably sufficient to falsify Christianity. Maybe, with a lot of heavy lifting and straining, you could overcome one or two, but all ten? You will find that quite a few problems are swept into each of the ten categories. This book is intended to help understand what the fuss is about with all these atheist books, and support atheists as they fight the good fight.

I also want to capture the attention of stray Christians who may show uncharacteristic curiosity. Christianity is plagued by multiple vulnerabilities, which have great shock value when people face them head-on.

Ten Tough Problems

The Brick Wall

Lest anyone suspect that I have constructed straw men to knock down, I should point out that I didn't imagine or invent the Ten Tough Problems that I will be covering. Some of them have engaged the attention of philosophers and theologians for millennia. Others are of more recent origin, but nonetheless have caused much theological hand-wringing. And, commonly, most of the people in the pews are simply unaware of them. Their pastors and priests don't bother to bring them up, and they aren't usually discussed during worship services or in Sunday school or catechism classes. Within all of those contexts, the goal is to explain and champion received dogma, not to challenge it: "Why draw attention to these problems if we don't have to?"

The Ten Tough Problems fall into two categories, grouped together in this book. In the first half, I discuss five problems that plague Western monotheism in general, (monotheism being the belief there is one perfect and powerful God). Then I go on to discuss five problems that are peculiar to Christianity.

It would be a wonderful thing if Christians were aware of these problems. It would be a breath of fresh air if they were able to discuss them knowledgeably–or even better have that wonderful *Ah Ha!* moment when they realize that Christianity just doesn't make sense.

It would be an improvement for the world if religion in general, and Christianity in particular, could become something that humans eventually talk about in the past tense–a relic of human development that our species should get beyond, lest we rush off the cliff into the sea, like the demon-possessed swine in Mark 5. If such self-destruction ever comes, it will surely be the fault of faith-fueled hatreds, human economic and political differences exacerbated by religion.

Notes

1. George Carlin, rense.com/general69/obj.htm.

2. Posted on his Facebook page, 18 January 2016. Boghossian is noted especially for his 2013 book, *A Manual for Creating Atheists* (Pitchstone Publishing).

3. Jack Nelson-Pallmeyer, *Jesus Against Christianity: Reclaiming the Missing Jesus* (Bloomsbury T&T Clark, 2001), p. 221.

4. I don't know whom to credit for one of the best atheist retorts to Psalm 14:1: "A fool says in this heart, 'There is no God,' but a wise man says it out loud."

5. Robert G. Ingersoll, *On the Gods and Other Essays*

6. Thomas Edison, *The Diary and Sundry Observations of Thomas Alva Edison*, atheism.about.com/od/aboutreligion/fl/Thomas-Alva-Edison-on-Religion-and-Faith.htm.

7. Andrew Carnegie, to Sir James Donaldson, Principal of St. Andrews University, June 1, 1905, Library of Congress Collection.

8. Charles A. Fecher, *Mencken: A Study of His Thought* (Knopf, 1978), p. 81.

9. Richard Dawkins, *The God Delusion* (Mariner Books, 2008), p. 373.

10. Speech in Toronto (1930); as quoted in "Breaking the Last Taboo" (1996) by James A. Haught, infidels.org/library/modern/james_haught/breaking.html.

11. In a letter 24 March 1954; from Helen Dukas and Banesh Hoffman, eds., *Albert Einstein the Human Side* (Princeton University Press, 1981), p. 43.

12. HarperOne 2008.

13. Bart Ehrman, *Did Jesus Exist? The Historical Argument for Jesus of Nazareth* (HarperOne 2013), p. 336.

14. Stephen Prothero, *American Jesus: How the Son of God Became a National Icon* (Farrar, Straus and Giroux, 2004).

15. alstefanelli.com/2011/12/04/my-story-why-i-abandoned-my-faith-and-embraced-atheism

16. christianitytoday.com/ct/2006/april/7.30.html.

17. John Loftus, *Why I Became an Atheist: A Former Preacher Rejects Christianity* (Prometheus Books, 2008), p. 24.

I

Evil and Human Suffering

> The whole Christian system, like every other similar system, goes to pieces on the problem of evil.
>
> —H.L. Mencken

> The problem of vindicating an omnipotent and omniscient God in the face of evil is insurmountable. Those who claim to have surmounted it, by recourse to notions of free will and other incoherencies, have merely heaped bad philosophy onto bad ethics
>
> —Sam Harris

A COUPLE OF YEARS before I was born, my mother lost a baby. Michael had been born too soon and lived only a day or two. Later, when I asked if my parents had meant to have me, my mother said, yes, my subsequent arrival had been planned. Indeed, I was conceived in the weeks following Pearl Harbor. My parents were bold enough, optimistic enough, to give it another try.

My oldest brother told me that the death of the baby had been the biggest trauma of his young life, and my mother never spoke of it. However, one of our family rituals every year was visiting the family graves on Memorial Day. Back then it was called Decoration Day, because decorating graves with flowers was the custom.

I have a keen memory of the look of deep sadness that always passed across my mother's face when she paused at Michael's grave. What could have been, what should have been . . . had been lost. She'd cherished a life within her for seven or eight months. She loved him—dare I say?—more than God did. She grieved through the years because her love for Michael had been forced to an abrupt end. Although she already had two children, the void left by the missing person must have been unbearable.

Pain Beyond Compare

If there's anything that sears the heart more deeply than this, it would probably be the death of a child several years old. By the time you've known your youngster for five or six years, he or she is an irreplaceable part of your being, precious beyond measure.

Thus the nation was wrenched to its core when a gunman shot up some elementary school classrooms in Newtown, Connecticut on 14 December 2012, killing twenty kids and six adults. The bullets mushroomed on penetration, ripping innocent six-year olds to shreds. Out of respect for the parents and the dictates of human dignity, the photos of that crime scene will never be released. Policeman Thomas Bean, one of the first responders, "has contemplated suicide, continues to have flashbacks, and is left crying some nights by memories of the bloodshed." Bean said, "Nothing could prepare you for that," the "worst possible scenes you could think of."[1] The parents of those children, no matter if they live for decades more, will never have even a day untouched by the crushing pain of that horrific loss.

President Obama responded to the crime by spending a day with the families at the Newtown High School. The experience was recounted by White House staffer Joshua DuBois, who was part of the advance team to make the arrangements. The families, he said, were asked to wait in various classrooms. Most were in still in silent shock, and some were angry. When the President arrived, DuBois briefed him on the names of the parents and their slain children.

> The president took a deep breath and steeled himself, and went into the first classroom. And what happened next I'll never forget.

> Person after person received an engulfing hug from our commander in chief. He'd say, "Tell me about your son . . . Tell me about your daughter," and then hold pictures of the lost beloved as their parents described favorite foods, television shows, and the sound of their laughter . . . In each room, I saw his eyes water, but he did not break.

> We spent what felt like a lifetime in those classrooms, and every single person received the same tender treatment. The same hugs. The same looks, directly in their eyes. The same sincere offer of support and prayer.

If being Commander-in-Chief is a tough job, is there a President who wouldn't prefer it to the Comforter-in-Chief role in such horrific circumstance? DuBois confessed that he worried about the toll on Obama, from what he called the "weekend when evil reigned."[2]

Unspeakable Evil? Always Look on the Bright Side!

Some Christians, abandoning all traces of decency, can't resist looking for a silver lining. Ten days after the massacre, at a Christmas Eve dinner at the home of a Catholic friend, the hostess made reference to the shooting–during grace, no less–by saying with a forced smile that "God must have wanted more angels." I wanted to leave the room to catch my breath because the comment was so grotesque. She was straining to exonerate God, and didn't even notice what she was doing.

One of the most troubling habits of the devout is that, so much of the time, they don't think about what they say. Something intended to be pious can be in shockingly bad taste. It comes out as ugly and bloodcurdling. And if we press them, we might even hear, "Well, I didn't mean *that*." Then why did you say it? Why didn't you think before you spoke? Had you no idea–really–how much you were trivializing things? Their thoughtless comments give Christianity a bad name, but, of course, there is a long tradition of Christians doing that in many different ways.

Trivializing the blasting of children into tiny bits doesn't "make it better." Oh that I could have arranged for my pious friend to be in the classroom with Officer Bean. Would it have occurred to her *on the scene* that the carnage was God's handiwork? Only pious folks whose grasp of reality has been shattered by unconscionable insensitivity can utter such excuses, and only at a distance from the horrors they wish to soften.

Comedians sometimes ask if it is "too soon" to joke about a tragedy. There will *never* be a time when it is okay to joke about the Holocaust, and there will *never* be a time when it will be okay to give a flip response to the savagery in Newtown. Ever. Let alone ten days after it happened."God wanted more angels" is a flip, unintentionally cruel answer, intended to evade to the all-too-obvious truth that a supposedly accountable god is incompetent and negligent.

He surely *must* be accountable if he provides the ultimate standard of morality in the Cosmos. It's enough of a struggle for preachers and theologians to explain why God would allow such a tragedy, but here was a Christian suggesting that God *engineered* it, because, uh, he wanted more angels.

How many of those Newtown parents would acknowledge God's right to get more angels by the slaughter of innocents? Even those who are deeply religious might question God's grip on morality (and omniscience) in allowing such a thing to happen. Most, I suspect, would sense the disconnect of this idea from our life on the ground on planet Earth. They raised their children in the real world, and then heard that their kids were beamed up to a realm of mythical creatures. Their kids are now angels? Why not unicorns skipping across rainbows? It's no consolation whatever. They want their kids back, and had reason to be angry.

In the face of such blistering, stinging pain, other Christians have been less cruel and shown more class than my Catholic friend did that Christmas Eve. They have grasped for more graceful, less ghastly, explanations. Sixteen years earlier, in March 1996, in Dunblane, Scotland, a gunman walked into a school and killed sixteen children and their teacher. Among the many flowers that were left outside the school in the days following, one bouquet was accompanied by a Teddy Bear with a note tied around its neck: "Wednesday 13 March 1996–the day God overslept."[3]

Let the Excuses Begin

For those raised to believe in a good god who also happens to be all-powerful, such evil is inexplicable. Theologians have given it their best shot–over and over, throughout the millennia–but none of their explanations really satisfy. As one of them, Uta Ranke-Heinemann has admitted, "The question of the origin of evil, of what causes the tears and deviltries of the world, the question that no theologian has so far managed to answer, is one that humans have always posed."[4]

Many serious thinkers have concluded from the existence of massive evil and suffering that there probably isn't a good god overseeing the Cosmos. Most believers can't go that far, and reach for other explanations. Hence one mourner in Dunblane chose the metaphor of oversleeping to excuse God's inattention. This metaphor is milder than Nietzsche's famous declaration that "God is dead," but "God overslept" is still just an attempt–tinged with cynicism it seems to me–to come to terms with God's absence or indifference. Why didn't God–almighty God who knows if even a sparrow falls to the ground (Matt. 10:29)–jam the gun that day?

Sounds so simple, doesn't it? God could have jammed the gun. Why not? But even many Christians would respond, "Well, the world doesn't work that way." Of course not. But why not, if "he's got the whole world in his hands"? The disconnect between such sentimental religious banalities and the real world can be very jarring. With so much evil and misery on this planet, how is it consoling, let alone *true*, that "he's got the whole world in his hands"?[5]

Many explanations have been offered to account for suffering in our tiny corner of a Cosmos supposedly supervised by a caring and all-powerful god. The result of this major theistic preoccupation can be labeled *The Litany of Excuses*. Most Christian lay people can usually round up a few of the standard apologies if asked point-blank why God tolerates so much evil and suffering.

But I've found that believers balk at any hard thinking that would require serious homework on this issue. They usually don't grasp how fraught with difficulties the common excuses are. The apologies sound okay only on the surface. Folks who blithely offer two or three excuses for God's tolerance for suffering and evil usually have not thought deeply enough about the excuses to see how vulnerable they are. For example, those who claim that free will lets God off the hook on a lot of suffering don't grasp how free will goes off the rails before it accomplishes much of anything (more on this later).

Nor do they seem to be aware that the standard excuses have been vetted by non-religious philosophers, and commonly found wanting. They seldom–if ever–ask where they can find the exhaustive theodicy literature that is available. I've never heard a Christian say, "I'd better read up on this. There must be lots of books on my favorite apology for God. Where can I find them?"

Secular philosophers understand that the excuses don't hold water–that's commonly why they *became* secular philosophers–and theologians differ as to which are worth clinging to, and offer strained and forced defenses of those that they prefer.

The Idiocy of Theodicy
Bring on the Big Guns, The Official Excuse-Makers

I put suffering and evil at the top of the list of ten problems, as the most serious challenge to Christianity, because Christians themselves agonize over this more than anything else. In the face of personal tragedy especially, even the most devout believers are stunned and want to know **why**. Why did a killer shoot up a classroom of six-year olds? How could that happen? We can explain that a man with a damaged brain was on the loose–and that assault weapons are as easy to buy as candy bars–but that really doesn't answer the profound question. How can such things happen if God is keeping watch, if God loves and cares, and has the power to protect us?

People in the deepest pain imaginable have looked their pastors in the eye, pleading for answers that make sense. The answers aren't there. In Chris Chibnall's superb BBC drama, *Broadchurch*, about the murder of an 11-year old boy in a small English coastal town, the parents sit with a young parish priest out of his depth trying to ease their anguish. The father stammers a few words: "Just need some answers, don't we? We need some help. You have a line to the Big Man, why don't you ask him? We're drowning down here."

In such moments, even staunch Christians may waver and suspect that H.L. Mencken was right: "The whole Christian system, like every other similar system, goes to pieces upon the problem of evil."[6] The pastor is usually at a loss for words, offering only a shoulder to cry on and platitudes like "God moves in mysterious ways" or "It's all part of God's plan that we don't know."

But theologians are paid to come up with something better than that, to be more profound; it is their business to work out answers. And they have tried, oh, how they have tried. The official term for this endeavor is *theodicy*, the purpose of which is to *dis*prove Joseph Daleiden, who observed, "looking at the mess the world is in, it might seem easier to prove a Devil than a God."[7]

I've never come across a better statement of the problem than that provided by George Carlin. Sometimes philosophers must stand aside to let a comedian make the point:

> Something is *wrong* here. War, disease, death, destruction, hunger, filth, poverty, torture, crime, corruption and the Ice Capades. Something is definitely wrong. This is *not* good work. If this is the best God can do, I am not impressed. Results like these do not belong on the résumé of a supreme being. This is the kind of shit you'd expect from an office temp with a bad attitude. And just between you and me, in any decently run universe, this guy would have been out on his all-powerful ass a long time ago.[8]

It's a big challenge to explain why God doesn't deserve to be fired. Some of his defenders specialize in theodicy. Barry Whitney labored away for years in his ivory tower to create a theodicy catalogue. One wonders if he was striving for some kind of Sisyphus Award–pushing the boulder uphill forever–searching for solutions to the insolvable, excuses for God that would hold up to close scrutiny. He even caught the attention of big-time media. In July 1993 the religion columnist for the *New York Times*, Peter Steinfels, reported the following:

> Whitney has constructed an annotated bibliography of more than 4,200 philosophical and theological writings on the problem of evil published from 1960 to 1990 –nearly one publication every 2 ½ days, and that is only in English. His book is titled *Theodicy* the term German philosopher Leibniz coined from the Greek words for "God" and "justice" for efforts to reconcile the goodness of God and the existence of suffering.[9]

Has the world beat a path to Mr. Whitney's door to get this book? You can find a copy on Amazon for $162. It probably didn't have a large print run, and its sales ranking– the last time I checked–was 5,643,466. No, that's not how many copies it sold; this is *how far down* on the bestseller list it is! This means that 5,643,465 *other* titles out there in the wide world have sold more copies than this book has. Just for comparison: The sales ranking of a book on the history of screws and screwdrivers is much higher at 418,682.[10] Dan Brown's *The Da Vinci Code* ranks 7,914, and Richard Dawkins's *The God Delusion* is at 1,821.

Certainly, failure to sell many copies says nothing whatever about the veracity of a book's content, and a scholarly anthology won't fly off the shelves in any case. But it can also mean that Mr. Whitney was *not* on to something that would be recognized and acclaimed by those who spend their lives thinking about such things. There have been no earth-shattering solutions to the problem of suffering among those 4,200 listed writings. Nothing in this catalogue has grabbed the world's attention. The book was a dud. It's a research tool for theistic academicians with too much time on their hands.

Screw the Excuses

"I'll Believe Anyway"

This tells me, among other things, that, outside the ranks of theologians and philosophers—who write for each other—people really don't give a damn about coming up with excuses that make sense; some may even suspect that there are none. They are content with excuses that satisfy on a superficial level. As philosopher Daniel Dennett has pointed out, they believe in believing. They *want* to believe in a good God, so they just do. Like petulant children, Christians commonly say—when God is so obviously negated by the agony and grief that we put up with in this world—"Well, I'm going to believe in God anyway."

But this can happen only at the price of intellectual cowardice, dishonesty, and egregiously bad theology. They decline to follow the logic of their excuses for God. They fudge the facts to show God in a positive light, and they utter nonsense like what one Christian actually said to me, "The Newtown massacre may have been God's way to give a boost to gun control."

Die-hard Christians are very resistant about letting anything stand in the way of holding onto their God. I had entitled an earlier version of this chapter, "Easy Acceptance of the Very Terrible," because Christians are willing to shrug off terrible things; they accept them easily while expressing appropriate distress: plagues, cancer, famine, earthquakes, tsunamis, floods, massacres, genocide, horrendous plane crashes: "Oh well, I can't let these things bother my faith too much. We're so sorry, of course, but that's just the way God allows history to unfold under his supervision. He's very mysterious, you know." Strange way to run a planet.

Believe it or not, Whitney—the master compiler of excuses for God—didn't reach his low point with his book *Theodicy*. He also wrote *Evil and the Process God*, which had a sales ranking of 12,402,806, far below *Theodicy*—well, it was written thirteen years earlier, so maybe it just slipped on the charts. I did manage to find a copy at the New York Public Library, and sneaked it to a photocopy machine (to avoid paying $110 on Amazon). I find most books on theology tedious: They are written by academicians for other academicians who understand dense theological shoptalk.

Do you need to be convinced that I'm not being snarky? Try to wrap your mind around this statement of his about process thinkers. He says they "envisage all things (from God to the lowest levels of sub-atomic life) as components of actual entities which continually synthesize the causal data which affect them into new units, new experience." Digging his shovel in again, he says, "Every new synthesis attains at least some minimal value, since with every new concrescence the 'many' of the causal data become a new and unified experience."[11]

No wonder a book on the history of screwdrivers has sold more copies. What, you may ask, is a "process thinker"? Mr. Whitney is a theodicy theologian who is also an advocate of a "process God." Wikipedia offers this explanation:

> [I]t is an essential attribute of God to affect and be affected by temporal processes, contrary to the forms of theism that hold God to be in all respects non-temporal (eternal), unchanging (immutable), and unaffected by the world (impassible). Process theology does not deny that God is in some respects eternal (will never die), immutable (in the sense that God is unchangingly good), and impassible (in the sense that God's eternal aspect is unaffected by actuality), but it contradicts the classical view by insisting that God is in some respects temporal, mutable, and passible.[12]

Yes, theologians actually argue with one another about such things. Since there are no data on God, if there is one supreme talent that theologians possess it is for making things up as they go along. They are masters of *ad hoc* arguments, and they commonly fail to notice that their endeavors have become supremely irrelevant.

Most lay people don't even know they exist, and that they like to argue endlessly—for centuries now—creating higher and higher piles of books with lower and lower sales rankings.

To Hell with Hell

Although there are no data about God, some hunches about God are considered better than others. I said earlier that believers want to hold on to God at all costs, but it's also important to hold on to a loving God. This has been my suspicion for a long time, and research backs it up.

In their 2010 book, *America's Four Gods: What We Say About God—and What That Says About Us*, Paul Froese and Christopher Bader report:

> Nearly all Americans (85 percent) feel that the term "loving" describes God well. In fact, the term "God" is almost synonymous with the idea of a loving deity. Americans overwhelmingly believe that God cares deeply for the safety of humanity, and even individuals with more abstract ideas about God tend to feel that the universe is guided by a loving force that does not seek to cause us pain.[13]

Hence, for the most part, I have to say that the instincts of lay people about what God *ought* to be like seem to be pretty decent. I suspect that the primary reason that the faithful hold on to religion so fiercely is that they want a friendly Cosmos. They want to know that there is a God who loves and cares for each one of us, who will take care of us when we die. The world is a pretty rough place, and wouldn't it all be a brutal joke if "this is all there is" with no welcome into God's everlasting arms?

But even before the inevitable Pearly Gates moment, God should be the Ultimate Comforter. It's nice to think that not a sparrow falls to the ground without God knowing about it, and that he even knows the number of hairs on our heads (Matt. 10:29-30). *The Man Upstairs* is never intended as a sinister image.

There's probably no more compelling concept than "God is Love," and hence "God so loved the world" from John 3:16 resonates so deeply with so many. While many brands of Christianity have no hesitation preaching hellfire and brimstone—and this is no metaphor as the New Testament presents everlasting torture as a real thing with real fire—even that is somehow construed as the working out of God's love. It really is a deeply troubling contradiction, so the "hell side" of God is commonly downplayed or denied.

I suspect that most lay people just can't stomach much stress on hellfire and brimstone. They know in their bones that it doesn't ring true about a loving God. The comforting, compassionate side of God is cherished above all; the New Testament guarantees of eternal fire—underwritten by Jesus himself—are discounted.

Keeping God Kind

Many years ago a touching story crossed my desk when I served in the parish ministry. I have no idea if the story is apocryphal, but there is nothing about it that seems far-fetched.

Once upon a time—the time and exact locale were not specified—a Quaker gentleman arrived in a very Catholic village in an Eastern European country to set up shop as a cobbler. He was a very good shoemaker, and the villagers were soon won over by his kindly manner and compassion. He charged modest prices for repairs or new shoes, and he commonly gave shoes to the poorest in the town. Of course, he never set foot in their church, but nonetheless he became a beloved member of the community. His differentness was taken for granted and he grew old making shoes for two generations of the villagers.

Upon his death, his non-Catholic status suddenly presented a dilemma: He could not be buried in the village cemetery since he was not a Catholic. The local priest searched the rulebooks and consulted with the bishop. But, no, only baptized Catholics could be buried in the sacred ground adjoining the church.

With heavy hearts, the villagers did the next best thing: They dug his grave as close as they could to the cemetery, just on the other side of the fence. Then later, after night had fallen, a few of them went to the grave and *moved the fence*. This story inspired me to preach a sermon titled, "Will They Want to Move the Fence for You?"

The villagers, the unlettered lay people, knew better than to trust the official theology that the priest and bishop were bound to uphold, that the good cobbler was in hell because he had not been baptized as a Catholic. Their cobbler in hell? That just couldn't be so. They wouldn't have been interested in quibbling about alternate destinations—maybe he was in Purgatory?—but they were certain that he deserved to be buried in their sacred ground. This speaks volumes about their concept of God.

They knew more about divine tenderness than all the theological hairsplitters in high places.

Not long ago, I heard another story that brings the comfort of God to the fore. An elderly woman recalled her traumatic experience of being shipped off to America during World War II. Her parents in England wanted her to be in safe harbor, far away from the anticipated German invasion, and sent her to live in New York with a welcoming family. One of her great consolations was learning to play the piano, and she mastered Bach's *Jesu Joy of Man's Desiring*. She cherished the music and its message all her life:

> Jesu joy of man's desiring,
> Holy wisdom, love most bright;
> Drawn by Thee, our souls aspiring
> Soar to uncreated light.
>
> Word of God, our flesh that fashioned,
> With the fire of life impassioned,
> Striving still to truth unknown,
> Soaring, dying round Thy throne.
>
> Through the way where hope is guiding,
> Hark, what peaceful music rings;
> Where the flock, in Thee confiding,
> Drink of joy from deathless springs.
>
> Theirs is beauty's fairest pleasure;
> Theirs is wisdom's holiest treasure.
> Thou dost ever lead Thine own
> In the love of joys unknown.

God is all consolation here; hell is not mentioned. Good-hearted believers sense that hell should be confined to fiery sermons, and the subject doesn't have much traction after school shootings. A kind and gentle God has to be the primary subject. He may have overslept, but banishing any of those assassinated kids to hell would be unthinkable.

Shortly after the twenty children were slaughtered in Newtown, one evangelical Christian wrote on his Facebook page that the kids had actually received an "early Christmas present" because they were now with Jesus. He apparently had a brain freeze, because he forgot about the certainty—according to evangelical theology—that some of them were in hell.

Within hours his Facebook page had disappeared, for at least two reasons, I suspect. It was a cruel, outrageous, insensitive thing to say, yes. But it was also bad theology from the conservative perspective, easily spotted by his fundamentalist pals who would have been alarmed at the suggestion of such "easy" access to Jesus, i.e., just by being gunned down. You don't get to be with Jesus unless you have accepted Jesus as your Lord and Savior, being born again.[14]

But, in the moment of deep distress, his instincts were right, and maybe he allowed the kids a free pass because they were too young to have accepted Jesus.

Deep down inside, most Christians want a friendly Cosmos, underwritten by the love of God that's not tainted by the idea of eternal torture awaiting those who don't believe the right way.

When I've pointed out the grim Bible texts that suggest a vindictive God (e.g. Romans 2), I hear Christians flatly overrule such theology: "That's not the God I believe in." Ignoring much of the strident message of the New Testament, they conjure a better God! If there's anything sinister or ugly about God, it is ruled out, which accounts for the popularity of the banal 23rd Psalm, the ultimate statement of saccharine piety.

"The LORD is my shepherd; I shall not want" (KJV). The rest of it is probably familiar to you. I could devote a chapter to careful analysis of the silly, delusional theology reflected in its few lines about acting like a kept sheep. But what's evident from its popularity is that folks like their religion to be comforting. Protestant hymnology, especially of the Victorian era, played on the wishes for God to be a celestial buddy. This sentimentality was captured nicely with titles such as *Leaning on the Everlasting Arms* (1887) and *What a Friend We Have in Jesus* (1855).

So, understanding now the overwhelming urge to keep God warm and fuzzy, we can survey the various ways in which positive thinking sabotages critical thinking about God's accountability for suffering.

The Litany of Excuses

Too Much Is Swept Under the Free Will Rug

The dictionary definition of free will, for example this one offered by Merriam-Webster, calls it "the freedom of humans to make choices that are not determined by prior causes or by divine intervention." The *Stanford Encyclopedia of Philosophy*, however, offers a peek into the complexity of the issue:

> "Free Will" is a philosophical term of art for a particular sort of capacity of rational agents to choose a course of action from among various alternatives. Which sort is the free will sort is what all the fuss is about. (And what a fuss it has been: philosophers have debated this question for over two millennia, and just about every major philosopher has had something to say about it.)[15]

Free will has commonly been seized upon to explain why it is unfair to blame God for bad things that happen; after all, we can "make choices that are not caused . . . by divine intervention." Largely isolated from the philosophical arguments about free will and determinism, the people in the pews have commonly assumed that the simple dictionary definition can be used as the foundation for a neat, slick explanation of free will.

Here's what that would look like: There is so much pain and suffering because, while God generously gave humans free will, we have not used it prudently. Our suffering is primarily *our own fault*. If we don't follow his will and laws, well, God can't be blamed for that; there are consequences. He wanted us to be happy and independent creatures–and gave us the rules to follow. God would spoil free will if he made obvious incursions into human affairs.

The people who rely on the free will argument seem to be pleased with its tidiness: God is exonerated, case closed. One anonymous Christian, responding to a blog, wrapped it up with a bow: "God gave us free will. If He were to intervene everywhere, we would lose that freedom. And without free will, we would not only be like automatons, but we wouldn't be able to choose to love Him."

Natural evil can't easily be swept under the free will rug–this will be discussed later–but a massive crime such as the Holocaust clearly had human origins. Thus the Holocaust is Exhibit A in the case against man, not God; it illustrates human error and failure on a massive scale. God wept, too. But the free will approach takes little account of the origins and complexity of human behavior, and the Holocaust especially had very complex origins.

In the next few years free will enthusiasts need to pay very close attention to the rapidly advancing field of brain science. Studies of the brain suggest how closely human behavior is tied to what's going on in our brains over which we have little or no control. It will become increasingly difficult to accept free will as an easy out.

Free Will Is Warped by Mental Illness

There is a very blunt question that we can pose to the free will excusers: Are you willing to argue that those who suffer from mental illness can just decide one day *not* to be mentally ill? As you drive by a mental hospital, would it be appropriate for you to wonder: "Why don't they all just snap out of it and leave the hospital? They've chosen to be mentally ill."

Free will runs onto the rocks when we consider psychopathy, for example. Psychopathy can be diagnosed, analyzed and medicated, but it cannot be cured. It is just a fact that there are bad brains, and the consequences can be lethal. So, no, it won't do to say that the shooters in Dunblane and Newtown were wicked people who turned their backs on God.

You can blame the construction of their brains on evolution–evolution allows for grievous aberrations–or on God. Take your pick. If you opt for evolution, then you have put free will in jeopardy and removed God from the equation. Please note, by the way, that theists who claim that a person has *God-given* talents are actually claiming that God *does* manipulate genomes and brains purposefully. If that's the case, how does he escape responsibility for psychopathy?

Free Will Is Warped by Brainwashing

There is a convent in my neighborhood in Manhattan, so from time to time I see full-dress nuns walking along the street–and I do mean wearing versions of the head-to-toe habits that I remember from my childhood. At the 42nd Street subway station I also see the Jehovah's Witnesses holding up their *Watchtower* magazines.

I have always resisted the temptation to say to these folks–the nuns or the subway witnesses–"You didn't get the memo? There is no God. You missed that memo?" But they are members of cults, and the brainwashing has been so acute that my taunt would have as much impact as shooting arrows at a tank. Most people–by no means all, but most–will remain in the cults that captured them. The oft-quoted Jesuit formula cannot be minimized: "Give me the child for his first seven years, and I'll give you the man." Jesuits, and all other brands of priests, are cult members–as are Jehovah's Witnesses, the Amish, Mormons, Seventh Day Adventists, Christian Scientists, Scientologists, Hasidic Jews. Well, let's face it, if you hold fast to the lessons taught in Sunday school and catechism, it's damn hard to accuse *others* of being cult members.

How common is it–how *possible* is it–to escape hard-core indoctrination? How is it that none of the nineteen men who hijacked the planes on 9/11 had the presence of mind to say, "You know, maybe this isn't such a good idea"? Any "presence of mind" was long gone for them. Their minds had been molded so profoundly that doubts could not break through. Their personalities had been tortured and twisted by environment and religion.

It may be tempting to say, "Aha, this is a perfect example of people disobeying God. There you have it: free will in action." But that won't do. Quite apart from the fact that the hijackers were convinced that they *were* following God's will (more about the problem of figuring out what God wants in the next chapter), the brainwashing had simply worked too well. Nature puts the hardwiring into the brain, but software installed by humans cannot be easily deleted. Darrell Ray uses the disease metaphor in his book *The God Virus: How Religion Infects Our Lives and Culture*.[16] There he demonstrates how tenacious and resistant the God virus is. Free will can be stunted.

We like to think that there's a level playing field, as in "all men are created equal." Hey, if you're born in America, you have a chance to grow up to become president. If you set your mind to it, you can do it. This is the ultimate free will fantasy. But people who grow up in grinding poverty, in circumstances of violence, abuse and malnutrition, have the deck stacked against them. Sometimes they defy the odds and build successful lives, but the playing field in anything but level.

The free will argument can't do the heavy lifting that its advocates assume when the variables of human life are considered."They have wandered too far from God's will" is hopelessly naïve. There is truth in the cliché, "There but for the grace of God go I"–which is a gracious way of admitting that life is not fair. God has little to do with it, much less grace: we are dealt a hand that undercuts confidence that free will is a useful concept. In the real world we are in a constant struggle to bring balance, to level the playing field, because choices are constrained by the hand we are dealt, by the *failure* of God's grace. We are all locked into something better or worse–or at least different–than the other guy has.

Ironically, the believers who argue most strenuously for free will as God's free pass are those who demonstrate that brainwashed minds have very little agility for critical thinking: they just don't have the free will to think outside the cult formulas that have been engraved in the minds; they are as good as carved in stone.

On my Facebook page for this book, I commonly find that Christians drop in to fume, protest and preach. It's pretty clear that the standard formulas have been locked into their brains. Consider this comment from April 2013 and its programmed accusation that atheists are selfish. Things quickly slide into Christian babble that has been pounded into the writer's skull since infancy:

> The first problem I see is that you can't see beyond self in your ponderings of ideological thinking. Jesus Christ the Lord who sits at the right hand of the Father proved by His death, burial & resurrection that its [sic] not about self but to humble ones self [sic]. If there was no hell to shun or heaven to gain, I'd still want to follow Jesus. His way is truth, His way is life and no other teaching will do. Like the ole preacher said, there's [sic] no atheists in hell. Repent ye and be baptized in the name of the Lord.

It is meaningless to suggest that this man has free will to think his way out of his doctrinal prison. His brain is locked.

In Fact, Free Will Hobbles Christianity

Another devout Catholic–not the one who turns slaughtered children into angels–clings to faith, she very candidly admits, because she wants to see her dead mother again in heaven. So she is highly motivated to save God from oblivion or irrelevance. In an email exchange with me, she glommed enthusiastically onto free will, assuring me that evil is rampant because, after God created, he "stepped back" (i.e., launched free will) in order not to impede human independence. She is proud of her training as a lay catechist, so this was probably one of the excuses that sounded right as she soaked up the wisdom of the priests. She also told me that she doesn't like to read books, so I gave up on expecting any depth to her thinking. Curiously enough, she is liberal on some social issues, but she is a non-reader who aches to see her mother again in heaven. On the doctrinal front, she is a Vatican wet dream.

The "God stepped back" defense that supposedly enables free will bristles with additional difficulties–beyond those I've already discussed. It's like water that freezes in the pipes, causing Christianity to crack, split, and leak. Here are some of the ways that free will kills most of her assumptions and practices as a devout Catholic.

- If you believe in a god who created, then stepped back–to let creation and its creatures run pretty much on their own–you are a deist, not a theist: A concerned, loving god, in any meaningful sense, is off the table. Christianity has been cancelled.

- Most Christians cherish the Bible, and would be reluctant to suggest that its picture of God is all wrong. The God of the Bible is very much involved in his handiwork, in fact is *intimately* involved. Of course the Bible is a book, and my Catholic friend doesn't read books, so the Bible probably isn't on her night table. If God had stepped back, in deference to free will, to let creation run on its own, most of the pages of the Bible would be blank. Why would God bother to know that a sparrow falls, and how many hairs are on your head, if he had stepped back? According to the Bible, God is the ultimate micromanager, e.g., Romans 2:16: "God through Jesus Christ will judge the secret thoughts of all." The concept of the Incarnation of God in Christ is destroyed by the suggestion that God stepped back.

- Prayer as approach to God–having God's ear–is seriously compromised by the argument that God, to safeguard our free will, watches creation with his arms folded or hands tied. Most Christians want to feel that God is accessible and responsive. They're ready to jump in to ask God to heal cancers, divert hurricanes and give a boost to the local football team. But what would be the point if God has stepped back? All those prayer circles to heal the sick are useless. The whole point of such prayer marathons is to coax God into tinkering in human bodies at the molecular level. Doesn't "please cure the cancer" imply just that?

What We Don't Know about God Won't Hurt Us

But here's one of the major snags in the free will excuse: if we don't *know* when God has intervened to stop evil–whether or not it derives from our free will–we'd be none the wiser. Thus we wouldn't be over-awed: Human freedom would not be compromised or tainted in any way. And obviously God's disguised almightiness would come in very handy in countless ways.

Yes, there might be circumstances in which God would use restraint to preserve free will, but if God is almighty, there must be ways, unknown to us, by which he could prevent evil. For example, how might he have prevented the Newtown massacre, assuming that the "He wanted more angels" argument is too obscene to take seriously? It's not hard to come up with ideas:

- God could have arranged for the shooter to have a flat tire and go off the road. Surely the God who parted the Red Sea can manage a flat tire. The cache of weapons would have been found in the trunk when the police arrived to investigate. So, off to jail with him–instead of to the classroom.

- Or maybe God could have used an even more subtle approach. Christians claim that God manipulated the brain cells of ancient authors to write the inspired books of the Bible. The Bible is a thousand pages long, so that's a lot of brain manipulation. Why couldn't he have tweaked a few of the shooter's brain cells to change his mind about shooting up a school? Is that really beyond God's power?

Philosopher and Bible scholar Richard Carrier, writing a full year before the Newtown horror, offered a more dramatic–even stunning–suggestion. Carrier was puzzled that any compassionate human would be more willing to take action than God:

> Think about it. A man approaches a school with a loaded assault rifle, intent on mass slaughter. A loving person speaks to him, attempts to help him resolve his problems or to persuade him to stop, and failing that, punches him right in the kisser, and takes away his gun. And a loving person with godlike powers could simply turn his bullets into popcorn as they left the gun, or heal with a touch whatever insanity or madness (or by

teaching cure him of whatever ignorance) led the man to contemplate the crime. But God does nothing. Therefore, a loving God does not exist.[17]

No, you can't have the personal God who takes care of your dead relatives in heaven if God adopted a hands-off policy regarding his creation. In every direction you turn, the contradictions smack you in the face.

The religious folks who are confident that free will trumps most accusations against God would do well to scan the literature. As the Stanford Encyclopedia quote mentioned earlier alerts us, free will has been the preoccupation of theologians and philosophers for centuries, and it is naïve to assume that the concept is within easy grasp.

A good place to start, a quick introduction into the voluminous literature, is Sam Harris's short book *Free Will*.[18] You can read this 75-page volume in a couple of hours, then follow the debate that has followed in its wake—Daniel Dennett especially has been critical of Harris—and dig into free will bibliographies that can be found online.

Free will fails to provide God with a get-out-of-jail card. Theists usually find themselves limping back to square one.

The "God Is Punishing Us" Excuse

The impulse that prompts this excuse is the fervent hope that people who do bad things will get what they deserve. We all say "life isn't fair"—but is that the way things are supposed to be?

And who better to settle accounts than God? The assumption that *God punishes* is actually rampant in the same popular culture that cherishes God's love so dearly. How could the Bible's overpowering message that God punishes not have seeped into Christian consciousness at some level?

We even joke about it. Most of us who watched TV in the 1970s remember Beatrice Arthur, in the sitcom *Maude,* snap out the words, "God'll get you for that." Tammy Wynette sang for an adoring public that had no trouble believing the sentiment behind her lyrics:

> God's gonna get 'cha for that
> God's gonna get 'cha for that
> There's no place to run and hide
> For he knows where you're at.

But God-the-punisher is too sinister to be taken seriously in healthy faith, if there is such a thing. Nietzsche's advice to "distrust all in whom the impulse to punish is powerful" is fair warning about the ugly theology we're going to encounter as we discuss this common theistic excuse for suffering.

God-the-punisher seems to be a natural fall-back explanation for people who detest sin and relish the idea of retribution. Muslim clerics suggested that the 2004 tsunami was a result of God's anger that European tourists were wearing bikinis on beaches in Thailand. And it's not uncommon for Christians to see mass suffering as

God's vengeful handiwork. Listen to Pam Olsen, founder of the Tallahassee House of Prayer. She could hold her own against any fervent Old Testament prophet:

> God is shaking. If anybody looks at the news and has just seen what's been happening recently with the floods, the fires, the tornadoes, God is shaking. Yeah I think you have God shaking, sure you have the Enemy shaking, you have both and I don't want to say oh that's the judgment of God or that's the Enemy. But the reality is God is judging us, and I think it's going to get worse.[19]

By "the Enemy," she means the Devil—we'll get to him later—and although she claims that she doesn't want to say that God is judging us, she can't resist citing "the reality is God is judging us." Pam Olsen seems to positively relish the idea of punishment and the prospect of things getting worse. Pat Robertson has likewise bookmarked too many of the punishment texts in the Bible.

> Mr. Robertson said tolerance of homosexual activity "could bring about earthquakes, tornadoes, and possibly a meteor." He warned Orlando, then festooned with flags marking the gay celebration: "You are right in the way of some serious hurricanes and I don't think I'd be waving those flags in God's face if I were you."[20]

The God-the-punisher excuse falls into the "Oh, give me a break" category. It's just bad theology, failing on at least four levels.

#1: Resistance in the Bible, of All Places

When's the last time you checked out Genesis 18? My guess is that it doesn't get a lot of attention, but it's an important patch of scripture because God *gets talked out of mass murder*. It's a glimmer of resistance to bad theology. Chapter 18 is a prelude to the famous story in Genesis 19 about the destruction of Sodom and Gomorrah. Because the Lord found great sin in Sodom (not specified as homosexuality, by the way), he "overthrew those cities and the entire plain, destroying all those living in the cities—and also the vegetation in the land."[21] This is typical dysfunctional behavior of the god who gave permission to the Israelites to wipe out the indigenous tribes in Palestine, and indeed who wiped out the whole population of the Earth—except for Noah and his family—at the time of the flood.

Bible scholar Hector Avalos has correctly identified this god as a moral monster. This tribal deity breathes threats against his own "chosen people" because they sin too much, e.g., Jeremiah 9:11: "I will make Jerusalem a heap of ruins, a lair of jackals, and I will make the cities of Judah a desolation, without inhabitant."

But Genesis 18 was obviously written by someone with more scruples and compassion, a theologian who was bothered by the moral monster, and sought to soften the prevailing concept of God. Thus he depicts a scene in which Abraham argues and negotiates with God, pouring on the flattery. This is clever, charming folklore. Of course, there never is actual data about God, but human sensibilities can come into play when people contemplate the divine. They imagine what God ought to be like, and this theologian saw the injustice in indiscriminate slaughter (Pat Roberson, take notice).

Even after the men turned away and went toward Sodom, "Abraham still stood before the Lord." He "drew near and said, 'Will you indeed sweep away the righteous with the wicked?'" Suppose, Abraham proposed, that there were "fifty righteous within the city." What then? Would God not spare the place for them? "Far be it from you to do such a thing," he told God, "to put the righteous to death with the wicked, so that the righteous fare as the wicked! Far be that from you! Shall not the Judge of all the earth do what is just?"

God relented. Sure, if you have fifty righteous, I'll back off. Then Abraham pushed the bargain. What if I come up five short of fifty? OK, God said, fine. Well, what if there are only forty righteous? Yep, that'll do. On and on it went until Abraham had a promise from God that he wouldn't destroy Sodom if just ten righteous were found there.

Would the ancient author of this story himself have stopped at ten? Who knows, but his conscience told him that God surely had to be better than the common rabble supposed, and the rabble included the other theologian who wrote Genesis 19: "[T]he Lord overthrew those cities and the entire plain, destroying all those living in the cities—and also the vegetation in the land."

Indeed, the author of Genesis 19 seems not to have known about the Lord's conversation with Abraham in chapter 18. This is evidence, by the way, that Genesis was cobbled together by editors who cared little for consistency. The same splicing can be found in the creation and flood stories, which both combine conflicting accounts.

Fast forward now to Matthew 18:21-22, a couple of verses that should be carved in stone above every church door: "Then Peter came to Jesus and asked, 'Lord, how many times shall I forgive my brother or sister who sins against me? Up to seven times?' Jesus answered, 'I tell you, not seven times, but seventy-seven times.'"

It really doesn't matter if Jesus actually said this or anything like it (as we will see later, it's virtually impossible to figure out what Jesus said). *Someone* in the early Christian movement believed it and felt strongly enough about it to put these words on the lips of Jesus. Here's a theological writer who believed that human affairs would be improved if people didn't hold grudges. Our constant approach to life should be forgiveness. Clearly the writer indulged in poetic hyperbole with his mathematical formula, but he appears to have valued compassion above almost anything else. God-the-punisher would have been a hard idea for him to take seriously.

So, those Christians who know in their gut that they don't love a vengeful God do have some scripture to back them up, and they have it worked out that The Man Upstairs is a benevolent figure. But cherry picking remains the primary methodology for using scripture to underwrite morality and faith, because Jesus and Paul said some pretty blood-curdling things about God.

#2: As Commonly Preached, God's Wrath Is Not Well Targeted

Pat Robertson mentions tornadoes, floods, fires, earthquakes, and meteors as God's way of getting even for Gay Day at Disney. But, unless the meteor scores a direct hit on Disney, isn't God being pretty scattershot in taking his revenge?

Pat seems to think that wildfires wiping out a trailer park a hundred miles from Orlando would be a sure sign that Gay Day at Disney has riled the divine temper. He doesn't seem to grasp that he is championing a sloppy, mean-spirited deity. The fire-and-brimstone tribal deity that strides through the Old Testament just doesn't translate well to the modern world. Does Robertson really think sane people will believe that an elderly couple dying in a trailer park fire makes sense as divine punishment for gay people having a good time at a theme park? Tornadoes, hurricanes, and meteors would be God's reckless anger with an exclamation point. Decent people see through such shallow theology; it's not really a helpful way to argue that God wants to teach people a lesson through suffering.

There was a priest in New Orleans who witnessed, in the wake of Hurricane Katrina, human suffering he'd never even imagined. He went on a spiritual retreat to try to patch his faith back together. He had been devastated by what he'd seen, and his faith was wrecked as well. The last thing he needed to be told was that New Orleans had been visited by God's wrath—for all that jazz, decadent night life and full-blown gay pride during Mardi Gras.

Some people who do embrace God-the-punisher usually back off when they consider the full implications of arguing that natural disasters are God's preferred instrument of terror. A tsunami kills 225,000 people because women were wearing bikinis? The best advice I can give is to put as much distance as you can between yourself and people who think that way.

#3: It's Delusional Thinking about How the World Works

It's painful how Christians so rarely dig beneath the surface of beloved Bible stories. For example, a swarm of questions arises in the wake of one simple gospel episode, from Mark 2. A charming, moving tale turns out to be, on deeper reflection, deeply disturbing. Because the visual is so impressive, this is a favorite story for illustrators, and every Bible storybook for kids includes an excerpt from the passage.

In verses 1-12 we are told that Jesus was so popular, so overwhelmed by the crowds, that friends of a paralytic couldn't get in the door of Jesus' house, so they lowered the guy on a stretcher through the roof.

When the stretcher landed on the living room floor, Jesus said, "Son, your sins are forgiven." That raised the eyebrows of the local theologians:

> Why does this man speak like that? He is blaspheming! Who can forgive
> sins but God alone?" And immediately Jesus, perceiving in his spirit that
> they thus questioned within themselves, said to them, "Why do you
> question these things in your hearts? Which is easier, to say to the
> paralytic, 'Your sins are forgiven,' or to say, 'Rise, take up your bed and
> walk'? But that you may know that the Son of Man has authority on earth

to forgive sins"–he said to the paralytic–"I say to you, rise, pick up your bed, and go home.

Put aside for the moment whether this really happened, whether these are actual words of Jesus (very real problems as we shall see later), or whether Jesus really did exist (which we'll also consider). Put aside that voice-activated healing of a paralytic is the stuff of fairy tales. Putting all of this aside, we have to ask: Is *sickness* really a legitimate punishment for *sin*?

This thinking is behind John 5:14 as well. After Jesus had cured a man who had been sick for 38 years–he was too weak to beat the crowds into a healing pool–Jesus cautions him: "Sin no more, that nothing worse befall you."

People can be overcome with guilt that sickness is a curse from God, but sickness as God's punishment is not our first reaction when we hear that a neighbor has been rushed to the ICU with a heart attack. "Gosh, what is God punishing *him* for?" Even if we know that he was a heavy smoker who ate a burger with fries every day, still we don't say, "Ah, the wages of sin is death." When we find out that a child has been diagnosed with leukemia, our first impulse is not to say, "Yes, we could have predicted this. His father has been cheating on his mother." We have a different worldview. We simply do not think–unless our minds have been severely warped by religious indoctrination–that people get sick because of their sins or the sins of others. But that was the understanding in New Testament times, with the assumption of demon possession thrown into the mix as well.

So our primary objection to the episode in Mark 2 is that it is delusional thinking and bad theology: **sickness = punishment for sin.** We now have a pretty good idea about how pathology works, and no researchers on neurological damage–those who study paralytics–have ever been willing to settle on sin as the cause.

Moreover, if these are the real words of Jesus, *he was wrong.* What else would we expect from a first century Galilean peasant? He couldn't and didn't think beyond the mythology of his time; he failed to bring new insights to the human condition. Shouldn't we expect new insights if he really had been tuned into God in a special way? It's actually better for Jesus' reputation if we assume that the story is a fabrication. Which it is.

#4: Why Would God Be Punishing You, Anyhow?

But think of the poor paralytic. Was he startled to be told that he was paralyzed because of his sins? Maybe the guy got kicked by a horse or fell off a wall. "What have my sins got to do with it? Give me a break. What sin?" That's the big problem with the idea that we suffer as punishment for sin. What good is punishment, what remedial, corrective role could it play, if God doesn't have some way to make it clear: "I have sent *this* punishment for *this* error, *this* violation"?

In the movie *Moonstruck,* devout Catholic Loretta was convinced that her husband died because they didn't get married in church. How much guilt and anguish have people suffered because of the pernicious suggestion that God is smacking us for something? We're left to draw our own conclusions, and human imaginations have run wild. It may have been that my mother wondered, when baby Michael died, how she had offended God, though I doubt it because she didn't think of God in those terms. But we can be sure that there have been countless women who have agonized over sins resulting in miscarried or stillborn children.

Once the thought has been planted that we suffer because we deserve it—our sins are catching up with us—humans are left to guess and face the torment, certain that bad things are their own fault. People conjure up sins and offenses against God that really aren't any such thing. This is *nasty theology*, and in its wake there has been so much human agony, grief, and bitterness. Human happiness has been diminished immeasurably. In fact, this is *evil* theology.

Well, Maybe God Is Testing Us

In Meredith Wilson's *The Music Man*, the very Irish mother of Marian the librarian is alarmed that her daughter is well into marriageable age with no suitors. Marian defends her slide toward spinsterhood: "I have my standards where men are concerned." Mother will have none of it:

> I know all about your standards and if you don't mind my sayin' so, there's not a man alive who could hope to measure up to that blend of Paul Bunyan, Saint Pat, and Noah Webster you've concocted for yourself out of your Irish imagination, your Iowa stubbornness, and your li'berry full of books!

Christian theology would have us believe that God has his standards where men are concerned—actually men, women, and children—and one of the ways to see if we measure up is to monitor our behavior and see how we handle suffering.

For the moment we will ignore the frightful brand of Christianity that maintains that there is no such thing as measuring up to God's standards: We are born evil, devoid of goodness, and can be saved only by God's grace via Jesus Christ. (See grumpy Paul's sinister view of people in Romans 3:3-19, "amazing grace, that saved a wretch like me.") We can be thankful that many people shudder at such vile theology, but even so they accept a God who measures . . . and tests.

When life smacks us, do we doubt, whimper, and fold—give in to the suspicion that God is missing in action? What better way to test our mettle and our resolve not to doubt God than to throw tragedy and trouble across our paths? And more than that: The tragedy and trouble are part of God's master plan to strengthen our character and give us backbone. So he keeps track of our daily lives to make sure we're measuring up. As George Carlin said, "Religion has actually convinced people that there's an invisible man living in the sky who watches everything you do, every minute of every day."

"God Is Testing Us" Presented as Bad Clichés

Why aren't people suspicious when clichés are passed off as theology? It is a slick move, a sleight-of-hand designed to divert attention from the God's negligence. It's the theological equivalent of making lemonade out of lemons, but it doesn't work all that well. It's the quintessential *ad hoc* argument: proposing an explanation when there's no evidence to back it up, and making it sound plausible. Clichés are clumsy guesses, and theologians and preachers having been saying them for such a long time that people have bought them and welcomed them into popular imagination.

One of the most commonly used clichés reflecting God-is-testing-us thinking is the doltish "everything happens for a reason," presumably meaning–actually it *has* to mean this–that there is a plan."For a reason" embodies the notion of *teleology*, i.e., everything is pushing toward a goal. God engineers our trials and griefs to see if we arrive, on the other side of the worst thing imaginable, healthy and whole, and with our faith in his goodness intact. That's the test. When I hear people say "everything happens for a reason," I sometimes respond, depending on the setting and circumstance, "No, it doesn't. That's a silly thing to say."

Think it through. This is in the same category as "God wanted more angels." You end up with evil theology if everything is meant to happen. On 27 March 1977, two Boeing 747s collided on a runway at Tenerife airport and 583 people were burned alive. It was the worst air disaster ever. Many aircraft had been diverted to Tenerife because of bomb scares at another airport, and were parked on the taxiway; heavy fog had also rolled in. So we know how it came to happen. But with an event like this is mind, it should stick in your throat to say, "Everything happens for a reason." I should think that any decent, compassionate person would be reluctant to claim this calamity was a way for God to test the faith of the loved ones left behind.

God-is-testing-us theology also lurks behind that other, equally silly cliché, "whatever doesn't kill you will make you stronger." This is intended to be comforting, a word of encouragement to appreciate the bad things that happen to us. Moreover, we should appreciate that God wants to see how we're going to bear up, and thus he uses our trials to make us better.

But sometimes Humpty Dumpty can't be put back together again. Many experiences and events that don't quite kill us *don't* make us better, stronger people. We see human wreckage all around us, those who are damaged and bitter, physically and mentally crippled by troubles they've encountered. Are we supposed to conclude that God has experimented on them, and they failed to bounce back?

"Whatever doesn't kill you will make you stronger" is sophomoric, and it's bad theology. Hence my quick retort is usually, "No, that's not true, think it through."

His Eye Is On the Sparrow–and Everything Else

In properly evaluating God-is-testing-us theology, it's helpful to consider the broadest possible perspective. A lot of people in this world are not Christian and don't fall into any of the Western theistic traditions. They haven't been introduced to the idea that God is watching and testing and might find the concept as foolish as it surely is. What kind of game is this? Is it really plausible that the God who runs the Cosmos is tracking and testing the 7.1 billion people on the planet, to make sure they're measuring up to, well, to what? Why would he even care?

Theists vary greatly in what they believe pisses God off, and what's going to send him off on a punishing binge to test our faith. A Mormon might fear that skipping the holy underwear for a day or two earns demerits; a Hasidic Jew knows that he has descended into impurity by touching a woman who's having her period; a radical Muslim may be afraid that failing to stone an adulteress will earn God's wrath. But doesn't God have better things to do than keep track of all the sins and shortcomings of every person on earth? There must be, at any given moment, millions of masturbating teenage boys: What a major challenge that would be to monitor (and does God consider the sin greater if the boys are fantasizing about other boys instead of girls?). If nothing else, the ever-watchful god becomes a petty voyeur. Surely such a concept of deity has outlived its usefulness.

That's the trouble with clinging to and trying to modernize and rationalize a religion that emerged in the Bronze Age, when people believed that God resided just a few miles overhead. They went to mountaintops to get closer to God and burned animals because the odor wafted upward and was pleasing to God.

You're not really that much better off if you've opted for a "deeply spiritual" understanding of deity: You close your eyes and think intensely to channel the deity (prayer). The channel supposedly works both ways: If you're making your soul transparent to God, isn't he watching you back? So you're right back to God the Voyeur who lives a few miles overheard. If you really do believe that God is personal and knows each one of us–knows even our thoughts (how else would prayer work?)– and that we are accountable to him (and will face that moment when we meet our Maker), then you must follow this idea to its logical conclusion and take the consequences. It's no good to protest that you "don't believe in that old-man-in-the-sky nonsense" *because indeed you do*, if you believe that God is keeping track of you. In some clever way you may have deleted "old man" and "sky" from your concept of God, but you haven't deleted the basic idea that Bronze Age thinkers invented.

"Hey, God is watching everything I do." Many serious thinkers have wondered how this is not arrogance: You've become the center of attention of the Engineer of the Cosmos? Such pious posturing is distasteful. Atheists don't buy the *pretended* humility that masks this arrogance. And how do you even know God is the Great Watcher and Tracker, the Great Voyeur? In the next chapter we'll see that the commonly assumed ways of knowing God fall far short of delivering the goods.

Fine, the Prince of Darkness Is Behind It All

In the gospel of Mark we read that Jesus had one encounter after another with demons and "unclean spirits." Perhaps the most dramatic confrontation is related in Mark 5. A severely tormented man who lived among the tombs, who "was always howling and bruising himself with stones," recognized Jesus as the son of God "from afar" and rushed to greet him. The realm of the good was about to tangle with the realm of evil.

As the story unfolds, the demons inhabiting the man converse with Jesus. The demons beg Jesus not to expel them from the country, but to send them instead into a herd of swine on the hillside. Jesus complies, giving them permission to do so, and the 2,000 frenzied swine run off the cliff into the sea. Not surprisingly, the local townspeople ask Jesus to leave.

It would be too much of a digression here to recount the reasons why this story fails as history, but the author was dead serious in this depiction of a realm of beings who could challenge the divine. The demon motif is a red flag that the gospels usher us into a Halloween-like thought world. We know that our ancient ancestors, well before Biblical times, invested nature with spirits. There was little understanding of causation, so human imagination supplied explanations of why things happened: it's not a stretch to conclude that a deranged man was possessed by demons.

People came to suppose as well that there could be a hierarchy in the realm of evil spirits. And the CEO of Evil–the devil, Satan or simply God's adversary–was invented as a desperate way to preserve the goodness of God above all else. When the weight of suffering becomes too great for theology to sustain (and explain), priests and theologians reach for whatever might seem to work–at least for a while, and until people see through it.

The Devil represents desperate speculation to explain why so much evil and suffering continue in a world that is overseen by a loving God. Accordingly–as I've stated before, theologians specialize in making things up as they go along–the evil isn't God's fault; other powerful and malignant agents are behind the wars, famines, plagues and all other manner of catastrophes, large and small. Thus we can breathe a sigh of relief that God's goodness remains intact.

By New Testament times, the CEO of Evil had emerged as a clear figure in the literature. It was an idea whose time had come when Israel faced centuries of setbacks by foreign conquerors. People commonly fantasized about a utopia that God would eventually establish when he was ready to make his move against Satan.[22] And, by the way, those champion New Testament preachers–John the Baptist, Jesus, and the apostle Paul–*all* fell for this shallow theology.

But why the delay? The most obvious question is: Why in the world would God tolerate an adversary, even for a minute? These theological mind games are utterly transparent. You have to shut down your mind, as so many Christians do, to resort to this expediency. At the very least you have to concede that God is not all-powerful, or that he breaches his own high moral standards to allow awful mischief to take place. If God is actually, in any meaningful way, all-powerful, how could there be an adversary with enough power to wreak havoc in human affairs for centuries?

One of the worst books of the Bible is Job, at least in terms of theological integrity. On a bet, God allows his adversary to test Job with unimaginable suffering to see if Job will crack. Job protests his innocence, but in the end he acquiesces when God pulls rank and plays the bully–"Where were you when I laid the foundation of the Earth?" (Job 38:4, RSV). Believers seem content with the answer "God is God, live with it." Of course, atheists really don't care about the mind games that Christians play, but is it too much to ask that Christians try to keep their theology honest?

So it simply will not do to account for evil and suffering by blaming it on God's adversary, as a way to keep God's hands clean. You only postpone God's accountability by blaming suffering on someone or something else that shouldn't even exist in the first place. At the end of Ludovic Kennedy's book, *All in the Mind: A*

Farewell to God, he wonders how long it will take for believers to give up on God, as they do on Satan, when they see the contradiction:

> There was a time in the history of the Church when the devil, Beelzebub or Satan, the king of evil, was as real and forceful a figure as for a diminishing number of people "God" still is today; a creation of the Jews and early Christians to give substance in half-human, half-bestial form to the wickedness they saw about them. Later Christians came to recognize that this was a fantasy figure with no basis in reality and quietly discarded him. How soon or long before they come to recognize that God is a fantasy figure, like Satan an idea in the mind, and learn to discard him too?[23]

But God has staying power, and, to hold on to him, some theologians do strive for honesty in grappling with the problem of evil: Maybe evil *is* stronger than God. Rabbi Harold Kushner, in his enormously popular 1981 book, *When Bad Things Happen to Good People*, frankly admitted that God isn't all-powerful. Giving up on God's goodness is unthinkable, so Kushner could live with the concession that God can't stop suffering. Speaking of a person's sickness, he wrote, "He can't make it go away. That is something which is too hard even for God."[24]

I suspect that most Jewish and Christian theologians recoil in horror at this bold step of deleting God's omnipotence: it's a violation of protocol to take nips and tucks here and there at God to suit your own sensibilities. You can make things up about God as you go along, as long as you *improve* the divine reputation, not diminish it.

To retain God's omnipotence most theologians resort to the "mystery excuse," i.e., our suffering is beyond our understanding (and I'll discuss this common dodge shortly). Christians especially are likely to cry foul at the good rabbi's suggestion. Faith healing is a big part of Christian piety, and Christians pray fervently–they organize aggressive prayer campaigns–to hound God to heal the sick. How could healing be "too hard" for God?

Your Theology Is Crumbling

You know you've lost . . .

. . . When It Hits You that Suffering Is Built In

Charles Darwin was a reluctant atheist. He abhorred the controversy that followed in the wake of his publications and deflected attention from his personal feelings about religion, especially because his wife remained very devout. But his powers of observation were acute and he saw too much. He observed nature up close for decades and his conclusions profoundly changed the way we think about nature and, indeed, the Cosmos. It struck him that a loving deity did not reconcile well with phenomena that he'd studied. While he "did not set out to demolish anyone's religious convictions," Darwin struggled

> with some things he saw in nature, from a religious point of view–such as parasitic wasps that slowly devoured their prey, and questions such as

"Why are so many animals created only to perish?" With respect to parasitic wasps, he observed that the adults lay their eggs inside their prey, which after hatching take days eating the host's non-essential body parts, such as muscles and gut, while the host remains alive, but dying. Such a life cycle discomforted Darwin and he wrote to the American biologist Asa Gray, "I cannot persuade myself that a benevolent and omnipotent God would have designedly created the Ichneumonidae with the express intention of their feeding within the living bodies of Caterpillars."[25]

It's very common for theologians, preachers and laypeople to romanticize nature, to deduce God from the beauty of nature and from the awe they feel in the presence of natural wonders. Paul berated people who failed to see God in the natural world (Rom. 1:20, ESV): "For his invisible attributes, namely, his eternal power and divine nature, have been clearly perceived, ever since the creation of the world, in the things that have been made." Barry Whitney, the theologian whom I excoriated earlier, earned my contempt on page one of *Evil and the Process God*. Instead of giving the reader confidence that he'd make a stab at suggesting credible means for knowing about God—well, credible at least to a mind soaked in theology (and I never expect much there)—we find mindless theological sludge about nature:

> We are fortunate indeed if we have experienced the serene beauty of a dampened forest or the majestic expanse of the open seas; or again, if we have been deeply moved and comforted by the awesome and mysterious vault of the starry heavens on a quiet evening, or shared the joys of intimate fellowship, or the indescribable love of a parent for his children. Such moments are to be cherished, for they somehow assure the longing soul of its communion with a Presence which animates all life by its love and care.[26]

This would make good copy for a Sunday School primer. Not a few theologians would wince at the suggestion that wet trees, lotsa water, starry nights and parental love are evidence of God that "somehow assure the longing soul." This is tedious writing and mediocre theology.

I invite Mr. Whitney to sit on the floor of a dampened forest for a few hours and watch what happens. Every square yard of the forest floor contains more organisms than there are humans on earth, and the struggle for survival is anything but serene. The message of nature is actually the opposite of what most people assume, as Darwin suspected. Guy Harrison explains bluntly:

> Right this moment, as you are reading this sentence, millions of creatures are being pierced, clawed, snapped in half, chewed and swallowed—while still alive. A constant and incomprehensible flow of pain and suffering is standard operating procedure, just the way life goes on this planet. If our world is finely tuned for life, then why is the overall extinction rate more than 95 percent?[27]

The suffering is incalculable. And we humans are at the mercy of the tiniest of creatures. As Mr. Whitney sits on the forest floor, the battle going on in the soil beneath him is matched by the battle within his own body. Every second of every day since the day we were born, our bodies fight the microbes that are out to kill us. We harbor many friendly microbes that enable our life processes, but they have nasty cousins. To fight the microbes, we take baths, wash our hands, brush our teeth, put on deodorant, get inoculations, and scrub the house from time to time. We may win most of the battles, but we *always* lose the war. And once the microbes have killed us, they eat our bodies.

All this looks far more like the unplanned, blind workings of natural selection than the intelligent design that many Christian apologists advocate. How would we possibly account for a good, compassionate God designing a natural world that operates this way?

Would Animals Have an Opinion?

As we have seen, theologians and preachers have demonstrated considerable ingenuity in explaining why humans suffer so much under God's watchful eye. Let's assume that they have it all wrapped up neatly with a bow, and we can breathe a sigh of relief: God is good, God is great, amen. Suffering is a necessary component of free will, maybe it's punishment for our sins, or a way to test our faith or improve our characters.

But none of these work at all as explanations for animal suffering. Bronze Age thinkers fantasized about a sky god who said, "Let there be light" and "Let the earth bring forth living creatures" and then pronounced the new creation "very good." But it's a good bet that the animals would have given a resounding *No* to that verdict. Any psychic energy radiating beyond our planet would carry the message that here, on the surface of this biosphere, is a natural order dominated by panic, terror, and pain as animals do their best to survive in their niche on the food chain.

This reign of terror has continued for billions of years, interrupted only by the greater terror of mass extinctions. It is hard for atheists to grasp how two or three billion years of suffering of such magnitude can be considered part of the plan of a compassionate God. It does make sense if evolution is the sole master: Genes are programmed to make copies of themselves relentlessly through endless eons. Energy pushes forward blindly, and individual organisms have no particular value in the scheme of things—from a genetic or cosmic perspective. And theology cannot modify that fact.

A sensitive child watching a nature program on TV, crying because a baby wildebeest is chewed alive by a cheetah, demonstrates far more compassion than any creator who would have set such a system in motion, to grind on without mercy for billions of years. Let evolution be the winner and take the blame in this debate; nature reflects very badly on God—no matter how much poetic eloquence has been triggered by technicolor sunsets and purple mountains.

What about Natural Evil?

Animal suffering is but one aspect of natural evil that theologians and philosophers have debated for centuries. Moral evil encompasses the suffering brought about by human failings and corruption–the bad things that we do, our sins. But natural evils are events beyond human control. They are just occurrences in the *natural* world– earthquakes, floods, volcanoes, tornadoes, tsunamis, hurricanes, plagues. It's been argued that God cannot be held responsible for these because he set the natural order in motion, and it takes its course, a vast machine that runs on its own. In fact, we all depend on regularity in nature. It must be constant, reliable, immune to divine tampering. The mechanics of nature must be what they are, and, well, it's too bad that tectonic plates slip and slide. The interior of the planet is dynamic–what could we expect God to do about that?–producing volcanoes, tsunamis, and earthquakes.

Although, oddly enough, we commonly refer to these and other natural disasters as "acts of God," we sense that the engine of nature is simply doing its thing. Theologians may think they've gotten away with something with this argument, that they've pulled the wool over our eyes. But this could be theism's third rail, because nature-taking-its-course *sans* deity comes dangerously close to saying that God is indifferent or doesn't have the power to stay nature's course. We sometimes hear that God is "there" to comfort people after a natural disaster, which is appallingly anemic. Is that all your god can do? We also hear, defying all logic, that *one* person saved out of a hundred casualties is God's miracle. Huh? The mind games can be numbing.

Theologians who take refuge in the nature-grinds-on-as-it-must argument run the risk of having to concede that the nature miracles in the Bible are, after all, fairy tales, and also slipping into deism. Impersonal Providence is watching–or not!–from afar. But if they protest otherwise–"No, no, we believe in an involved God"–then other feeble excuses must come into play. The mind games appear more and more desperate and trivial, and even devout believers might wince and squirm.

The day after the 2004 tsunami, a Catholic colleague expressed appropriate sadness and regret, to which I responded, "Ah, yes, it seems that God overslept again." A look of shock and anguish crossed his face. Had anyone ever talked to him about God like that? It was seemingly unthinkable to blame God, but if you believe in an involved God, you have to work hard to make God-is-good plausible in these most horrific situations. There's a reason that even Christians are at a loss for words.

. . . When Your Own Religion Is Part of the Problem

When Christopher Hitchens died, many Christians gloated that he was most certainly roasting in hell as he so justly deserved. Their reaction proved that Hitch had been right all along: Religion *does* poison everything. It certainly spoils Christian charity.

Hitchens was once asked if he intended the subtitle to *God is Not Great* as hyperbole. No, he said, religion *does* poison everything. He does a pretty good job in the book demonstrating the disastrous impact of religion, and it is indeed true that Christianity does have a lot to answer for. Not the least of which is the Christian arrogance to claim that, without God, we would not know how to be moral. With only the feeblest understanding of the Ten Commandments and the Sermon on the

Mount, Christians posture themselves as the guardians of moral standards; with only the shallowest grasp of Western history, Christians pretend that the church has been primarily a force for good.

Tirelessly, atheists have pointed out the flaws in the Ten Commandments–the Hitchens update of the Big Ten on a YouTube video is superb. But we haven't been as tireless as we should in exposing the defects in the Sermon on the Mount. We've insisted that the Crusades, the Inquisition, and slavery show Christianity in its true light, but contemporary Christians brush aside these crimes of the past. They claim that these are not indictments of their own religion as they know it; the egregious sins of the church were long ago and far away: "Those horrendous things are not my fault. My religion is better than that. Our version of Christianity has come a long way, so quit harping on those things."

If we walked into any church today, we would find a high level of confidence that Christianity now is a force for good in the world, and that the church is a bulwark against "the moral decline and decay that threaten our society."

They shouldn't be allowed to get away with that smugness. There are many ways in which Christianity operates as a *force for evil*, and is part of the problem of evil. I will add this disclaimer: Of course we know that many Christians are virtuous, decent, and generous people. They've invented a positive image of Jesus to follow, and they do their best to live accordingly. But the big picture is not a pretty one, and good Christians commonly do a very poor job of pushing back against the bad Christians.

The evils of Christianity in the contemporary world are palpable and demonstrable. We don't need to rub Christian noses in the crimes of the past. There's plenty of nastiness and villainy happening right now.

––––––

Televangelism is a good place to start. This is the sewer of Christian piety. Slick hucksters live well by extracting millions of dollars from credulous folks who are ignorant enough to take them seriously. They defile Christianity with patriotism and capitalism and unctuously spread hate. Why isn't there a Society of Decent Christians against Televangelism?

Christians can't resist building, endlessly, and the ongoing colossal waste of resources is a scandal. The lure to erect churches has proved irresistible. If you plan to step inside the Archbasilica of St. John Lateran in Rome or St. Peter's, expect to be overwhelmed by the insane excess. But maintain perspective and ask, "Why?"

There's nothing impressive about the banal theology that compelled the construction of these monuments and thousands of other churches throughout the centuries. Search the gospels for the slightest clue that Jesus had such obsessive-compulsive construction in mind.[28] For centuries, precious resources that could have been used to improve the human condition have been squandered to cater to ecclesiastical ego and vanity, under the guise of "glorifying" God. This is soulless religion. The disregard for human need, to help God feel good about himself, is evil.

The **crusade against knowledge and science** (I choose the word deliberately) is a scandal in the United States. Frightening percentages of Americans have contempt for science, believe in creationism, and expect the return of Jesus in their lifetimes.

The **anti-gay crusade** in the U.S. is fueled by Christian ignorance, which is anchored in a medieval understanding of sexual orientation. Homosexuality has been studied and researched extensively since the 1950s, but the fact that homosexuality is natural and benign is brushed aside in favor of a few Bible texts.

The **condemnation of contraception and population control** is commonly an obsession of the super pious, and this posture has earned the contempt and opposition of the people working overtime to reduce the threat of overpopulation catastrophe. Exhibit A: In January 2015, when Pope Francis visited the Philippines, a country overwhelmed with homeless "street children," he condemned birth control, urging Philippine families to be "sanctuaries of respect for life."[29] This strikes me as stunning example of evil: theology oblivious to massive human suffering.

Sexual abuse of children is not exclusively a Christian sin by any means, but the ugly spectacle of the Vatican orchestrating cover-ups to protect guilty priests and the reputation of the church is especially worthy of contempt.

The **oppression of women** is a hallmark of Christian theology, especially as embodied in Catholic dogma and practice. Tell me again: Why would any woman agree to be a Catholic? The idealization of female saints counts for nothing when we grasp the imbedded misogyny of the Catholic brand. That old boy's club disdains the ordination of women, and regards the female body as a portal to sin; priestly celibacy is a nod to the apostle Paul's conviction that even touching a woman is bad business. So much abuse and suffering are locked into the lives of Catholics worldwide by the church's mean-spirited opposition to abortion and contraception, "driven almost wholly," as Valerie Tarico has said, "by archaic theologies."[30]

———

On many fronts, Christianity promotes evil and suffering, and this reality–the examples could be multiplied many times over–makes the case that Christianity itself is part of the problem of evil.

Feeling good about your religion, glowing with confidence that you and Jesus get along just fine, really doesn't cut it. Atheists don't want to hear, when we point out all of the above evils, "Well, that's not my brand of Christianity." Good Christian people who claim to distance themselves from these sins of their "brothers and sisters in Christ" don't earn points if they're not on the front lines of opposition, along with atheists and secularists.

And we do have to ask: "What were God's plans for Christianity?" Since he is all-knowing (few theologians want to delete this either), he must have seen how it would play out in human hands in the real world. Would all the good that supposedly has come from believing in Christ outweigh the enormous catalogue of Christian crimes? It doesn't seem to be a well-thought out plan.

. . . When You Resort to "God moves in mysterious ways"

The immensity of human suffering and agony is too much to handle with reasoned arguments, if you're trying to explain why God maintains a hands-off policy.

Christians feel stymied when they are pressed for explanations, and when they feel their own faith buckling under the weight of tragedy and evil. Yet, unable to yield on the conviction that God must be good, sensing that the common excuses are shaky and shallow, they proclaim that God's purposes are beyond human understanding. Thus "it's-a-mystery" is the last resort of desperate, frustrated believers. It's the last resort of lazy thinkers who don't want to face the consequences of giving up on "God is good"–and even "God *is*." "Mystery" is the dark cave into which theologians and preachers retreat.

They seek refuge from the slings and arrows of serious thinkers, and do their best to convince the world that the mystery cave is a noble place. In fact they seem to think that mystery is a precious thing. Mystery makes God more majestic, untouchable, and unreachable: the holy of holies, the hocus pocus that has worked so well on the masses for millennia. They don't *want* mystery to be dispelled."Pay no attention to the man behind the curtain" is their motto, even if they deny that the fraudulent Wizard of Oz is a role model! The curtain is vital to avoid having to answer hard questions. Theology is crippled by the problem of evil, hence "God moves in mysterious ways" is a favorite dodge.

Humans ought to be in awe of the mystery, we're told. Christian apologists sometimes ask atheists and skeptics to keep the big picture in mind (never mind that this suggestion actually works against them, as we shall see in the next chapter). By the *big picture*, they mean eternity and the vast Cosmos that we're imbedded in.

We cannot possibly see things from God's perspective. Human existence, stretching back even a few hundred thousand years, is but a blip on the cosmic screen, a blink on the cosmic time scale. How could we possibly know and understand God's grander plan and purpose? That is, we shouldn't be too troubled by suffering as a theological problem, because everything that unfolds on Earth does so as part of God's plan, however grim it may seem to us. Hence it must be good, since it derives from God, even though we can't see how it fits into the big picture. We must not judge God; we can assume that whatever he allows *must* be good.

This approach means, however, that God is a bravado artist, and it has a familiar ring to it, doesn't it? When Job had hurled his protests at God, for being made a pawn in God's bet with Satan, God's rude response was, "Where were you when I laid the foundations of the Earth?" In other words, sit down, shut up, don't ask questions.

But this won't do. It's slick, but not slick enough. It flies in the face of Christianity's 2,000-year old message that God *cares*. You can't have it both ways. Is there any theologian who would welcome the task of dropping in at Dachau or Buchenwald in 1944 to buck up the inmates with the assurance that they shouldn't take their suffering too seriously: It's part of God's big-picture plan, so cheer up, it must be okay: "Not helping you is part of God's plan." Why do theologians think they can get away with such callousness and cruelty? There is much more authenticity in the words scrawled on a wall in one German prison: "If there is a god, he must beg my forgiveness."

Of course, the ugly stepsister of the theological banality, "It's all part of God's plan," is the requirement that we "take it on faith" that God is good and ultimately has our best interests in mind. Thus we can supplement Nietzsche's conclusion that God is dead with his warning that "faith is not wanting to know what is true." But what's true is this: The assurance that God's master plan can encompass and excuse massive suffering is an utter failure in the context of the Christian message itself.

God the Incompetent or God the Improbable

The person who wrote that message attached to the Teddy Bear, following the Scotland school massacre–suggesting that God had overslept that day–may have reconciled the horror with faith and retreated into Christian piety and orthodoxy. But it's also quite possible that the person might have said, eventually, "Overslept? No, that's too generous. God is incompetent." And then it's but a short step to "God is improbable." Given much opportunity to think about it–or being forced by inexplicable tragedy to think about it–many people will agree with Bertrand Russell when he suggested that the existence of God is on the same level of probability as finding a teapot in orbit around the sun. The arguments for it are just too farfetched.

It is my contention that any one of the Ten Tough Problems that I write about in this book is enough to falsify Christianity, and it certainly collapses under the weight of all ten. But Tough Problem Number One is usually the deal breaker for many people.

Why is Europe so secular today? My guess is that 50 million deaths during World War II knocked the starch out of "God is good" theology. World War I, with 300,000 killed at the Battle of Verdun alone, was probably the beginning of the end for the faith-based view of the world, at least in Europe.

But religion is extraordinarily tenacious. When asked to think deeply about their faith, most of the devout take a pass. They perform whatever mental gymnastics are required to keep the faith. And part of this is "the easy acceptance of the very terrible," no matter how much compromise with reality and honest thinking is required. When asked to grapple with the tough problems, sooner rather than later they make a dash for the mystery cave.

However, we have a right to ask which is better:

- a cruel world without God, **or,**
- a cruel world with a loving God who seems–inexplicably, even to the theologians–to be indifferent and impotent?

Would there be much difference? Would there be *any* difference?

The apologies for God that we hear from Christians turn out to be shallow and contrived, concoctions of wishful thinking. If a compelling explanation cannot be made why a good, all-powerful god allows suffering on the scale we witness–why our world looks so much like another planet's hell, as Aldous Huxley put it—this concept of god collapses. ***God loses.***

Notes

1. *Haunted by the Newtown massacre, police officer faces firing over PTSD*, CNN website, 13 November 2013.

2. Joshua Dubois, "What the President secretly did at Sandy Hook Elementary School," *Vox Populi: A Public Sphere for Politics and Poetry*, voxpopulisphere.com/2015/12/11/10733 (accessed 12 December 2015).

3. *New York Times*, 23 March 1996.

4. Uta Ranke-Heinemann, *Putting Away Childish Things: The Virgin Birth, the Empty Tomb, and Other Fairy Tales You Don't Need to Believe to Have a Living Faith* (HarperCollins, 1994), p. 62.

5. This is not a text from scripture, but a line from a beloved spiritual, made famous especially by contralto Marion Anderson. But the sentiment certainly reflects the good and caring god that most people *want* to find in the Bible—but can do so only by ignoring the cruel god that lurks in the New Testament as well as the Old.

6. H.L. Mencken, *Treatise on the Gods* (A.A. Knopf, 1946), p.272.

7. Joseph Daleiden, *The Final Superstition: A Critical Evaluation of the Judeo-Christian Legacy* (Prometheus Books, 1994), p. 136.

8. rense.com/general69/obj.htm

9. *The New York Times*, 31 July 1993.

10. Witold Rybcznski, *One Good Turn: A Natural History of the Screwdriver and the Screw* (Scribner, 2001).

11. Barry Whitney, *Evil and the Process God*, Toronto Studies in Theology, Book 19 (Edwin Mellen, 1985), p. 134.

12. Wikipedia, Process Theology [en.wikipedia.org/wiki/Process_theology] (accessed 6 May 2016).

13. Paul Froese and Christopher Bader, *America's Four Gods: What We Say About God—and What That Says About Us* (Oxford University Press, 2010), Kindle loc. 284.

14. But at what age? Are those under 6 exempt from the born-again rule? Catholics and evangelicals would probably tangle over this, since the former insist on baptism as soon after birth as possible.

15. plato.stanford.edu/entries/freewill

16. IPC Press, 2009.

17. Richard Carrier, *Why I Am Not a Christian: Four Conclusive Reasons to Reject the Faith* (2011), p. 21.

18. Free Press, 2012.

19. thelibertytree.me/tag/pam-olsen

20. *New York Times*, 30 July 2001.

21. There is no evidence that people way back then saw it as being about homosexuality. See Ezekiel 16:49: "This was the guilt of your sister Sodom: she and her daughters had pride, excess of food, and prosperous ease, but did not aid the poor and needy."

22. See T.J. Wray and Gregory Mobley, *The Birth of Satan: Tracing the Devil's Biblical Roots* (Palgrave Macmillan, 2005).

23. Ludovic Kennedy, *All in the Mind: A Farewell to God* (Hodder & Stoughton, 1999), p. 274.

24. Harold Kushner, *When Bad Things Happen to Good People* (Schocken, 2001), p. 142.

25. *The New World Encyclopedia*, newworldencyclopedia.org/entry/Charles_Darwin.

26. Whitney at p.1.

27. Guy P. Harrison, *50 Popular Beliefs that People Think Are True* (Prometheus Books, 2011), p. 280.

28. St. Francis (not to be confused with Pope Francis) was tuned in: when he returned from a trip to help the poor, he found his disciples erecting a building. He was furious, and climbed onto the roof, throwing tiles to the ground: for their mission, there was no need for a building.

29. NPR Website, 16 January 2015: "Pope, On Visit to Philippines, Defends Catholic Ban on Contraception." In 1998, the number of street children was estimated to be 1.5 million.

30. valerietarico.com/2016/05/10/a-tidal-wave-of-zika-brain-damage-it-doesnt-have-to-go-that-way

II

How Do You Find Out About God?

God by Popular Demand

THEOLOGIANS SAY that God is present everywhere, and Americans are hell-bent on making God seem as real as possible. Chances are, right now you have God in your pocket or purse. The affirmation that we trust God is on our money, every piece of it. From the cradle we are taught to brag, in public and in unison, that our country is one nation under God. Presidential addresses must end with the chief executive asking God to bless us.

The original Pilgrims set foot on our shores driven by fervent devotion to their faith, so it's hardly a surprise that even today the Boy Scout oath includes the words, "To do my duty to God." What would the seventh inning stretch at Yankee Stadium be without Kate Smith singing our unofficial national anthem, *God Bless America*? (Ironically enough, it was written by atheist Irving Berlin, who also gave us *White Christmas* and *Easter Parade*.)

Ours is a steeple-studded landscape, burdened with hundreds of thousands of tax-exempt shrines. Every town and city has several, dozens or even hundreds. How could we endure the unconscionable tax impact of this indulgence—we all pay more to the government as a consequence—if God were not real? If you're raised American, it just seems so unlikely, from the get-go, that our national-protector god could be fiction. As Americans, God is something we do, and faith is the default position expected of good citizens.

How dare we question something as patriotic as the worship of God? Atheists are challenged—and people are usually in quite a huff about it—to prove the negative, that God does *not* exist. The weight of tradition is against us; the momentum of thousands of years of piety should flatten us. A mighty fortress is their God. The burden of proof is on the atheist naysayers: Put up or shut up. We can't just ridicule and scoff; we have to show why everyone has been so wrong for so long. Of course, we have been doing exactly that, but precious few pay attention.

Believers have dominated the discussion for a very long time, and they usually have a lot to tell us about God. They've filled in most of the blanks about what God is like, what he wants and does. Anything that defies explanation or definition is just, well, God being his mysterious self.

How Do you Know, Really?

In God we trust? How do you know that he can be trusted, indeed, what does this even *mean* in a world where suffering is so randomly distributed? How does a Scout know–a memorized oath is hardly a source of knowledge–that we each have a duty to God and what it might be? How do we know that God is in the business of blessing nations, and what does that mean?

Religious folks have gotten away with a lot; the bulk of our citizenry nod approval as believers tell us what God is like. On the surface, many of the attributes of God may seem reasonable enough, perhaps because we've all heard them so long:

- God is good, and if we read the gospels superficially, ignoring so many details, isn't Jesus evidence for that?

- He knows and sees everything (even science fiction has helped us get used to the idea since Arthur C. Clarke introduced us to the supercomputer Hal in *2001: A Space Odyssey*).

- He is omnipotent. Well, we do have problem with that, as we saw in the last chapter, given so much evil that has happened on his watch for billions of years, but maybe all the contorted arguments could force us to throw in the towel here too.

- God is, of course, invisible.

But not so fast. Usually, in the real world, when we're told that a person is invisible, we assume that the person is imaginary. Only in fairy tales do we accept storylines that involve real things that are invisible.

Of course, there are invisible realities, and believers commonly champion these as god-analogies. Electricity comes to mind, but this provides no analogy for God, since electricity can be generated, measured, stored, bought, sold, shipped, and especially, verified. And of course, physicists and cosmologists are trying to figure out dark matter, which is notoriously difficult to grasp precisely because it is invisible. But scientists don't have to take it on faith that dark matter exists; its influence can be observed in the way galaxies hang together and rotate. There are no physicists who are willing to add "god" to the four invisible fundamental forces of nature–gravity, electromagnetism, the strong and weak nuclear forces–to account for the operation of the Cosmos. In the religion sphere, invisibility is trickery.

Is There a Dragon in the Garage?

How can the invisibility claim not make us suspect that religions are pulling our leg, and that believers dwell in fairytale land and want us to join them? No one who reads Harry Potter believes for a second that his Invisibility Cloak is anything other than fantasy. The god whom Christians claim is good, all-knowing and all-powerful, is all everything–except visible. Why is the invisibility game so important to God? Why the Cheshire cat routine throughout the millennia? Hell, even a hologram would do. You can feel his presence, we are assured, and you can see evidence of his presence in nature and in events–and in people's hearts–but God is invisible. You're a churlish brute if you hint that invisibility is grounds for dismissal; how foolish was the Soviet Cosmonaut who returned from orbit and declared the he didn't see God up there. He was ridiculed for being naïve: Of course you can't *see* God.

But we ask believers to grasp the problem that the Invisibility Cloak presents when God is wearing it. And there's no better way to illustrate this point than Carl Sagan's parable where the narrator is your neighbor claiming there is a dragon in the garage. You don't see anything in there except the usual junk, and ask where the dragon is.

> "Oh, she's right here," I reply, waving vaguely."I neglected to mention that she's an invisible dragon." You propose spreading flour on the floor of the garage to capture the dragon's footprints.

> "Good idea," I say, "but this dragon floats in the air." Then you'll use an infrared sensor to detect the invisible fire.

> "Good idea, but the invisible fire is also heatless." You'll spray-paint the dragon and make her visible.

> "Good idea, but she's an incorporeal dragon and the paint won't stick."

Every proposed test gets countered by a "special explanation of why it won't work." That leads Sagan to ask just what the difference is "between an invisible, incorporeal, floating dragon who spits heatless fire and no dragon at all." What does it mean to say *the dragon exists* if there's no way to disprove that contention, "no conceivable experiment that would count against it"?[1]

If believers want to know what makes atheists tick, why the God followers get so much pushback from us, they have to help us understand *how they know* about their gods. We suspect that their gods rank about as high on the probability scale as that dragon in the garage.

Christians Also Ask for More, Sometimes

The invisibility of the gods, by the way, has always been a tough concept for ordinary believers. This is why gods, angels, and saints have always been big business in religious art. In their guts people know that seeing is believing, so the church purchasing departments, the preachers and builders, have gone along: "Let's give 'em pictures. Anything to help the cause, right?"

The faithful know that relying on faith is supposed to be sufficient, but visual aids are welcome, and thus churches–at least outside of stark Protestant traditions–are big on stained glass, statuary, costuming, music, and jumbo TV screens. In short, sensory overload. This is all meant to compensate for the gnawing feeling that being invisible comes too close to being imaginary.

I have a vivid memory of a thought that flashed through my mind, when I was a kid sitting in a very plain, unadorned church."How do we know that there's anything *there*, wherever God is supposed to be? Maybe the sky is empty." How I wish I had pursued that doubt.

When people glance to the sky, hoping that the genial Man Upstairs is looking out for them, they perhaps come closest to wanting to clap eyes on him themselves. After all, that doesn't seem so unreasonable when we read that Adam and Eve "heard the sound of the Lord God walking in the garden in the day" (Gen. 3:8, ESV), and that the Lord "used to speak to Moses face to face, as a man speaks to his friend" (Exod. 33:11, ESV). A popular Protestant hymn draws on these images:

I come to the garden alone,
   While the dew is still on the roses,
   And the voice I hear, falling on my ear,
   The Son of God discloses.

And He walks with me, and He talks with me,
   And He tells me I am His own,
   And the joy we share as we tarry there,
   None other has ever known.[2]

The folks in the pews may sense that shock and awe before God are appropriate. But Michelangelo's God is as big as life on the ceiling of the Sistine Chapel because believers really don't like it that God is invisible. Maybe they suspect, as much as anybody else in weaker moments, that this is all a ruse. And, wait a minute, didn't Jesus "come into the world" precisely to be real flesh and blood, for people to *see God* up close and personal?

Sometimes theologians speak of the *hiddenness* of God, which is a variation on invisibility. For example, in Mark 9 (also Luke 9 and Matthew 17), we find the story of Jesus going to a mountaintop to be "transfigured." In this piece of religious fantasy, Jesus glowed in the presence of Moses and Elijah who had dropped by for a visit. The implication here is that Jesus is in good company. According to tradition, Elijah had been taken to heaven in a chariot, and Moses, of course, had the ultimate mountaintop experience. We are told that God spoke from a cloud: "This is my beloved Son, listen to him" (Mark 9:7, NASB).

This is considered one of the high points in Jesus' life, and believers love the story. Here the invisible God, hiding in a cloud no less, at least *speaks*. The aim of this episode is to authenticate Jesus. But shouldn't we be suspicious? Why isn't the authentication announced at large, instead of in a hush-hush ceremony with a private glowing Jesus? This story is the product of overheated religious imagination, as well as shrewd theological plotting to draw people into the myth. The very devout will even settle for audibility. But, of course, they suspend judgment and critical thinking: How is a voice generated by water vapor?

Is it true that God is invisible but not imaginary, and present everywhere? He does not communicate with us with anything like perfect clarity (even believers freely confess this) so there is a high level of mystery about God.

Or is it true, instead, that the mystery comes from trying to figure out something that isn't actually there at all? Trying to understand something that doesn't even exist will appear to be a great mystery!

Getting Messages from the Invisible Beyond

If God is invisible, if we just can't get around that fact, then there must be some very good ways to communicate with this invisible deity. So atheists ask that believers *please* convince us that the means of getting messages to and from God are beyond reproach."It's all very mysterious, you know," just won't do, because that's precisely the point: We *don't know*. Saying we have to take it on faith is useless as well, because there are any number of things that believers of all stripes routinely ask other people to take on faith, e.g., that cats go to heaven, that believers get their very own planets when they die, and that blood washes away sin. Would you waste *your* energy "taking it on faith" that there is an underground holy city on the far side of the moon, undetectable by our satellites?

Atheists think all of the mystery is manufactured, and there's enough mystery about the Cosmos already without adding the mystery of a god behind it all. The devout are willing to embrace mystery so long as they get to keep their gods. Theologians make their living trying to explain at least some of the mystery, at least enough to make it bearable. And thus they're in charge of keeping the mystery, *the dragon*, alive and well. They go into the depths of a cave at midnight on a moonless night, with no flashlight, searching in the darkness for a black cat that isn't there, and then yell, "I found it!"[3]

But the cat is not there and never has been. Neither are any of humanity's many gods. The burden of proof operates in exactly the opposite way that believers assume.

Atheists are not obliged to demonstrate that God doesn't exist, any more than Carl Sagan has to show that the neighbor's dragon doesn't exist. It's a no-brainer: I can safely assume that there is no such grandiose mythological creature unless you offer some very convincing proof to the contrary. Yet atheists are asked to humor believers that they've got it right."Come on, believing in God is something we ought to do—besides, it's good for us—and you've got no proof that God isn't real."

If believers sincerely want us to come on board and take their ideas and affirmations about god(s) seriously, we must insist that they put their sources of God-knowledge under the closest scrutiny imaginable. They claim their ways of knowing about God are reliable. In fact they're pretty sure about it. But do these ways indeed hold up? Have believers examined them closely, carefully, skeptically? Have they tried to poke holes in their sources, and do they understand why *we* do?

It gets mighty suspicious when believers buckle under the pressure of questions and brush them aside impatiently, sometime contemptuously, and tell us that we just have to "take it on faith." Not even believers would do that if their neighbor was trying to convince them that there was an invisible dragon in his garage.

Claiming to Know What They Don't

It can be quite an adventure to get believers to explain how they know about a god. When Christians visit my Facebook page to tell me about God's love, or his wishes, or what makes him angry, sometimes my simple response—knowing full well that I'm just playing with them—is, "What is your epistemology?" And they shoot back some variation of, "Stop using such fancy words. That doesn't prove you're so smart."

The sad thing isn't that they don't know the word *epistemology*—few lay people do—but that they don't grasp that doing epistemology is crucial, even if you don't know the word. A belief, doctrine, or dogma usually has a long history behind it, and doing the epistemology means digging to find out where it came from, to determine its legitimacy. Intellectual honesty about one's belief requires understanding *how* you know what you know. You have to peel away layers of assumptions.

This problem is rarely grasped because people fail to think analytically about the sources of God-information. Commonly, they simply don't bother to ask, "Where do I get my beliefs about God?" This is one area of life in which the failure of curiosity is most conspicuous."I like my beliefs, "or as I heard one person affirm, "I love my religion," so why not just let it go at that? We might hear this default position: "People have lived by these truths for almost two thousand years. How wrong can they be?"

These are the questions to be posed:

- Where did, or do, I get my information about God? The curious believer who makes any claim to intellectual integrity must try to trace a belief back to its original source. Who thought of an idea or belief *for the first time*? After all, there had to have been someone who was the very first to have the idea, "God is love" or "God doesn't want me to steal" or "God wants me to pray to him." All three of these ideas, for example, are widely accepted Christian beliefs.

- Then, once that first person with that idea has been identified, or at least reasonably conjectured, we can ask: "Where did that person get the idea?" Did it come from God, or did it emerge from his own imagination? Actually there is another way to put this question: Is the human brain with its three or four pounds of organic matter an instrument for channeling accurate information from God about himself? Christians commonly fail to recognize that claiming that a belief is from God is simply unverifiable, which is not a value or a virtue.

An old Sunday school song has the lyric, "Jesus loves me this I know, for the Bible tells me so."[4] There is, in fact, serious theology (and epistemology) here: the claim that God-information is derived from the Bible. But people rarely pursue the thought: How *do we* **know** that the Bible is reliable? How do we know, for example, that John 3:16, "God so loved the world that he gave his only begotten son," wasn't just dreamed up by someone?

Let's take a look at some of the sources that supposedly yield *bona fide* information about God.

God Knowledge, Source #1

"It's common knowledge"

In the wake of his popular TV series *Cosmos*, Carl Sagan did a lot of public speaking. In one lecture, "A Sunday Sermon," he described what often happened during Q&A. Almost as common as inquiries about UFOs and ancient astronauts, especially after he's discussed evolution, is the question,

> "Do you believe in God?" Because the word "God" means many things to many people, I frequently reply by asking what the questioner means by "God." To my surprise, this response is often considered puzzling or unexpected: "Oh, you know, God. Everyone knows who God is." Or "Well, kind of a force that is stronger than we are and that exists everywhere in the universe." There are a number of such forces. One of them is called gravity, but it is not often identified with God. And not everyone does know what is meant by "God." The concept covers a wide range of ideas.[5]

This gives us a good idea of what we're up against in trying to pin people down on how they know about God. Christianity was in the drinking water when I grew up, so we had no reason to question our assumptions. God was just *there*, a given. We've seen that American popular culture is saturated with God–at the ballpark, in the Scouts, on our money. God is common knowledge. Critical thought is not even considered necessary.

Source of God Knowledge #2

Revelation via a Sacred Book

I enjoy finding those Gideon Bibles in hotel rooms. Usually I write on them, "Please read this book carefully. There is no god, and this book is all the proof you need." Gideon missionaries would come to our church when I was a kid, collecting money so that they could keep up their good work. Since 1908, they've given away more than 1.7 billion Bibles. So, not only is the Bible (supposedly) the best selling book of all time, it's also the book that has been given away the most.

We can be thankful, however, that it's probably the least read book of all time. That was especially true before modern times. Just how did God think this was going to work? In the time of Jesus, perhaps five people in a hundred could read. Lay people weren't even allowed to reading the Bible until the Reformation. When Luther finally made the Bible available to the masses, it still cost the price of a good horse to get your hands on a copy. Mass publication at reasonable prices took quite a while even after Gutenberg's printing press.

One of the reasons we doubt that we have authentic words of Jesus in the gospels is that very few people in his audiences would have known *how* to write them down even if they wanted to, and they certainly didn't carry around pads of paper.[6] No one outside Jewish communities read Biblical Hebrew. In fact, most Jews didn't speak it as Aramaic had replaced it. So the Old Testament eventually got translated into Greek that Hellenistic Jews could read.

Since the vast majority of the population couldn't read, and even those who did had limited access to books, why would God have imagined that revelation through a new one was such a good idea? And then, for the next 1,500 years, his new book remains inaccessible to most everybody but his self-designated priests. Doesn't this seem a little suspicious?

A Holy Book Full of Holes

In the next chapter we'll look at the major problems that the Bible presents, how far it falls short of qualifying as revelation. But here I can point out two reasons for suspecting that the holy book idea is a sham and a scam.

First, notwithstanding all their posturing, Christians don't themselves *really* believe in revelation via sacred text. Once they bump into the books of Leviticus and Numbers, they hem and haw. They've already put the Old Testament into a second-tier position, a trend that the writer of Matthew 5:18 (pretending to quote Jesus) was already resisting back in his day: "For verily I say unto you, till heaven and earth pass away, not one jot or one tittle shall in any wise pass from the law till all be fulfilled" (KJV). Obviously there were already Christians discounting Old Testament revelation. And modern Christians don't given any credence whatever to the Qu'ran or to the Book of Mormon; why don't *those* holy books qualify as revelation?

When we back Christians into a corner, they confess that the precious status of *revelation* is reserved for the parts they like. Most of their own holy book is ruled out. Any atheist who has boned up on the New Testament can easily point out at least ten items in the teaching of Jesus, and just as many in the writings of Paul, that Christians admit are wrong.[7]

Just spend an hour or two wading through the books of Leviticus and Ezekiel, Paul's Letter to the Romans, and the tedious theology-soaked gospel of John—especially chapters 14-17. How would you rate them in terms of advancing the human condition? How would you rate them even for their *spiritual* value? Frankly, God's skills as an author fall far short of what we would expect of an omni-competent being. Revelation through the sacred text? It's a phony claim.

Second, it's actually a dangerous theological move to claim that God took the trouble to give us a book. If he left his comfortable perch "outside time and space" to inspire a few dozen authors to write a 1,000-page tome, why not give us a head start on understanding something as important as why we get sick? If God had been concerned about human welfare, why not a book about microbes and hygiene? Why didn't God drop hints about how to prevent infant deaths?

For century after century, half of all human infants died before their first birthdays. That's an awful lot of anguish for moms and dads. Did God care? Mankind has been engaged in a long struggle to understand nature and our place in it. Why couldn't God have given us a massive book about biology, astronomy, cosmology, agriculture, or oceanography. Instead, he told us that epilepsy is caused by evil spirits. God has *failed*, utterly, as mankind's mentor in getting a grip on how the world works.

Source of God Knowledge #3
Visions

Who Is Seeing What?

Those who believe in God accept visions as *bona fide* revelation events. Those who don't believe in God accept visions as *bona fide* imagination and hallucination events. Who is right?

Christians should give serious thought to how, why, and when reports of visions should be taken seriously. It's not a stretch to argue that the apostle Paul was a primary architect of Christian thought and can even be considered one of the inventors of Christianity. He claimed that his knowledge of Jesus, whom he apparently had never met, came through visions. But how do we know if the resurrected Jesus actually spoke to Paul? Of course there was no doubt about it for Paul, but reliance on visions should make Christians more than a little uneasy. Christians may say, "Well, I'm fine with just taking it on faith that Paul's visions were the real thing"–that Paul was channeling divine truth. But where, and how, do they draw the line?

If visions are the real thing, then why not become a Mormon because Joseph Smith had visions in the Sacred Grove in New York State in the 1820s? Why don't Quakers and Baptists become Catholics because of the visions of Joan of Arc, which she testified were personal visits to her by saints Margaret, Catherine, and Michael?

Catholicism should win hands-down in the "truth based on visions" department. There have been countless visions of the Virgin Mary over the centuries, perhaps the most famous of which were the six monthly appearances of the Lady of Fatima in Portugal in 1917. Pope John Paul II credited her with saving his life when he was struck by an assassin's bullet in 1981. He had the near-fatal bullet inserted into the crown of the Lady of Fatima statue. If you're really big on visions, why not trust the pope?

If we accept the logic of those who believe in God, how could the Lady of Fatima visions have been anything less than authentic? Yet many Protestants question and even ridicule these claims. Believers seem to put themselves in the dubious position of doubting the visions claimed by other faiths. The Jews, it is said, don't recognize the divinity of Jesus; the Muslims don't recognize that the Jews are the Chosen People; and Baptists don't recognize each other at the liquor store. And none of them recognizes the visions claimed by the others.

Listening to a Dead Man
What Are the Chances?

If some believers can robustly doubt the visions of other believers, why shouldn't we apply the principle of reasonable doubt to **all** visions? Are there ways to explain visions without resorting to the supernatural? In Paul's case, is there any other explanation for his visions? Did Jesus really speak to him, as many Christian theologians and biblical scholars urge us to accept?

Medical professionals who have studied the texts do indeed have other suggestions about what might have happened. They have noted that people suffering from temporal lobe epilepsy have reported many of the same experiences and feelings that Paul spoke of. Of course, at a distance of almost 2,000 years and without the man himself available to examine, it is impossible to say, "Ah ha! This is what happened!" But experts have noticed similarities, and Christians would be well advised to be skeptical.

Australian comedian Tim Minchin has said, "I know that Christianity's origins lie more in Paul of Tarsus' mental illness and the emperor Constantine's political savvy than in the existence of the divine." Whether mental illness is part of the mix in Paul's case is beyond our capacity to judge, although many commentators have noted his very disturbed personality. But Tim Minchin reminds us that religions don't need a god to get off the ground. Which is more likely: that Paul had major mental issues, or that a man who had been killed and then resurrected spoke to him from the sky–or through the "still small voice" in his head?

For people outside the Christian fold, this is not really a tough call.[8] Even liberal Christians, who know that resurrection is more trouble than it's worth (as I discuss in detail in Tough Problem VII), sense that hearing voices isn't worth defending. Visions are just too shaky for grounding theology.

Background

Medical Opinions about Paul's Visions

In a 1987 article, *St Paul and Temporal Lobe Epilepsy*, we find the topic examined carefully. Two researchers "reviewed the literature on the religiosity of the epileptic" and "described six cases of religious conversion which followed forthwith upon ecstatic religious auras" of temporal lobe epilepsy (TLE). Another researcher studied the personality characteristics of people subject to epileptic episodes.

> This personality structure includes increased concern with philosophical, moral and religious issues; increased and extensive writing on religious philosophical themes, lengthy letters, diaries, poetry; diminution of sexual activity; aggressiveness. Paul's personality would seem to bear some resemblance to this description.[9]

Dr. David E. Comings, a physician, neuroscientist and molecular geneticist, has devoted a long chapter to "The Spiritual Brain" in his major study of the origin of the religious impulse in humans. He discusses the visions of Paul and concludes:

> Interpretation of parts of the epistles of Paul suggest his facial motor and sensory disturbances were coming after ecstatic seizures and that his religious conversion occurred as a result of ecstatic visions associated with TLE.

If the role of TLE in Paul's conversion is correct, it could be argued that without TLE Christianity would never have become the dominant religion of the Western world.[10]

We certainly cannot say, "For sure, this is what happened," that Paul was an epileptic. But it is an explanation that is consistent with the biblical texts, and more grounded in reality than some report of a voice coming from the sky. What are the probabilities? It's not outrageous or rude to suggest that we're dealing with elements commonly found in religious fantasy literature: The "event on the Damascus road was the historically embellished record of the experience of a visionary dreamer."[11] Paul reports in his letters that he had many "revelations," and he relied on these more than on any facts he might have been able to collect about Jesus the historical person.

Any Christian who claims that visions are valid, that they are a way for God to communicate with humans, must provide evidence that visions are not simply a product of brain chemistry, and reasons for rejecting the visions of other religions and denominations."Oh, those other visions are just products of wild imaginations," is just a lame version of "My religion is better your religion."

Source of God Knowledge #4

Prayer

Believers are convinced that some of their thoughts fall into the category of "communication with God." Supposedly God knows all of our thoughts–nothing is hidden from him, especially not our lusts, unspoken profanities or evil intentions. There are those moments when, by custom, believers bow their heads, close their eyes and think with more intensity and focus: These thoughts are ***prayers***! Now God must really be paying attention.

Presumably prayers have special oomph or flying power when they are done in unison, perhaps in church, or standing, holding hands in a circle–or when they are done by a preacher at a microphone. And believers are confident that God answers prayers: favors are granted, results are achieved, guidance is provided, information flows from heaven to Earth. Even Christians who dilute "heaven" into a metaphor for "a special relationship with God" (it's not *up there*) believe that prayer is two-way contact with a deity.

But there are fundamental problems with prayer that undermine its credibility as a source of God knowledge. Why would we have the private channel that believers claim? How would the private channel work? What is the mechanism? Why can't the people who pray so earnestly even agree on what God wants?

Cosmic-Sized Hubris Passing for Piety

When the Bible was written, gods were thought to be a few miles overhead, literally close enough to get a whiff of burning animal sacrifices, close enough for Jesus to ascend to join him, disappearing through the clouds. Human chants and incantations, and even private thoughts, were close to the heavenly realm. I suspect that most people who take prayer seriously haven't come to terms with where we actually are; they have failed to internalize the modern Cosmic perspective, summarized in a meme that has made the rounds on Facebook for a while:

> Christianity: the belief that a god created a universe 13.75 billion light years across, containing 100 billion galaxies, each of which contains an average of more than 100 billion stars, just so he could have a personal relationship with you.

Theologians have scrambled to make ancient theologies square with science-based cosmology. Hence Biblical references to heaven being *up there*, including Jesus ascending through clouds, become mere metaphors for "spiritual truth." Maybe Pope Pius XII was trying to defy this trend by issuing the dogma of The Assumption of Mary into heaven in 1950. Metaphors be damned, the pope declared that she went up there, soul *and body*.

Nevertheless, the theological campaign to salvage the ancient imagery from the dustbin has moved ahead. Perhaps the most prominent spokesman for this trend was the liberal Lutheran theologian Rudolf Bultmann (1884-1976), who popularized the "demythologizing" of the New Testament: Don't even try to take the stories literally. Who cares if they are historical or not? Dig to find the "spiritual truth" behind them. Generations of theologians in his wake have tried to distance themselves from the naïve Biblical narratives and now push God as a reality "outside space and time," though that bristles with contradictions, as we'll see later.

But isn't this just another wild ride into theobabble? It sounds erudite and sophisticated, but what does it *mean*? Where's the evidence that God is "outside space and time"? It's another grand thing that theologians love to say, to make an end run around our increasing knowledge of the Cosmos. But how do *they* know? How can the very personal understanding of God rooted in the ancient world view—he's close by to hear my prayers—be made to work as we come to grips with 100 billion stars in each of 100 billion galaxies?

We're riding on one planet that accompanies one star. What better way to describe our plight than "lost in space"? And God is paying attention to, and sending signals, to each one of the seven *billion* of us? As Richard Dawkins has said, "What bandwidth!" It is the height of ego-centrism for anyone to insist that he or she has a private channel to God, that God is waiting for human opinions and pleading. Is this really the way the Cosmos works? Pardon our skepticism.

What Is the Mechanism for the Communication?

An article in *The Onion* offers crucial information on this point:

Scientists Discover 90 Percent of Earth's Atmosphere Made from Thoughts, Prayers

Following a litany of tragedies occurring over the past year, a report this week from scientists at Princeton University confirmed that 90 percent of the Earth's atmosphere is made up of thoughts and prayers. Researchers confirmed that, with the rise of tragic events occurring all across the world each and every day, the

Earth's atmosphere is seven percent nitrogen, three percent oxygen and 90 percent emotional pleas begging for everything to be okay.[12]

Given the overwhelming affirmation of the devout that prayer is real, and their supreme confidence that it works, it is not cheeky for us to ask *how* this form of communication operates. Finding, by some means, that 90 percent of the atmosphere is saturated with prayers is perhaps too much to ask. But we do have a right to ask for *something* of substance, since believers claim that information about God comes through prayer. When they assure us that it is a source of data (e.g., George Bush supposedly saying that God told him to invade Iraq–probably not, but would we be at all surprised?), then they're not just blowing smoke. Pious believers have done some pretty bad things because God told them to.

If a devout friend says to us, "Tonight my little group of true believers is going to get together to commune telepathically with a conclave of priests that lives in a holy city on the far side of the Moon," most of us would roll our eyes and say, "Well, have a good time. You didn't forget your meds today, did you?" How does this differ from our good Christian friends going to a prayer meeting to ask the head priest of the Cosmos, presumably much farther away than the far side of the Moon, to ask him to heal a sick friend? In any case, we're willing to be kind and indulge the fantasy. But when the people who pray come back to us claiming that the priests on the Moon, or the Head Priest of the Cosmos, has provided them with information, or guidance or– more ominously–instructions, then we have a right to ask for *verification* that there really is a mechanism by which this communication happens. No, we do not believe that Uri Geller could bend spoons by staring at them; the mechanism is not there.

If God is "outside space and time," how do prayers reach him, and how does he answer back? You can't have "outside space and time" while still claiming that human brains, which exist very much in both space and time, have a means of breaking that barrier. Where is the slightest scrap of evidence that the lump of living tissue in our skulls is an instrument for channeling an invisible-but-not-imaginary being?

Why Can't People Agree?

If prayer is an authentic means by which God communicates information to humans, then it is exceedingly strange that Christians can't agree on much of anything. The prayer channel running through mammalian humanoid brains seems to get garbled by imbedded doctrine and uncritical thinking; reception is spotty and fades in and out. The old black-and-white TVs used to have "snow" when the channels went off the air. No picture, no patterns, just black and white confetti dancing around. God's messages to people seem to come in with about as much clarity.

Christians tell us they arrive at their devoutly held positions and opinions through prayer. There are Christians who endorse capital punishment, and others who oppose it. Some Christians think that abortion is murder, one of the greatest sins. Other Christians feel that there are circumstances in which abortion is justified. Name any major social issue–gay marriage, the equal treatment of women, climate change–and you will find Christians deeply divided, and deeply convinced that *they* know God's will because prayer yielded the desired results. There's even disagreement on spiritual issues. Thousands of Catholic women have prayed very hard about their roles in the church, and—guess what—God told them to become priests. But the hierarchy of the church has said, "No, you've got the message wrong." In other words, *their* prayers can't be trusted. Isn't that a bit suspicious?

When the Boy Scouts decided to lift the ban on openly gay boys, troops were kicked out of churches. One church that slammed its doors was Louisville's Southeast Christian Church. Its executive pastor Tim Hester called it "a difficult decision for the church to sever its relationship with the Boy Scouts," and confessed there was a "lot of prayer, a lot of thought and a lot of discussions." Many other churches have also prayed about the issue, and decided to adopt a policy of welcome and charity. So who got God's message right? Who's fooling whom about the value of prayer as evidence? Human brains are saturated by doctrine and prejudice, hence any confidence that prayer provides evidence for God is destroyed."I distrust those people who know so well what God wants them to do," Susan B. Anthony said, "because I notice it always coincides with their own desires."

Couldn't God have foreseen this fatal flaw? Couldn't he have designed a way to get around human brains to make his messages clear and unequivocal? As Carl Sagan suggested, a gigantic message board on the Moon might do the job. When human prayers about gays in scouting reach a critical mass, God could light up the message board and make his will clear: "Gay scouts are cool, get over it." Or, if God is less compassionate than many humans are, the message could be mean and nasty. After all, we can't rule out a wicked god; that's part of Tough Problem IV.

We should note as well the role of confirmation bias in convincing the faithful that prayer works. When things turn out as hoped, as prayed for, it is so easy to give God credit for granting our wishes, and assume that it was heartfelt praying that did the trick. Disappointments and even really horrible outcomes are not allowed to erode confidence in prayer and God's attention and benevolence. Enthusiastic prayer-practitioners never allow themselves to become discouraged or biased against prayer when their requests fall flat. It's not that prayer didn't work—God forbid—it's just that humans can never see our world and our lives from God's supreme perspective. God knows best, even if we must accept disappointment. The positive outcomes are all that count; God and the process remain unscathed.

Source of God Knowledge #5

My Personal Feelings

The atheists who attended the American Atheists National Convention in Austin in March 2013 were surprised to find that local Christian pastors asked for a discussion session, and that it turned out to be a cordial event. But there were no conversions, in either direction. It would've been highly unlikely for the Christians to give ground, because, no matter how much evidence and logic the atheists mustered, the Christians rested their case on their personal relationships with Jesus. The reality, intensity, and beauty of that trumped everything else. They knew Jesus in their hearts.

They were, in essence, arguing that touchy-feely sentiment is a basis for making claims about how the Cosmos works. Christians want us to believe that Jesus plays a role in running the Cosmos, and some even carry this idea to the subatomic level. Fundamentalist radio empire owner Bryan Fischer has argued that physicists have been looking in the wrong place trying to figure out the force that holds the nucleus of atoms together. According to Fischer, it's none other than Jesus.[13] I suspect that most Christians don't give much thought to physics, but they would probably nod in approval, based on John 1:3 ("Through him all things were made; without him nothing was made that has been made"). And it's the same Jesus who is prepared to be friends with those who love and accept him ("welcome him into their hearts").

But something is obviously askew here, and atheists have noticed it, even if Christians are oblivious: Very devout, deeply spiritually Jews and Muslims–who have also prayed and meditated–dismiss the Jesus claim out of hand. All of *their* prayers and meditation have resulted in a concept of God and the Cosmos that is radically at odds with Christian affirmations. It's hard to disagree with John Loftus's analysis:

> The number of believers who claim they have had a personal experience with their particular cultural god are a dime a dozen. It doesn't matter if believers say their religious experience is real and the others are not. You would expect them to say that. The honest truth for honest people is that these subjective experiences provide no evidence at all.[14]

I usually get looks of shock when I say to Christians that personal opinions don't count, no matter how deeply felt. They are *not evidence*. When we're trying to figure out how the Cosmos runs, I don't care what you feel in your heart. It would make as much sense for me to ask, "What is your personal feeling about the Giant Red Spot on Jupiter, the huge storm that has been raging there for a couple of centuries?" Why would I care about how you feel about that? Loftus points out that "believers deny the need for sufficient objective evidence because they intuitively know their faith does not have it." If it did, he says, those believers "would be the first ones crowing about it."[15]

As much as religious folks hope and assume that their personal feelings are a source of God-knowledge, they have to do much more than "give testimony" to make the claim stick. We're back to the issue of verification, and deep feelings won't do. In fact, their deep feelings make us suspicious that objectivity and the quest for truth have been subverted. You have a personal relationship with Jesus? Well, great, but billions of non-Christians have claimed the same thing with respect to the gods in their own pantheons. The ancient Romans enjoyed intimate friendships with their multiple household gods. Christians are keeping this brand of piety alive and well, but please don't expect others to accept it as a genuine source of knowledge about God.

Source of God Knowledge #6

The Wisdom of Theologians

Astronomer and planetary scientist David Grinspoon begins his 416-page book, *Lonely Planets: The Natural Philosophy of Alien Life*, by admitting that "a book summing up everything we *know* about alien life would contain only one word: *nothing*." To that, he's "managed to add an additional 150,000 by following our quests for aliens through history, speculative science, philosophy, and fantasy." After all, he says, "if Jerry Seinfeld can do a sitcom about nothing, why can't I write a book about something we know nothing about?[16]

Theologians are masters at the craft of make-believe, and have also risen to the challenge of writing about nothing. Grinspoon's book about nothing manages to be entertaining because it's actually rich in information. He had a lot of data to talk about, as preface to what we don't yet know about alien life. The reader is left with the impression that we are close to finding out something soon.

We never get the feeling that the theologians are on the verge of something. They relish mystery, that mysterious something hovering somehow outside of space and time, and don't want or expect breakthroughs. Unlike Grinspoon with his abundant knowledge of planets, theologians don't have any data about God, just speculation masquerading as certainty and–of all things–eternal truth.

Their Gray Eminences

From time to time, pre-eminent theologians from important Catholic, Protestant, Jewish, and Islamic traditions gather for major interfaith conferences. The costumes are elaborate and eccentric; as lyricist Jerry Herman would have put it, they "hustle out their highest drag." Funny hats and beards are *de rigueur*, and we can see from their bearing and demeanor that they are held in high esteem by their respective flocks. But we know for sure that the theological points held in common by these august divines could be counted on one hand.

They are experts in their own elaborate and eccentric ideologies, and no matter how much conciliation and politeness are the order of the day at such gatherings, they *absolutely do not* agree about God. With no data about God, what could they possibly agree on? And how could their speculations be counted as evidence? Their very lack of agreement is evidence that theology long has been running on empty.

In Mark Twain's *Letters from Earth*, he describes an experiment in which he tried to determine if, as he puts it, "man is a reasoning animal":

> In an hour I taught a cat and a dog to be friends. I put them in a cage. In another hour I taught them to be friends with a rabbit. In the course of two days I was able to add a fox, a goose, a squirrel and some doves. Finally a monkey. They lived together in peace; even affectionately. Next, in another cage I confined an Irish Catholic from Tipperary, and as soon as he seemed tame I added a Scotch Presbyterian from Aberdeen. Next a Turk from Constantinople; a Greek Christian from Crete; an Armenian; a Methodist from the wilds of Arkansas; a Buddhist from China; a Brahman from Benares. Finally, a Salvation Army Colonel from Wapping. Then I stayed away for two whole days. When I came back to note results, the cage of Higher Animals was all right, but in the other there was but a chaos of gory odds and ends of turbans and fezzes and plaids and bones and flesh–not a specimen left alive. These Reasoning Animals had disagreed on a theological detail and carried the matter to a Higher Court.[17]

Theologians just *know* what they know, and grimly, when they are allowed any measure of political or military power, "not a specimen is left alive." Many believers have been burned at the stake because they happened to be on the wrong side of the right theology in power. No one really knows anything about God, but those who think they do employ all sorts of tricks to fool others.

Top-Notch Theology at Its Worst

Catholic theologian John F. Haught is a particularly grim example of the Tough Problem of finding out about God. He's one of the experts, so shouldn't we expect really good stuff from him? Not like, say, C.S. Lewis (*Mere Christianity, The Screwtape Letters*), an amateur for whom most theologians offer weak smiles when lay people ooze praise on him.

Haught is one of those fine academicians folks look up to, educated at The Catholic University of America, teaching at Georgetown, the kind of guy who might get invited to sit down for a chat with Charlie Rose. He's held in esteem because of his erudite theology—well, fellow academicians might consider it so. But his theology is obtuse and nearly impenetrable to even well-educated lay people. Two of his books that I have ploughed through have enticing titles, *What Is God: How to Think about the Divine* and *The Cosmic Adventure: Science, Religion and the Quest for Purpose*. Throughout both, I scrawled in the margins, over and over, "How does he know this?" and "How do theologians learn to talk like this?" The promised cosmic adventure was anything but.

From his perspective atop piles of theological tracts and tomes dating back centuries, Haught writes for modern readers, always keeping an eye on the accumulation of Catholic Dogma that marks the outer limits of theological speculation. It's a dangerous business, actually. Theologian Uta Ranke-Heinemann didn't last long when she denied the Virgin Birth; in 1987 she was fired by Pope John Paul II. From inside his academic cocoon, Haught projects his guesses as knowledge; he is held in such awe that his theobabble is mistaken for wisdom. These highfalutin theologians probably hope that people will say, "I can't understand it because it's so profound."

A Sneaky Move on Page One

I got the first inkling that the wool was being pulled over my eyes on page one of *What Is God? How to Think About the Divine*:

> Thinkers ask questions like "What is nature?" "What is man?" "What is time?" "What is space?" "What is history?" etc. They cannot help asking also, "What is God?"[18]

Haught is being sly here. Yes, thinkers do ask about these realities: nature, man, time, space, history. They are real, we know they're real, and we are curious about how they work. But then he slips in the final item, "God," which does not qualify for this list of certainties. It is the reality of God that is up for grabs: the Great Invisible One whom we are assured is not imaginary. It seems like an attempt to lull readers into thinking that God is a real player in the real world. Perhaps tacking God onto the list along with nature and history might do the trick?

Frankly, I doubt that many people do wonder what God is. Most of those who do probably would get lost in this book after just a few pages. The obfuscation is deep indeed, and you know what kind of a pile I'm talking about:

> If we are interested in referring to God at all it is probably because we have had a "feeling," a "premonition," and "sense" or "intuition" of what is referred to as God. But feelings, premonitions and sensations are not yet what I mean by thought. Even though the term may have a much broader application, by thought I mean here the *theoretical* mode of consciousness. By theoretical consciousness I mean the type of cognition in which we step back from the immediacy of an experience and place that experience in a conceptual framework. Once we have placed our immediate experience in such a network of ideas the original experience can be mediated to us in a way that allows us to relate it to other experiences and ideas.[19]

It's no page turner, and there is no promise of excitement to come. Theologians write for other theologians.

Most "worshipers find it difficult to relate to a cosmic principle that appears totally impersonal," Haught admits. But, then, amazingly, he shows his hand, and why he can't be taken seriously. He *admits* that his goal is to *design a God* that the devout want and need! Note the give-away words that I have emphasized.

> I am unable to deal here with the complexities of this problem. But I shall proceed under the *assumption* that a transcendent reality that does not possess at the very least those qualities which constitute the dignity of human persons, that is something like intelligence, feeling, freedom, power, initiative, creativity, etc. (though to an eminent degree) *could not adequately inspire trust or reverence in human beings*. In this sense God *would have to be* "personal" to be God. It is doubtful whether believers could be *fully satisfied* religiously by surrendering to something that is *less intense in being than they are*, that is, to something that does not *have at least the stature of personality* (which is the most intense form of being of which we have any direct experience).[20]

This paragraph illustrates why I regard schools of theology as blights on the academic landscape. For all his admirable knowledge of science, Haught ultimately makes his living by coming up with answers that are in line with dogma. He's guided by what worshippers want to hear. He will follow assumptions regarding his ideal of a "transcendent reality," and he must avoid descriptions of God that would fail to adequately satisfy and inspire.

And he acknowledges that he will run up against the objections that serious thinkers have always posed regarding theism. He states that one of his tasks is "to make sense of the main problem associated with talk about God, namely God's apparent absence and unavailability." If God is a reality, he asks, frankly acknowledging the challenge,

> why is this reality so unavailable, so unverifiable, so elusive? Why, as Freud asked, should that which holds the most importance for believers, namely God, be so lacking in immediate obviousness to themselves as well as to non-believers? I shall contend that an examination of the transpersonal dimensions of God's life, that side of God's being which cannot be fully represented in personalistic terms, may help us to make some sense of the "scandal" of the divine hiddenness.[21]

I couldn't have used a better word than *scandal*. But he thinks there's a way around it because of "the transpersonal dimensions of God's life"? How do theologians learn to talk like this? Why are they allowed to get away with such gibberish in academia? What are his sources for *knowing* about the "transpersonal dimensions of God's life"?

The best explanation for God's "absence and unavailability," which, Haught confesses, has always gnawed at believers, is that believers have always been on a fool's errand. God's absence is really a big clue *that he doesn't exist*. The Little Engine That Could comes to mind, chanting "I think I can! I think I can! I think I can!" Theologians chant "There must be a god! There must be a god! There must be a god!" huffing and puffing to make it so. The Little Engine finally succeeds, "I knew I could!", but theologians have never made it to the top of the hill.

They convince no one outside their narrow preserves and the pious church folks who pay their salaries. They may have studied and prayed and meditated far more than ordinary people, but that doesn't mean they've tapped into divine reality. The "wisdom of the theologians" as a source of knowledge about God is no such thing. The respected, revered, adored religious thinkers of the various faith traditions inspire awe because they've mastered dogma and theobabble, and because people like to be awed. The learned theologians manage to fool some of the people all of the time.

God Knowledge Undermined by Perspective

Let's Remember Where We Are

I grew up looking at the night sky from the flat Indiana prairie before artificial satellites had been invented. (Yes, I'm that old.) Little did I know how much would be discovered about the heavens during my lifetime alone, things that not even the most optimistic astronomers at the time could have predicted.

But there is an irony here. We now know so much, yet still we know almost nothing. And tragically, most of seven billion humans who look at the night sky don't know how much we've learned. Human ignorance is one of the most durable and abundant commodities on the planet, and thus religions remain. Religious awe is vastly outclassed by the awe that emerges from our telescopes, at *seeing*.

The How-Much-We-Know Side of the Equation

We can be thankful that some humans are intensely curious about what's going on "out there" and have put so much energy and brainpower into trying to find out. Two of the most important instruments that we've put into space are the Wilkinson Microwave Anisotropy Probe (WMAP), which was launched in 2001, and the European Space Agency's Planck mission, launched in 2009. Never before in human history have we known what we do now, thanks to these probes. Their data show that the Universe is 13.82 billion years old, expanding a bit slower than we expected. It's made up of 4.9 percent normal matter, 26.8 percent dark matter, and 68.3 percent dark energy.[22]

A few years ago, the Kepler spacecraft was launched into an Earth-trailing orbit of the Sun, with the goal of finding planets around other stars. It has been staring at 100,000 stars that are several thousand light years away. As of February 2013, it "found a total of 2,740 candidate exoplanets" and "114 confirmed exoplanets in 69 stellar systems." In January 2013, "astronomers at the Harvard-Smithsonian Center for Astrophysics (CfA) used *Kepler's* data to estimate that 'at least 17 billion Earth-sized exoplanets reside in the Milky Way Galaxy.'"[23] We are living in a Golden Age of knowledge about the Cosmos.

The We-Know-Almost-Nothing Side of the Equation

And yet. Take a long hard look at this image of the Andromeda Galaxy, taken in 1923 by Edwin Hubble. He used the 100-inch Hooker telescope on Mount Wilson. It's one of the most important photographs ever taken.

In the upper right hand corner, his handwriting is visible: "VAR!" This means that he had discovered a Cepheid variable star in the Andromeda galaxy, which was momentous. With this identification, because of the peculiar behavior of Cepheid variable stars, Hubble was the first human to determine the distance to this other galaxy. It was far outside our Milky Way Galaxy. We now know that it is about 2.5 million light years away. Because of their gravitational attraction, Andromeda and the Milky Way are

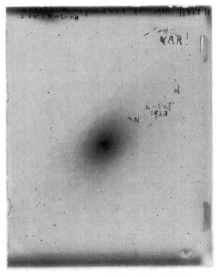

Andromeda Galaxy by Edwin Hubble
(negative, 1923)[24]

moving toward one another at the rate of about four million miles per day, and will merge in a few billion years.

Edwin Hubble's discovery settled a great debate among astronomers, and it changed forever the way we can think about ourselves. It became immediately clear that the Cosmos is vastly more immense than had been previously understood. Until that time, astronomers assumed that the Milky Way Galaxy *was* the Universe. We now know that there are perhaps 100 billion other galaxies.

Yes, this prompts the feeling that we are very small. We knew that even before this photo was taken. In 1923, however, our isolation in the Cosmos was magnified incredibly. Science writer Timothy Ferris imagines "an atlas of our galaxy that devoted but a single page to each star system in the Milky Way." Just one page for our solar system, with Earth and Mars and all the rest of it that we've seen depicted in those fascinating space probe photos. This

> atlas would run to more than ten million volumes of ten thousand pages each. It would take a library the size of Harvard's to house the atlas, and merely to flip through it, at the rate of a page per second, would require over ten thousand years. Add the details of planetary cartography, potential extraterrestrial biology, the subtleties of the scientific principles involved, and the historical dimensions of change, and it becomes clear that we are never going to learn more than a tiny fraction of the story of our galaxy alone–and there are a hundred million more galaxies. As the physician Lewis Thomas writes, "The greatest of all the accomplishments of twentieth century science has been the discovery of human ignorance."

From this perspective of radical isolation, we are forced to acknowledge that we know virtually nothing about the cosmos. *Theologians should take the hint.* Our ignorance, Ferris notes, "has always been with us, and always will be. What is new is our awareness of it, our awakening to its fathomless dimensions, and it is *this*, more than anything else, that marks the coming of age of our species."[25]

If they wrote very small, many of the thousand pages in each of those ten million volumes could describe what other intelligent beings in the Cosmos think about what we would call religion. But we have not been able to compare notes with any other thinkers in the Milky Way, to say nothing of all those other galaxies. We are profoundly isolated. So how can we be so confident about *our* god ideas?

Just how isolated are we? The nearest star system to earth is Alpha Centauri (it's actually three stars that orbit each other), which is 4.37 light years away. Because it is the nearest, it has played a role in science fiction writing; perhaps it too has planets with civilizations, and could be the first for Earthlings to visit. So why don't we aim a spaceship at Alpha Centauri and go find out? NASA has no plans to do so. NASA doesn't even have a division called Milky Way Exploration Projects. It has launched hundreds of planetary probes, but not a dollar has been spent for going beyond.[26]

Why not? What's holding us back? Star Trek and Star Wars make it look so do-able, but there's a harsh reality in the way. If, say, the Space Shuttle were sent speeding toward Alpha Centauri at about 18,000 miles per hour, the journey would take about *160,000 years*. And that's to the nearest star! The Cosmos is mostly nothing. When the Milky Way and Andromeda eventually merge, no stars will collide or even come close.

Perhaps some super-advanced means of travel will be invented. In the meantime, though, our isolation is absolute, and our ignorance is staggering. *Theologians should take the hint.* Our knowledge of the Cosmos is threadbare, and we have seen that all of the ways to know God claimed by religious folks—revelation, visions, prayers—are evidence only of what's going on inside human heads. We should maintain perspective and realize that we really are lost in space.

Let's Remember Where We Are in the History of Thought

In 1946, Henri Frankfort and several others published an essay entitled *The Intellectual Adventure of Ancient Man.* The title became a part of our intellectual heritage. Just when did the adventure begin? Surely Neanderthals and the earliest *Homo sapiens* gave thought to matters of life and death, beginnings and endings.

But perhaps one of the best ways to mark the true beginning of the adventure was the invention of writing, when stories and speculation could be preserved and shared in tangible form. In the West, we credit the Sumerians with the invention of writing, some 5,000 years ago. They began to write things down for keeping financial and commercial records, but soon more important thoughts and reflections, myths, epics, and poems came into existence. The intellectual adventure had begun in earnest. So it's not unreasonable to say that our quest to understand the Cosmos got under way about 5,000 years ago. It's less than a blink of an eye since the moment our universe burst into existence about 13.82 billion years ago.

Imagine there are intellectually advanced civilizations on just a tiny fraction of the 17 billion Earth-size planets that scientists suspect lurk in our galaxy alone. We could have galactic neighbors who have been thinking about the Cosmos for a million years. Our 5,000-year quest is a joke compared to that. Some of our very smart neighbors wouldn't even grant that we're at the first grade level.

Yet there are those among us, seized by religious certainty, who claim that they've got it figured out. For some reason, a few billion Earthlings remain in the grip of a sky-god idea that was born in remote deserts thousands of years ago. The sky-god idea is known formally as monotheism and has morphed, like a virus, into many forms in broad categories, e.g., Judaism, Christianity, Islam, Mormonism—all of which have splintered endlessly. But monotheism is fundamentally wrong-headed in all of its manifestations, no matter how much sophisticated thinkers have labored to make it intellectually respectable.

Is it really likely that we know as much about God or gods as religions claim, and that god-information was channeled to Earth at the time and place that Christians claim? "A further difficulty," Christopher Hitchens has pointed out, "is the apparent tendency of the Almighty to reveal himself only to unlettered and quasi-historical individuals, in regions of the Middle Eastern wasteland that were long the home of idol worship and superstition, and in many instances already littered with existing prophecies."[27]

The intellectual adventure of ancient man stalled with the emergence of monotheism, especially the mind-numbing sort preached by the apostle Paul, who detested curiosity and learning; he warned the Corinthians that the "wisdom of this world is foolishness before God" (1 Cor. 3:19, NASB). He had figured out how to escape death by believing in Jesus, and that's all he needed to know. He urged his followers to get ready to meet Jesus returning to earth through the clouds. History would end at that moment, so for Paul there was no intellectual adventure; he set the tone for Christian thought for a thousand years. With the Renaissance, the adventure would be reborn and accelerate.

The Realm of the Ridiculous

George Bush's handlers and apologists have insisted that he never claimed that God told him to invade Iraq. George, who found God after his alcoholic youth, became the darling of conservative Christians, but even his most faithful followers might squirm at the suggestion that God spoke directly to him. After all, according to one old proverb, "If you speak to God, it's called prayer, but if you claim that God speaks to you, it's called insanity." It's best to be cautious about that kind of claim. A therapist friend reminded me once that reality is what happens *outside* the patient's head.

In trying to figure out God, should we rely on revelations, visions, prayers, and all of those other religious sensations that take place *inside* our human heads? I'll leave the last word on this to Bob Schieffer, the dean of American television broadcasters who offered his opinion on the vile preaching of the Westboro Baptist Church about American soldiers dying in foreign lands because God wants to punish us for tolerating gay people. With one comment, he put down the whole project of Western theology:

> That anyone would have the audacity to claim knowledge of God's reasoning is ridiculous.[28]

Theologians really should take the hint.

Notes

1. Carl Sagan, *The Demon-Haunted World: Science as a Candle in the Dark* (Ballantine Books, 1997), p. 171.

2. Charles A. Mills, 1913

3. I've heard the theologian-as-spelunker analogy attributed in various forms to Ambrose Bierce and Oscar Wilde.

4. Anna and Susan Warner, "Jesus Loves Me," lyric 1860, tune 1862.

5. Carl Sagan, *Broca's Brain: Reflections on the Romance of Science* (Ballantine Books, 1986), p. 281.

6. More about this with respect to Tough Problem VI.

7. For starters, Luke 14:26, in which Jesus says that hatred of family is a prerequisite for being one of his followers; and Romans 13:1, Paul's warning to his readers not to resist rulers because they are appointed by God.

8. John Loftus has written extensively about the Outsider Test of Faith, which we'll discuss later.

9. D. Landsborough, "St. Paul and Temporal Lobe Epilepsy," *Journal of Neurology, Neurosurgery, and Psychiatry*, 1987; 50, pp. 661-62. The researchers were K. Dewhurst and A.W. Beard, and N. Geschwind.

10. David E. Comings, *Did Man Create God? Is Your Spiritual Brain at Peace with Your Thinking Brain?* (Hope Press, 2008), pp. 363-64.

11. Landsborough at p. 663.

12. Transcribed from *Onion* video at youtube.com/watch?v=goSvNTcZ6gU.

13. Bryan Fischer, "What Holds an Atom's Nucleus Together? Jesus!", examiner.com, 7 June 2013.

14. "Why I Am an Atheist, My Statement vs Dr. Rauser," debunkingchristianity.blogspot.com/2013/06/why-i-am-atheist-my-statement-vs-dr.html (posted 6 June 2013).

15. Ibid.

16. David Grinspoon, *Lonely Planets: The Natural Philosophy of Alien Life* (Harper Perennial, 2004), p. xiii.

17. *Mark Twain's Book of Animals*, pp. 121-122.

18. John Haught, *What Is God? How to Think about the Divine* (Paulist Press, 1996), p. 1.

19. Haught at pp. 1-2.

20. Haught at pp. 6-7.

21. Haught at p. 7.

22. From astronomer Phil Plait's blog, 21 March 2013.

23. foxnews.com/science/2013/01/08/at-least-17-billion-earth-size-planets-are-in-milky-way-new-estimate-says.html

24. Photo: Carnegie Observatories.

25. Timothy Ferris, *Coming of Age in the Milky Way* (Harper Perennial, 2003), p. 383.

26. The Voyager Spacecrafts I and II, launched in 1977, are indeed leaving our solar system—after exploring the outer planets—but reaching other stars was never the intent.

27. Christopher Hitchens, *God Is Not Great: How Religion Poisons Everything* (Twelve Books, 2007), p. 98.

28. Bob Schieffer, *Face the Nation* (6 March 2011).

III

The Bible's Revelation Ripoff

> [The Bible] is also a dangerous book because we often ascribe divine will to the many human distortions it contains. We undermine the sacredness of the Bible and fuel its dangers whenever we fail to discern the difference between distortions and revelation, whenever we give its words and its writers too much authority, or whenever we abandon or fail critically to examine the contents of its pages. Simply stated, the Bible can inform our religious experience, but it is often wrong about God.
>
> —Jack Nelson-Pallmeyer, *Jesus Against Christianity: Reclaiming the Missing Jesus*

> [T]he Bible is a self-destructing artifact.
>
> —Randel Helms, *The Bible Against Itself*

God Wrote a Book

HOW DO PEOPLE OF FAITH overcome the conundrum of our profound isolation in, and ignorance about, the cosmos? It renders theological speculations highly suspect. They are so commonly based on subjective and suspect ways of channeling God, e.g. prayers, meditation, visions, personal intuitions and feelings. And our limited time on the planet as self-aware, thinking creatures also makes it doubtful that our ideas about deities are trustworthy. Most humans remain under the spell of crude guesses about God that we owe to ancient thinkers.

Theologians in the Western tradition, however, argue that we have been rescued from isolation and ignorance by God's intervention through revelation *in written form*. God supposedly has revealed his thoughts and wishes for humanity through sacred text; the very words of God are there on the paper for all to see and believe. Jewish, Christian, and Islamic believers have trusted their respective scriptures–the Old Testament, the New Testament, and the Qu'ran–for information about God. And they're usually adamant.

But a sacred book is just a gimmick.

Trust Me

One of Billy Graham's closest friends was fellow evangelist Charles Templeton, who, as it turned out, played the Judas role.[1] As Billy's career as an evangelist was taking off in the 1950s, Templeton admitted that he had too many doubts and gave up preaching. It would be forty years before he published *Farewell to God: My Reasons for Rejecting the Christian Faith* (1995).

The loss of this good friend to atheism was traumatic for Graham, and he had to hold onto the Bible as a lifeline to withstand Templeton's invitation to slide with him into apostasy. Lee Strobel, probably one of the most popular Christian apologists of our time, tells the story, shedding light on the mediocrity of Graham's thinking.

> Templeton argued: "Billy, you're fifty years out of date. People no longer accept the Bible as being inspired the way you do. Your faith is too simple." Templeton seemed to be winning the tug-of-war."If I was not exactly

doubtful," Graham would recall, "I was certainly disturbed." He knew that if he could not trust the Bible, he could not go on. The Los Angeles crusade–the event that would open the door to Graham's worldwide ministry–was hanging in the balance.[2]

So how do you find out if you can trust the Bible? The table below has a few obvious tests. But Graham was sure that the *Bible itself*, along with prayer and some meddling of the Holy Spirit, would provide all the evidence he needed.

Some Bible Trustworthiness Tests

Does it look like it was written by divine guidance, e.g., with the original manuscripts of the gospels still around, as pristine today as when their authors handed them off to be copied? (*No, not even close.*)
Are its books seamless, without errors and contradictions? (*Far from it.*)
Are all its books authentic, exempt from suspicion of being forgeries? (*Of course not.*)
Are its stories confirmed by other documents from the ancient world? (*There's no confirmation at all.*)
Are its laws, ethics, and morality of the highest possible caliber, without exception applicable today? (*Not by a long shot.*)

He searched the Scriptures for answers, he prayed, he pondered. Finally, in a heavy-hearted walk in the moonlit San Bernardino Mountains, everything came to a climax. Gripping a Bible, Graham dropped to his knees and confessed he couldn't answer some of the philosophical and psychological questions that Templeton and others were raising.

> I was trying to be on the level with God, but something remained unspoken," he wrote."At last the Holy Spirit freed me to say it."Father, I am going to accept this as Thy Word–by *faith*! I'm going to allow faith to go beyond my intellectual questions and doubts, and I will believe this to be Your inspired Word.[3]

Poor Billy. There was the big Los Angeles crusade at stake, so he had to go on. He hunkered down and, damn it, decided to *just believe* that the Bible could be trusted, despite philosophical and psychological questions. We can suspect that Graham didn't have the intellectual tools to tackle the challenge. Faith was his tool for guaranteeing the Bible.

During his televised sermons, showman Billy dramatically waved the Bible above his head, thus helping nail its status as a reassuring talisman. The custodians of religion have always counted on hero worship–in this instance, a book is just as much the hero as the preacher–to command the adoration of vast numbers of people. In Western monotheism, a book–well, different books, depending on which monotheism you believe in–can be trusted to deliver God-information. But this approach buckles on close examination. The revelation-via-scripture claim is crippled by some serious flaws. Since my focus in this book is Christianity, I will describe those flaws as they pertain to the Bible.

Can the Bible Prove Itself?

It doesn't seem to have dawned on Billy Graham that his methodology was defective as well as juvenile. The Bible's validity can't be derived from the Bible itself. Thus my suspicion that he didn't have the intellectual tools that were up to the task. Gripping the Bible on your knees in the moonlight (on a mountain, no less, like Moses?) and waiting for a soothing "there, there" from the Holy Spirit is simplistic self-indulgence. It falls far short of rigorous, relentless pursuit of tested methodology.

The most obvious flaw in the revelation-via-scripture claim is that it is an article of faith, just as "Jesus is the son of God" and "Neptune is the god of the ocean" are articles of faith. Anyone can choose to believe it or not, but those outside the circle of believers want to see evidence that such faith is warranted. There must be an ironclad case to begin with that the Bible can be trusted. So-called "revealed information" gained from the sacred text isn't information at all if the holy status of the text can't be verified in the first place.

The God's-Word-via-the-Bible idea is used as if people were totally unaware that they are indulging in intellectual laziness and sleight of hand. This flaw finds its ultimate expression when believers quote one of the lesser books of the New Testament, 2 Timothy 3:16, "All scripture is inspired by God and profitable for teaching, for reproof, for correction, and for training in righteousness" (RSV). Never mind that the author of this verse certainly didn't have his *own* writing in mind (it would be a couple of hundred years before 2 Timothy was considered canonical), and never mind that he couldn't have been referring to the New Testament, which didn't exist yet. But the faithful commonly and confidently point to 2 Timothy 3:16 with great satisfaction, as if to say, "There you have it, what more could you want, case closed." And why should we believe the author of 2 Timothy, anyhow?

The fallacy can usually be driven home to Protestants by asking if they believe that the Pope is infallible."Of course not!" is the usual response, but then we ask, "How can you not believe it? The Catholic Church says it's so." I was raised among Protestants whose rude retort would be, "But I think the Catholic Church is full of crap. Why should I believe anything it says?" *The parallel here is precise*: If you don't believe Catholic dogma to begin with, then its authority is null and void. If you don't believe in the Bible to begin with, its authority is likewise null and void. Citing some book of the Bible adds nothing to your argument.

It's not hard, though, to get away with the idea that the Bible is the credible and reliable Word of God. Almost 80 percent of Americans believe that the Bible is God's Word, although according to Gallup in 2011, only 30 percent understand this in a literal sense. The Bible enjoys the status of a talisman; it would be unthinkable for the president of the United States to be sworn in without his or her hand resting on it. But no matter how high the level of confidence in the Bible, which would probably slip substantially if people actually *read* the thing, no document on the planet can be self-authenticating.

Mind of God or Mind of Man?

Let's suppose, however, that God's-Word-via-the-Bible is not just a faith idea, some romantic fantasy that God touched ancient authors in a special way. Even if we grant that this is a real phenomenon, where does that leave us? How do we proceed to find the true words of God? That is, how do the advocates of this idea determine which texts are inspired? Which texts can we point to in full confidence that they reveal the mind of God to us?

Of course, as soon as we pose these questions, we realize that we confront serious difficulties. True believers will fight each other, sometimes to the point of bloodshed, about which texts are God's very words. Do Christians, Jews, or Muslims have the true scripture? Christians are prepared to acknowledge that the Word of God can be found in both the Old and New Testaments, but Jews certainly won't say the same thing for the New Testament. Most Jews would vehemently deny the claim that, say, the gospels—propaganda pieces about Jesus—are as holy as the Torah. To return the favor, Christians have always relegated much of the Old Testament to an inferior status. And the Qu'ran holds no value whatever as the word God for Jews or Christians. If it did, they would read the Qu'ran with as much zeal as they read the Bible. This lack of devotion is an insult to devout Muslims who consider it the very word of Allah. It must be anguish as well for Mormons that their treasured word of God, The *Book of Mormon*, is not taken seriously by almost anyone besides themselves—indeed is commonly considered a joke. Yet generations of Mormons have earnestly believed that God's message was written on the golden tablets "discovered" by Joseph Smith.

This irony is not lost on atheists. The theists, in fact, are among those who deny that the word of God comes in book form—when it's the other guy's book. They are like kids in a playground taunting others, "My book is holier than yours!"

Which Words Are God's?

But let's humor the Christians, conceding for the sake of argument that the Bible contains the Word of God. The heavy lifting is still ahead of them to make this claim stick. We need specifics and criteria for verification.

My old Bible, which I've had for more than fifty years, is almost 1,300 pages long. Do Christians really expect us to believe that every page, every verse is the true Word of God? There are some Christians who do make this claim, and there are scholars who have written books in an attempt to prove it (e.g., Norman Geisler's 841-page *Baker Encyclopedia of Christian Apologetics*). But most mainstream Christians are smart enough to know that they can't get away with the idea that *every* last word is God's, and they don't want to even try. So then they face the heavy lifting: Which texts out of those 1,300 pages qualify as *God's* words? How do they decide that?

Just because a text is famous or a favorite doesn't mean that it passes scrutiny. How do you tell, objectively, that a text passes muster as a *bona fide* word of God?

The quality of the material in the Bible varies dramatically. As any serious reader of the Bible knows, there are many embarrassing, disturbing and puzzling texts in its pages. The Bible on the altar in church is a thing of beauty: large, leather bound—white leather in many cases—with gold trimming and a large red satin ribbon bookmark. The folks in the pews have no problem assuming that this beautiful artifact must be chock full of holiness. Except for the most fervent defenders of biblical inerrancy, though, most devout Bible readers would be uneasy with the idea of throwing the Word-of-God mantle over everything in it. That would cause far more problems than it solves. One becomes mired in tedious and fanciful explanations as to how God could possibly have inspired this or that verse, e.g., the famous lines, "Thou shalt not suffer a witch to live" (Exod. 22:18, KJV) and "Slaves, be obedient to those who are your masters according to the flesh, with fear and trembling, in the sincerity of your heart" (Eph. 6:5, NASB).

So just within the Bible, if you've ruled out the Qu'ran and the *Book of Mormon*, how do we determine which texts are the Word of God? And this brings us to the essence of this flaw: What is claimed is, in fact, beyond our grasp, out of reach. For anyone committed to exploring reality with intellectual honesty and integrity, it is shocking that revelation-through-the-written-word can be taken seriously. How, exactly, would that work?

The Barrier of the Human Brain

The Bible's advocates know very well, or should, that it's beyond verification. But faith-laziness commonly obscures this fact. Believers are accustomed to just taking it on faith that their particular favorite verses are the true Word of God.

But faith is not a reliable methodology; it won't do when such extravagant claims are being made. And it is an extravagant claim that words or verses on a page have come from the Mind of God. Any reasonably skeptical person has a right to ask (and those skeptics include people from rival religions as well as atheists): How do we know what is inspired and what isn't, who had conversations with God, and who just imagined it? Isn't it bizarre that people are willing to make life decisions and huge emotional investments based on words of God that could, in fact, be nothing more than the product of someone's fertile imagination?

We don't know the process of this alleged phenomenon, but let's try to trace it as far as we can. Even the most conservative Bible believers acknowledge that the texts, the actual words, were written down on paper (well, the ancient equivalent thereof) by men.

The human brain cannot be extricated from the process, which presents us with a troubling ambiguity, one that occurred to me at the time that I wrote my cheeky essay in seminary: How can we be certain that the words that flowed onto the paper were stimulated by a deity? Were they merely traveling *through* a brain functioning as a conductor, from an external or superior source? It's not so outrageous or unreasonable to suggest that we really ought to have criteria for judging what is of human origin and what is of divine origin. How can we be so sure that any particular sentence, chapter, or verse really does come from God? Well, here's the kicker: *We can't*. There are no criteria for doing so.

Theologians do no more than make guesses based on their own traditions and theologian biases, while trying to convince the world that God has guided them to the authentic God-texts through prayer.

Revelation theists claim that certainty, of the kind that outsiders expect, is a false expectation. In fact the desire for certainty is ridiculed: Anyone who won't make the leap of faith and simply believe that God was the author is guilty of spiritual cowardice. But we can reply that faith may be prompting believers to accept the product of imagination or hallucination, not revelation. Christian author Jack Nelson-Pallmeyer is fully aware of the problem: "We undermine the sacredness of the Bible and fuel its dangers whenever we fail to discern the difference between distortions and revelation." Sounds good, Jack, but how exactly can we do that?

Getting Away with Truth from Olden Times

God's-Word-in-a-book is a game of guesswork played by theologians, clergy, and devout laity who are bound by doctrine to find God's writ where they want to. Steeped in tradition and wishful thinking, believers argue that revelation is a reality, while non-believers suspect that a less fanciful explanation for the ancient writings will do just as well. Revelation is no more plausible than the use of tarot cards or tea leaves in trying to fathom the secrets of the Cosmos.

How have they been able to get away with it? How is it that the theists have been so successful in convincing the world that their claims are true? As with the concept of God itself, people are comfortable with the idea that the Bible is the word of God, and that it is holy, perhaps because such a link with the divine is a reassurance. I suspect that theists also have gotten a pass due to people's willingness to give the benefit of the doubt based on the passage of time. It's become believable that the Bible is revelation, God's Word, because it is ancient. That's convenient, because the Bible is from an era long gone when God was imagined to have moved more easily in human affairs.

But the passage of time, placing the Bible in the "sacred" past, really solves no problems as far as *verification* is concerned. If our next-door neighbor claims to have conversations with God, or to write down messages from God, we don't take it seriously. If anyone today makes such a claim, it is considered evidence of instability or insanity, not revelation, and, except for a few crazies, nobody listens. Bishop John Shelby Spong has described the hate mail that he has received because of his liberal views. The angriest mail he receives, he says,

> comes from those who claim to be the most religious and who think that they speak with the very voice of God. Indeed, some of these letter writers even state that their hostile missives do not contain their own fallible words but the divine words spoken directly by God to me through them.[4]

Even most of the people who don't like Bishop Spong's liberal views would ridicule the suggestion that his angry dissenters are directly inspired by God, and are passing on God's word to the Bishop.

The Role of Ancient Holy Men

A different aura attaches to the idea of God conversing with people when the scene is shifted to the ancient past. It's more respectable and an easier sell if the "inspired" people had a reputation for being holy, with names like Moses, Isaiah, Matthew, Mark, Luke, and John.

People are considered holy because they were inspired, and they were inspired because they were considered holy. Just as we'd be unwilling to drop our critical eye toward the people who wrote hate messages to Bishop Spong, we must use the same criteria of evidence and verification to evaluate any revelation claim from the ancient past. It's no different than believing that your neighbor is having conversations with God. If we could divest the "holy" men of the Old and New Testaments of all the holiness baggage attached to them as an article of faith (sustained brilliantly by the images of Western art and, in no small part, by Cecil B. DeMille), we'd see the reality: They were someone else's next-door neighbor, too.

They shouldn't be granted immunity from scrutiny and skepticism just because they lived long ago and far away. And I wonder how many of the ancient authors would themselves have made such a claim, anyhow. I suspect that many of them would've been shocked that their writings would one day be considered the very Word of God. There was probably much more humility at the level of the original authors. Only the devout of later generations read their words and made the article-of-faith decision that the word of God could be isolated in a pure form in a canon of inspired texts. The author of 2 Timothy 3:16 was certain that the ancient authors of the Old Testament were inspired. Could he have imagined that his humble letter would someday be granted similar status?

Great Expectations

There is another level on which the whole revelation process is deeply suspect. Revelation theists, those who champion the idea that God wrote a book, ask us to believe in a process that is farfetched. Can God, *has* God really operated in this way? If so, we would be dealing with an arbitrary God who is irresponsible and negligent. We certainly can level this accusation on other grounds. Why the tsunamis, earthquakes, plagues, and massive hunger when God supposedly "has the whole world in his hands"? But theists unwittingly invite ridicule when they make the revelation claim.

If revelation truly were a means by which a deity could break through to humanity with crucial insights and information, directly agitating or energizing brain matter in such a way that human beings are able to write down the thoughts or messages from God, it is almost an inescapable conclusion that God *has let us down* on innumerable occasions. God has missed opportunities to use this technique to good advantage since the days when the Bible was written. The process is implausible because of the many times and circumstances in which a supposedly good deity *hasn't* used it. Why didn't God keep up the good work?

Grievous human suffering could have been averted if God could plant ideas in human heads, if the revelation process really existed. Is it true that an ancient author was moved directly by God to write down, "God so loved the world that he gave his only begotten son" (John 3:16) or, "And Samson found a fresh jawbone of an ass, and put forth his hand and seized it, and with it he slew a thousand men" (Judges 15:14-15, KJV)? If so, then why on earth didn't God work on the brain of Adolph Hitler to change his way of thinking about Jews? During the 14th century, when the Black Plague was killing a quarter of the population between India and Iceland, perhaps God might have whispered in a few ears, "It's the fleas!" That piece of information, planted in a few thousands minds, could have reduced human agony significantly. For generations scientists have been trying to find a cure for cancer. Why doesn't God just give us the answer already?

Theists commonly retort to such questions, "Wait a minute! You're second-guessing God. You don't know his ways, his wisdom and plans." After all, God yelled at Job (when Job questioned his goodness), "Where were *you* when I laid the foundations of the earth?", which is the ultimate "because I'm the daddy, that's why" response. If the revelation process is real, and God has used it, there certainly have been a lot of missed opportunities for a demonstration that God "so loves the world."

Most of the Bible Is Not Worth Reading

Here's the dirty little secret that every Biblical scholar knows: The Bible is mostly *dead weight*. Who would suspect this when we look at that leather-bound, gold trimmed book sparkling on the altar? And when we realize how much the Bible has been probed and analyzed to death?

Most lay people, the average folks in the pews, are unaware that thousands of scholars make their living studying and writing about the Bible. Without question, it is the most researched and minutely studied book ever written. There are countless books, articles, scholarly journals, doctoral dissertations, and sermons about the Bible. John ended his gospel (21:25) with the boast that, if all of Jesus' deeds could be written down, "the world itself could not contain the books that would be written." Bible specialists seem to have taken this as a challenge and have done their best to fill the libraries of academia many times over.

Bible scholar Hector Avalos makes the case that this can now be considered a colossal waste of time. He added his own book, *The End of Biblical Studies,* to that vast pile of writings. In this case, however, he argued that there is no longer any point to all of the Bible idolatry, even the kind that passes itself off as legitimate scholarship. Why bother? He is pretty blunt in his essay, "Why Biblical Studies Must End," in the John Loftus anthology, *The End of Christianity*: "If we were to go verse by verse, I suspect that 99 percent of the Bible would not even be missed."[5]

How could that possibly be true? The book gleaming on the altar is a fraud? Those billions of Gideon Bibles placed in hotel rooms since 1906 are 99 percent wasted paper? The Gideons hope that an occasional tired tourist or lonely businessman will find solace in the pages of endless tedium, but the chances are slim, especially now that hotel rooms offer hundreds of TV channels. Reading the Gideon Bible or watching the adult channels? That's probably not a tough call for a lot of people.

But, even without the adult channels, the Bible will almost always be left in the drawer simply because it is *so boring*. So little of it has any relevance whatever to our lives today. And saying this is not just atheist cattiness. I suspect that very few churchgoers who have tried to read the Bible cover-to-cover would disagree, at least in anonymous polling. It is a form of self-flagellation to pursue the promise, "I'll get through it all."

The Catholic Church doesn't even try to get lay people to read the Bible, mainly because the hierarchy doesn't want the laity thinking about the faith. But the priests also know that the Bible is simply too daunting and uninteresting. Protestants are constantly prodded to read the Bible because of its central theological role. Hence Bible "study guides" are provided by the thousands by Protestant denominations. All of the drivel and dross have to be defended and given a positive spin, and no lay person can begin to understand the abstruse ramblings of the Bible without a lot of tutoring provided by the spin doctors.

The Daily Agony

Many Protestants have taken up the challenge of making it all the way through the Bible, often on a chapter-a-day plan. It's a tough slog. Boredom is one factor; anyone who doubts this should try getting through the books of Chronicles, Isaiah, Jeremiah, and Ezekiel. But shock and disgust also come into play as well. In the story of the destruction of Sodom and Gomorrah—you have to wade into Genesis only to chapters 18 and 19 to find this—Lot and his family make an escape. Except for his wife, that is, who got turned into a pillar of salt for glancing back over her shoulder.

Lot is the hero of the story, despite offering his two daughters to the town mob to be raped. At the end of the story, he's in a drunken stupor for two nights in a row and gets laid by his daughters. (It's a part of the myth, I suppose, that, totally wasted on wine, he could still get it up.) Thus he fathered his own grandsons. Oops, where does this tale fit into the scheme of traditional family values? Fundamentalist Bible believers are trapped by such stories. They can't just come clean and admit that the Bible includes bawdy folklore. An ancient Balzac was having a good time.

These stories require a lot of theological spinning. Left on their own, many readers have concluded that the Bible presents shoddy morality in too many of its pages. After all, God didn't step in to scold Lot, or his daughters. But this failure pales in comparison to other crimes and savagery in the "good" book.

Avalos has rightly called the Old Testament god a "moral monster" because of his bloodthirstiness. Anyone who soldiers on through Leviticus, Deuteronomy, Joshua, and Judges comes face to face with a brutal, capricious deity who deserves no respect whatever. Philosopher and Bible scholar Richard Carrier remembers that he was "regularly pestered by a Christian" to read the whole Bible."When I finished the last page, alone in my room, I declared aloud: 'Yep, I'm an atheist.'"[6]

Crappy Commandments

The Ten Commandments are perhaps the most famous Old Testament contributions to world culture. Generations of believers who saw Cecil B. DeMille's film *The Ten*

Commandments sense that DeMille got it right when he depicted that awesome finger of fire blasting the words into the stone tablets. Yes, that's the way it was done! It did seem that way to me as a teenager. There can be no doubt for the faithful: Here are the *very words* of God himself.

But are they? Supposedly, this was one of God's great chances to communicate a helpful message to humanity. After all, it was the ultimate mountain-top experience: Moses stood there in front of God getting the word directly from the horse's mouth, so to speak. So we might expect God to have covered the most important items on the human agenda, right? Well, with just a little reflection on this famous law code, we can suspect the lowly human origin of this "revelation"–and how far it falls short of being directives from a competent, responsible manager of the Cosmos.

With the first three commandments, we come face-to-face with cosmic narcissism: No "other gods" are to be worshipped, idols are forbidden, and swearing (using God's name) is outlawed as well. These edicts are in line with the belief that God is jealous, a concept that derives from an era when tribal gods fought for territory and status. Are these really the highest-ranking principles for humanity, revealed by the Ruler of the Cosmos?

After this groveling before a jealous tribal god, there are some commandments that make good sense for quality of life and social stability. Rest one day per week. Honor your parents. Don't kill, commit adultery, steal, bear false witness, or covet your neighbors' possessions. If God wanted to pass on words of wisdom for human conduct, this list is a good beginning. But human lawmakers of the ancient Near East had come up with these guidelines *well before* Moses supposedly received the tablets from old Yahweh on Mt. Sinai. People had figured out that social stability is enhanced if people don't kill, steal, and commit adultery.

And then there's what's missing from the Ten Commandments, something a lot of ethicists have commented on. Remember, this was one of God's great chances to hand down supreme laws to humankind, the fundamentals to guide our common life together on this planet. However, on balance, the list disappoints us because of what *isn't* there.

We would expect true revelation to be of the highest quality, focused on the essentials. But there are at least three commandments missing that deserve top billing, that would have had a much greater positive impact on human history than the first three devoted to the flattering of a petulant narcissistic deity. Can there be much disagreement that humanity would have fared much better with these three commandments at the top of The Ten?

- Thou shalt not engage in war, tribe against tribe, nation against nation, race against race. War is abhorrent to the Lord thy God.

- Thou shalt not enslave other human beings; thou shalt not own slaves, neither shall thine relatives or employees own slaves. Slavery is an abomination to the Lord thy God.

- Thou shalt not hate, mistreat or malign other human beings because of the color of their skin.

One doesn't have to be a Moses to come up with these three prohibitions. War, slavery, and racism have brought unimaginable suffering to the human race, yet these are not banned in the Ten Commandments. In fact, they are not unequivocally condemned anywhere in the Judeo-Christian scriptures.

Did God have a brain freeze? He seemingly didn't think to mention them in his conference with Moses on Mt. Sinai. Was that really a revelation event? The Ten Commandments appear to be of very human origin, about on a par with other lists of laws from the ancient world.

For yet another reason, the Bible is not worth reading.

A Glaring New Testament Example

The New Testament has preserved the thoughts, the writings, the *madness* of Paul, a tortured character who followed his hallucinations like a North Star. He deserves to be ignored and forgotten, but we were not that lucky. Rank and file Christians commonly fail to grasp how much their religion derives from Paul, instead of from Jesus. And there is the Christian bias that the New Testament is better than the Old Testament, but, sad to say, it would be hard to make that case. The tedium is there too: the bad theology, the lame-brained ideas.

One such idea that both Jesus and Paul seemed to have shared, that truly drags down the quality of the New Testament, is that Jesus was going to return to Earth. Jesus appears to have promoted this idea ("You will see the Son of Man coming on the clouds"), and Paul was counting on it. His consistent message to his congregations was, "Get ready for it!" It is probably the most pathetic of his delusions, and Christianity has come in for quite a bit of ridicule over the centuries because of Paul's glaringly wrong texts about Jesus-is-coming-soon. It is one of the central ideas of the New Testament that makes it not worth reading.

For hundreds of years, Christians have resorted to tortured evasions to escape the clear meaning of Paul's words about Jesus' imminent return. For example, it has been suggested that God's concept of time differs from ours—and Paul's. The favorite text to prove the point is Psalm 90, a somber piece of scripture if ever there was one. It speaks of God's wrath and man's insignificance. But the key verse (90:4, RSV), which plays a role in the effort to get Paul off the hook, is this: "For a thousand years in your sight are but as yesterday when it is past." Of course it was later Christians who landed on this text to make excuses for Paul. Yet, despite quoting a lot of Old Testament passages in his letters, Paul doesn't mention Psalm 90:4 in his discussion of Jesus' return. And it's not a stretch to say he would have been shocked at the suggestion that Jesus would be delayed for a few thousand years.

Paul was clearly thinking that the wait would not go on much longer when he wrote his letter to the congregation at Thessalonica. He was obsessed with the ghoulish idea that dead Christians—newly alive, in transformed bodies—will float up from their graves into the clouds. There, with trumpets blasting and an archangel screaming, they will meet Jesus when he returns. What prompted Paul to give this assurance? The Thessalonian Christians were worried that their dead relatives would be left behind, left out of the new Kingdom of God, when Jesus comes back. Hence

Paul assures them that the dead relatives will emerge from their graves to join the party. And here's the crucial line: "Then we who are alive, who are left, will be caught up in the clouds together with them to meet the Lord in the air" (1 Thess. 4:17). Paul expected to be alive himself when it happened. He was wrong, dead wrong.

Paul was very pleased with the good report he'd received about these believers, that they had remained steadfast in the faith. At the end of the first chapter of this letter he wrote, "For what is our hope, our joy, or the crown in which we will glory in the presence of our Lord Jesus when he comes? Is it not you?" (2:19, NIV). He fully expected that these people would be alive when Jesus returned. On this point he seems to be in line with the teaching of Jesus that "the end is near": "Truly, I say to you, this generation will not pass away until all these things take place" (Mark 13:30 NASB, Matt. 24:34, Luke 21:32). Both Jesus and Paul were wrong.

Who needs to read such trash? Believing in God is bad enough. Why add layers of nonsense about bodies coming out of graves to meet a hero coming down from heaven? This is an extra helping of bad theology that isn't worth reading. It is cult craziness that falls within the 99 percent of the Bible that Hector Avalos says wouldn't be missed.

The Trouble with Words

Another flaw in the revelation claim really is an extension of one discussed above, though in some ways it's even more troubling: What's it *mean*? Just as we have no way of telling whether a particular biblical text has come from the Mind of God or the mind of man (did it come *through* or *from* the brain of the author?), we commonly have no way of discerning the meaning of the text.

Despite the fact that much of what we read in the Bible seems clear and straightforward, the ambiguity of words–the *slipperiness* of words–is a real handicap to the Word-of-God claim. Even if we could somehow arrive at a consensus as to which texts can be considered the word of God, where does that leave us?

The pious can claim that we are guided by the Holy Spirit as an aid to understanding, but "Holy Spirit" is as much a faith assumption as "Word of God" itself. Hence, more arguing in circles, more guesswork. If the Holy Spirit has been playing any role, it's been a very indecisive and ambiguous one. The interpretation of scripture has flown off in all directions. Jews and Christians, Catholics and Protestants, conservatives and liberals–to name just six broad categories–have been deeply divided on the meaning of important passages of scripture. And yet all would claim at some level to be guided by the Holy Spirit in arriving at their interpretations (although Jews probably wouldn't use that term).

There is actually nothing esoteric or academic about this trouble with words. We are confronted with the dilemma on a daily basis in the real world. In March 1993, for example, an anti-abortion activist driven by religious fervor murdered a doctor at an abortion clinic. *New York Times* columnist Anthony Lewis opened his commentary on the incident as follows: "The murder of a doctor in Pensacola, Fla., tells us the essential truth about most anti-abortion activists. They are religious fanatics, who want to impose their version of God's word on the rest of us."[7]

Lewis's observation about religious fanatics is true, of course. But it would be a mistake to assume that it is only religious fanatics who have "their version" of God's word, as if it varies from the "right" version that might be kept in an ecumenical temple for everyone to consult. There is no "right version," any more than there is the "original" copy of the Bible in a monastery or museum somewhere in the Middle East.

Very seldom can religious or moral arguments be settled by quoting scripture, for the simple reason that the "word of God" in the Bible means different things to different people. Where does that leave us in the quest to probe the Mind of God through scripture? We are, in fact, in a wilderness, without a compass.

A Guessing Game

The Mind of God perceived through scripture is much too elusive to be taken seriously. It's like trying to catch smoke with a sieve. Several months before the Pensacola murder, a rabbi wrote his views on abortion to the *New York Times* and in so doing made a very revealing comment that goes to the heart of the issue. He concluded an eloquent letter with a simple observation that "abortion is an immensely complex spiritual issue. No one truth emerges from the sacred texts or religious conscience. Thus, how can we ever consider the mandating of a single position by the state?"[8] The rabbi nailed it: "No one truth emerges from the sacred texts," partly because texts may not be clear, and partly because people do not agree on what is "emerging" from the texts.

The ambiguity of the texts is not necessarily a problem in itself. It can be a plus in the sense that it stimulates thinking and questioning. In fact the process of examining the texts–dwelling on them, pondering them, having lively debates–can be very helpful. Insights do come, understanding is deepened. But the ambiguity of the texts–"no one truth emerges"–does become a problem if the reader is trying to make a revelation claim, trying to infer from the words on the page that we are actually grasping the mind or will of God.

The Word of God eludes us because human beings disagree on the meaning of words. There is no arbiter, no Supreme Court to render the *definitive* meaning, to let us know what God really has in mind. Indeed, thoughtful people will always resist the tendency of popes, cardinals, ministers, and rabbis to claim that they have the inside track to the right meaning.

Embarrassing Words of Jesus

How acute this problem is can be seen more clearly by moving beyond the abortion issue, since abortion is not even mentioned in the Bible, let alone treated as a moral issue. The problem is immediately apparent when we examine scriptural texts that state ideas very clearly but still have evoked heated debate and disagreement.

Many Christians have squirmed when reading the words of Jesus as presented in Mark 13:24-31 (RSV):

> But in those days, after that tribulation, the sun will be darkened, and the moon will not give its light, and the stars will be falling from heaven, and the powers in the heavens will be shaken. And then they will see the Son of

man coming in clouds with great power and glory. And he will send out his angels, and gather his elect from the four winds, from the ends of the earth to the ends of heaven. From the fig tree learn its lesson: as soon as its branch becomes tender and puts forth its leaves, you know that summer is near. So also, when you see these things take place, you know that he is near, at the very gates. Truly, I say to you, this generation will not pass away before all these things take place. Heaven and earth will pass away, but my words will not pass away.

These are very vivid, clear words, conveying sharply-etched images that any reader can grasp. And, if indeed these are the words of Jesus, it is clear from them that he was immersed in the parochial Messianic eschatology that flourished in Judea in the first century.

But this eschatology in Mark 13 is manifestly wrong, about as wrong as any theological idea could be. It is a prophecy with a date attached that didn't happen. Christians have spent the better part of two millennia trying to explain these and similar verses in such a way to save Jesus from being wrong. So we are entitled to ask: How are these verses the Word of God? A variety of answers has been offered, of course, but they put us back to square one: Which interpretation of God's Word is the "right one"?

The problem also confronts us when we encounter sections of scripture that, unlike Mark 13:24-31 above, do *not* present a clear picture of what is meant. For example, in Mark 9:47-50 (RSV) we read words attributed to Jesus:

And if your eye causes you to sin, pluck it out; it is better for you to enter the kingdom of God with one eye than with two eyes to be thrown into hell, where their worm does not die, and the fire is not quenched. For every one will be salted with fire. Salt is good; but if the salt has lost its saltness, how will you season it? Have salt in yourselves, and be at peace with one another.

The original meaning and intent here are not clear at all, thus leaving the way open to a variety of explanations and interpretations. No doubt countless preachers over the centuries have offered countless opinions, based on their own biases, times and circumstances, about the meaning of this supposed Word of God.

When Pigs Fly

Flights of Fantasy

The problem becomes especially acute when the New Testament obviously violates basic standards of historical reporting. The ancient worldview intrudes and takes over, and then what are we to make of it as the Word of God? Mark tells us the story of Jesus arriving by boat and meeting the "Garasense demoniac":

And when he had come out of the boat, there met him out of the tombs a man with an unclean spirit, who lived among the tombs; and no one could bind him any more, even with a chain; for he had often been bound with fetters and chains, but the chains he wrenched apart, and the fetters he broke in pieces; and no one had the strength to subdue him. Night and day among the tombs and on the mountains he was always crying out, and bruising himself with stones. (Mark 5:2-5, RSV)

Now, we really cannot fault the New Testament authors of the first century for believing that mental illness was demon possession. In this case, the man is described as being possessed of an "unclean spirit." The story itself, even allowing for some exaggeration, is believable *until* the text reports that the demons in the man bargain with Jesus, and they persuade Jesus to transfer them into nearby pigs.

So he gave them leave. And the unclean spirits came out, and entered the swine; and the herd, numbering about two thousand, rushed down the steep bank into the sea, and were drowned in the sea. (Mark 5:13, RSV)

If this part of the narrative is historical, then 2,000 pigs ended up at the bottom of the sea and the owner of the herd was probably ruined, his livelihood destroyed. Might we not question Jesus' judgment in bringing about this catastrophe? No wonder the people of the region asked him to leave.

Why is this story worth reading? It's obviously open to debate that the Bible is the Word of God when it is guilty of false reporting, when it passes off as historical narrative the figment of someone's imagination (i.e., demons carrying on a conversation with Jesus). Certainly, there's no denying that this is fertile ground for making observations about the human condition. Preachers and psychiatrists alike can draw a variety of lessons from these verses.

We can see how the revelation claim is in fact undermined. How are these verses the Word of God? Who is to say what they mean as a communication from God? Whose version will be the "right" version? We might have insights into dysfunctions of the human psyche, but how can the Mind of God be discerned with any confidence from the story itself and from all the diverse commentary that such a passage is likely to provoke?

What the Hell Was Paul Talking About?

The ambiguity of texts is even more of a problem with Paul. His letters make up a significant portion of the New Testament, but they're a mess. Even readers who want to understand Paul, approaching his letters eager to learn and with great generosity of spirit, can find the patches of dense, obtuse theology very perplexing.

Classical historian Michael Grant brought abundant fairness and scholarly curiosity to his study of Paul. But I've sensed some frustration in Grant's writings about trying to decode Paul. His observations are absolutely on target and have devastating consequences for any argument that Paul's writings are the Word of God.

The question of how we can know what a text is supposed to mean hits us with full force when we read Grant's analysis in his book, *St. Paul*. He calls Paul's letters

vividly varied and lively, but unrounded, unarranged and muddled, making their points not by any orderly procedure but by a series of hammer-blow contrasts and antitheses. Paul is far too impulsive and enthusiastic to standardize his terms or arrange his material. *He is often ambiguous*–with results that have reverberated down the centuries. And he commits flagrant self-contradictions, which caused Augustine, among many others, the deepest anxiety.[9]

The problem of understanding Paul is "a daunting one," Grant says, because of his "highly idiosyncratic ways of thinking and expressing himself." Making the problem worse is Paul's "blend of Jewish thought with Greek expression–a forcible bringing together of two alien cultures." Thus he says, "it has always been possible to take widely differing views of what he intended to say."

Grant tells the story of guests dining

at the house of John Colet, Dean of St Paul's, early in the sixteenth century. While guests ate, "a servant would read aloud in a clear, distinct voice" a chapter from Paul's Epistles or the Proverbs of Solomon–and then their host was accustomed to ask them what they believed the significance of the passage in question to be. Even Martin Luther would have found this an awkward predicament, for *he was not always at all sure what Paul really meant*, though he "thirsted ardently to know.'[10]

Paul's "equivocal" teachings include his "utterances on Original Sin, which "encouraged an immense diversity of opinion on their meaning":

Some of these ambiguities arise from the random contexts in which Paul threw out his views, with haste and emotion, to meet special circumstances. But others are basic and intrinsic to his thought: these are due to *unresolved contradictions in his philosophy.* Sometimes, too, one feels some things were left unresolved quite deliberately, because Paul realized, for all his apparent confidence, that some philosophical problems were insoluble.[11]

Christian and secular thinkers have been agonizing over Paul's meanings for centuries. Obviously this can be good philosophical exercise, but it's something else entirely to argue that the Word of God is within our grasp when we approach the writings of Paul. They are disqualified because they are a mess.

Sometimes even very conservative scholars goof by admitting more than they should. By any standard, Ben Witherington is an impressive scholar of Paul's Letter to the Romans, a monumental work of bad theology. On the first page of his 400-page commentary on Romans he warns that "the goal of understanding this formidable discourse is not reached for a considerable period of time."[12] *What?* His point is very true, of course, but this admission is a curious one for an evangelical scholar to make. It carries implications about the accessibility of the Word of God to ordinary readers.

Why did God provide his word in a form that people can't easily understand? Why isn't God's word more transparent? Paul's Letter to the Romans is one of the charter documents of the Christian faith, yet most lay people find it an uphill battle to get through and grasp. Scholars spend years trying to figure it out. Couldn't God have found a better author?

A Historical Flop

Another flaw in the revelation claim is that the Word of God simply hasn't worked very well. An "inspired book" that was cobbled together thousands of years ago turns out to have been a bad choice. It hasn't been the kind of success one would expect of God.

Indeed, the Bible has been suspiciously ineffective as the instrument of a supposedly omnipotent, omniscient Supreme Being to get vital ideas across to the human race. The Word is anything but clear, even to those who believe in it. And the majority of humankind has always been, and still remains, outside the Judeo-Christian heritage, and is thus totally untouched by this revelation–some 2,000 years after its final installment. Apparently people in Asia thought it weird that they had been kept out of the loop for such a long time: "One recalls the question that was asked by the Chinese when the first Christian missionaries made their appearance. If god has revealed himself, how is it he has allowed so many centuries to elapse before informing the Chinese?"[13]

Muslims claim, by the way, that God gave the "holy book idea" another try with the Qu'ran; the Church of Jesus Christ of Latter Day Saints argues that the *Book of Mormon* is the most recent attempt. Those who are outside Islam and Mormonism give these claims a shrug, and while Jews and Christians have argued for centuries about the meaning of scripture and what God is trying to say through it (and come up with dramatically different conclusions), most of the people on the planet couldn't care less.

This shortcoming was summarized eloquently by Columbia professor Robert Gorham Davis, in a 1992 letter to the *New York Times*. Davis wrote in response to John P. Meier's review of Robin Lane Fox's *The Unauthorized Version: Truth and Fiction in the Bible*.

> Obviously the sacred texts of the major world religions do not have intrinsic credibility as God's self-revelation. Adherents of rival religions can read them and remain unpersuaded, unperturbed. Religious Jews have lived in often painful proximity to Christians for 2,000 years without accepting Jesus, son of Joseph, as the promised Messiah.
>
> The God who "revealed Himself" in the Scriptures knew no more of the world and its future than those He presumably addressed. Jesus warned that the final days of tribulation were near: "Truly, I say to you, this generation will not pass away till all these things take place." But they did not take place, and have not yet.
>
> On no clear evidence theologians and philosophers declare God to be omniscient and omnicompetent. Plainly if there were such a God who really wished to reveal Himself to mankind, He could do so in a way that left no doubt.[14]

Precisely. No one has ever offered a truly satisfying explanation as to why God is being so coy, presuming that the Judeo-Christian claim is true that God wants to communicate with us, and yet remain mysterious. Why be so subtle? "God moves in a mysterious way, His wonders to perform."[15] But why? And if the Designer of the Cosmos is really trying to get through to us, an ancient book that is unknown or ignored by most of the human race, often bitterly disputed by those who do revere it, hardly seems the way to go.

The Bloody Word of God

It can be noted as well that the Word of God hasn't worked very well because it has proved to be too dangerous. It plays into the hands of authoritarian personalities, breeding intolerance and arrogance. When Christians have taken it upon themselves to spread the Word, they've often done so with brutality.

How much blood has been shed because zealots in possession of God's Word have felt an obligation to impose it on others? After all, it's God's word, isn't it? Anything goes. In the film *Auntie Mame*, young Patrick Dennis's conservative trustee is determined to rescue him from the aunt's unconventional lifestyle: "I'm going to make a God-fearing Christian out of that boy if I have to break every bone in his body." This gets a good laugh, but this is an attitude that has worked itself out with horrible consequences in world history. Bishop Spong has commented on this ugly aspect of the Word of God idea:

> My understanding and knowledge of the history of religious systems convinces me that whenever a group of religious folk begin to believe that they possess God's truth, almost inevitably they become those who in the name of their version of that truth persecute, excommunicate, purge, burn at the stake, or justify cruel religious wars against any who will not salute their tradition or acknowledge their rightness in things religious.[16]

Couldn't God have foreseen that this was a dangerous idea to entrust to human beings? It is one of those ideas in human history, which, like *Chosen People* and *Promised Land* (supposedly good ideas, but not really) has a very sinister side. Violence to advance God's word, or a particular version of truth based upon it, has been perpetrated on the scale of wars and crusades—and on the scale of everyday life in America. The anti-abortionist murdered the doctor because "he wanted him to stop doing things the Bible says is wrong, and start doing what the Bible says is right."[17]

The Bible That Isn't There
The Way of All Flesh, and Papyrus

There's one final situation to mention, which deepens our skepticism that God had anything to do with making the Bible. Christian bragging about the Bible, positioning it as God's primary message to humanity about salvation and morals, tempts us to imagine that God would take steps to protect it from damage or harm. Shouldn't the original Bible be in safekeeping somewhere? After all, it's a very important book! Some believers may even assume that the original Bible is kept under lock and key in a museum or monastery for access by scholars and theologians. A large percentage of

American Christians say that they believe in angels. Maybe they think that angels are on duty protecting the original Bible.[18]

But here's the startling fact: There is no original Bible, anywhere. None of the original manuscripts of any of the books of the Bible have survived. How's that for divine carelessness? The originals probably perished within a few years or generations after they'd been written; perhaps they became worn out from being rolled and unrolled for reading and making copies, or they were lost in fire or flood. The oldest manuscripts that we possess are in fragmentary form. It's a very painstaking business, for the scholars who devote their lives to this effort, to try to reconstruct the exact wording of the original manuscripts based on comparison of third, fourth, or fifth generation copies, of which there may be dozens or hundreds.

When you see footnotes in the Revised Standard Version, for example, these usually refer to manuscript variations that the editors of the RSV deemed worthy of mention. Here are two footnotes to Luke chapter 17: "Other ancient authorities omit 'in his day'" and "Other ancient authorities add verse 36." In other words, it is impossible to know *for sure* the wording of chapter 17 as it left Luke's hands. The ancient manuscripts disagree.

The most famous example of manuscript variance is that of Mark 16:9-20. These twelve verses that end the gospel are missing from the earliest manuscripts of Mark, which means that they weren't part of Mark's gospel when he handed it off to others. They were tacked onto the gospel at a later date. Without these eleven verses, Mark's gospel ends abruptly with verse 16:8. It is possible, therefore, that the original ending of Mark was somehow lost. Maybe the end of the scroll, being on the outside of the roll, was ripped off or damaged and is lost forever. The abrupt ending at verse 8 bothered someone enough—who knows how long after the gospel had been written—to write new material (now in verses 9-20) to make up for the lost ending. Another author created a one-verse ending that appears in some manuscripts. Some scholars think that the original gospel ended with verse 16:8.

If God had indeed been guiding men to write down inspired words in this holiest of books, one would suppose that God could have taken precautions to preserve the manuscripts. He could also have guided generations of copyist not to make mistakes, and would have preserved the manuscripts from damage and destruction. With God in charge of getting the Bible ready for human enlightenment, it's a bit strange that he dropped the ball when it came to protecting the book from corruption and error. It's also mighty suspicious that all of the original books of the Bible have perished.

Scholar Bart Ehrman, who was driven to his career of studying biblical manuscripts because he believed that the Bible was the literal and accurate Word of God, describes how his suspicions were aroused:

> The more I studied Greek, the more I became interested in the manuscripts that preserve the New Testament for us, and in the science of textual criticism, which can supposedly help us reconstruct what the original words of the New Testament were. I kept reverting to my basic question: how does it help us to say that the Bible is the inerrant word of God if in fact we don't have the words that God inerrantly inspired, but only the

words copied by scribes–sometimes correctly but sometimes (many times!) incorrectly? What good is it to say that the autographs (i.e., the originals) were inspired? We don't *have* the originals. We have only error-ridden copies, and the vast majority of these are centuries removed from the originals and different from them, evidently, in thousands of ways.

His doubts drove him "to dig deeper and deeper, to understand what the Bible really was."[19] And he realized there was a big problem here. Why couldn't God have preserved the original words of scripture, if he'd been able "to inspire them in the first place"? If preservation of the words was God's goal, he could have conveyed them in a language the people "could understand, rather than Greek and Hebrew." God did *not* in fact want to preserve the words for us, Ehrman figured, since we don't have them.

> And if he didn't perform that miracle, there seemed to be no reason to think that he performed the earlier miracle of inspiring those words. In short, my study of the New Testament, and my investigations into the manuscripts that contain it, led to a radical rethinking of my understanding of what the Bible is. This was a seismic change for me.[20]

The Processed Word of God

I suspect that many of us, at least those of us of a certain age, have an image of Billy Graham etched in our minds: the patriarch of TV evangelism standing in the pulpit and holding the Bible aloft as the very Word of God. However, few of those in Billy's audiences, few of those who gaze reverently at the Bible on the altar every Sunday at church, realize that the richly bound, revered book isn't the real thing. *It is the* **processed** *word of God.*

What do I mean by that? Can't we just pick up the Bible, open it and read God's Word? No, it's not that simple, even if you believe that the Bible is God's Word. Everything we see on the pages of any modern Bible is the product of countless hands and minds that were involved after the original authors wrote the books in it. So there are many uncertainties that stand between the reader and the original Bible authors and texts. It's processed material.

For example, the earliest Greek manuscripts were written with no separation between the words and no punctuation, which can lead to confusion. Someone later made the word separations and added the punctuation.

There is a complex history of manuscript copying and recopying, and an enormous number of scribal errors to deal with. There is also the matter of translation, the meaning of words, and which manuscripts to rely upon. These issues required thousands of decisions–some informed, others not. All divisions into chapters and verses came later. Some Bibles print the words of Jesus in red, which may give the impression that these are the very words of Jesus, which is misleading. We are reading English translations of Greek manuscripts that purport to record words spoken by Jesus in Aramaic, perhaps a generation or two earlier. Was a stenographer present? It is false advertising to print the (supposed) words of Jesus in red.

And now we are confronted with many contemporary translations that attempt modernization and paraphrasing of the text, which allow the biases, prejudices, and agendas of the translators to have a voice. There have been blatant, egregious distortions. Beware: The translators are commonly conservative theologians who do have their own agendas.

It is a theological affirmation that the Bible is the Word of God. But even if you do believe that, it is important to remember that the modern Bible you hold in your hands is the product of ongoing adjustment and manipulation over the centuries. Some of the pious handlers of the "holy text" have been competent and conscientious, but far too many have not been.

No modern copy of the Bible is the real thing.

Found Wanting

All these flaws rob us of any confidence that claims of biblical revelation can be taken seriously.

1. You can't use the Bible to prove that it is the Word of God, any more than you would accept the Pope's opinion that Catholicism is the true religion.

2. There are no criteria for determining which words in the Bible derive from the Mind of God, as opposed to the mind of the author who wrote the text. There is no way to tell. Period.

3. Most of the Bible is not worth reading, as anyone who has slogged through it knows, if honest enough to admit it.

4. There never has been, and never will, be agreement on the meaning of even the most "important" verses. And there never has been, and never will be, an agreed-upon arbiter to hand down rulings on meanings.

5. The Bible has been a flop historically. It has failed to convince the human race, either of its authority or the truth of its narrative.

Hence we do not have the solid foundation of God's Word that believers like to claim.

"Revealed truth" turns out to be an article of faith at best, wishful thinking or hallucination at worst. It does nothing to lift theology out of the realm of speculation and guesswork. To anyone not already committed to defending the Bible as Word of God (in some cases, down to every chapter and verse), fair, open-minded and even sympathetic study reveals its patchwork quality, its evolution in the tumult of human history, its weaknesses and strengths, the unworthy ideas alongside the great ideas.

Earlier in Western history, the Bible as a whole could stand without qualification as God's Word, but intensive research has destroyed this notion. By doing their job so well, generations of Biblical scholars—usually devout believers—face the irony that the Bible misses the mark as reliable history, and isn't all that great even morally or spiritually.

Notes

1. Not to be confused with John Templeton, who created The Templeton Foundation in 1987, hoping through scientific research to boost the credibility of religion.

2. Lee Strobel, *The Case for Faith* (Zondervan, 2014), pp. 11-12.

3. Ibid.

4. John Shelby Spong, *Rescuing the Bible from Fundamentalism* (HarperOne, 1992), p. 170.

5. Hector Avalos, "Why Biblical Studies Must End," in John Loftus, ed., *The End of Christianity* (Prometheus Books, 2011), p. 109.

6. Richard Carrier, *Sense and Goodness without God* (2005), p. 17.

7. nytimes.com/1993/03/12/opinion/abroad-at-home-right-to-life.html

8. *The New York Times*, Robert N. Levine Rabbi, Congregation Rodeph Sholom New York, June 19, 1992.

9. Michael Grant, *St. Paul* (Crossroad Publishing Co., 1982), p. 6 (emphasis added).

10. Grant at pp. 8-9 (emphasis added).

11. Grant at p. 34 (emphasis added).

12. Ben Witherington, *Paul's Letter to the Romans: A Socio-Rhetorical Commentary* (Eerdmans, 2004), p. 1.

13. Christopher Hitchens, *God Is Not Great*, p. 262.

14. *The New York Times*, 5 July 1992.

15. This opening line of William Cowper's poem has become a favorite Christian saying—or, in some ways, even a lament when God doesn't seem to rise to the occasion in preventing catastrophe and suffering.

16. Spong at p. 170.

17. Anthony Lewis column, *New York Times*, 12 March 1993.

18. And what, by the way, *is* the "original" Bible? By any reckoning, the current collection is a hodgepodge, and many books were left out. Catholics and Protestants can't even agree on which books should be included.

19. Bart Ehrman, *Misquoting Jesus: The Story Behind Who Changed the Bible and Why* (HarperOne, 2007), p. 7.

20. Ehrman at p. 11.

IV

The Absurdity of Western Monotheism

> People sometimes say to me, "Why don't you admit that the humming bird, the butterfly, the Bird of Paradise are proof of the wonderful things produced by Creation?" And I always say, well, when you say that, you've also got to think of a little boy sitting on a river bank, like here, in West Africa, that's got a little worm, a living organism, in his eye and boring through the eyeball and is slowly turning him blind. The Creator God that you believe in, presumably, also made that little worm. Now I personally find that difficult to accommodate . . .
>
> —David Attenborough

Truths That Are Not, After All, Self-Evident

SINCE MY TEENAGE YEARS are now more than fifty years in the past, the words *old time religion* now evoke memories of the church I attended in the 1940s and 1950s. The folks of that congregation, their faith unsullied by the devastating critiques of Bertrand Russell and H.L. Mencken, accepted a simple-minded version of Christianity. Their practice of religion was also unsullied by the crass televangelism and big business, show business mega-churches, none of which had been invented yet, although Billy Sunday and Herbert Armstrong had started blazing that trail earlier in the century. These small town parishioners may even have enjoyed the banal version of Protestant worship that flourished in Indiana at that time, droning-style sermons notwithstanding. Everyone shook hands with the preacher as they filed out of church.

Their rural community values included wearing their Sunday best to church: suits and ties for men, and even suits or best dresses for women—and hats; this was well before the era when lyricist Stephen Sondheim could wonder, "Does anyone still wear a hat?" Air conditioning, except for the local cinema, was unknown, so on sweltering summer Sundays every pew was provided with paddle fans. On one side there was a commercial-art rendering of Jesus praying in the Garden of Gethsemane, and on the other an advert for the local funeral home; an oversized Popsicle stick was the handle. Worn hymnals littered the cushionless pews.

On communion Sundays, in a tame knockoff of the Catholic Mass, the blood of Jesus was served in thimble-sized glasses. For these teetotalling Methodists, pungently sweet Welch's grape juice was the reasonable facsimile of blood. Squishy Wonder Bread, cut into tiny cubes, was the body. There was no transubstantiation on our Protestant side of the tracks; the Welch's and Wonder Bread resisted alchemy and retained their middle-American identities all the way into our stomachs.

Those were the days! Nostalgia kicks in, even for me, an atheist, as I recall those Sunday services and the good people who populated that northern Indiana congregation so long ago. They were under the spell of that old time religion. Somehow the contradictions escaped notice, as did the unabashed silliness of swallowing juice and bread to commemorate an ancient execution. If it's any consolation, there is virtually no chance that Jesus commanded such a blatantly pagan ritual as the Last Supper.

It was probably in the 1880s that the song *Gimme That Old Time Religion* originally became popular. Presumably, even sixty years before my birth, there was yearning for an earlier version of the faith. But it is impossible to imagine how the religious practice of my youth in the 1950s could smack of modernity, even remotely. The building itself embodied antiquity, at least by American standards.

During my teenage years, a new "educational wing" eyesore was added. I can remember the creak of the floorboards under the carpeting of the old building and the cool dampness of the church basement. I can almost smell the mothballs emanating from a religion that was so naïve and—here's that word again—simple-minded. No matter how much glitz and racket have been grafted onto the ancient frame (Christian rock music comes to mind), more than two billion people today seem content to be trapped in various quaint and musty versions of Christianity.

One preacher I know worried, as her 100-year old father was nearing death, that his dementia-tainted brain was putting his eligibility for eternity in jeopardy. He had been uttering swear words, which she had never before heard him do. It was risky business, as she put it, to be saying such things as he was about to "meet his Maker." Of course, "Are you ready to meet your Maker?" is a warning that preachers have uttered ever since they discovered that threats might be a motivator to keep people in line. Be prepared: You'll have to face the music. That's a chilling thought if it means actually facing God and being held accountable for every word and deed.

I suppose it's easy to convince people that they have a Maker. After all, the god-who-made-everything is the god of last resort for people who sense that they are desperate to defend their faith, especially if it is the least bit wobbly. When they become rattled by precise and rational arguments against gods, they remind us that the natural world must be accounted for."Look at that beautiful sunset, those awesome mountains and the spectacular expanse of the night sky. Did those things just happen? How did they get here without God? Don't be daft." And they usually throw in the "miracle" of the newborn infant: something like *that* doesn't just happen. Case closed, there is a Maker. *You* have a Maker. But when I hear the faithful smugly, even naively, claim that there must have been a Maker, and thus Christianity, supposedly, falls neatly into place, my retort is, "You don't want to go there. It will not enhance your case for God in the least."

Let's examine what happens when we thoughtfully consider the big picture—the expanse of the heavens—and the smaller, more intimate picture, the miraculous newborn infant that we hold in your arms. Awe is appropriate for both, but both are *dead-ends* for theists and their cherished fantasies about a Maker.

The Maker God

Atheists can concede ("Let's suppose, for the sake of argument . . .") that there was a creator (*sans* all the Christian baggage, however), because we know that this is a way to set a trap for Christians. We can ensnare them in their own arguments, because this concession raises more questions than it answers and leads eventually to the scuttling of theological hubris.

What's the first challenge that Christians face when they argue that there is a creator god? The most natural question that arises (how many Sunday school children have asked it in all innocence?) is, "Where did God come from?" Christians regard this question as just so much foolishness. God just *is*, and was from the beginning. His existence is a given, a self-evident truth, an assumption that doesn't need to be explained, defended, or justified.

But no, we can't let them get away with this. We can't allow the shutdown of curiosity, especially on so important a matter. Given what some of the best minds on the planet have discovered about the Big Bang (and the expansion of the Cosmos in the milliseconds following), no cosmologist would be satisfied with saying we don't need to know more, with the lazy take-it-for-granted suggestion that a god just did it. Physicist Sean Carroll's 2003 essay has one of the best, in-your-face titles I've seen, which should give Christians pause, reflecting scientific impatience with canned theological formulas: "Why (Almost) All Cosmologists Are Atheists."

What's the evidence warranting god-came-first thinking? Cosmologists are honor-bound to go only by the evidence and they don't buy it. God-came-first is a knee-jerk faith answer, a gut reaction that counts for nothing in the search to discover what actually happened. Bertrand Russell, with classic clarity, showed the shallowness of this approach. He pointed out that it's just as easy to believe in an eternal universe as it is to believe in an eternal god. What's the difference? Why would one be more plausible than the other, and why would a god be preferred or even matter?

The word **god** in this context is devoid of meaning. One could just as well say that "xyz-factor" caused the Big Bang (or à la *Star Wars*, The Force). Christians believe that "god" has meaning in this context because they hang biblical baggage on "god." They *assume* that the god they're used to, the god of "Let there be light" fame waved his magic wand, spoke those magic words, and voilà. But there is *no evidence whatever* for this scenario.

A Christian friend once told me that the energy that suffused the Cosmos after the Big Bang was the Holy Spirit. It was a nice little pop-theology attempt, but magical thinking is not a solution in cosmology. If something falls into the *it-has-always-existed* category, why would it have to be a god? And there's a serious betrayal of curiosity involved, as Ludovic Kennedy explains:

> The heavens whose wonders science has opened up for us today is a much vaster affair than the one the Ancients knew, so vast indeed, with its billions of galaxies divided by billions of miles, that it defied mental attempts to formulate it. To say that "God" created this immensity out of nothing insults the imagination and adds nothing to the store of human knowledge.[1]

The non-answer of "God did it" is just a comfort zone for theologians. They think that mystery is honorable, but people who are consumed by curiosity abhor mystery, and *are driven to dispel it*. They feel the compulsion to find out what happened. Resorting to a god undermines that, and ironically, means that curiosity should kick in even more, i.e., where did a god get *its* start? Who gave Christians permission to get away with, "We'll just agree to take it for granted that a god always was"? We need data, not theobabble. We want the cosmologists to keep digging, probing, and abhorring mystery.

Theologians retreat into mystery to hide and escape having to answer tough questions. They wallow in it much like a pessimist wallows in misery. Mystery makes God majestic, untouchable, unreachable, the holy of holies. It's hocus pocus that has worked well on the masses for millennia. Mystery plays an important role in Christian attempts to bully people into believing, because priests and preachers claim to be custodians of the mystery. Hence, as we have seen, "God moves in mysterious ways" is a favorite dodge, the last recourse of theology hobbled by difficult dilemmas, contradictions, absurdities, and silliness.

The Big Bang

In one of the ironies in the history of twentieth century cosmology, it was a Belgian *priest*, Georges Lemaître (also a physicist) who, in the 1920s, proposed the "creation event" that would become known later as the Big Bang. Lemaître's proposal was a way to come to terms with the theories of Einstein that implied an expanding universe, which baffled astronomers at the time. Lemaître suggested that the Cosmos had been expanding from an explosion at a single point in the unimaginably distant past. In the decades since the 1920s, the discovery of cosmic background radiation, with increasingly refined measurements of it, have verified his theory.

Not surprisingly, Pope Pius XII was delighted that a Catholic priest had made such an important contribution to cosmology and confidently announced that Lemaître had provided confirmation of the Genesis story, i.e., "Let there be light." God had triggered the creation event! It was a nice idea that seemed to meld theology neatly with scientific fact. But Lemaître was uneasy with this inference. It was reckless and unseemly for a theologian, even a pope, to jump in with speculation for which there was no evidence whatever. It was a faith idea polluting rigorous scientific inquiry.

Lemaître sensed the danger in this because science could eventually find a cause for the Big Bang that had nothing to do with a god. Once again, theology would be embarrassed. The Pope was satisfied that God was lurking in the mystery that lay behind the Big Bang, but what would happen when that mystery was dispelled?

Now, is it true, as theologians so earnestly wish, that there is deep mystery about the Cosmos that our science will never, ever penetrate? A mystery that a god presides over and that we are not *meant* to understand? If so, then theologians could be able to get away with the claim that "Where did god come from?" is not a legitimate question. At present, however, it just seems to be a ploy or ruse betraying intellectual laziness—or cowardice. After all, as I pointed out earlier, our intellectual journey as humans has been under way for only about 5,000 years, and our understanding of the Cosmos has accelerated dramatically in only the last century.

People who are acutely curious, and suspicious of flip, faith-based answers, are compelled to envy the intellectual achievements that we hope might have been made by other thinking creatures out there in the Cosmos. There may be others who have been probing, measuring and analyzing data for 100,000 years. With such a head start, *they* could have figured out the ultimate mysteries of the universe. Have they relied on religious intuitions and speculations? Of course we have no way of knowing, but look what happened on this planet. When secular thinkers and scientists have worked up the nerve and mustered the clout to say to preachers and theologians, "Go to your room. Mind your own increasingly irrelevant business," our knowledge and understanding of the natural world have advanced exponentially.

There is another possibility to be considered as well: Our brains may be too puny to "get it." We are endowed with mammalian brains that evolved to survive in our specific and peculiar biosphere, and we're pretty small scale. Einstein's theories of General and Special Relativity, which must rank as among the grandest of human insights, are tough for even the best minds to grasp. Maybe the mysteries of the Cosmos are just impenetrable to us, not because a god designed things that way to keep us in the dark, but because evolution has provided us with–*cursed* us with– brains that are not up to the task. We may be the simpletons of our galaxy.

The great geneticist of the early twentieth century, J.B.S. Haldane, speculated about this in his 1928 book, *Possible Worlds*:

> Now, my own suspicion is that the universe is not only queerer than we suppose, but queerer than we *can* suppose. I have read and heard many attempts at a systematic account of it, from materialism and theosophy to the Christian system or that of Kant, and I have always felt that they were much too simple. I suspect that there are more things in heaven and earth that are dreamed of, or can be dreamed of, in any philosophy. That is the reason why I have no philosophy myself, and must be my excuse for dreaming.[2]

Our excuse for dreaming is the desire to discover the origins of the Cosmos, and settling for the "God did it" non-answer just isn't good enough. It's settling for too little, something too humdrum. No matter how many superlatives preachers and theologians come up with–their god is all powerful, all knowing, all wonderful, yada, yada, yada–they are just piling on silly flattery without substance, in the absence of evidence and understanding. The confident assumption that there is an everlasting god who doesn't have to be accounted for is a symptom of intellectual bankruptcy.

Some Alternate Possibilities

Believers get whiney and petulant when we delete God from "in the beginning," so let's wipe their tears and soothe their troubled spirits by granting that a god must have launched the Cosmos–pending the latest updates from cosmologists. But give Christians that inch and they'll take a light year. They overreach and rush in with assumptions and faith babble. Right away, like Pope Pius XII, they'll want to push the Bible agenda. Their swarms of ideas about their god are as deeply entrenched as the belief in god-the-originator. They leap to the conclusion that the God described in the Bible is the one that triggered the Big Bang. And they're shocked to be told that *this doesn't follow at all*. God is God . . . what's the problem?

Well, here's the problem: The Christian god, the jumble of ideas about God in the Bible, was a little late arriving on the scene. According to the latest refinement of the data, the Big Bang took place 13.82 billion years ago. The Earth formed from galactic dust and debris about 9.3 billion years after that. The Cambrian Explosion is now dated at about 550 million in the semi-distant past. *Homo sapiens* came along maybe 1.5 million years ago, and religious impulses probably emerged as soon as these sentient beings learned to be afraid of death. The Sumerians invented writing some six or seven thousand years ago, thus allowing for the dispersion of ideas, especially in the form of religious texts. Perhaps as early as 1,500 years B.C.E., the people whom we now call the Hebrews began worshipping a jealous tribal god who was in a bad mood most of the time: The record of his nasty disposition is called the Old Testament. He was known as *Yahweh* (put in different vowels and you get *Jehovah*).

Over the centuries, the Hebrews, especially after they had become the Jews in the 6th century B.C.E., arrived at the conclusion that Jehovah was the one and only god. Their major contribution to Western thought was monotheism, most brands of which have shown a remarkable capacity for intolerance.[3] One especially malignant version insists that a human sacrifice, of a backwoods Galilean peasant, no less, was required to deflect the wrath of the god. That this peasant might have claimed to be the son of a god—the texts are unreliable—only compounds the silliness.

Theologians have been massaging, refining, and knocking the rough edges off this idea for more than two millennia. But the tribal god behind it all was one of many, all of whom were the brain droppings of illiterate desert nomads. They lived long ago and far away from us—though only *very* recently on the cosmic scale of time. They were making guesses about the gods, as were all other ancient peoples.

Why should we trust them? There is no reason to suppose that they were on to something or had special insights into cosmic origins. The Hebrews thought that their god spoke out of a burning bush. Give me a break. Their religion fails the test of cosmic respectability. It doesn't fit the big picture. *This* is the god who ignited the Big Bang and launched billions of galaxies?

Adding to the bafflement provoked by the suggestion that old Yahweh has been in charge all along, the Bible does not present a unified and consistent view of God. Theologians have acknowledged for a long time that it's virtually impossible to write a *theology of the Bible* because there is such a tangle of different god-ideas in the Old and New Testaments. Many thinkers and writers have their say in the Bible. There are 66 books in the Protestant canon (of course, there is even disagreement on which books should be included). It should be no surprise that the authors' guesses about gods differ so substantially.

However, those who insist that there *must* have been a creator don't get to arbitrarily decide the nature of the creator, based on cherished theological traditions. It just cannot be that the problematic god of the Bible is the only candidate for The Maker of the Cosmos. So it's not all that radical to urge Christians to consider other gods that may have created the Cosmos. It's a bit narrow-minded to be exclusive on this issue.

For the sake of argument, perhaps we might consider that a god indeed may have kicked things off. But, even so, we'd still have to be open-mindedness about what *kind* of god that was. Here are some alternative possibilities to consider.

#1: An evil Maker

A good god is considered a self-evident truth by Christians, but nothing about the Cosmos mandates this conclusion. I've mentioned Joseph Daleiden's observation that, given the state of the world, it would be easier to prove a Devil than a god. Is there anything that rules out an evil god as Creator? In fact—and how embarrassing is this for Christians?—many of them *already* believe in an evil god; those of the evangelical variety take Satan very seriously. As does Pope Francis, who employs a staff of exorcists. And Justice Scalia, good Catholic that he was, stingingly rebuked people who denied the reality of the devil.

Jesus spoke of Satan (he even spoke *to* Satan), so what more could the Bible-believer want to prove Satan's existence? Throughout Western history Christians have credited Satan with enormous havoc and evil, positioning him as their god's adversary and as a cunning, irresistible tempter of humans. Christians may protest that Satan is not a *god*, but that's splitting hairs. They're convinced that Satan is a being who can stand up to and hold his own against their god. That is *de facto* acknowledgment that Satan has supernatural powers; he must enjoy *some* rank as a god. So why would it be such a stretch to believe that the chief god of the Cosmos is evil, perhaps none other than Satan himself? Or that the Satan who gets so much airtime in the New Testament is his deputy?

Frankly, the seriously defective god of the Bible would be a major disappointment as the Creator Deity. He is overtly and covertly evil, camouflaging his evil with talk of love. But an aggressively evil god would have to be a possibility.

#2: An Unaware Maker

Christians maintain that their god is all-knowing, no doubt inspired by words attributed to Jesus that a sparrow doesn't fall to the ground without God knowing about it. People apparently draw comfort (and too much guilt, I would think) from the thought that God is keeping a close eye on everything. But it could very well be that the god in charge of the Cosmos is not a microwatching micromanager. What if god doesn't (or can't) notice stuff below the level of planets? Nothing whatever requires a creator god to be omniscient, knowing everything, though that's a favorite *sine qua non* of our monotheist heritage.

Let me suggest an analogy of a bread maker. The baker who shuffles that paddle of dough into the oven knows all there is to know about flour, yeast, sugar, and salt, and can whip up a perfect semolina baguette. But she remains absolutely unaware of the individual atoms and molecules in the baguette and couldn't care less.

The god of the Cosmos might be a master confectioner, conducting an experiment of sweepingly grand proportions. Over aeons, the galaxies swirl gracefully after an initial push from the Big Bang, with vast swaths of dust distilling into stars and planets. It just so happens that a byproduct of this on the extreme micro level, all of those elements of the periodic table swirling around, is life and evolution on countless planets. But, for the god in charge, life isn't even noticeable or worth noticing. Most of it is microbial, after all, even on our planet. Some of the life may evolve into self-aware creatures, billions of them on billions of planets, many of whom develop egos and delusions of self-importance, who crave the attention and approval of the *grand fromage* of the Cosmos.

But what a disappointment they'd be in for if they knew better! The concern and gaze of the Cosmic Baker god doesn't penetrate that deeply. It feels no love or any of the other human personality traits and emotions that Christians commonly assigned to their God.

A god whose eye is *not* on human beings, let alone sparrows, would explain nature's utter indifference toward us. It occurred to me a long time ago that planet Earth, in one way at least, was poorly planned in that it was not a comfortable habitat for humans. Our ancestors evolved very late in one small area of the world, requiring communication, tools, clothes, and agriculture to become the world-dominating creatures we are now. Contrast that reality with Christian belief in a personal, loving God, with humans beings as the crowning achievement of his scheme for life here on this world. After all, we alone are made in his image. Shouldn't that count for something in being given a safe place to live?

Even now, we sit uneasily on Earth's surface while tectonic plates shift beneath us, causing earthquakes, volcanoes, and tsunamis. New islands are formed and new life may emerge in the heated waters around the lava tubes on the ocean floor, but millions of humans are crushed, burned, and drowned by these planetary growing pains. The crust of our little rock is a hazmat zone, unbeknownst to a god above—*way* above! "There are creatures down there made in my image? Who knew?" This god doesn't have a clue. Nature is indifferent because, despite having baked the stars and planets into existence, it is, and must remain, unloving and oblivious.

#3: A Council of Makers

Christians are smug about their one true god, assuming that monotheism is the inevitable culmination of proper god-building. But since our species emerged on the African savannah, many billions of people have taken it for granted that there are many gods. How can those who argue for the existence of the spiritual realm be so sure about how it is populated? Jews, Christians, and Muslims are dead certain that their understandings of the one true God cannot possibly be wrong. But if they're not wrong about who their god is, that would mean that there must be at least three major gods, because their three gods are definitely different. They just have one tiny part wrong, i.e., that their god is the *only* one; monotheism would be wrong after all.

Catholics have certainly wandered into questionable territory, accepting a seriously compromised monotheism. The Catholic faith is infested with minor deities whom it camouflages as "saints," hundreds of them, to whom Catholics bring their pleas and petitions. The Virgin Mary is one of the super-sized saints. In Catholic thinking, these grateful dead are more than just good people who have "passed to the other side." The saints are endowed with special powers to help people; God's power seems to be siphoned off into many tributaries.

This is dangerously close to believing in a vast crowd of minor deities who help carry the divine load. Monotheism has flirted with such subversive ideas since its first advocates found it necessary to rail tirelessly against the worship of false gods and idols. There's a reason for the plural pronoun in Genesis 1 ("Let us make man in our image"): It's a vestige of an earlier polytheism. So on what grounds can we rule out a Council of Gods that manages the Cosmos?

Indeed, there could be a god for each galaxy–after all, each one is huge–and in the aggregate they form the Council of Gods. *Oh now you're just being ridiculous* may be the retort, but theology is just guesswork. A Council of Gods might be a wild guess, but what's wrong with a few wild guesses? After all, a human sacrifice–that Galilean peasant again–to escape the anger of the one true god is about as wild as you can get, and it has worked pretty well for two thousand years.

And Christians wonder why we think that their religion is silly.

#4: A Science Fiction Maker

Maybe it's time to think outside the box . . . really outside. I propose that twenty-five of the top-ranked seminaries in the world initiate formal dialogue with the world's top ten science fiction writers. For millennia, theologians have exercised their imaginations on the question of god or gods, and the results have been dismal. Isn't it time for the monopoly to end? I'm pretty sure that science fiction writers have far sharper, more robust imaginations than theologians do. And science fiction writers are more informed by scientific sensibilities. Let's have input from these creative minds that have thought about the twisting of time and space at black holes horizons, wormholes, parallel and alternate universes, the universe as a computer model, perhaps serial universes as well, i.e., one Big Bang after another. These are the people we should be talking to.

The objective of this formal dialogue could be the development of new ideas about god or gods, purged of silliness, cult craziness (e.g. the sacrifice of a Galilean peasant just won't do), barbarism, intolerance, and sappy sentimentality about divine love. Would it be hard to convince the world that a new, better god has been imagined? The Cargo Cults blossomed in the South Pacific as soon as U.S. military supply aircraft had disappeared. The apostle Paul, Joseph Smith, and L. Ron Hubbard were very good at startup religions. Most of the people on the planet might soon have iPads, so massive conversions to a SciFi-WiFi god should be a breeze.

––––––

The god possibilities are endless as soon as we concede to theists that there *must* have been a creator. We have humored them, and their foul mood will get worse. They should be careful what they wish for.

Mutations as Maker

Before my oldest brother John reached his teenage years, he had developed a keen interest in opera. This was in rural Indiana in the 1940s, mind you. Our father was born on a farm, and our mother–before becoming a full-time housewife–was a stenographer and a beautician. Yet their oldest son was composing at the piano at an early age, and when I was growing up, he had us all listening to the Saturday afternoon radio broadcasts from the Metropolitan Opera. I learned that Wagner was easy listening; to this day, I am allergic to Country & Western music.[4]

How did John turn out that way? The town folks marveled at his musical genius, and explained it as his God-given talent. Like everyone else, John had a Maker who had mixed just the right ingredients to create a musical prodigy who, inexplicably, had entered the world in, of all places, northern Indiana. Given how much we hear about individuals having God-given talent, we can assume that people take the concept seriously. God gets the credit, but the implications of this boast are catastrophic for the idea that God is good.

The idea of God-given-talent leads, inescapably, to God having tinkered with each person's DNA. Of course, nurture plays a major role, but we are elaborately programmed to be what we are. We turn out to be blue or brown eyed, left or right-handed, big or small boned, musically gifted or not. And we even know enough now to say, "It's all in the genes." To claim that God has twisted all the right knobs to insure all of the God-given-talents that humans display means that God knows the DNA of each person and—wouldn't this be a full time job?—tweaks everyone's genes to get what he wants for each one of us.

Well, God be praised for the musical prodigies, but, hold on: That's only a small part of the big picture on this small scale. There are thousands of genetic *diseases*. Why isn't God held accountable for these as well? I never hear Christians speak about God-given muscular dystrophy, God-given Alzheimer's, God-given cystic fibrosis or hemophilia. What about God-given birth defects? And our aging process? We are built to bio-degrade while we're alive, and the process is commonly painful, debilitating, and humiliating. We have to assume that God planned it that way.

Those who speak about the Maker of each person have painted themselves into a corner: God has a lot to answer for. How smart is it, really, to talk about Intelligent Design? Why would God arrange for billions of people to be imprinted with thousands of horrible diseases? Christians give their Maker credit for God-given-talent, but a free pass for the dreadful flaws in the genetic codes. That won't do: The creator has to own up to everything. If Christians were smart, they would eagerly embrace evolution as the culprit.

On the cosmic level, God-the-Maker fails to command much respect, and on the individual level you have to take the bad with the good. It hardly seems worth it. That new-born baby—so perfect, so awesome—could very well be programmed for suffering. This is evidence of blind evolution doing its thing, or God's blunders—take your pick.

But let's be honest. Smart, educated people know that we are the product of genes passed on through thousands of generations, and Darwin's astute observations of nature laid the foundation for removing gods from the process. One of the silliest claims of theists—well, those who make a stab at sophisticated thinking aligned with science—is that God set evolution in motion and manages it. Evolution is "his way of doing things." Anyone who understands that, by definition, evolution is directionless knows that's rubbish. Random mutations, selection pressure from myriad environmental variables, and genetic drift do all the tinkering; there is nothing for a Maker to do.

The British scholar A.N. Wilson has commented on the watershed moment that Darwin represents in the history of human thought. The two-word summary is: "God loses." But this eloquent quote of his about the irrelevance of a Maker is also worth sharing:

> Milton's picture (based on Genesis) of fixed species arriving on the surface of the planet by divine decree was not borne out by the evidence. And what Darwin was able to demonstrate beyond reasonable doubt was not merely that species mutate, evolve, change, but that they do so within a system which requires for its "explanation" no theory of volition by a creator–no Watchmaker, coming in from outside to "make" what is. On the contrary, what is, is. And "this"–this immense continuum of time and space–is what there is. All the pictures which humankind had crudely made for itself of the here and now–depending for their existence on some exterior agency– had to be discarded.[5]

Dependence on an external agency discarded: *God loses.* But people want to hang on for dear life to their Maker.

One of the popular memes floating around gay-oriented Facebook pages is the affirmation: "God made me gay and God doesn't make mistakes." Thousands of medical textbooks, however, provide evidence of God's mistakes. There has been speculation that same-sex attraction has a genetic component; it may be part of the programming of our species. I'll grant you that, but spare us the goofy pop theology.

One of the truly irritating habits of the pious is their making breezy assurances about God. Gee, he doesn't make mistakes? Because God is God? Zero thought–*zero* thought–has been put into how such God knowledge could have been obtained. Why would such sentimental confidence count for anything?

God the Narcissist

Why Worship?

The faithful admit it: They are there on Sunday morning to worship God. A friend of mine once defined himself and his status as a believer."I am a *worshipper*," he said. Why would that be important or appropriate?

Schools are for learning, offices are for business, stadiums are for sports, hospitals for healing, and we all agree that they answer legitimate human needs (even stadiums). Churches, however, are dedicated to that most baffling of human obsessions: getting together frequently to boost God's ego. When priests raise funds to build churches they always claim that the real purpose is to glorify God, which can only mean that there is a divine ego that must be stroked. My friend the worshipper had gulped the Kool-Aid. He has bought into this peculiar, warped view that our feelings of wonder and awe must be directed at a Supreme Being who isn't satisfied unless the awe and wonder are directed *at him.*

The faithful will accuse me of egregiously misunderstanding what's going on in church; they're just showing proper respect and humility before The Almighty. But pardon my cynicism. What they're doing is pouring on the flattery, often with congregational singing. In 2001, *How Great Thou Art* was ranked the second most popular hymn (behind *Amazing Grace*). So we can assume that millions of Christians every Sunday lift their voices to *assure God* that he is great. Isn't that a curious thing to do? How can it be necessary? God likes to be sung to?

Obsequiousness is usually associated with pleasing a moody, egocentric monarch. In *The King and I*, the story of an English woman serving as tutor at the court of the king of Siam, Anna was appalled that the king expected his subjects to bow before him, face down, flat on the floor, as priests sometimes do during ordination ceremonies:

> **A**ll that bowing and kowtowing, to remind you of your royalty
> I find a most disgusting exhibition
> I wouldn't ask a Siamese cat to demonstrate his loyalty
> By taking this ridiculous position.

Worship, as a human obligation to conjectured higher powers, is a ridiculous position.

Does God need to be worshipped for some reason? Does he get off on it? Is that really what God is like? The need to be worshipped, the craving to be praised suggest a narcissistic, insecure deity who can be manipulated and mollified by flattery. Are we dealing with a case of colossal cosmic narcissism? If there is a god who created the universe, why would this god demand to be loved and worshipped by mere humans?

Anyone not under the spell of religion quackery should find this idea astonishingly absurd, but it has been discussed, apparently with a straight face, by Francis Collins, the scientist who headed the human genome project. It's hard enough to endure theobabble when it comes from professional theologians, but when a scientist tries it, the results can be alarming.

In *The Language of God: A Scientist Presents Evidence for Belief*, Collins proposes that God created humans to keep him company, although he dresses up this idea a little by saying that God wants to have "fellowship" with people. Of course, this is a Christian code word for "being in this cult together." Here, believe it or not, is how Collins makes the case in his chapter, "The Origins of the Universe":

> If God exists, and seeks to have fellowship with sentient beings like ourselves, and can handle the challenge of interacting with 6 billion of us currently on this planet and countless others who have gone before us, it is not clear why it would be beyond His abilities to interact with similar creatures on a few other planets or, for that matter, a few million other planets. It would, of course, be of great interest to discover whether such creatures in other parts of the universe also possess the Moral Law, given its importance in our own perception of the nature of God.[6]

Yes, you read that right; he seems to feel that the Moral Law is important "in our own perception of the nature of God." This is what he counts as *evidence?* No wonder he fails utterly to deliver on the promise of evidence for God. Humans may be religious, but the Judeo-Christian god certainly has not won the hearts and minds of six billion earthlings.

According to the gospel of John, Dr. Collins should recall, the only way to get to "interact" with God is by believing in Jesus, an idea the apostle Paul pushed with a vengeance. So the percentage of humans available for interaction doesn't even come up to half. And this minority arrived on the scene more than 13 billion years after the Cosmos was blasted into existence. That's a long time for a god to wait to have company. He also wants fellowship with beings on billions of planets, so maybe he had others to keep him company while he was waiting for humans to show up. Which provokes a disturbing thought: If the experiment on other planets has been as dismal as on ours, does Jesus have to travel from planet to planet, aeon upon aeon, to be sacrificed repeatedly to save other beings?

But wait a minute. Collins suggests that God wants fellowship, while the tradition of Christian worship appears to assume that God expects to be worshipped, praised and flattered. *God doesn't want friends; he wants sycophants.* Presumably each person who praises and flatters is noticed by God for doing so and is given credit."Hey, I'm earning points!" In fact, isn't worship–not the *failure* to worship–a symptom of arrogance? Isn't it monumentally presumptuous to suppose that each one of us receives the personal attention of the force that manages the Cosmos? There are perhaps a hundred million galaxies in the observable universe. *Who do we think we are?*

Naturally such presumption makes us feel important: "God is interested in me! God is guiding my life and has a purpose for me. I'm here to do God's work. God finds me so interesting and irresistible–he can't ignore *me*–so I'd better return the favor and let him know how totally terrific *he* is." How great thou art! And Christians wonder why we think their religion is silly.

In truth, of course, churches have been built not to satisfy God's ego, but human egos. Worshippers want a place to go to be confident that God is really paying attention to them: "I'm in God's house. I will kneel and be noticed." And priests, whose careers depend on presiding over bigger and better churches, are always in the construction business. Cathedrals are the ultimate excess, the whoring of art and architecture for priestly egos using the divine ego as a front: "We must glorify God."

As much as we cherish the art and architecture–Europe is my favorite destination, and I spend a lot of time admiring churches–the world would be much better off if schools, offices, hospitals, and stadiums had been built instead. Worship is theatre– some done magnificently, I will grant you–and that requires the venues. But all theatre is illusion, and when done in church, it's a scam. The faithful have been fleeced and fooled for centuries."Religion was invented," an anonymous cynic has suggested, "when the first con man met the first fool." The con man knew that hero worship was a human failing that could be easily and profitably exploited.

The God Who Has to Be Reminded to Be Good

Lettuce Pray

In the musical *Chicago*, prisoner Roxie Hart mutters to the prison matron, "Jesus, Mary and Joseph" upon hearing about the history of hangings in Cook County. Mama Morton retorts, "That's your problem, you're talking to the wrong people."

For millennia, humans have been having conversations with their gods—many thousands of them. For those who believe that there's only one true god, it's obvious that those who aren't tuned in to that singular deity have been talking to the wrong people. Christians, however, are confident and proud that they speak to the *only* god, the *right* God, though Protestants think that the Jesus-Mary-Joseph formula isn't quite right. Praying to the Virgin Mary just isn't done.

But let's not quibble about which god is the right one. Atheists find that discussion tiresome, and we'd like to get people to think about what they're doing when they pray. There are so many ways in which the prayer concept fails, the least of which is *which god* a prayer is aimed at. So what if you've had a robust prayer life for years and are sure it "works"? Most folks have never heard of confirmation bias. Bad habits die hard.

Returning to an example I've used earlier, if someone claims to be communicating telepathically with a race of priests who live in holy cities beneath the far side of the moon, we wonder if they've skipped their meds. Why should I'm-praying-to-a-**god** be taken any more seriously? Sam Harris illustrates the folly of the practice:

> The president of the United States has claimed, on more than one occasion, to be in dialogue with God. If he said that he was talking to God through his hairdryer, this would precipitate a national emergency. I fail to see how the addition of a hairdryer makes the claim more ridiculous or offensive.[7]

Praying comes naturally, as easily as breathing. Our parents taught us to say our prayers at bedtime, and taught us how. What could be wrong with that? Well, a lot.

For starters, what is the mechanism by which prayer works? I argued earlier that believers want a friendly Cosmos—indeed, that's why God is important—and they cozily refer to God as The Man Upstairs. The theologians who are paid to think seriously about such things know that the idea of a Man Upstairs is untenable. In fact, they join their secular philosophical colleagues in shooting Him down.

Ironically, there might be a mechanism by which prayer could work if God *were* The Man Upstairs; that imagery suggests closeness. But theologians have worked hard to give God respectability, and to vigorously defend the idea that God cannot be subjected to tests of verifiability (how convenient). They do so by arguing that God is a being (or even the Ground of Being) who resides "outside space and time." God "inhabits eternity." That's why we humans can't detect any evidence for him, although he's there just the same . . . outside space and time. But this is theobabble, and theologians have created a god that laypeople don't recognize. Their friend, the cosmic buddy, is gone: *Their prayer buddy is gone.*

Laypeople don't read theology because they're not interested in ethereal definitions of God; they're not embarrassed by The Man Upstairs. They're not the niche market for the dense, abstruse tracts and dissertations that theologians churn out decade after decade. As I asked in Chapter II regarding the problems of finding out about God, how can prayer penetrate the barrier that theologians have imposed? God is supposedly outside space and time, but the faithful are very much *in* space and time. It would be a piece of cake to communicate with those priests in the holy cities beneath the far side of the Moon, because the priests and the Moon are *within* space and time.

How do prayers leave space and time, especially as propelled by the human brain? There is no basis for believing that our mammalian brains can establish communications with gods. We may hear, "Oh, it's a spiritual thing," but that's not good enough. It's a non-answer. For prayer to be credible we would have to know the mechanism. The "spiritual thing," as a mechanism for making prayer credible, is pious fiction and pretense.

There are even bigger theological problems with prayer as well. It's astounding how these deal breakers are just shrugged off by believers. Consider the assumption, usually hotly defended by monotheists, that God is omniscient. How else would he know the secrets of our hearts? He wouldn't be all-powerful and perfect if even the tiniest fragment of Creation escaped his attention; that would mean that there are deficiencies. As we have seen, the New Testament authors assumed that the hairs of our head are numbered and the fall of a sparrow is registered in the divine database. So, what could any human being tell God that he doesn't already know?

There may be a huge pain or crisis in one's personal life, and the impulse is understandable, for the religious person, to "take it to the Lord in prayer," as a popular hymn from my childhood puts it. God is there to be your comforter. I get that. But there's a lot more to prayer, and this is where we wander into dangerous theological territory.

When people go into a prayer mode, they usually have an agenda other than securing comfort. They want stuff, they want help; they're in the "gimme gimme" mode, although they're not that blunt about it. They have the good sense to slip into the obsequious florid beseeching style of prayer: "Oh merciful and everlasting Lord, who knows our thoughts and needs before we ask, grant wisdom and courage to our elected leaders" (as if that ever happens). And, of course, they deny that they're praying for anything too trivial like victory in a football game. Perhaps too many unanswered prayers even give people pause about what they're doing. One meme floating around Facebook says, "I asked God for a bike, but I know God doesn't work that way. So I stole a bike and asked for forgiveness."[8] George Carlin claims that he decided to pray to Joe Pesci instead of to God ("Pesci looks like a guy who can get things done") and the success rate was the same.

The faithful ask God to change course, change his mind, and do what they want; they don't blush at the thought that their need or request *hadn't occurred* to God. How else would they explain their behavior? Churches commonly organize prayer vigils or marathons–hundreds of parishioners pleading with God–to heal a member just diagnosed with cancer: "We'll storm the fortress to get God's attention and badger him to do the right thing." You mean it didn't already dawn on God that there's a sick Christian needing help? So much for a God who knows everything.

Maybe, for some reason, it's just important that we beg shamelessly. Mildred and her sister in Peoria pray that their brother will come through a serious operation. Perhaps God says, "I was waiting for your opinion on that. Wasn't sure what to do." How many millions of people pray for peace in the Middle East? Has God been waiting for their input? "Actually, I wasn't sure what to do about the Middle East. Thanks for the tip!" Is God grateful to get all these nudges? The pious folks who are confident of their direct line to God might be startled with hear him respond:

> Thank you for reminding me to help you do your best during the football match. I appreciate that you didn't ask to win, because the other team is praying too. I've been tied up comforting a few survivors of a supernova blast in the Andromeda Galaxy. It was a beauty, but what a mess . . . . I lost a lot of planets.

This Prayer Phenomenon is a cause for multiple puzzlements. Here's a brief summary:

- Does suffering have to be brought to God's attention?
- Does God cure people only when prayers reach critical mass?
- Does God let another cancer patient die if there aren't thousands of prayers for him? Too bad for the guy in the next bed.
- Why are all outcomes rationalized? If the person is cured, God be praised. The person dies? Well, God "took" him. She's with God now, and we can't question his omniscient wisdom. God moves in mysterious ways and knows the overall plan. To those whose minds are so clouded by Pollyanna theology, God always wins; his reputation never takes a hit.
- The person gets well. Wonderful. God did it? Wonderful. If God *can* cure one person of cancer, why not cure *all* people who have cancer? Cheering that God has cured one cancer victim puts Christians on the brink of embracing bad theology: He cured *only* one? Christians rush in with excuses, but God stands indicted of sins of neglect and omission.

See what I mean by dangerous territory? The impulse to pray is just *there*. Has there ever been a time when humans didn't look toward the sky and say, "Oh, help!" or "Why Me?" It's been our habit, I suspect, since we began walking upright. But just a little thought should drive sensible people to conclude, "No, this can't be right. Let's get over this massive indulgence in wishful thinking." Praying long and hard for something is wishful thinking on steroids.

The first time I saw a Catholic prayer card promising that holy people will devote years to praying for a dead relative, the word that came to mind was *scam*. Seriously? A bunch of monks will pray for the soul of the dear departed, every day for however many years the fee has been paid? The waste of human effort is staggering. A disinclination to do anything useful gets justified by pitiful piety, religion gone off the rails. There is the scam part—horrible enough—but the theology behind the practice is simply bizarre. How will the soul of the person or the patience of God be affected?

It's hard to imagine that any reasonable person has thought it through. Priests are exploiting those who are grief-stricken and catering to the avarice of those who run the cloister treasury. Once upon a time, the Catholic Church invented purgatory and used it to rake in the coinage by selling indulgences. This was a despicable way to prey on the gullible, and the brisk sale of prayer cards means that priests still have a robust appreciation for what they can get away with.

But thinking it through rarely works with the prayer crowd. The few studies of prayer that have been done, on anything approaching a scientific basis, have shown that prayer doesn't work. Yet that hasn't slowed the prayer vigils.

And then there's the famous study of prayer in relation to the well-being of the British royal family. This was done in 1872 by Francis Galton. His tongue may have been in his cheek, but he was following rigorous logic. He decided to take the faithful up on their assumptions, hypothesizing that intercessory prayer, if effective, would have shown some results.

> He had good information for a statistical analysis, that of comparing the health and longevity of the general population of England vs. that of the Royal Family. In England at the time (perhaps even now), tens of thousands, probably more, prayed every Sunday for the well being of the British Royal Family.
>
> The English kept good records of health and life spans of the general population along with that of the Royal Family. Comparing the life expectancy of both the Royal Family and the general population should show (if prayer works) that the Royals lived longer life spans than that of the general population.
>
> The reasoning would be that constant prayer for the Royal Family, if effective, would certainly contribute to that long lifespan. In addition, the Royal Family then and now would have had absolutely the best in physicians, hospitals and medical care.

You can guess what the result was, can't you? It didn't work, because prayer doesn't work: "The results from statistical tables were that there was no difference at all in the life span of the two groups. And certainly, the prayers of tens of thousands should have accounted for more weight with God than the occasional prayer for those of the general population."[9]

What's So Great about the Lord's Prayer?

A Digression

Putting aside the question of the authenticity of the Lord's Prayer (Does it derive from Jesus? We just don't know), the question of which version of the prayer is the "right" one (they differ in Matthew and Luke), and the problem of textual variants (due to mistakes made by copyists, we don't even know the wording of the original written form of the prayer), we can scrutinize and critique the prayer as it is found in Matthew 6:9-13. In the parallel passage in Luke we are told that the disciples asked Jesus to teach them how to pray.

If this is the best the son of God can do–echoing George Carlin's reaction to God's résumé–I am not impressed.

Our father, who art in heaven, hallowed be thy name.

This is standard liturgical formula and flattery of the male deity who resides overhead. Why would a god need to be told that his name is holy? Many years ago I first encountered the Jewish practice of writing G-d, instead of God, because "God" was too sacred to be spoken or written. This ranks high on the scale of silliness, and derives from the Old Testament belief that the name of the old Hebrew god, YHWH, should not be uttered. We really don't know how it would have been pronounced, because the vowels are not included in written Hebrew. Nonetheless we should reassure God that his name is holy. Huh? What's the point?

Thy kingdom come, thy will be done, on earth as it is in heaven.

Apparently, if the gospel texts are to be trusted even a little bit–and granting that Jesus existed–he expected the cataclysmic arrival of the kingdom of God on Earth sometime soon. Check out Mark 13 for a really scary version. Matthew 24:30 says the Son of man will appear in heaven, "and then shall all the tribes of the earth mourn, and they shall see the Son of man coming on the clouds of heaven with power and great glory" (RSV). This didn't happen, of course, and John Loftus is probably not far off the mark in calling Jesus "at best a failed apocalyptic prophet."[10] In fact, Jesus was one of many failed messiahs that we know of from ancient Palestine.

It is now common for Christians to understand "thy kingdom come" in a softened metaphorical sense–an "internal spiritual reality," as the spin-doctors might say (more about them shortly). But there's little reason to doubt that Jesus was thinking literally. He was hoping for God's kingdom to be lowered through the clouds into our biosphere, following which God's will would be done on Earth. A naïve fantasy, no? And he taught people to pray for this.

Well, Jesus died and childish Christian mythology maintains that he went up to heaven, and hasn't been seen since. It's not all that radical to suggest that we are long past this prayer's expiration date. But how many billions of times has God had to listen to Christians praying that his kingdom will come? (We can imagine God saying, "*Why* did that kid tell them to say that?")

What a waste of breath. And for some reason God hasn't budged. There seems to have been a snag in the plans as Jesus imagined them, and there's no sign at all that God's will has been accomplished on our long-suffering Earth. Do Christians ever *think* about this line as they utter it by rote year after year?

Give us this day our daily bread.

In his book *Life in Year One*, Scott Korb points out that, at the time of Jesus, the Romans had created a precursor of agribusiness in Palestine to keep the cities fed and accommodate Roman lifestyles. Peasant farmers were the big losers. The rich got richer in cities such as Sepphoris, the city nearest to Nazareth. The poor got poorer, and, for the common people, the struggle for food and survival intensified. Thus this line in the prayer reflects a primary concern of ancient peoples who commonly lived on the brink of famine.

Forgive us our trespasses, as we forgive those who trespass against us.

This is the best item in the prayer, and it stands the best chance of having come from Jesus, if we can trust Jesus' words as reported in Matthew 5:23-24: "[I]f you are offering your gift at the altar and there remember that your brother has something against you, leave your gift there before the altar and go. First be reconciled to your brother, and then come and offer your gift" (RSV). The message seems to be: You don't have any right to worship God, and be forgiven, if there's bad blood between you and someone else. The deal with God is this: He will forgive your sins as long as you forgive the sins of others.

So, listen up Christians! If you're in church and praying this prayer, but can't stand somebody in the next pew or in your neighborhood or continue to be pissed off at your brother-in-law, the magic isn't going to work. The charge is often made that churches are filled with hypocrites. The hypocrisy starts when people say this prayer, but really don't take it seriously. In my stint as a parish minister, serving two churches, I soon learned where the fault lines were, the factions that didn't get along, the members of the congregation who despised each other.

The faithful like to claim that their morality is anchored in religion, to the teachings of Jesus, but this particular moral guideline is one of the most universally ignored; the Lord's Prayer is held in contempt. Knowing how much Christians don't *like* each other (think Baptists vs. Catholics), we can safely say that Christians thumb their noses at Jesus when they give lip service to this line in the prayer that he taught them to pray.

Lead us not into temptation, and deliver us from evil.

This is perhaps the worst item in the prayer. Do Christians really believe that it is God who leads them into temptation? The Old Testament story of Job is the God-damning story of God giving Satan permission to ruin Job's life, to see how Job will handle the horrible things that happen to him. Will he cave in and curse God? God is the bad guy in the story, as he would be if he willfully tests people or plays with them. More innocently, perhaps this line is intended as an impulsive plea to God that the worshipper can muster the moral fiber to be on best behavior.

But this has the strong aroma of magical thinking: pleading with a god to boost willpower rather than owning personal responsibility. And, of course, begging to be delivered from evil, in a world rampant with evil, is wasted breath. God is going to arrange for you to dodge the bullets? Only those who utter this prayer will be so privileged?

It's an understandable impulse, but it's worthless. Christians have been saying this prayer since word got out that Jesus had recommended it. What is the success rate? Fifty-fifty? Are Christians tempted less than other people? Have they suffered less evil than other people? This line is a fragment of liturgical theobabble; it's a magical formula, an incantation, wishful thinking disguised as a pious plea.

For thine is the kingdom, and the power, and the glory forever.

When I was growing up, this was the ending of the Lord's Prayer that we recited, but the Catholics didn't include it. We wondered why they left it off. Clearly they weren't saying it right! But it turns out that they were. This last flourish of flattery–massaging the divine ego, assuring God that he has power and glory–is missing from the oldest manuscripts of Matthew. The Revised Standard Version puts these words in a footnote, and tries to comfort readers who wonder why they are missing: "Other authorities, some ancient, add, in some form, 'for thine is the kingdom, and the power and the glory forever.'" The phrase "Other authorities" sounds pretty grand, but it actually means manuscripts that have been tampered with, i.e., the words were added by copyists. The word *authority* is used to disguise that fact; just because a manuscript is ancient, doesn't mean that it qualifies as an *authority*. And "in some form" means that *different* versions of the final words were added to different manuscripts.

The God Who Takes His Own Sweet Time

The seeds of atheism are spread widely throughout scripture. There are Bible verses that should make even pious readers stop dead in their tracks: "How can this *possibly* be true?" Genesis 15:13 is an arresting, breathtakingly embarrassing text, a sharp stick in the eye for anyone who wants a good god.

First, a little about context. Genesis is one of the literary masterpieces of the ancient world. It tells the sweeping epic of the origins and progress of the Hebrew people. It is an elaborate patchwork of folklore. (Not a scrap of it is history, but this fact is not relevant to the point to be made here.) The Old Testament as a whole tells a story of the triumph of the Israelites, their high point being the kingdoms of David and Solomon, supposedly in the 9th century B.C.E. But the folklore also tells about slavery in Egypt and the heroism of Moses in rescuing the chosen people (not a scrap of that is history either, by the way).

By the time Genesis was written in the 7th century B.C.E., the theologians who preserved the epic needed to clean up the story. How could it be that the chosen people had been slaves? Their solution was that God had planned it all along, right from the beginning. Theologians had to sanitize the folklore, or at least try. That's why we read in Genesis 15:13 that

> God said to Abram, "Know for certain that your descendants will be strangers in a land that is not theirs, where they will be enslaved and oppressed four hundred years." (NASB)

This story is set in a time when there were many gods, and supposedly Abraham had options. Wouldn't slavery have been a deal breaker? Who could have blamed Abraham for tossing back a stiff drink and saying, "What the hell does it mean to be the chosen people? How is slavery part of that bargain? Can't this god do better than that? Maybe other gods would try harder to take care of my offspring." But even more staggering is the part about slavery lasting four centuries. Yes, it is folklore, and thus we expect predictions from gods and *sturm und drang*, but four hundred years? It didn't dawn on the author of this Genesis text that he had wandered into bad theology.

One of my teenage moments of doubt was occasioned by this verse. Why would God allow the slavery of the Hebrew people to go on for such a long time? He planned that? It didn't make sense. Doesn't this puncture the idea that God is loving and powerful and can get things done? We're supposed to believe the story about his Really Big Stunt at the Red Sea, but God is powerless to stop four centuries of slavery? This is the conundrum: The Biblical narrative is about a god who is not in a hurry when a whole lot of pain and suffering are happening right under his nose.

Now fast forward to the last few centuries before Jesus. The catastrophe for the ancient nation of Israel was the destruction of Jerusalem in 586 B.C.E. by the Babylonians; their history went downhill after that. For the most part, Palestine was under the control of a succession of empires: Persians, Greeks, Seleucids, Romans. (Jewish self-rule under the Hasmonean dynasty was a brief exception.) This too was inexplicable theologically for the chosen people. Something must have gone terribly wrong, and the tendency was to blame their own sin. The thundering Old Testament prophets took this approach, and the ground shook as they delivered their blistering sermons against the sins of the Israelites and their whoring after other gods.

Even if they deserved the suffering, it was just impossible to imagine that God would abandon them forever; there *had* to be a solution to their dismal history and national humiliation. The theology of denial gave birth to simplistic imaginative solutions, including the expectation of a messiah who would come to the rescue and the belief that God would step in to end history altogether. There was no evidence whatever for these ideas. They're based on theological hunches and unwavering faith in the promises that old Yahweh had once made. The theologians weren't daunted that there were inexplicable delays. John the Baptist, Jesus, and the apostle Paul appear to have bought into this messianic end-of-the-world delusion, and they all preached that the end was near; the kingdom of God was at hand. But John, Jesus, and Paul went to their graves without it happening. God, it turned out, was still not in a hurry.

A favorite theme of Christian preachers is that, *when things get bad enough,* God will step in. They can't let go of the New Testament texts that promise Jesus' return. The Bible can't be wrong, so God is still biding his time. But how bad do things have to get for a compassionate God to say "enough is enough," and usher in his kingdom on earth? "C'mon God, split those clouds and come on down so that your will can be done on Earth." Such delay is a major contradiction for those who passionately argue that God is good and omnipotent.

But we're not that dumb: We can see magnitudes of human suffering that should be unacceptable to a good God, and should have made him stop taking his own sweet time. There was the Black Plague in the 14th century that killed a third of the human population from Europe to India, the mass extermination of the native population of the Americas, the Battle of Verdun that left 350,000 men dead in 1916. The flu pandemic from 1918 to 1920 killed at least 50 million. And then came World War Two, with another 50 million dead, and the Holocaust, and Hiroshima. All of these episodes of colossal human suffering should have been attention grabbers and prompted God to act: "*Now* is the time for my will to be done on Earth."

Let's face it, history has not been kind to God. In the superbly crafted 2004 play by Alan Bennett, *The History Boys*, we follow the angst of eight young men studying with all their might to qualify for Oxford.[11] One of their teachers, Mrs. Lintott, is irked that only men are in the intense preparation course, and calls attention to the male bias of history, both the making and writing of it:

> History's not such a frolic for women as it is for men. Why should it be? They never get around the conference table. In 1919, for example, they just arranged the flowers then gracefully retired.

> History is a commentary on the various and continuing incapabilities of men. What is history? History is women following behind with a bucket. And I'm not asking you to espouse this point of view, but the occasional nod in its direction can do you no harm. You should note, boys, that your masters find this undisguised expression of feeling distasteful, as, I see, do some of you.

Maybe we should blame God, too, for putting men in charge. The male bias of scripture can lead to no other conclusion.

Rudge, the only working class boy in the group, is counting on his golf prowess to get into Oxford; his interest in history hovers just above zero. Mrs. Lintott asks him to role-play the upcoming interview at Oxford:

Mrs. Lintott: Now. How do you define history, Mr. Rudge?

Rudge: Can I speak freely, miss? Without being hit.

Mrs. Lintott: I will protect you.

Rudge: How do I define history? It's just one fucking thing after another.

Human history is indeed the story of God-missing-in-action, just one fucking thing after another. The same-old, same-old nature of history, the unending chronicle of brutality and suffering, is an indictment of God, *The Supreme Procrastinator*.

Just what is it going to take to get him to snap out of his complacency? The promise of the New Testament is that he plans to put a stop to it. But we now know that those billions of Christian prayers for God's will to be the rule on Earth are based on another of Jesus' delusions. God taking his own sweet time doesn't give us much confidence that it's even worth having a god. Part of our cultural heritage is Handel's magnificent setting of Job 19:25 in the oratorio, *Messiah*: "I know that my redeemer liveth." Ironically, Job 19:25 had nothing whatever to do with Jesus, and this sentiment about a living redeemer has no relevance whatever to human hope that history and life will get better.

God Only Knows Who Goes to Heaven

In 1993 the Southern Baptists found themselves in a major dustup when they announced that 46.1 percent of the residents of Alabama were going to hell. The *New York Times* reported (20 September 1993):

> The Southern Baptists have done such demographic research for years, said Martin King, a spokesman for the denomination's Home Mission Board. The study took each county's population and subtracted from it the membership of all churches. After that, Baptist researchers used a secret formula to estimate how many people from different denominations and faiths were probably going to heaven.

A secret formula? Here's a clue: "The Southern Baptist Convention's county-by-county breakdown of who is bound for heaven and who is not, unless they are born again." The phrase *born again* is a Christian cult formula for escaping death, more specifically escaping hell, a concept that probably seeped into Christian thought from Zoroastrianism.

Humans have feared death far longer than they feared hell, because the prospect of oblivion has been more obvious, less speculative, than the existence of a place of eternal torture. Humans probably began suspecting an afterlife when they saw departed friends and relatives in dreams; it occurred to them as well to provide for the journey "on the other side" by putting supplies in graves. However, it also dawned on some people that maybe, just maybe, they could find a way to *get* to the other side. Perhaps it could be engineered. As soon as hell as punishment was part of the formula, then priests could argue that a pleasant afterlife depended on good behavior.

But Christianity has always been conflicted on this very issue. Believers who take their faith very seriously have been sharply divided on how to get to heaven, largely because the Bible can be quoted to support differing ways to prepare for the pearly gate moment.

One of my favorite stories about Jesus is one that has caused more than a little Christian discomfort over the centuries. This is found in Mark 10:17-22 (NIV):

> As Jesus started on his way, a man ran up to him and fell on his knees before him."Good teacher," he asked, "what must I do to inherit eternal life?"

> "Why do you call me good?" Jesus answered."No one is good–except God alone. You know the commandments: 'You shall not murder, you shall not commit adultery, you shall not steal, you shall not give false testimony, you shall not defraud, honor your father and mother.'"

> "Teacher," he declared, "all these I have kept since I was a boy."

> Jesus looked at him and loved him."One thing you lack," he said."Go, sell everything you have and give to the poor, and you will have treasure in

heaven. Then come, follow me." At this the man's face fell. He went away sad, because he had great wealth.

Christians have shown great ingenuity in explaining why they don't have to take Jesus too seriously here."What, sell all my stuff?"

Consider Jesus' response when he was asked point-blank how to get to heaven. His answer was, essentially: Be a good, compassionate person, and don't be so attached to *stuff*. For most of their long history, the Jews did not put much stock in an afterlife. There may have been a soul that survived for a while after death, but then it gradually faded away. But when afterlife became a standard expectation, obeying the law of the Torah–being a good person, a law-abiding Jew–was required to qualify. And Jesus, as a good Jew, agreed.

So what happened in the Christian camp? I think a case can be made that the apostle Paul had a major role in poisoning the well. Apparently Paul never heard Mark's story of Jesus and the rich young man–the gospels had not been written when Paul wrote–and he believed that following the law of the Torah was virtually impossible. He was scared to death of death, and had to find a way around the Torah. Paul settled on a magical formula, based on his obsession with the magical properties of Jesus' resurrection. (This makes no sense at all, as we will see in later chapters.)

Here is Paul's magic formula, about as convincing as a Harry Potter spell, Romans 10:9-10: If "you confess with your mouth that Jesus is Lord and believe in your heart that God raised him from the dead, you will be saved. For with the heart one believes and is justified, and with the mouth one confesses and is saved" (ESV).

We can safely say that the Galilean peasant, Jesus of Nazareth, beneath all the layers of theological invention in the gospels, would have been nonplussed at this farcical exaggeration of his importance, that his dying and rising was a neat trick for getting people into heaven. Christians forget–correction, they never learn–that the gospels are highly biased accounts of Jesus. Indeed they are propaganda pieces with heavy theological agendas, created by writers who assumed that Jesus was in some sense divine. That's not a good formula for writing reliable history; the purpose of a gospel is to *sell*, not to tell.

What are the chances of finding the historical Jesus, and how he might have felt about getting to heaven, beneath the heavy helpings of theology that the gospel writers serve us? The chances are ruined because the gospel writers were, to varying degrees, under the spell of Paul's deranged theology of magic. After the destruction of Jerusalem in 70 C.E., the community of Jesus followers there was decimated. Knowledge of the real Jesus, if he was real, was lost forever.[12]

The Bad Theology of John 3:16

In John's gospel there is no doubt that Jesus is a fictional character, and any discerning lay person notices that the Jesuses of Matthew, Mark, and Luke are different characters. John's Jesus speaks in an entirely different vocabulary and raises bragging about himself to unprecedented levels, e.g., "I am the way, the truth and the life" and "No one comes to the father except through me." In that most popular Bible verse, John 3:16, Jesus talks about himself when he says, "God so loved the world that he gave his only son ..."[13] This egocentric Jesus, a caricature of a religious zealot, takes too seriously Paul's theology about the magical properties of his resurrection. As one of my old professors pointed out, "Jesus of the fourth gospel always walks three feet above the ground. His feet never touch it."

John 3:16 is an echo of Romans 10:9-10 mentioned above. The verse in its entirety: "God so loved the world that he gave his only son, so that whoever believes in him shall not perish but have eternal life." This is the gimmick; here religion is reduced to a cheap bargain. Just believe and you're in, you've won the prize. With just a little thought, the absurdities pile on. The apologists who think that John 3:16 is the essence of Christianity, the pinnacle of Christian thought, also are obliged to work overtime to explain away the crudeness of it all. So you mean that anyone who has never heard of Jesus is excluded from eternal life? No Jews or Muslims are eligible? Well, certainly no atheists.

Back to Square One

Human beings are out of their depth when they try to figure how to get to heaven. May I be so rude to point out that there's *no evidence whatever* for an afterlife? All the hoopla about NDEs (Near Death Experiences) has been pretty neatly dispatched by scientists who study brain activity. And since there's no correlation between NDEs and religious loyalty, Christians who claim that only Jesus gets you to heaven are left explaining the NDEs of all those other Jesus-less people.

Any way you slice it, any way you try penetrate the conundrum, you can't win. There's no data for doing the figuring, despite the Southern Baptist claim to have a secret formula. And thus Christianity finds itself in such a tangle of contradictions, a morass of God ideas that just don't work.

Why don't we just throw in the towel and go with the approach that seems to resonate with decent people. If there's anything they *don't* want to delete from God, to iron out the contradictions, it's God's love. After all, in 1 John 4:8 (not to be confused with the gospel of John) we read: "Anyone who does not love does not know God, because God is love" (ESV). How much more Hallmark Cards can you get than "God is Love"? This is cult talk, by the way. What can it mean to say that God *is* love? Only the cult members have a clue. But if God *is* love, why and how would he exclude anyone from heaven? Well, maybe Hitler, but he's the extreme outlier.

Father Andrew Greeley explained how a God-welcomes-all policy could work. In an article in the *New York Times* (10 July 1994), he suggested that Catholics stay with the church because it has such good stories. Here's a darned good one, in Father Greeley's article:

> When I was in grammar school in the mid-1930's, the nuns told a story that sums up why people stay Catholic. One day Jesus went on a tour of the heavenly city and noted that there were certain new residents who ought not to be there, not until they had put in a long time in purgatory and some of them only on a last-minute appeal. He stormed out to the gate where

Peter was checking the day's intake on his Compaq 486DX Deskpro computer ... next to which, on his work station, was a fishing pole and a papal crown.

"You've failed again, Simon Peter," said the Lord.

"What have I done now?"

"You let a lot of people in that don't belong."

"I didn't do it."

"Well, who did?"

"You won't like it."

"Tell me anyway."

"I turn them away from the front gate and then they go around to the back door and your mother lets them in!"

That supersized saint, Mary—God bless her—can't resist the ultimate open door policy. And few Christians can resist the comfort that is offered, although Protestants would give no credit whatever to the heavenly mother.

The Tale of Two Deathbeds

When they tout the value of religion, and brag about the good it does, Christians usually rank *comfort* as a primary benefit. My former friend, who believes in Christ with all her might, does so because she wants to see mom again in heaven. Coming to grips with reality is not her strongest suit, and she would turn a deaf ear to cautious theologians who warn that we really don't know what heaven is like."What? You mean I might not get to see Mom again?" We have no more evidence about heaven than about God. Yet there can be ferocious reliance on the comfort of the idea.

The bizarre notion that dead relatives, their personalities intact, will be re-accessed after we "cross over" can lead to dysfunctional, painfully daffy behavior. A Catholic woman (this is a darned *creepy* Catholic story) told me that when her mother was about to die, in a semi-conscious state, she gave her mother a little coaching about what would happen next. I hope that she told her that she loved her, because then she gave her mom messages to deliver to the dead relatives.

Had God really intended such moments to be used so opportunistically? If Aunt Mildred and Uncle Wayne had been "looking down" as the pious so commonly assume, why send messages to them anyway? It requires a special brand of stupid to exploit the moment of death in such crass fashion; this is tacky, trailer-trash religion at its worst. The woman told me that her mom became agitated; unable to speak, she began thrashing her legs wildly, a sure sign, the daughter felt, that Mom was anticipating the walk to heaven. I think it's just as possible that, if this woman in her final ordeal was able to hear, it was a moment of panic or terror for her. She might have been trying to flee the room, to get away from her babbling idiot daughter. As Steve Jobs famously said, even the people who want to go to heaven don't want to have to die to get there. Maybe her mother was totally freaked: "Die? You mean I'm about to *die*? I don't want to die." A cynic friend of mine wanted to know why this deranged daughter didn't ask Mom to take along packages as well as messages.

On the morning that my own mother died, in December 1998, she was in a peaceful sleep when I left the house on an early errand. When I returned, I found that the health care attendant had put a boombox on mother's bed, blasting whoop-and-holler gospel music, the kind of racket that my Mozart-loving mother detested. She was awake and hyperventilating. It was as if the breathing switch in her brain had been moved to the highest setting. I yanked the radio off the bed and restored silence to the room, except for the alarming rattle of mother's accelerated breathing. We had known for several days that the end was near, and it is no cliché to say that this was the blessing we had hoped for. Her short-term and long-term memory had been gone for a couple of years, and for many months she had been immobilized by a stroke.

Now I sat with her, held her hand, and kept repeating, "This is David, I'm here. This is David, I'm here." Did she have any grasp of what was happening? I have no idea. But if anything could penetrate, I hope it was the assurance that her last-born son was at her side. By late morning her breathing had become relaxed, then stopped shortly before noon. She died 51 days into her 94th year.

I needed no assurance that she was in heaven, and my mourning had already taken place for a delightful, compassionate woman who had disappeared long before her physical death. Her mind and personality had been destroyed by disease. *What*, exactly, would have gone to heaven? I have no doubt that I, an atheist, showed far more decency, far more respect, to a person on her deathbed who was relinquishing the precious, fragile gift of life. That moment deserves to be free of foolish, inflated dogma, free of the poison that religious fanatics add.

God only knows who goes to heaven, but let's review the options that fever-pitched theological speculations have come up with:

- People who are good and compassionate, no matter what their religion, get in.

- People who believe in Jesus, even if they've not been good people, get in. They bought the cheap ticket.

- God lets (almost) everyone in, if the Virgin Mary has anything to say about it.

Silliness has clearly won the day. Preachers and theologians should be ashamed of themselves for giving even a moment's thought to figuring out the getting-into-heaven formula.

I've long considered Christianity, Catholicism in particular, to be a cult of the dead. It is so focused on escaping our final and obvious fate by creating a fantasy hereafter. Christians can be so god-damned certain about it. Bravado, however, counts for nothing. *Huis Clos*, No Exit. The title of Jean-Paul Sartre's 1944 play expresses the truth that religious delusionists have done their very best to hide, disguise, and deny. **There is no exit from death.** Period. It is unbecoming to be so afraid of death, and it's disgraceful that religions have specialized in marketing ways to get out of it. They don't have the product, but they hawk it shamelessly anyway.

I appreciate the candor of atheism, and thus loathe that favorite euphemism of Christians who want to avoid saying what really happens; supposedly it softens the blow to say that *he passed away*. No, please be honest enough to tell it like it is: He *died*. He's gone.

Christian apologists of every stripe, from professorial theologians to lay Sunday school teachers, rhapsodize about how wonderful the mystery of God is, and they willingly park so much there that they don't understand. So, please, park heaven there as well, and let it go at that. We don't know for sure what happens when the brain dies, although there is no reason whatever to suspect anything other than oblivion. God only knows, and he's a fictional character.

The Dead Rodent and the Spin Doctors

Occasionally Christians visit my Facebook page for this book, *10 Tough Problems in Christian Thought and Belief*. They display various degrees of indignation, but one man was just puzzled. *Problems?* What problems? He couldn't think of one, let alone ten. He set a new standard for shallowness. I responded that he was not ready for serious discussion of the issues that I deal with. I told him that he had a lot of homework to do. Had he thought so little about his faith?

I pointed out that Christian theologians have been wringing their hands about these problems for hundreds of years. They have written libraries full of books trying to argue away the problems. The formal term for this endeavor is *apologetics*. It comes from a Greek word, *apologia*, which means *to speak in defense of*. Of course, in English, it sounds like *to apologize for*. Maybe someday Christians will graduate from defending to apologizing, since Christianity has foisted so many bad ideas onto its credulous followers, and caused so much harm along the way.

But the whole business of apologetics should give Christians pause; there is so much in their religion that just doesn't make sense. Maintaining a staff of spin-doctors is a clue that too many gaffes and mistakes have been made. The doctors should lift the rug under which so much has been swept, and acknowledge the mess. Yes, my dear Facebook visitor, there are problems, lots of them.

One of the great atheist spokesmen of our time is former minister John Loftus. On his Facebook page on 3 August 2013 he marveled at the work of the spin-doctors:

> Do you ever wonder, seriously wonder, why it takes so many Christian apologists to defend their faith with a multitude of books, essays, lectures and debates? It's as if God has left the one true faith in their hands, and that, without them, people would believe differently. C.S. Lewis said good philosophy must exist because bad philosophy needs to be answered. Okay. But why did the Christian God make it so hard to defend his one true faith against so many thoughtful and serious objections to the contrary? No, really. It's as if God shot himself in the foot and these apologists are called upon to heal his self-inflicted wound. This makes no sense at all, none.

As of 2016, Loftus had published ten books deconstructing Christianity: "I think I've said all I need to say. I've kicked this dead rodent of the Christian faith into a lifeless blob so many times there is nothing left of it."[14]

Oh, that we should be so lucky. The apologists are relentless; one of the images that comes to mind is Mickey Mouse's broom. As the Sorcerer's Apprentice (in Disney's *Fantasia*), Mickey puts a spell on a broom to get it to carry a water bucket for him. But the spell turned out to be a curse: The broom won't stop hauling the water, even after Mickey frantically smashes it to bits. The splinters become brooms and keep carrying water, until the sorcerer's chamber is under water. I could push the metaphor and say that the world is drowning in religion, but suffice it to say that the accursed apologists don't stop coming!

And sad to say, all of their energies are so misdirected; they pursue a niche industry committed to propping up dilapidated ancient ideologies. This endeavor provides adrenaline rushes to Christian academicians and fawning clergy, but brings no benefit whatever to the human condition.

Ironically, it usually takes a lot of brainpower for the spin-doctors to do their jobs. They have to be very clever and adept at designing arguments that don't look shallow. Samuel Walter, writing in the Facebook group *Atheist Friend Center* (30 Nov 2013), puts it well in referring to "the madness that is Christian apologetics." It is, he says, "painfully difficult to read, especially for those of us who value logic and consistency with reality." Not surprisingly, the church has commonly enlisted academicians for the job, but there is a major downside to this approach. The academicians may come up with arguments that prompt other academicians to nod in approval, but few people beyond the university understand what the hell they're talking about.

Earlier I have referred to Karl Barth, the Swiss theologian (1886-1968), who is considered one of the giants in the field. He is famous among the theological elite for his 8,000 page treatise about God (*Church Dogmatics*, 13 volumes), but not one in a million laypeople has read it, or could stand to read it. Theologians write for other theologians. Hundreds of them, for decades to come, will write scholarly papers about Barth's theology for their academic associates, trying, endlessly, to refine and legitimize an esoteric concept of the Christian God that somehow escapes the silliness. Even short works of theology can be torture. Painfully good examples are John F. Haught (Catholic), *What Is God? How to Think About the Divine*, mentioned in Tough Problem II; B.L Hebblethwaite (Protestant), *The Problems of Theology*; Richard Swinburne (Protestant), *Is There a God*; and C. Robert Mesle (Protestant), *Process Theology: A Basic Introduction*.

Sometimes the apologists go off their reservations. Catholic theologian and religion historian Uta Ranke-Heinemann was fired by Pope John Paul II because she denied the Virgin Birth. This would be a safe departure from orthodoxy on the Protestant reservation, at least the *liberal* Protestant one. But Catholics won't hear such talk about their super-sized saint. Uta was too much of a rebel in other ways as well, for example, by thinking out loud in trying to square the circle with God's compassion vs. his omnipotence:

> The theologians prefer to deduct points from God's compassion rather than from his omnipotence. A powerful God finds more supporters than a compassionate God. This is because people model their image of God on their own image. And potency and power mean a great deal to them–sometimes they mean everything–while compassion means less, and sometimes nothing at all. But we should rethink this.[15]

Do you see what she's doing, other than rethinking, which has been the tiresome habit of theologians for millennia? She's trying to figure out God when there are no data, only hunches. It's guesswork 100 percent of the time. She speaks of an idea about God having "more supporters," as if the nature of God is decided by consensus among those who specialize in the guesswork. Furthermore, and very dangerously, she admits that "people model their image of God on their own image." With friends like this, God doesn't need enemies.

Protestant theologians can go too far as well. The liberal Lutheran theologian Rudolf Bultmann (1884-1976) popularized the "demythologizing" of the New Testament. Don't even try, he argued, to take the stories literally–who cares if they are historical or not?–dig to find the "spiritual truth" behind them. This is pretty risky. If you don't care if there's any history in the gospels, Jesus may turn out not to be there at all (as some scholars now argue), or merely a disappointing Galilean peasant. Nonetheless, many theologians in Bultmann's wake have tried to distance themselves from the naïve Biblical narratives and now, as we have seen, advocate that God is a reality "outside space and time." Most pastors would find themselves in hot water if they used this approach from the pulpit. Lay people remain quite content with The Man Upstairs who helped Moses part the Red Sea and his son Jesus walk on the Sea of Galilee. They want the miracles, and happily believe them.

The spin doctors will keep on doing their thing. But it's an indictment of the Christian faith that they are obliged to stay in business, apologizing endlessly for silly religious speculations that are so hobbled by contradictions and improbabilities.

Suspending Thought Instead of Suspending Belief

At the Scopes Monkey Trial in 1924, three-time presidential loser and fundamentalist William Jennings Bryan was the state prosecutor, while famous atheist attorney Clarence Darrow ("I don't believe in God because I don't believe in Mother Goose") defended John Scopes, a teacher who had violated the law against teaching evolution. Portions of the transcript ended up in the text of the 1955 play *Inherit the Wind*. High drama was achieved when Darrow, outmaneuvered by the judge, did the unthinkable: He called Bryan as a witness to testify as an expert on the Bible.

It was a calamity for the overly confident Bryan; Darrow put him on the hot seat by quoting naïve texts from Genesis. Since Adam and Eve were the first and only couple on Earth, where did their son's wife come from? "Did someone pull off another creation over in the next county?" He asked Bryan what he thought of the contradictions, and he responded, "I do not think about the things I do not think about," which brought the retort, "Do you ever think about things that you *do* think about?" Darrow was appalled by Bryan's shallowness: "It frightens me to imagine the state of learning in the world if everyone had your driving curiosity."

Christianity survives because Christians lack driving curiosity about their religion and its origins, and they don't mind being obtuse and myopic. Jesus once likened faith in his message to a house build on rock (Matt. 7:24-27). But that house has seen better days; Christians don't see that the roof leaks, the paint is peeling, the windows are broken, and the carpets are frayed.

It is astonishing that the failings of their faith don't *bug the hell* out of believers. Even if they vaguely grasp that there are problems–doubts gnaw here and there–they shrug them off, yearning for a friendly Cosmos and escape from death. Christianity chugs along as it has for centuries, with the faithful not realizing that The Man Upstairs has left the building.

Notes

1. Ludovic Kennedy, *All in the Mind: A Farewell to God* (Hodder & Stoughton, 1999), p. 261.

2. goodreads.com/quotes/4082-now-my-own-suspicion-is-that-the-universe-is-not

3. Jewish monotheism is a muddled business. The idea of a lone god could have been a borrowing from Zoroastrianism, and even among the Jews this concept did not exist in unsullied form. There are plenty of complaints among the Old Testament prophets that other gods than Yahweh were being worshipped, and by New Testament times Yahweh had to deal with a rival god who headed the realm of demons.

4. Not my line, sad to say. It was the great jazz drummer, Buddy Rich, who said it first while being wheeled into emergency surgery and asked if there was anything he was allergic to.

5. A.N. Wilson, *God's Funeral: A Biography of Faith and Doubt in Western Civilization* (W.W. Norton & Co., 1999), p. 223.

6. Francis Collins, *The Language of God: A Scientist Presents Evidence for Belief* (Free Press, 2007), p. 71.

7. Sam Harris, *Letter to a Christian Nation* (Vintage, 2008).

8. Posted by the FB page "Philosophical Atheism," 24 November 2013.

9. examiner.com/article/population-statistics-on-the-efficacy-of-prayer-show-prayer-does-not-work

10. See Chapter 12 of John Loftus, ed., *The Christian Delusion: Why Faith Fails* (Prometheus Books, 2010).

11. *History Boys* won the Laurence Olivier and NY Drama Critics awards for best new play.

12. Reza Aslan, *Zealot: The Life and Times of Jesus of Nazareth* (Random House, 2014), pp. 214-215. Aslan's shameless attacks on certain prominent atheists make it unappetizing to cite him about anything, but his observation about the destruction of the Jerusalem temple does bear mentioning.

13. Well, maybe. There's a problem with John 3; there was no punctuation in the original written Greek, so we can't be sure if verse 16 was supposed to have been spoken by Jesus, or is part of the author's commentary.

14. From the Prologue to Loftus' book, *Unapologetic: Why Philosophy of Religion Must End*, posted to his blog, 5 May 2016.

15. Uta Ranke-Heinemann, *Putting Away Childish Things*, p. 61.

V

Which Monotheism? Which Christianity?

> In the absence of a spiritual Supreme Court (or papacy) to adjudicate competing
> scriptural interpretations, all believers were free to interpret the Bible for themselves.
> This new Christian liberty resulted—as Catholics predicted it would—not in unity but in
> near-anarchy, an endless splintering of Protestantism into a Babel of competing beliefs
> and practices.
>
> —Stephen Prothero, *American Jesus: How the Son of God Became a National Icon*

Why Not a Registry of Certified Religions?

WHEN Richard Nixon ran for the Senate in 1950, his opponent, Helen Gahagan
Douglas, nicknamed him Tricky Dick. Because of his sinister appearance, it was hard
for photographers to be kind to him, and even harder for political cartoonists. Ten
years later, during Nixon's campaign for the presidency, Democrats created a poster
to exploit his shady-character image: "Would you buy a used car from this man?" In
the history of dirty tricks in American politics, it remains a classic. Nixon eventually
got his wish to be president, but he lost the 1960 race by a razor-thin margin to John
Kennedy. People knew that buying a used car is tricky business.

There is so much emotional and financial investment in the purchase of a car that
consumers usually become consummate fact checkers. When they're forced to settle
for a used car, they are especially careful; these days they can check the registry of
certified pre-owned vehicles. Thousands of dollars are at stake, as well as their self-
image and reputation in the neighborhood. You are what you drive, it seems, and
buyers have to live with their decision for years. Nobody wants to get burned.
Rigorous due diligence is usually applied to the purchase of other big-ticket items as
well, such as houses, insurance, and college educations.

There's another big-ticket item, however, that usually receives no more than a
shrug. There is commonly a major emotional and financial investment, but nobody so
much as kicks the tires. In fact, people already own it: the religion into which they are
born. They take for granted that they've got the best model ever made.[1] When
Mormons or Jehovah's Witnesses come knocking at their doors, they send them
packing because—well, above all because they're a nuisance—but also because it's
assumed they're hawking inferior wares."I already know what I believe, and I've got
the true religion."

There has been no demand for a registry of certified religions. Wouldn't that be
handy? With thousands of religions swarming the Earth—Stephen Prothero has called
it "a furiously religious planet"—why not create an independent authenticating body
to sort it all out? The consumer could shop for religions with confidence that she is
not getting shoddy goods. A certifying body would weigh religious claims against
reality.

Certainly Mormonism and Scientology—both of which are bogus, totally made-up
by con men—would stand to lose, as would the Virgin Mary on toast or tree bark.

I learned recently that there is an American Association of Professional Psychics, and it welcomes website visitors to "consult a guaranteed authentic certified psychic." Wow: *Guaranteed*. Authentic and Certified, even. Why can't we have that for religions? I suspect that even some of the most devout believers on our furiously religious planet would agree that "guaranteed, authentic, certified" is overreaching.

But never mind looking for certified religions. Most believers follow in the faithsteps of their parents. How wrong could Mom and Dad be?

Religion and Baseball

Surely, though, that shouldn't be good enough. Who were Mom and Dad, after all, and how much did they really know? Should we trust them on ultimate, fundamental questions?

When I once asked a Christian to trace her beliefs back to their origins, it was clear that she didn't understand what *origins* means. She said that she learned them from her mother, who had received them from her grandmother. She smugly assumed that I should be satisfied with this solid matriarchal lineage. But why would that be a reliable pedigree? There were approximately eighty generations between Grandma and Jesus. That's a lot of time for garbling, and for the intrusion of doctrinal flotsam and jetsam. Of course, eighty generations is also enough time for loyalties to become entrenched, and the more entrenched they are, the less rational analysis there will be.

There is a parallel here to another kind of family tradition. Dad inherited his loyalty to the Yankees, Mets or Boston Red Sox from his mom and dad, and passed that on to his kids. Baseball is one of the comfort zones of youth. Religious loyalties are passed on in much the same way, clothed in a mantle of seriousness that parents and preachers encourage. Although outings at baseball stadiums are recalled fondly, the painful hours in church, Sunday school and catechism classes are endured and perhaps even resented. A lot goes in one ear and out the other, but there is a substantial residue that sticks in the brain and stubbornly resists removal later.

What would have happened, what religious certainties would have been engraved on the brain, if my Christian friend had had another set of grandmothers? Our identities derive from chance, from accidents of birth and location, far more than is commonly realized. If I had been conceived a day earlier later than I was, I would be a different person. In fact, if Sperm No. 205,012 had arrived at the egg instead of the sperm that resulted in me—say, No. 213,576—I would be a different person. As I would if my great-great grandfather had immigrated to Minnesota instead of Indiana, and had married someone other than my great-great grandmother. Most importantly, in the context of this discussion, if I had been born in Croatia instead of Indiana, I would have been taught that *another* religion is the only one that is worthy of my full devotion.

In one of the more memorable confrontations between Richard Dawkins and a devout Christian during a Q&A session, the gentleman claimed to have a personal relationship with Jesus. Dawkins bluntly pointed out that the fellow would not even have been a Christian if he'd been raised in another culture or another era. Instead of believing in Jesus, he might believe in Thor, Wotan, or Allah. The man repeated that he had a personal relationship with Jesus and seemed to feel that was verification enough. Jesus might as well have been standing there beside him, he was so certain. How could the learned atheist doubt that?

A God-Inventing Species

Dawkins does not suffer fools gladly, or even those who can't absorb a cogent point in a rebuttal, and he suggested that the man was a victim of hallucinations. That response probably weakened Dawkins' argument, because the point that *should* be made is that years of indoctrination and ceremony dig deep grooves in the brain. The emotional investment, the spell under which the man lives, seems, for all the world, like Jesus relating to him personally. It doesn't have to be hallucination for the fellow to believe that the warm devotion in his heart is the embrace of Jesus.

Dawkins's point about timing and geography is a crucial one and has been made by countless observers. Why is it lost on Christians? Why doesn't it occur to them, and stop them in their tracks? "Gee, I'm a Christian because Mom and Dad convinced me to be one." Parents team up with determined ecclesiastical lobbyists, putting colossal effort into making sure that the young don't stray from the religion of their clan.

Some Christians may protest that they were not raised in religious homes at all but came to Christ later. That should be the occasion for another "Aha" moment, because they didn't come to Allah, Yahweh, or Neptune. Why was it *Christ* that won their attention? We live in a Christianity-soaked culture, and the marketing of Jesus is a multibillion-dollar business. So it really is a no-brainer that, when most people in modern America "get religion," it is Christ that they "find."

Why don't people think about the how this all comes to pass? There's nothing divinely inspired or guided about it at all. A special arrogance is required to believe that one's own religion, the one that Mom and Dad got from their parents, or that predominates in our culture, just happens to be the one that is right, out of all the thousands of religions that have been invented. To Guy Harrison, there is just one thing suggested by the "great number of gods that we humans have confidently believed in since the dawn of history and probably deep into prehistory." It is that

> we are a god-inventing species. We see divine beings everywhere and then imagine that we know their desires. The fact that there has never been agreement on who the real gods are and what they want of us hints to the likely source of our tales. The gods have not spoken to us. Most likely it is we who are simply speaking to one another, in their names.[2]

It takes only a thimbleful of common sense and a glimmer of objectivity to see that the chances are very slim that any one religion, including one's own, has stumbled upon the truth. Intellectual integrity and self-respect would seem to demand putting one's own religion under full scrutiny."Hey, Mom and Dad gave me this, but moms and dads all over the world in all religions have done the same thing. I'd better check this out, with far more passion, and following far more stringent standards, than I'd bring to buying a used car." But this is precisely what most devout people studiously avoid doing. Harrison says that

> very few of the world's people are doing much thinking, if any, when they first become tied to a religion. There is virtually no comparison shopping going on when it comes to the adoption of religions throughout the global population. There is no weighing of evidence and assessing of arguments. There is no time given for fair hearings of alternate beliefs or counter explanations for religious claims.[3]

Education, Loosely Defined

The irony is that now, well into the 21st century, there are unprecedented resources for people to check out their own religions. The irony is compounded for Christians because Christianity above all–because of its high profile and high quotient of silliness–has been scrutinized more intensively than most religions by scholars and serious thinkers.

For example, no other documents from the ancient world have received as much thorough, painstaking study as the four gospels. The scholarly writing on these accounts of Jesus is so extensive–most of it generated in just the last two centuries–that it could fill libraries. Yet most Christians remain unaware of this, because they're not interested in checking out the gospels. Taking the story of Jesus at face value is good enough for them; curiosity about their faith hovers just above zero.

Well, maybe this is too harsh. Christian education is a thriving business because churches *do* push study of the faith; continual propagandizing has long been seen as a major factor in passing along the core beliefs. Even parents who are lukewarm about their religion feel, for some reason, that the kids "ought" to get the straight scoop about it. Hence every church has a Sunday school, or catechism classes, even adult Bible study groups. But the words "school" and "study" must be used loosely in these contexts because there is a firm commitment *not* to probe deeply, question authority, or to distrust dogmas and liturgies.

Pastors and priests are not in the business of stirring up doubt. They are not about to open up the hornet's nest of real gospel study, because there is just too much to undermine faith when people study the gospels at more than a superficial, devotional level. *None* of what goes on in Sunday school qualifies as due diligence.

The Weird World of Christian Devotional Books

Just as libraries could be filled with the works of authentic scholarship about the gospels, librarians could also fully stock their shelves with Christian devotional literature. These books are churned out, decade after decade, by Christians who are so in love their faith, so in love with Jesus, that they want to share the good news, without a glimmer of critical thought. *Reading this genre of books is not due diligence*, however much it may masquerade as study.

The Christian authors who produce these books by the barrelful are the used car salesmen of the religion world. They don't want you to kick the tires. The last thing they want is for their readers to show the least spark of curiosity or suspicion that all is not as it should be. Moreover, these authors and their publishers possess enough killer instinct to target vulnerable people. At a big chain drug store in my neighborhood, there is a rack of Bibles and Christian devotional books in the *pharmacy* department.

Fairly typical is a book by Adam Houge, *The 7 Most Powerful Prayers that Will Change Your Life Forever!* It has sold more than 600,000 copies and is free for the Amazon Kindle. Houge has found his niche market with those who are especially credulous. How far short of due diligence we're going to fall with Houge's approach is clear in the opening sentence of his book:

> God wants to connect with you. He is an intimate and loving God who seeks you fervently, daily. He is always looking for an opportunity to be a part of your life and a part of your day. He wants to know you perfectly and intimately.[4]

How cool is that! God wants to be friends. This is probably the ultimate statement of God the Cosmic Buddy. It probably doesn't occur to the folks who lap up this stuff that they should ask Adam Houge to explain how *he* knows all this about God. They trust his more than a used car salesman with a slick pitch.

The question that always comes to mind when I hear such extraordinary claims is the one I've posed repeatedly: What is your epistemology? For goodness' sake, learn this word! Religion gets away with so much because people don't know to ask this question. This is basic due diligence. How has Houge verified that these seven prayers are the most powerful? He would have us believe that he has figured out that some word formulas are better than others at nudging God to do something, to coddle and cuddle with us. How does this differ from magic incantations? *The Seven Most Powerful Prayers* could be a course description at Hogwarts.

Perhaps one of the most high-profile spiritual used car salesmen of the last decade is Squire Rushnell, retired TV executive, a former CEO at ABC. His books have thrived on the *New York Times* bestseller list. Rushnell invented the term *godwink*– Yes, you may roll your eyes–and pushes the idea that coincidences are actually God winking at people:

> Every time you receive what some call a coincidence or an unanswered prayer, it's a direct and personal message of reassurance from God to you– what I call a *godwink*. It's similar to when you were a kid sitting at the dining room table. You looked up and saw someone you loved looking back. Mom or Dad or Granddad. They gave you a little wink. You had a nice feeling from that small silent communication.

> What did it mean? Probably–"Hey kid . . . I'm thinking about you right this moment. I'm proud of you. Everything is going to be all right."

> That's what a godwink is.[5]

Rushnell gives this definition of *godwink*: "An event or personal experience, often identified as coincidence, so astonishing that it could only have come from divine origin."

Astonishing coincidences can only be of divine origin? He can count on impressing people who are not trained in critical thinking, trading on the yearning for a friendly Cosmos. Comfort rules in this genre of faith.

Here's an example, in a story that Rushnell tells. When the great clown Emmett Kelly died, his daughter Stasia boarded a flight to Sarasota, where Kelly had lived at the winter home of Barnum & Bailey. Kelly's brand was the sad clown, and he had always been careful never to be photographed smiling. But on the day that he got word of Stasia's birth, his broad smile was captured by United Press International photographer Frank Beatty, and the picture was carried by newspapers around the world. Now it *is* a startling coincidence that the man seated next to her on the flight to Sarasota turned out to be Frank Beatty."Instantly, a peace flowed over her," says Rushnell."It was as though this incredible wink from God was delivered at this very moment to bring comfort, that her daddy was at God's side–looking down on her."[6]

Are we really compelled to conclude that the coincidence of Stasia and Frank sitting together could only have been of divine origin? It cannot escape notice that here we have full-blown belief in The Man Upstairs that remains so popular. Daddy is at God's side, looking down. Rushnell's God is intimately involved, micromanaging everything, including where people sit on airplanes.

But is Rushnell blind to the implications of this? God must also be accountable *for everything that goes wrong.* Why aren't *horrible* coincidences also godwinks? "An unidentified man in South Carolina was killed on December 22 when he hit a cow in his 2006 Ford Ranger and metal from a ruptured [airbag] inflator sliced his neck."[7] It is so phenomenally unlikely that any one of us will be killed in a car-cow collision. What a coincidence, surely an astonishing coincidence by Rushnell's definition, that the poor victim of this crash just happened along when a cow wandered onto the road. How could God *not* have arranged that?

Rushnell's smarminess extends to misuse of scripture. He is fond of putting out-of-context Bible quotes in sidebars, all designed to construct a feel-good religion (e.g., Jeremiah 1:5, "Before I formed you in the womb I knew you") whose primary message is "God will buck you up when you're down." Occasionally Rushnell stoops to shocking sappiness, e.g."I have long held the secret notion that when my tear ducts become involuntarily activated, it is substantiation that the Holy Spirit is moving through me."[8] No wonder he earns big bucks as a motivational speaker.

I suspect that the devotional books by Houge, Rushnell, and many others have wide appeal because they reinforce belief in the cosmic-buddy god, and they enable Christians to *think* that they're studying their faith. And this, ironically enough, forces me to have more respect–well, at least some respect–for the official apologists whom I mentioned earlier, i.e., the paid theologians who recognize the staggering problems of the Christian faith. Those folks cringe as much as I do at Rushnell's claptrap. They know that there's a lot of defending of the faith to be done, and that a stab at due diligence may lend respectability to Christianity.

Faking Honesty

There is also, however, the phenomenon of *faux* due diligence. Earlier in my discussion of Billy Graham, I mentioned Christian apologist Lee Strobel, a journalist who turned from atheism to belief in Christ. He warmed the hearts of many Christians with his 2000 book, *The Case for Faith: A Journalist Investigates the Toughest Objections to Christianity*. A number of Christians urged me to read it, and since I've read a lot of Christian theology, why not? Having done so, I am more confident than ever that many Christians, certainly those who are Strobel fans, are a gullible lot. How can they avoid noticing Strobel's faulty methodology?

His mission was to verify the claims of Christianity, so he set out to do this by interviewing the most conservative Protestant theologians and scholars on the planet, those whose minds have soaked in Christian brine for decades. He posed eight objections to Christianity to these people, and they all dug deeply into their barrels of *ad hoc* arguments, and came up with clean answers. Strobel was relieved and suggested to his readers that they no longer needed to lose sleep over any doubts they might have about their one true faith.

Please note that this methodology will work just as well with *any* religion. Do you want to know if Roman Catholicism is the one true faith? Well, just pick out ten of the most conservative members of the College of Cardinals to interview–Pope Francis is so accessible you might include him on the roster of experts, too–and you'll be able to write a book reassuring Catholics that *they* have the one true faith. Then move on to the Mormons, those most ridiculed of monotheists. Ten top Mormon theologians will have you convinced in no time that those Golden Plates really did exist and that Mormons have the inside track to God.

As a journalist by training, Strobel should be ashamed of following such shoddy methodology and then broadcasting the results on the assumption that, what? . . . no one would notice his trashy approach? There's nothing wrong with interviewing the most conservative Christians, but then he should have interviewed liberal Christians and secular thinkers who have marshaled the evidence that Christianity has been falsified. The Christian who wonders if Mom and Dad inducted him into the right religion must listen to critics as well as apologists; this is the most honest approach for digging out the truth.

Maybe we can cut Strobel some slack, because *The Case for Faith* was written (2000) before major atheist authors landed on the bestseller lists, e.g. Dawkins, Hitchens, and Harris. It would be a far greater challenge for Strobel to make his case for faith now. Due diligence would require addressing the critiques of the new atheists. But there's another name as well that should prompt Strobel and other apologists to circle their wagons.

Which Monotheism?

The Outsider Test for Faith

I have mentioned John Loftus in previous chapters. He was an ordained minister, and from that perspective brings penetrating insights to his deconstruction of Christianity. Dan Savage, commenting on his own journey out of Catholicism, said that he didn't lose his faith; he saw through it. Loftus is the champion with piercing vision; he qualifies as a force of nature in marshaling the evidence against Christianity. If there is an eleventh tough problem for Christianity it would be withstanding the Loftus challenge.

In 2008 he published *Why I Became an Atheist: A Former Preacher Rejects Christianity*, then followed up with three hefty anthologies, *The Christian Delusion: Why Faith Fails* (2010), *The End of Christianity* (2011) and *Christianity Is Not Great: How Faith Fails* (2014). These titles were modeled on Dawkins's *The God Delusion*, Harris's *The End of Faith*, and Hitchens's *God Is Not Great*.

His onslaught continued in 2013 with the remarkable volume: *The Outsider Test for Faith: How to Know Which Religion Is True*. Richard Carrier provided one of the back-cover testimonials for this volume: "Superbly argued, airtight, and endlessly useful, this should be everyone's first stop in the god debate. Loftus meets every objection and proves the Outsider Test for Faith is the core of every case against religious belief and the one argument you can't honestly get around."

Lee Strobel would do well to study this Loftus volume to learn how to evaluate one's own faith critically, and then turn for further instruction to Loftus's 2015 book, *How to Defend the Christian Faith: Advice from an Atheist*.

Storming the Mighty Fortress

It's very hard to break down the immune system of any religion; the pro-faith propaganda arsenal can be impressive. At the beginning of the previous chapter I mentioned my nostalgia for the church and worship services of my youth. These were a comfort zone, and one item I remember especially was Martin Luther's invigorating hymn, *A Mighty Fortress is Our God*. It is a mighty experience to hear it done well in a big church with thundering organ bass; it's a rousing number, more or less the *Star Spangled Banner* of Christendom. The gist of the hymn is that God is the mighty fortress against Satan and will triumph. It sets the tone for Christian confidence about the faith. How do you break down that confidence? How do you find a way to outwit the immune system?

One way to begin is to point out that the other major monotheisms have their own pro-faith arsenals and are just as confident. Loftus urges Christians to gather all the tools that they use to deconstruct *other* monotheisms and apply them to their own faith. By no means is this a difficult concept. Surely Christians would be able to articulate why they aren't Jews or Muslims. Well, maybe not, because most Christians have not bothered to study these other faiths. As Guy Harrison points out, there has been precious little comparison shopping going on.

But it's a fairly good bet that if Christians do try to articulate why they aren't Jews or Mormons, they might be honest enough to point out, first of all, that they were *born* Christian. Obviously that's a feeble way to defend one's religion, and that is one of the main points that Loftus makes. If you were born into it, you've probably not thought very deeply about it; there is no incentive to do so.

If there is a next step to be taken beyond "I was born that way," then it might be for the Christian outsider to demonstrate why Judaism and Islam can't be true. Jewish and Muslim theologians have worked out, with as much certainty as Christian theologians, why *their* religions are true. How is the Christian going to counter that? There has to be skepticism about how these other monotheisms back up their claims.

Perhaps a Christian might argue that Jewish and Muslim prayer experiences are simply bogus. The Jewish and Muslim miracles that supposedly prove the truth of those faiths are bogus, too, just made-up stories, exaggerations, fairy tales. All of the deep, meaningful meditations that pious Jews and Muslims attest, from which they derive information about God, are faulty and flawed. How could a Christian argue otherwise? If, say, all these Muslim religious phenomena are valid, why not convert to Islam? Loftus recommends the only appropriate methodology for finding out which faith is true (Lee Strobel pay attention):

> Christian believers should examine the specific extraordinary claims of Christianity using the same kinds of skepticism. The OTF [Outsider Test of Faith] calls on people to do unto their own religious faith as they do unto the other faiths they reject. It is the Golden Rule for testing religious faiths."Do unto your own faith what you do unto other faiths." It calls on believers to subject their own faith to the same level of reasonable skepticism they use when rejecting other faiths, which is the skepticism of an outsider, a nonbeliever.[9]

One Big Happy Family?

Many Christians sense that they're on thin ice if they denigrate the religious experiences and testimonies of the other monotheisms. There's a danger that this approach will backfire; it strikes too close to home. It smacks of the pot calling the kettle black. Besides, it would just be bad manners to tell Jews and Muslims that they've got it all wrong. So why not argue that we're *all* right? The common approach, at least for believers of a more liberal bent, is to slide into sentimental and superficial assurances that "we're all worshipping the same God." Aren't Judaism, Christianity and Islam all branches of the same tree? Perhaps it's comforting to think that the same God is behind it all.

Except he isn't. It's a phony solution. This sleight of hand is attempted in the hope that theological sloppiness won't be noticed. Earlier I demonstrated that revelation mechanisms are highly suspect—how do we know who's getting it right?—and this problem now comes charging back at full strength. These three major monotheisms are very different in their understandings of God, so how can we let Christians get away with the massive papering-over of those differences to preserve the fiction that the same god is behind it all? For starters, why has this god given such different revelations? Loftus points out that the one-God approach is "empty rhetoric with no substances at all":

> If Allah is the same deity as the one worshipped by Christians then that deity duplicitously revealed two different religions. This means God, by whatever name is used, helped to instigate the wanton slaughter of Muslims by Christians and Christians by Muslims because of his conflicting revelation. It also means that God duplicitously promised salvation to believers in one of them who will end up being condemned to hell for not believing according to the other one's creed(s). These are two different gods, each of whom denies doing some of the things the other one claims to have done, especially with regard to the resurrection of Jesus.[10]

If Christians were really sincere that they worship the same God that Muslims do, the Qu'ran would be in high demand in Christian bookstores. Christians would esteem it as highly as the Bible. After all, the Hebrew Bible is there already, the bulk of the pages. To Christians, it is known as the Old Testament. It is massively ignored, yes, but it is bound together with the New Testament. Why not slip the Qu'ran in after the New Testament? And while they're at it, add the *Book of Mormon* as well. After all, the official name for Mormonism is The Church of Jesus Christ of Latter-day Saints. Why not make it just one big happy family album?

Religion scholar Stephen Prothero explains the problem. Yes, he says,

> it is comforting to pretend that the great religions make up one big, happy family. But this sentiment, however well-intentioned, is neither accurate nor ethically responsible. God is not one. Faith in the unity of religions is just that—faith (perhaps even a kind of fundamentalism). And the leap that gets us there is an act of the hyperactive imagination.[11]

Perhaps some believers assume that the piling on of revelations adds gravitas to monotheism. Holy people from the Jews to the Mormons keep hearing from God.

But of course it doesn't. For those of us who are outsiders, the question is inescapable: Why are all of these updated revelations necessary? God couldn't get it right the first time? It's not gravitas, it's clutter and aberration. These "updated revelations" come from the imaginations of theologians who keep spinning more and more tales about the "one true God." The Jews don't agree with what they find in the New Testament and correctly point out there are no predictions of Jesus in the Old Testament. The Christians don't agree with that they find in the Qu'ran (Jesus wasn't the son of God?) or with the *Book of Mormon* (Jesus visited North America after his resurrection?) With each iteration, the concept of God becomes more confused, and the way he interacts with humans is re-imagined.

Ironically, it is *honesty* that is missing in this tangle of monotheisms. Belief in the one true god is supposed to make us better people, with respect for the truth. Believers claim this moral high ground, but then settle for standards that don't meet the most basic honesty tests. It's neither honest nor intellectually respectable to stake the claim that *your* monotheism is true because you were born into it. Who can't see through this ploy and recognize its weakness?

Christians settle for "I'm used to it. It makes me feel good, it's my comfort zone, so, of course, it's true." Atheists cry foul. Jews and Muslims cry foul, as well, although they are victims of exactly the same faulty methodology. Every religious person who has ever lived has recited the same litany—"I was born into it (or found it), I'm used to it, it makes me feel good, it's my comfort zone, so it's true"—while failing to grasp that familiarity and feelings can't and don't deliver the goods. Which monotheism is true? Everyone is dead certain that their own one-true-god is the real thing, but they've not found convincing reasons for cancelling the revelations, visions, and meditations of those who have another god, also considered one and true.

One Great Fellowship of Love

The words "gentle Jesus meek and mild" are the opening line of a children's poem written by Charles Wesley in 1742, and this misunderstanding of the gospels contributed to the saccharine piety of the Victorian era a century later. This piety found expression in the common artistic theme of Jesus surrounded by children and holding a lamb.

In 1908, William Dunkerley wrote another poem that was as detached from reality as Wesley's lyric. It was one of the beloved hymns of my childhood:

In Christ there is no East or West,
   In Him no South or North;
   But one great fellowship of love
   Throughout the whole wide earth.

Correction: The history of the church is a chronicle of disagreements and hatreds. The Catholic-Protestant divide, marked by so many wars, persecutions and executions, is *Exhibit A* in the case against "one great fellowship of love." The body count—Christians killing Christians for Christ's sake—is incalculable, but the splintering can be measured.

By one reckoning at the turn of the century (the 2000 *World Christian Encyclopedia*), there were 33,820 Christian denominations. A couple of billion people raise their hands that they believe in Jesus, but then they fight and draw blood about what that means. Rodney King once lamented, "Can't we all get along?" but Christians don't seem to care about getting along even with each other. Even as Christianity was being born, Paul scolded his flock at Corinth, "Is Christ divided?" (1 Cor. 1:13). The resounding answer can now only be *Yes*, with most Christians adding *Yeah, so what?*

When did it all start, the infighting and scrapping over turf? Apparently before Jesus was even dead in his grave. We read about it in Mark 10:35-41 (RSV):

And James and John, the sons of Zebedee, came up to him and said to him, "Teacher, we want you to do for us whatever we ask of you."

And he said to them, "What do you want me to do for you?"

And they said to him, "Grant us to sit, one at your right hand and one at your left, in your glory."

Jesus said to them, "You do not know what you are asking. Are you able to drink the cup that I drink, or to be baptized with the baptism with which I am baptized?"

And they said to him, "We are able."

And Jesus said to them, "The cup that I drink you will drink, and with the baptism with which I am baptized, you will be baptized, but to sit at my right hand or at my left is not mine to grant, but it is for those for whom it has been prepared."

And when the ten heard it, *they began to be indignant at James and John.*

So much for the one great fellowship of love.

Not that any of this is history: Mark is a contrived theological tract. If nothing else, though, this episode is a glimpse of cult infighting. Here are two disciples jockeying for position, and Jesus was nonplussed, "You don't know what you are asking," which is actually one of the themes of Mark's gospel; the disciples, with Peter leading the pack, are a pretty dense lot. I'm not making this up. It would take you only a couple of hours (or less) to read Mark's gospel and find out for yourself.

After Jesus' death, the turf war intensified. It's in full view in the New Testament. Christians commonly sift through their scriptures looking for choice fragments of love and sunshine while missing the big picture. They don't notice the bad blood between the apostle Paul and the original crowd that surrounded Jesus. Paul was a zealous persecutor of the early church, so the deep distrust of him by Peter and others was understandable. Paul avoided contact with these folks, but when their paths did cross, sparks usually flew. Paul reports in Galatians 2:1 that, when he ran into Peter in Antioch, he "opposed him to his face" on the matter of Jews mixing with Gentiles.

Even after Paul's famous conversion, he made a point of not having much to do with the people who knew Jesus personally. He didn't return to Jerusalem for three years and spent only 15 days there "getting to know Peter." Then he stayed away for fourteen years. Paul's obsession, of course, was preaching about Christ–*his concept of* Christ derived from visions–to the Gentile world far from Palestine. He left a trail of new converts and new congregations behind him as he traveled the Mediterranean basin, but he couldn't control the infighting that seems to be in religion's DNA.

In his first letter to the church at Corinth, he shows annoyance that *his* version of Christianity is already slipping:

I appeal to you, brothers, by the name of our Lord Jesus Christ, that all of you agree, and that there be no divisions among you, but that you be united in the same mind and the same judgment. For it has been reported to me by Chloe's people that there is quarreling among you, my brothers. What I mean is that each one of you says, "I follow Paul," or "I follow Apollos," or

"I follow Cephas," or "I follow Christ." Is Christ divided? Was Paul crucified for you? (1 Cor. 1:10-13, ESV).

The severe splintering of Christianity found its precedent here, and since theology is based on imagination and speculation, it's no surprise that beliefs about Jesus galloped off in many directions. In the second century, alternative versions of the faith abounded, as Bart Ehrman has shown in his book, *Lost Christianities: The Battles for Scripture and the Faiths We Never Knew*.

The irony is that Christianity wasn't even supposed to exist at that point. Both Jesus and Paul predicted the arrival of the kingdom of God on earth; there would be no need for religions at all, with Jesus and God ruling the saved remnant of humans together. But as Christianity endured, partially by ignoring how wrong Jesus and Paul had been, nobody could agree on what Christianity was. As Philip Jenkins has pointed out, "In any theological struggle, the first thousand years are always the bitterest." A professor of history and religious studies at Penn State, Jenkins has made his mark as an historian of Christianity. I'm tempted to recommend one of his books, more than Dawkins or Hitchens, to jar people out of Christianity, although the faithful don't seem to care all that much about the incriminating history of Christian origins.

Jenkins tells the messy and barbaric story in *Jesus Wars: How Four Patriarchs, Three Queens, and Two Emperors Decided What Christians Would Believe for the Next 1,500 Years*. Those first thousand years were not pretty: "By 500 or so, the churches were in absolute doctrinal disarray, a state of chaos that might seem routine to a modern American denomination, but which in the context of the time seemed like satanic anarchy."[12] And by 600, the Christian world was "divided into several great transnational churches, each with its own claims to absolute truth. This was an ugly reality for those who idealized the church as the seamless, united body of Christ."[13]

You Pays Your Money and You Takes Your Choice

Christianity has had the capacity to morph into so many different shapes and deformities because people could find whatever they want in the Bible, and thus create a Christianity that suited their personalities, outlook on the world, and level of sanity. What kind of Christianity could *you* build on the following statement?

> Those who believe in Jesus–who are baptized "in Jesus"–"will cast out demons, they will speak in new tongues, they will pick up snakes with their hands, they will drink any deadly thing, it will not hurt them, they will lay their hands on the sick and they will recover."

This is a startling list. How many people in the pews these days would take it seriously? According to this text, if you're a Christian, you will be able to cast out demons, speak unintelligible languages, pick up snakes, drink poison, and heal people by touching them.

Who came up with this? It may come as a surprise to many people that these are the *words of Jesus*.[14] And not just Jesus, the *resurrected* Jesus. Isn't this ultimate authentication? Isn't this good enough for most Christians? But I suspect that most Christians, even evangelicals, are hesitant to embrace this agenda. If you go down that road, you end up in Appalachia with snake handlers getting killed by copperheads.

It may be some consolation, of course, that these verses are a fraud. They are in the forged ending of Mark, i.e., 16:9-20. These twelve verses are missing in the oldest manuscripts of Mark; someone tacked them on later (hence, many modern translations put them in a footnote). Person or persons unknown, who disliked the abrupt ending of Mark at verse 16:8 (it's bothered a lot of people) just made them up. But nut-case versions of Christianity have nonetheless flourished because these verses are "in the Bible."

Here's another example, and by almost any standard you want to use, this reflects a far better religion. What kind of Christianity can you build on these verses, also words attributed to Jesus (Matt. 5:38-42), found in the Sermon on the Mount?

> You have heard that it was said, "An eye for an eye, and a tooth for a tooth." But I say to you, do not resist an evil-doer. But if anyone strikes you on the right cheek, turn the other also; and if anyone wants to sue you and take your coat, give your cloak as well; and if anyone forces you to go one mile, go also the second mile. Give to everyone who begs from you, and do not refuse anyone who wants to borrow from you.

There is little doubt that this text strikes a higher moral tone; it has to do with treating others with decency and generosity. But even so, most Christians ignore—indeed, even ridicule—these verses as well:[15]

- Don't resist an evildoer? If someone hits you, let him hit you again.
- If someone sues you, give her more than she sues you for.
- If you're coerced to do something, just keep doing it.
- Never refuse to give money to a beggar or refuse someone who asks to borrow money.

These verses may be imbedded in the beloved (and overrated) Sermon on the Mount, but they are not imbedded in the hearts and habits of most Christians I know."Don't be ridiculous" would be the reaction of most of the faithful, until you spring the news on them that these are the words of Jesus. They don't take these words of advice any more seriously than the verses about drinking poison and handling snakes.

There are some Christians, however, who argue passionately that these Sermon on the Mount verses should actually be put into practice. Quakers try to embrace some of them, and build a kind of Christianity that the majority of those who claim to follow Jesus, in fact, reject. In the history of Christian thought, in the history of sweeping awkward and embarrassing Bible verses under the rug, we usually hear some version of, "Well, what Jesus *really* meant was . . ." and the contorted excuses pile on.

Which Package Did You Buy?

There's no escaping this reality: The two examples just given, from Mark and Matthew, illustrate that "believing in Jesus" can mean different things to different people, and they draw vastly different conclusions about God as a result. *Many different religions* function and thrive under the name of Christianity. It may be an exaggeration to suggest that the 33,820 denominations cited by the World *Christian Encyclopedia* are different religions, but clearly there have been enough disagreements to cause a lot of splintering.

As we have seen, the apostle Paul asked the Corinthians, "Is Christ divided?" He had no way of knowing that Christians would specialize in quarreling, often to the point of bloodshed, for many centuries to come. He had no way of knowing that Jesus was not coming back and that history was just going to keep rolling along, benignly neglected by heaven.

For two millennia, the divisions have multiplied, especially in the wake of the Protestant Reformation, when the Roman Catholic Church lost its grip. As Stephen Prothero has observed, "This new Christian liberty resulted–as Catholics predicted it would–not in unity but in near-anarchy, an endless splintering of Protestantism into a Babel of competing beliefs and practices."[16] So there are now 33,820 different Christian packages, each of which has moms and dads who want to make sure their kids buy the right package. If we were to pick out *any two* of the denominations and say, "Hey, why don't you folks just shake hands and bury the hatchet," we might hear some very unchristian snarling. *Christians don't mind not getting along.* Christ is divided. There are no rumors of minor or mass reconciliations.

For anyone who wishes passionately to defend Christianity from the assaults of atheists, it will first be necessary to defend the Christian package that *you* happened to buy, the package that your parents sold to you or that you bought after shopping around. There are so many thousands of options. Which one is the "right" Christianity? To make the case that *your* brand of Christianity, the package you bought (Catholic? Baptist? Quaker? Pentecostal? Greek Orthodox?) has cornered the truth: Now, *that's* a tough problem.

It would be so refreshing–sadly, too much to expect–if Christians in these 33,820 denominations would show some embarrassment about the failure to agree. Why don't they ask themselves and each other: Why can't we get along? Just as the jumble of ideas about God in Judaism, Christianity, Islam, and Mormonism is staggering proof that monotheism is a hopeless mess, so 33,820 denominations demonstrate that Christian is a hopeless mess as well.

Why aren't Christians ashamed of this? They seem to feel no incentive to work for and achieve reconciliation. Why don't they want to brush away the clutter and get to the bottom of it all? Shouldn't there be a way to find out what "true Christianity" is? Is it too much to ask that "being a Christian" should mean *just one thing*?

Why Not Go Back to Jesus and Get It Straight?

It is impossible to just go back to Jesus and leave it at that. *You can't get there from here.* Christians owe it to themselves to find out why this is so. As an atheist, I plead with Christians to pick up the New Testament and do some basic homework, and resist the temptation to turn back when serious brain-hurt sets in. Find a copy of the gospels with the words of Jesus printed in red, and plow through them slowly, thoughtfully, and critically. This is a daunting exercise, and very few Christians do it. They are satisfied with upbeat sunshiny verses that they hear from the pulpit: Blessed are the peacemakers, suffer the little children to come unto me, God so loved the world. These are the texts that show up in Christian coloring books and on stained glass windows.

Brain hurt sets in when Christians find that *they disagree* with so much of what Jesus supposedly said. If they didn't know that Jesus was the speaker, they would bluntly declare, "This can't be right"–or even, "What a lot of nonsense." Furthermore, a lot of the Jesus material is unclear, and too much of it can be categorized as cult craziness. The good verses are there, but they are overshadowed and overpowered by end-of-the-world-coming-soon creepiness. If you are skeptical that Jesus said creepy things, take a break right now to read Mark 13, which is rarely read from the pulpit except in those churches that embrace the creepiness. The careful reader will also discern that the Jesus of Mark's gospel doesn't sound anything like that Jesus of John's gospel. These are two different fictional characters. I have more to say about these problems later, but the point I want to stress here is that Christians don't have the option of deciding which denomination is the right one by harking back to Jesus to "get it right."

There are so many denominations because the teachings of Jesus and Paul are a jumble and are fertile ground for overactive theological imaginations. The New Testament documents themselves are a mess; they reflect the original failure to agree on who and what Jesus was. Each of the four gospel writers had his own theological biases and created a Jesus to suit those biases. Peter and Paul couldn't get along, the congregations that Paul founded couldn't get along, and the hope of having one true Christianity was lost forever.

Laughing Off the Scandal

Until you can agree on the right monotheism, until you can agree on the right Christianity, *please go away.* Don't show up in the marketplace of serious ideas and expect to be treated with respect. Sam Harris's comment that theology can now be regarded as a branch of human ignorance may seem too cynical for some; does it cross the line into ridicule? Well, yes it does, but Christians themselves have often indulged in self–ridicule to deflect attention from the scandal of so much quarrelling and disagreement about Jesus.

Humor defuses criticism, and anyone who knows anything about Protestantism gets a chuckle from the observation that "a Baptist is a Christian who has learned to wash; a Methodist is a Baptist who has learned to read; a Presbyterian is a Methodist who has gone to college; and an Episcopalian is a Presbyterian whose investments have turned out well."[17] This deflects attention from long-standing theological orneriness.

In the days when people travelled on horseback, it is said that a Baptist preacher once encountered a Methodist preacher on a path in the woods."Sir," the Baptist demanded sternly, "is it true that you believe in infant baptism?"

To which the Methodist responded confidently, *"Believe* in it? Man, I've *seen* it." And a heated dispute ensued.

In the long run, smart folks see through the silliness of imagining Jesus the Baptist way, or the Methodist way—or the thousands of other ways that thousands of denominations claim.

How is it that God is so misunderstood? Ideas about God proliferate, flourish, and then collide because ideas don't have to be grounded in anything other than fertile human imagination. Let me repeat: There are *no data* about God. None, zero, zip. Period. Hence "Which monotheism?" is an unanswerable question, as is "Which Christianity?" The only people who feel that they have secured the right answer are those who are willing to be fooled. When that happens, the theology approach to reality appears victorious because it evades reality. But "god" fails as a defensible concept.

Again, God loses.

Notes

1. Some people do indeed switch religions, but those who stay put remain uncritical. And even those who flee to other faiths commonly fail to kick the tires. What would be the compelling *evidence* to switch from Methodism to Catholicism, for example?

2. Guy P. Harrison, *50 Popular Beliefs that People Think Are True*, pp. 248-249.

3. Ibid., p. 251-252.

4. Adam Houge, *The 7 Most Powerful Prayers that Will Change Your Life Forever!* (Living Tree Publishing, 2014), Kindle loc. 43.

5. Squire Rushnell, *When God Winks at You: How God Speaks Directly to You Through the Power of Coincidence* (Thomas Nelson, 2006), p. 3.

6. Rushnell at pp. 60-63.

7. blog.caranddriver.com/takata-airbag-recall-10th-death-reported-more-recalls-expected, accessed 24 Jan 2016.

8. Ibid., p. 163.

9. John Loftus, *The Outsider Test for Faith: How to Know Which Religion Is True* (Prometheus Books, 2013), p. 23.

10. Loftus at p. 41.

11. Stephen Prothero, *God Is Not One: The Eight Rival Religions that Run the World* (HarperOne, 2011), p. 3

12. Philip Jenkins, *Jesus Wars: How Four Patriarchs, Three Queens, and Two Emperors Decided What Christians Would Believe for the Next 1,500 Years* (HarperOne, 2011), p. 242.

13. Jenkins at p. 231.

14. My paraphrased translation of Mark 16:17-18.

15. For more on this, see Tough Problem IX.

16. Stephen Prothero, *American Jesus: How the Son of God Became a National Icon* (Farrar, Straus and Giroux, 2004), p. 169

17. James B. Twitchell, *Shopping for God: How Christianity Went from in Your Heart to In Your Face* (Simon & Schuster, 2007), p. 31.

VI

The Gospels Fail as History

> All the tales of miracles, with which the Old and New Testament are filled, are fit only for impostors to preach and fools to believe.
>
> —Thomas Paine

> The earliest evangelist was not writing a historical biography, as many interpreters suppose, but a novel, a prose anti-epic of sorts.
>
> —Dennis R. MacDonald, *The Homeric Epics and the Gospel of Mark*

The Passion of Jesus

How Not to Do History

ONE OF THE STRANGEST DETOURS that piety can take is the erotic, and there has probably been no greater taboo historically than the eroticizing of Jesus. Yet the marketing of Jesus these days is big business, and savvy peddlers know that they need to kick it up a notch. While the traditional depictions of Jesus holding a lamb may still have appeal, it would seem that sex appeal as a tool is not lost on the hucksters. Hence some modern portraits present Jesus as if he were a soap opera idol or model for the cover of a Harlequin romance novel. It's a bit jarring to see a hunky Jesus with his hair properly moussed.

Craving the body of the Lord beyond the wafer on Sunday morning, it seems, would be the ultimate forbidden lust. Talk about sacrilege! Perhaps there are precedents. In 1652, Bernini completed his masterpiece *The Ecstasy of St. Teresa* for the Cornaro Chapel, the Santa Maria della Vittoria in Rome. This stunningly graceful sculpture honors St. Theresa of Avila, known for intense contemplative prayer, during which she lost herself in her adoration of Jesus. In Bernini's interpretation she swoons, head back, eyes closed, betraying perhaps a bit too much rapture. She looks for all the world like she's having an orgasm. For some this has been off-putting, as much as the full-frontal depictions of Adam and David *sans* fig leaf.

While a saint having an orgasm is bad enough, what about Jesus? Would this really be such a shock if Jesus were a *bona fide* human being? To avoid the ancient heresy of *Docetism*, whose advocates considered Jesus so totally divine that was an apparition only seeming to be human, Christian orthodoxy has maintained that Jesus was fully human, a real person who lived and breathed in first-century Palestine.

So did God cancel his sexuality when he made Jesus? Christians would rather stare at the sun than think about a sexually active Jesus. No, this just won't do. Anthony Pinn, in his escape-from-faith story, explains the mandatory neutering of the Galilean preacher:

> Jesus, the savior of the world, had a penis (typically not depicted in the images), but his sexual ethic—what he did with that penis, who received pleasure by means of it, and how Jesus received pleasure as a result of it— was never spoken of. To even think of Jesus having sex with men or women

was construed as sinful because it meant reducing the God/man to a human controlled by a sex organ. Doing so was to point away from the ministry of the Christ and instead to replace his saving work with the yearnings of a physical body.[1]

Such built-in biases have a big impact. It's tough to penetrate piety, the cherished and chaste views of Jesus, to achieve a grasp of *who Jesus really was.*

The great French Jesus scholar Charles Guignebert wrote in 1935, "It was not the essence of Jesus that interested the authors of the Gospels, it was the essence of Christ, as their faith pictured him. They were exclusively interested, not in reporting what they know, but in proving what they believe."[2]

The author of John's gospel is candid about having such narrow interests. Jesus did lots of things not written about, he says, but what's written is there so his readers "may come to believe that Jesus is the Messiah, the Son of God, and that through believing you may have life in his name" (John 20:30-31). This is the agenda of a theologian, not a historian. When John assures his readers that "Jesus did many other signs in the presence of his disciples," he sounds a little forced. We suspect that he faced a shortage of actual sources—not that he even cared.

The authors of the gospels wrote a highly idealized Jesus to promote him as the son of God, and they bent history (if there is any at all preserved in their writings) to advance their cause. Ironically, though, their ideal may not always be *our* ideal. Texts that embarrass modern Christians seemingly didn't bother the gospel writers.[3] What we can only regard as flaws remain in full view.[4] Modern readers avert their eyes from these negatives and invent ingenious excuses. They don't want their wonderful Jesus to be tainted or reduced to the least degree.

Accordingly, Christians have taken for granted, based on the gospels accounts, that Jesus never approached the marital bed. So, he of all people, since he was moral and holy, remained pure. No erections for Jesus. Well, erections are involuntary, but you know what I mean.

Is it true that Jesus never married? Again we see how hard it is to tease history from the gospels: They provide no hint whatever about Jesus' marital status, let alone his sexuality. Many observers have pointed out that it would have been rare for a man of his era and culture *not* to have been married, but that's inference, not information.

So are the suggestions that Jesus might have been gay. Based on what? Well, one famous text, John 13:23, has raised eyebrows: "Now there was leaning on Jesus' bosom one of his disciples, whom Jesus loved." That's from the *King James Version,* but the *New International Version,* produced by the conservative Zondervan publishers, removes any hint of intimacy that some modern readers might find jarring, saying "the disciple whom Jesus loved was reclining next to him." Get that man off Jesus' bosom!

If this text hints that Jesus had a male lover (as some gay activists have inferred, going beyond what is stated in the text), why does this show up first in this latest of the gospels? There's no hint of it in Matthew, Mark, or Luke, who fail to mention a beloved disciple at all. The Jesus-was-gay advocates also point out that he chose to hang out with twelve men, but that was hardly unusual in a highly misogynistic culture. And the gospels do report that his circle of followers included women.

The gospels writers had a theological agenda to fulfill. They showed no interest in what Jesus did for sex, which may have been nothing at all. This is often the case with religious fanatics, except those of the Joseph Smith variety. We can make all sorts of guesses, but we have no information at all on Jesus' marital status and sexuality.

History or Invention?

Earlier we considered the reasons why the Bible cannot be considered revelation. There is no such thing as the Word of God delivered in book form. But can't the gospels at least stand on their own as accounts of the life and teachings of Jesus? Weren't they written by people on the scene who recorded what happened?

For many centuries that was just taken for granted. Then, about 200 years ago, serious research on the gospels got under way. Although most of the researchers have been devout Christians and Jews, the general consensus of New Testament scholarship now—outside of lockstep fundamentalist circles—is that the gospels cannot, after all, be considered reliable *historical* documents. There may be authentic remembrances of Jesus captured here and there, but the fictional and fantasy elements virtually smother the history. So, how in the world are we supposed to separate the wheat from the chaff? Which stories are authentic, and which are make-believe? Did Jesus even *exist*? (We'll discuss that shortly.)

Christianity turns out to be not as securely anchored to historical events as had once been assumed. Most of the stories of Jesus (even if we concede that he did exist) may very well have been made up to match Old Testament patterns. A good brief introduction to this topic is the 1988 book by Randel Helms, *Gospel Fictions*. Some conservative scholars have resisted this conclusion, but most New Testament scholars acknowledge that retrieving history from the gospels is very problematic. This turns out to be one of the toughest problems that Christianity faces.

The New Testament Scholar's Lament
No Idea Where it Came From

Some New Testament scholars devote their careers to comparing ancient gospel manuscripts (thousands of them) to eliminate errors (thousands of those as well) to figure out the exact wording of the very first documents (the "autographs"), as they were worded at the minute the authors blew on the ink to get it dry. For those who care about the New Testament, who cherish the thought of attaining the correct original versions, that seems a worthwhile pursuit.

It has nothing to do, however, with a much more profound issue: Are the gospels accurate in their portrayal of Jesus? Is the *content* reliable? Are they history, or something else? Unfortunately the gospels do not measure up to their reputation for "telling it like it was." The story of Jesus seemed solid for centuries, recorded in four gospels that everyone knows (plus many others that were left out of the canon), hefty documents chock full of information about Jesus—or so everyone thought. They were the bulwark of Christian thought for all these centuries, backed by their stature as the

Very Word of God. Out of respect, many congregations stand when verses from the gospels are read aloud in church.

In the wake of the Enlightenment, however, curious thinkers took up the challenge of examining the gospels as historians would, not as the theologians and preachers do. That's when things began to fall apart, because it became clear that sources were unknown.

It's commonly assumed that Jesus died about 30 C.E., so we would dearly like to know how soon after his death the gospels were written. How how many decades after Jesus' death were they written? Sources and dating are of primary concern in analysis of the gospels. After all, we want to find out *what really happened*–not what theologians fondly wish had happened, and have a vested interest in insisting happened. The tools and protocols of historians must be used.

A Divine Abraham Lincoln

To grasp what we're up against, let's consider a scenario about a person closer in time to our own era. Abraham Lincoln was murdered in 1865, and he is one of the most written-about figures in human history. What if you were trying to write the story of Lincoln *for the first time* 40 years later, in 1905. I chose 40 years because that is generally the estimate that scholars give for the creation of Mark, the first gospel, after Jesus' death.

Here's my interview with the guy who wants to write the Lincoln story in 1905:

Lincoln Enthusiast: It's about time that we got this inspiring story down on paper.

David Madison: Great idea. I guess that's going to be a lot of work. There must be hundreds of letters to go through.

LE: Letters? Gee, I don't know of any letters that Lincoln wrote.

DM: Really? Did he keep a diary? Or write any articles, books, essays? Those will be crucial.

LE: You got me there. I don't know of any.

DM: You'll have to spend a lot of time in newspaper archives, to find all of the articles published about Lincoln.

LE: Gosh, I never heard of any newspapers stories.

DM: Then you'll probably have to work hard to track down eyewitnesses. Especially after you've written your Lincoln book, you'll want to check the facts with people who knew him.

LE: Well, that won't happen. They're all dead by now.

DM: Gee, it sounds to me like you've got a real problem here. How are you going to write this book? What are your sources?

LE: Not a problem, I've got loads of stories that have been handed down since 1865. His followers are great storytellers.

DM: *Handed down*? You mean by word of mouth? But how reliable is that? Each time a story is retold, details drop out, other are added–basically things are made up.

LE: Oh, I don't think there's much danger of that. All these people who handed down the stories were inspired by God to get it right.

DM: Come again? How would you know that? That would be hard to verify. What would give these people such extraordinary powers?

LE: Because they *believe* in Lincoln. I'm writing this story because we know that Lincoln was divine, our lord and savior. He was the Son of God, after all. And I'm sure we're going to get the story right. I want to convince people that they should worship Lincoln too.

DM: But, maybe, if they're sure Lincoln was divine, that might have influenced how they remembered what he said and did. They might have exaggerated and embellished.

LE: But God would not have let that happened. God is all about truth. Everything you'll read in my Lincoln book will be trustworthy. I'll make sure of that myself.

DM: Check. Sounds like a plan.

It's a very poor plan, with predictable, lamentable results. In no other area of life would we accept this method, certainly not when it comes to nailing down what actually happened in the ancient or even recent past.

I'm not really being unfair in suggesting that there is a parallel between how the gospels were written and how that Lincoln enthusiast plans to write his story. Not only is the methodology deficient and defective, but the motivation should make us skeptical. Many New Testament scholars, especially evangelicals, would deny that my Lincoln scenario is accurate with respect to the lack of eyewitnesses. They are confident that the gospels derive from eyewitness, people who knew, saw and heard Jesus. But there is *no evidence* for this fond hope, and it is a very thin reed indeed to lean upon.[5]

Every verse and chapter you cover in a careful reading of the Jesus story in the gospels floats free of any grounding. History, as opposed to folklore and novels, cannot be written without contemporary documentation. Historians rely on letters, diaries, inscriptions, newspaper accounts, articles, and testimonies written as closely as possible to the events described–and even those must be evaluated critically. In the case of Jesus, we have absolutely *no* such sources. Without at least a few of these missing items to make the case that the gospels are *bona fide* accounts of the real Jesus, the gospels-are-history crowd is left with nothing.

Decades of Study, Overkill, and Some Consensus

In the 200 years since Bible study based on critical analysis rather than piety got under way, thousands of historically trained scholars–most of them devout Christians and Jews–have pored over the New Testament texts in excruciating detail. There are now countless books, articles, doctoral dissertations, and journals devoted to understanding and explaining every word, verse, and chapter. This colossal scholarly endeavor has been accomplished in academic seclusion, largely out of the view of ordinary lay people. At least one biblical scholar, Hector Avalos, has suggested, "Enough already."[6]

So much study, going on decade after decade, seems like overkill. Is the Bible really worth it? Here's the delicious irony: The intense analysis by religious scholars has confirmed that hunch. If most of the faithful could grasp the result of all this study, most of them would probably say "enough already" as well. The Bible has been de-glamorized, demoted from its holy pedestal.

What the Bible study industry has produced is consensus among scholars about some basic New Testament facts. It is agreed, with very little dissent, that Mark was the first gospel to be written, and that great chunks of it were later copied and modified by Matthew and Luke. Dating these documents has been notoriously difficult, but most scholars feel that Mark 13–a dreadful piece of scripture if ever there was one–reflects the destruction of Jerusalem and the Temple by the Roman army under Titus in the year 70 C.E. Hence the dating of Mark about 40 years after the death of Jesus. Maybe the author of Mark gathered early fragments of the Jesus story to include in his gospel, maybe not. Again we hit that brick wall: his sources are unknown. Without contemporary documentation, it's all guesswork. Which part is history, which is folklore, which is just unrestrained theological fantasy?

Wouldn't it be nice if gospels came with the same sort of documentation that works of art do? Art dealers and curators want to know the provenance of any painting or piece of sculpture, to be able to prove it's not a fake. They want to see the paper trail, the records of ownership since it left the artist's hand. That is precisely what we *don't* have with a gospel.

So the educated guess about Mark's date, made by people who have studied it the most, is about 70 C.E., with some scholars landing on slightly earlier or later dates. Matthew and Luke were produced maybe a decade or two later, with John being composed toward the end of the first century. It might have been even later than that, as is the view of Dr. Robert M. Price.

Most New Testament scholars are comfortable with this range of dates. I have heard some atheist skeptics claim that the gospels were written "hundreds of years" after Jesus, but that cannot be the case.[7] We can confirm that all four gospels were known by the end of the second century for sure, since they are mentioned by other writers, e.g., the Church Father Irenaeus about 180 C.E. and in the list known as the Muratorian Canon, about 190 C.E.

Wasting Red Ink
The Words of Jesus Are Gone for Good

That the gospels were written decades after the death of Jesus should be alarming to Jesus devotees. It's an awfully long delay if you're trying to get the facts straight, if you want to end up with history instead of hearsay. Think about it: If you go to a family reunion, concert, sports event, and want to get an accurate report about it down on paper, "I'll wait forty years to write it down" would be considered a feeble approach. It fails the test of *contemporary documentation*. Most of the faithful, of course, give no thought to this test. The gospels are like comfortable old slippers, and they're quite happy to take them as they are. It's no surprise that ecclesiastical authorities, the priests and bureaucrats in charge of keeping the Jesus brand going, have about as much use for Bible scholars as laypeople do. They encourage the old-slipper thinking. Church bosses want seminaries to turn out preachers who will proclaim The Word, not nitpick the gospels.

Laypeople seem to have an uncanny level of trust that they're dealing with the real thing when they pick up their Bibles. One pastor who was interviewed by Daniel Dennett and Linda LaScola for their book *Caught in the Pulpit*–about clergy who have become atheists–reported her encounter with one Bible-toting parishioner:

> When I got to my church where I had to preach every week, it was hell on wheels very quickly . . . I was really stunned and shocked when a woman said to me, "I know what Jesus said in the Bible, because it's written in red." I remember just kind of sitting there, thinking, "Oh my God, what am I doing here?"[8]

It's well nigh impossible that the gospels got the words of Jesus right. *There may be no real words of Jesus at all.* The obstacles to taking the "words of Jesus" seriously, that they are authentic (and thus warrant red ink), are considerable.[9] Here are some of them.

#1: No Motivation

One of the reasons that the gospels were so late in appearing, perhaps 40 to 60 years after Jesus died, is that the early Christians *had no motivation* for writing things down. If the general thrust of Jesus' reported message can be trusted, he was sure that the Kingdom of God was going to be lowered from heaven in the very near future. The early Christian cult was expecting Jesus to return to bring history and Roman oppression to an end. The rule of Satan would be over, no one would ever die, history would flatline. There would be no posterity to record memories for. Archives and libraries, biographies, and reminiscences would be unnecessary.

John Loftus is surely correct in calling Jesus a "failed apocalyptic prophet," and the apostle Paul was a primary champion of the macabre theology about the general massacre of humanity at the end of the world. Only when the failure of this prophecy became painfully obvious–Jesus didn't come back, though some Christians are pathetically still watching the skies–was the need felt for "memories" of Jesus to be preserved. But had most memories evaporated by that time? The destruction of Jerusalem in 70 C.E. meant that the original Jesus followers, if there were any, were killed or scattered. The apostle Paul, of course, had run around the Mediterranean basin for a couple of decades preaching about the risen Christ, but he neglected to say anything about the life of Jesus. Hence his letters contain no memories, let alone quotations, of Jesus. Paul simply wasn't interested.

By the time Jerusalem had been laid waste in 70 C.E., there were Christians far afield, in Damascus, Antioch, Greece, and even Rome, but we have no way of knowing if *authentic* memories of Jesus travelled with those who were scattered. Even if this was the case, how did the memories of Jesus diverge and become garbled as Christians scattered, time passed, and the stories were told to new converts? How could the stories *not* have been altered with each retelling?

It is unlikely that letters flew back and forth comparing notes on who recalled what about Jesus and his message, as it is also exceedingly unlikely that there were designated fact checkers. How many of these Diaspora Christians had even been eyewitnesses? Historically trained scholars know we're on very thin ice here. There has been some speculation that the gospel of Mark was written in Rome. If so, any confidence about Mark "getting it right" sinks even further. We aren't surprised that Mark contains so much blatant fantasy.

#2: Literacy Limitations

Even if Christians did see value in preserving memories of Jesus, despite the imminent end of the world, how would that have been accomplished? We're seeking that rare thing from the ancient world, documents *written at the time* to verify the real words of Jesus. It is the fond hope of evangelical scholars that written records of Jesus' teaching occurred almost on the spot, but we have little confidence that this happened. The illiteracy rate in first century Palestine was perhaps 95 percent, and Jesus preached to the common people. It is possible that even the disciples themselves were illiterate. Writing materials were very expensive, out of reach for most of the peasantry that followed Jesus around—if indeed that happened (there are no records whatever outside the gospels of massive crowds following Jesus). This was long before an era when people could carry around pads of paper and pencils. We have no clue when people began to write down the supposed words of Jesus.

So, were the words of Jesus just remembered and passed along orally? It's sometimes claimed by conservative scholars that this was an era when oral traditions could be very accurate, but, again, we would need *evidence* to demonstrate that this was the case for the words of Jesus. Perhaps oral traditions could be accurate if ethnic folklore is being handed down, or epic poems. But the words of a wandering preacher? Did people really listen more attentively then than they do now? Could they have gone home after hearing Jesus and accurately have recorded, word for word, what he had said? And then recall those exact words of Jesus a day or a week later, and be certain that any people they reported them to would have gotten them right—totally right? This is what we would have to count on for those red-letter words of Jesus in modern Bibles to be warranted.

It is very hard to get the spoken word transcribed correctly. Robert Ingersoll, a major champion of secularism in the 19th century, spoke widely in the U.S. following the Civil War. Newspaper reporters followed him around scribbling his words to print on their front pages. He was a sensation, an atheist with a bracing message for Americans. But they made mistakes and misreported his words, so badly in fact, that the Robert Ingersoll estate felt compelled to publish a multi-volume edition of his addresses to set the record straight. When professional reporters get things wrong, we have a right to be suspicious that the words of Jesus were recorded accurately in written form—whenever that might have taken place.

Then there's the matter of who heard what, if there were large crowds and no means of amplification. Consider a modern example: President Calvin Coolidge was known as Silent Cal, famously a man of few words. One Sunday, so the story goes, he came home from church and his wife asked him, "What did the preacher talk about?"

He replied, "Sin."

"Well, what did he say about it?"

"He's against it."

Sure, Cal got the gist of the sermon, but could he have repeated with dead accuracy even two or three sentences of the preacher's sermon? Chances are, if a few members of the congregation had been asked to repeat verbatim, accurately, those few sentences, none of them would've been able to do so, and none of the versions would be exactly in accord. Is it possible, *really*, that we have the real words of Jesus?

#3: Anonymous Authors

The titles of the gospels give them an aura of authenticity, and most folks might assume that Matthew, Mark, Luke, and John were standing right there beside Jesus. But the gospels are anonymous works. We don't find the authors' names in any of them, nor do the writers even position themselves as participants or eyewitnesses.[10] There is no surprise here, since the gospels were written in Greek, which was not the native tongue of most of the earliest followers of Jesus. (He spoke Aramaic.) The traditional gospel titles were assigned to them in the second century, and we have no idea—no *contemporary documentation*—to help us understand when, how, and why copyists somewhere along the way came up with the names, Matthew, Mark, Luke, and John.

This has not stopped conservative scholars from leaping to conclusions. At the close of Paul's letter to Philemon (1:24), he includes the name *Luke* in his list of colleagues. In two other epistles, a Luke is also mentioned: In Colossians 4:14 he is referred to as "the beloved physician," and he is mentioned as well in 2 Timothy 4:11. It is not relevant to my argument here that scholars doubt that Colossians and 2 Timothy were written by Paul (i.e., they are probably forgeries). But since the name is *there*—and golly, since the traditional name of the gospel is Luke—that must be our man!

But that's just grasping at straws, because—need I say it again?—there is no *evidence* to underwrite this claim. There is no Luke mentioned in the gospel itself, and Luke was not one of the twelve disciples. Furthermore, it would be a true curiosity that a colleague of Paul had such a treasury of information about Jesus, but this information *never shows up in Paul's letters*.

Landing on *this* Luke as the gospel writer is a guess, a *wildly improbable* guess. That doesn't stop the true believers from claiming certainty to which they are not entitled. Here's evangelical scholar Ben Witherington being happy to resort to guesses and assumptions, trying to bolster the credibility of the gospel. He caters to the ignorance of the people in the pews in an inexcusable breach of sound scholarship:

> If the information we have in Luke 1-2 reflects an authentic recounting of what happened at the beginning of the Jesus story, it could ultimately have come only from Mary herself (or perhaps Joseph). So what should we make of these chapters? I have suggested elsewhere that Luke was privy to this material because he spent two years in the Holy Land in the late 50s while Paul was under house arrest in Caesarea Maritima, during which time Luke surely must have gone to Jerusalem and interviewed many persons, which may well have included Mary.[11]

New Testament Scholars who are not bound by piety to defend everything in scripture conceded long ago that the birth narratives in Luke and Matthew are fiction. These stories have been studied, analyzed, and parsed endlessly and exhaustively. They turn out to be religious fantasy literature, pure and simple. They can be assigned to the genre known as *hagiography*: stories that idealize and idolize. They bristle with inaccuracies, contradictions, and improbabilities, and are not worth defending as historical narratives. In trying to figure out the life of Jesus, scholars leave them out of the equation completely, abandoning them to thrive in church pageants.

Yet here is Witherington, in a stunningly inept ploy, suggesting that Luke 1-2 is based on interviews with Mary, conducted by Paul's colleague Luke who had gone to Jerusalem for two years. There is no evidence *whatsoever* for any of this."Luke must certainly have gone to Jerusalem" is utter rubbish. Witherington should know better. He is functioning here as a novelist, not as an historian. It's deplorable deception to pass this off as scholarship, yet it's given approving nods by his niche market of credulous evangelicals.

This is the kind of thing that happens when people cling to the pious tradition that Matthew, Mark, Luke, and John were the actual authors, instead of names that bubbled up out of early Christian imagination. It is troubling that *honesty* is a virtue that conservative Christian scholars sometimes fail to achieve.

Jesus Didn't Even Exist

The New Gang of Mythicist Rebels

What are we up against as we try to figure out what really happened in first century Palestine? We're swimming upstream against a strong current of faith bias. Ben Witherington dedicated his massive, 400-page 2004 commentary on Paul's Letter to the Romans to "Dr. A.W. Gwinn, a very present help in difficult times, and a very able expositor of the Good News which Paul brokered for Gentiles like us." This is Ben's true confession that he is a member of the Paul cult that became Christianity. His love for the Letter to the Romans, a toxic brew of bad theology,[12] is the dead giveaway.

Without going to Witherington's extreme, it is indeed the case that most of the world's experts on the New Testament are people of faith who were motivated to study the Bible, at the graduate level no less, because they believe in Jesus. Some, I would guess a small minority, end up losing their faith as a result of their study. For me faith evaporated completely. While others do not undergo this extreme metamorphosis, they do find that their faith moderates–they can no longer "accept Jesus" as they once did–because they understand that the real Jesus is not as accessible as they had assumed. The red-letter words of Jesus have to be rubbed out, and one of Witherington's titles probably resonates with scholars whose faith has been compromised by study: *What Have They Done with Jesus?*[13]

Now, it *is* possible to hold on to Jesus, even as scholarship has undercut a literal reading of so many texts and stories. But just how far are you allowed to go before you end up with a minimalist, threadbare Jesus?

As I pointed out in the Prologue, my mother–no fundamentalist, but no flaming liberal either–could say of some Bible stories, e.g., the Genesis creation accounts, "Well, it didn't really happen like that. You can't take that literally." This has become the mantra of liberal Christian scholarship about so much of the Bible. Did Jesus *literally* ascend to heaven? "Well, you can't take that literally; it's a metaphor for Jesus' close relationship with God." Did Jesus *really* turn water into wine? "Well, you can't take that literally; it's a symbol of Jesus' power to transform your life." Did Jesus really transfer demons into a herd of pigs that then ran off a cliff into the sea? "Well, that's meant to capture the truth that Jesus conquers evil."

Soon the scales begin to tip: Fiction outweighs almost everything else. What does that tell you about the accounts of Jesus? Astute believers who know that so many of the Bible stories are hard to swallow–and who don't care for the creepy advice that they just have to believe hard enough–may find some of this theological sleight of hand convincing, if they're in the mood to be coddled and hoodwinked.

But please notice what's happening: The historical part of the Jesus story is eroding. Great chunks of the elegant old façade have crumbled."Well, you can't take that literally" is a coy way of saying that *the story didn't happen.* It was just made up by someone.

Enter The Mythicists. The people-of-faith New Testament scholars, those who cling to Jesus, even if only by a thread, now face a phalanx of scholars who argue that the *whole story* of Jesus could be fiction; Jesus, they say, may belong to the rich tradition of mythical divine beings worshipped in the ancient world. These new rebel scholars have been dubbed The Mythicists.

When I worked on my Ph.D. in Biblical studies in the 1970s, we freely accepted that the gospels were fair game for critical analysis. We knew that they are flawed and often ineptly written, but no one at Boston University seriously suggested that *there was nothing there*, that Jesus was a myth. That idea was nowhere on our horizon.[14]

Another Force of Nature

I've suggested that ex-pastor John Loftus ranks as a *force of nature* against Christianity. He is a Christian escapee who has, in several books, amassed the data and the arguments that demonstrate beyond reasonable doubt that Christianity has been falsified. Hence, with a nod at the title of this book, I said earlier that Loftus is an eleventh Tough Problem. But he has to share the status of force of nature against Christianity with the amazing scholar Richard Carrier, who is a specialist on the

Greek and Roman literature of antiquity. The time may come when scholars of religion will write the history of Christianity's demise, and I suspect that Carrier will get high ranking for demonstrating in such sweeping and detailed fashion the errors upon which it is based, and the bankrupt strategies of its apologists.

It seems to me that Carrier blindsided the world of Christian academia. He is a New Testament scholar who did not come up through their ranks, and his command of the field is staggering. You can almost hear the old-school scholars inhaling in alarm, "Who is this guy?" Because of his PhD from Columbia University in ancient literature and his demonstrated powers of scholarship, Carrier was recruited and funded by private individuals to undertake a major study of the historical Jesus.

It was becoming increasingly clear that Christian academicians have made a royal mess of Jesus studies. They have studied and studied and studied the gospels *ad nauseam*, yet no consensus has been achieved about who and what Jesus was. The Quest for the Historical Jesus has gone on for generations and come up empty–or rather come up with a lot of *real Jesuses*. It's one of the major scandals in New Testament studies.

Hence there were those who felt that maybe another stab at it should be entrusted to a scholar who doesn't have any level of faith commitment to Jesus–*whatever*. Carrier states the case in the opening of *Proving History*:

> I have always assumed without worry that Jesus was just a guy, another merely human founder of an entirely natural religion (whatever embellishments to his cult and story may have followed). I'd be content if I were merely reassured of that fact. For the evidence, even at its best, supports no more startling conclusion. So, I have no vested interest in proving that Jesus did not exist. It makes no difference to me if he did. I suspect he might not have, but then that's a question that requires a rigorous and thorough examination of the evidence before it can be confidently declared. Believers, by contract, and their apologists in the scholarly community, cannot say the same. For them, if Jesus didn't exist, then their entire worldview topples. The things they believe in (and *need* to believe in) more than anything else in the world will then be under dire threat. It would be hard to expect them ever to overcome this bias, which makes bias a greater problem for them than for me. They *need* Jesus to be real; but I don't need Jesus to be a myth.[15]

A good introduction to Carrier's thinking is a short volume (82 pages), *Why I Am Not a Christian* (2011). In 2005 he published a major work that helped establish his reputation as a philosopher and scholar, *Sense and Goodness Without God: A Defense of Metaphysical Naturalism*.

Carrier's major works on Christianity and Jesus studies include *Not the Impossible Faith: Why Christianity Didn't Need a Miracle to Succeed* (2009), *Proving History: Bayer's Theorem and the Quest for the Historical Jesus* (2012), and *On the Historicity of Jesus: Why We Might Have Reason for Doubt* (2014). He also has an ongoing presence via his blogs and YouTube.

As I've said before, the folks in the pews usually shrug their shoulders–when and if they do hear about such books–and say *so what?* They have no clue that there are problems with the Jesus gospel stories, so they can remain aloof from the scholarly scuffling and believe what they want to believe.

Serious-minded believers, however, who don't want to have the wool pulled over their eyes, laypeople and clergy alike, *should* want to find out what serious Jesus research has come up with. There is a rising chorus of dissent to the easy assumptions that have so long prevailed. Other Mythicist scholars include:

- Thomas L. Brodie, *Beyond the Quest for the Historical Jesus: Memoir of a Discovery* (2012).

- Earl Doherty, *Jesus: Neither God Nor Man - The Case for a Mythical Jesus* (2009).

- David Fitzgerald, *Nailed: Ten Christian Myths That Show that Jesus Never Existed at All* (2010).

- Robert Price, *Deconstructing Jesus* (2000), *The Incredible Shrinking Son of Man* (2003), *Jesus Is Dead* (2007), and *The Christ-Myth Theory and Its Problems* (2012).

- Thomas L. Thompson, *The Messiah Myth: The Near Eastern Roots of Jesus and David* (2005).

Bart Ehrman, one of the top Jesus scholars of our time, has his heels dug in against Mythicism. Nonetheless, he's written several books on Jesus that pose a major threat to Christian belief. His large body of work leaves Jesus heavily damaged. Ehrman entered the fray to defend the historicity of Jesus with *Did Jesus Exist? The Historical Argument for Jesus of Nazareth*. This volume provoked a sharp response from Carrier and others, e.g., Price and Fitzgerald, but also Earl Doherty, Frank Zindler, René Salm, and D.M. Murdock. They shot back with *Bart Ehrman and the Quest for the Historical Jesus: An Evaluation of Ehrman's Did Jesus Exist?* (2013). It's a harsh critique, but most Bible scholars remain in the Ehrman camp.

These skeptical scholars make a compelling case (the information provided by Carrier is staggering), urging people who are seriously interested in the Jesus problem to consider *probabilities*. In terms of the historicity of Jesus, their work has moved the needle significantly toward the "improbable" end of the spectrum.

Wary Christians owe it to themselves to find out why the Mythicists say what they do. I will mention here only three major points that they advance, these three highlighted by Price:

1. There is no evidence for Jesus–no *verifiable contemporary documentation*–outside the faith-generated and heavily faith-biased gospels, which were written decades after Jesus supposedly lived.[16] Jesus just isn't *there* at the place and time that the gospels suggest.

2. In the earliest of the New Testament documents, penned long before the gospels, Jesus is missing in action.[17] That is, the epistles by Paul and

others don't speak at all about Jesus of Nazareth (their focus is a divine Christ). There seems to be no awareness of Jesus' preaching and parables, his miracles, his disputes with religious authorities, or even the Passion narratives. It's almost as if the real Jesus hadn't been invented yet, which would not happen until the gospels had been created. The focus of the epistles, with Paul being the giant presence, is salvation through believing in a resurrected Jesus. Inexplicably, they skip over everything else.

3. While the gospel writers prove to be adequate novelists, the basic framework of the Jesus story was not theirs. It is *not* unique. In a sense, it's the same old story. Truly an eye-opener is Carrier's discussion of the Rank-Raglan Hero-Type, named for scholars Otto Rank and Lord Raglan who formulated it, and Jesus' place on this scale, along with fourteen other heroes from the ancient world.[18] These heroes share many attributes, e.g., born of a virgin, thought to be son of a god, escaped death as a baby, hailed as a king. The story of Jesus in the gospels includes *twenty* of these hero features.

For example, Carrier points out that the "Thracian deity Zalmoxis was also anciently believed to have died and risen from the dead." Like Jesus, he won "salvation for all who share in his cult (including a ritual eating and drinking), as attested by Herodotus in the fifth century BCE."[19] Carrier draws attention as well to the striking similarities between Jesus and Romulus, the mythical founder of Rome. This recap especially should give Christians pause:

> There were, in fact, numerous pre-Christian savior gods, who became incarnate and underwent sufferings or trials, even deaths and resurrections. None of them actually existed. Neither did Romulus. Yet all were placed in history, and often given detailed biographies.[20]

Christians: *Your gospels look suspiciously like rehash.* There were swarms of religious ideas that had a long shelf life in the ancient world, and many of them—for whatever reason—got dumped onto the story of a Galilean preacher, who may or may not have even existed.

When the day comes that New Testament scholarship is less in the grip the church lobby, the mythicist case—especially Carrier's formidable assault—finally may be considered on its merits.

Alarmist Reaction
How Dare You!

Why are we not surprised that the Mythicists have been ridiculed? In a 2012 preview of his forthcoming *Jesus: Mything in Action*, David Fitzgerald points out:

> Most historians aren't biblical historians; so when the question of Jesus' historicity comes up, it's only natural that they'll turn to the majority opinion of bible scholars. But who are the majority of biblical scholars?

Biblical history has always been an apologetic undertaking in the service of Christianity; even today it remains perhaps the only field of science still overtly dominated by believers. So to begin with, how many of them do you suppose are open to entertaining the idea that the lord and savior they depend on for their salvation might never have existed?

Fitzgerald notes that the output of the Mythicists has been called "historical revisionist nonsense, fringe pseudo-scholarship, junk history, crackpottery, the atheist equivalent of creationism." The theological establishment is digging in. It's just name-calling by apologists who

> love to parrot the old lie that "no serious historians reject the historicity of Christ," but fail to realize (or deliberately neglect to mention) that the "Historical Jesus" that the majority of historians *do* accept is at best no more than just another first century wandering preacher and founder of a fringe cult that eventually became Christianity—in other words, a Jesus that completely debunks their own.[21]

Serious Jesus Erosion

Just Another Wandering Preacher

Christians, please take note of that last sentence: The Jesus that survives scrutiny by secular historians is a *debunked* Jesus, a shadow of his former self. Even some religious scholars have been leaning in this direction. By tolerating the erosion of Jesus, freely admitting that so many gospel stories must be transferred from the realm of history to the realm of metaphor, symbolism, and—take a deep breath—mythology, they have moved dangerously close to embracing the mythicist case, or at least portions of it.

They can't quite cross the line, though. They still want to hang on to "the first century wandering preacher and founder of a fringe cult," the Galilean peasant. They cling to the hope that there is enough in the basic framework of the Jesus story to command respect and reverence, enough to still be a Christian.

After all, aren't there Jesus stories that are entirely credible—no miracles or flashy stunts—those that don't have to be downgraded to metaphor or myth? (Theologians, fond of turning reality on its head, would call it *upgraded*.) Yes, of course, but then we run into that brick wall again, the lack of *contemporary documentation*.

Two charming stories that I recall fondly from my childhood, from listening to my mother talk about them in Sunday School, are of Martha and Mary (Luke 10:38-42), and Zacchaeus (Luke 19:1-10). Calling at the home of Martha and Mary, Jesus is pleased that Mary listens intently to his teaching, but scolds Martha for being too preoccupied with her duties as hostess. In the other story, Jesus calls to Zacchaeus, a short man who had climbed a tree to see him passing by; Jesus invited himself to Zacchaeus' home, even though the latter was a despised tax collector.

No, there is nothing at all implausible about these stories, and they fit perfectly well into ideal image that many people have conjured of Jesus. The problem: They are found only in Luke, and we don't know what Luke's sources were. If Luke was written

50 or 60 years after Jesus died, who can vouch for these stories? A writer with the instincts of a good novelist could have created these scenes. We have no obligation now to treat them as history instead of folklore. We cannot take the gospel accounts as gospel truth. The Jesus-really-did-exist crowd has very little to base their case on, not even the charming stories that may *seem* so authentic.

Moreover, these stories that could be taken as historical (if we had enough *evidence* to do so) are overshadowed by episodes that alarm us because they clearly are fantasy literature. So many of the stories in the gospels would be laughed off as tall tales if we hadn't grown accustomed to hearing them in church—and if Christians didn't have the kneejerk reaction to leap to their defense. Right away, in the first chapter of the New Testament, we are told that Joseph took instructions from angels. This doesn't qualify as history.

Faith-Based Fairy Tales
If It Walks Like a Duck and Quacks Like Duck

I'd love for Christians to take a highlighter and mark the gospel verses that would be treated as just good fun *if seen in a Disney movie*: A woman is healed by touching Jesus' garment, he heals and raises the dead by touch or voice, he heals a man's blindness by applying spit mixed with mud, he sends demons into a herd of pigs. Jesus talks to the devil, walks on water, changes water to wine, multiplies food supplies a thousand-fold, stills a storm, glows on a mountain top, floats up to heaven after the resurrection.

All these items are rooted in the ancient Near Eastern worldview, and they undermine our confidence that the gospels are history. The strong impulse among theologians and preachers to interpret these stories metaphorically, to salvage their "sacred meaning," is totally understandable, but it is also sleight-of-hand; it's cheating. Did the stories happen as the gospels report them or not? If it looks and sounds like a fairy tale, it's a fairy tale.

"But," the establishment insists, "the core story *must* be true, there *was* a real Jesus, no matter how many barnacles have to be scraped off." They can't stop grasping at straws, hoping they can get away with the argument that the gospels surely must be rooted in eyewitness accounts and oral traditions that go back to "the beginning," despite the absolute lack of *contemporary documentation.*

Were the Eyewitnesses on Holiday?

Here's one test of the cherished eyewitness hypothesis. The fond hope of conservative New Testament scholars is that Matthew, Mark, and Luke preserve, however imperfectly, reports made by the people who actually saw and heard Jesus. Well, I invite Christian folks to do some basic homework here; it shouldn't be too painful if they love the Bible as much as they're supposed to. In one sitting, or maybe two or three at the most, read Mark, Matthew, and Luke, in that order. Take a break, have a glass of wine, and ponder what you're just read. Then turn to John's gospel.

What a shock. Who is **this** Jesus in John's gospel? Scholar Burton Mack states bluntly, "What a somersault, turning the page between Luke's life of Jesus and the

Gospel of John."[22] Louis Ruprecht makes the case that John's gospel "explicitly intends to *replace* the Synoptic gospels," and refers to "the howling conflict between Mark and John."[23] Peter Brancazio, who has written a massive book recapping the entire Bible, declares that John's gospel "will come as an astonishing surprise. Here the reader will encounter a radically different portrait of Jesus, both in terms of his message and his person."[24]

Can it possibly be the same person, let alone the same preacher? In John we encounter, for the first time, the famous "I am" sayings of Jesus: He claims to be, variously, the bread of life; the light of the world; the good shepherd; the resurrection and the life; the way, the truth, and the life; and the true vine. Moreover, John 14-17 is a stand-alone block of dense theology found nowhere else—all those red letters "guaranteeing" that they are the words of Jesus. The curious reader should ask: If eyewitnesses preserved the words of Jesus in Mark, Matthew and Luke, how did they miss all these things that Jesus supposedly said in John's gospel?

We have to wonder where these strikingly different sayings came from. There's hardly a chance that a stenographer was tagging along behind the Galilean peasant. It's almost certain that they were written by a verbose theologian late in the first century, or later, whose obsession was Christ-creation and inflation.

Carrier has pointed out how speeches of public figures in the ancient world were "recorded." Today, he says, "we certainly eschew any blurring of the line between dramatic narrative and objective history." But it "was routinely blurred in antiquity, even by the best historians of the day."

> This is exemplified by the fact that Thucydides and all his successors felt at liberty to *invent entire speeches*, based on limited data in conjunction with assumptions about what they themselves thought was "probable" (and that would depend on their religious, ideological, personal, and philosophical commitments).[25]

John's Jesus is a figure of his own invention, a tedious, arrogant theological automaton, who speaks streams of theobabble. The author's artistry as a windbag reaches apogee in chapter 14-17. Have another glass of wine to help you slog through those four chapters.

The Jesus-was-real crowd has to fess up to the truth that the Jesus of John's gospel *is* a mythical character. You can't have it both ways, i.e., that the Jesus of Mark, Matthew, and Luke is real, and that the Jesus of John is real, too. So the pro-Jesus people, if they choose to hold on the former Jesus, have to confess that they are Mythicists about the latter Jesus.

Poor old C.S. Lewis, perhaps the most beloved Christian apologist, took it for granted that John's egotistical Jesus was the real one. Jesus *must* have been the son of God to get away with such arrogance, he inferred. Otherwise he'd have been a liar or lunatic. This is perhaps one of Lewis' silliest statements, made in *Mere*

Christianity. He recoils at the idea that Jesus can be demoted from a divine being to a great moral teacher:

> I am trying here to prevent anyone saying the really foolish thing that people often say about Him: I'm ready to accept Jesus as a great moral teacher, but I don't accept his claim to be God. That is the one thing we must not say. A man who was merely a man and said the sort of things Jesus said would not be a great moral teacher. He would either be a lunatic–on the level with the man who says he is a poached egg–or else he would be the Devil of Hell. You must make your choice. Either this man was, and is, the Son of God, or else a madman or something worse. You can shut him up for a fool, you can spit at him and kill him as a demon or you can fall at his feet and call him Lord and God, but let us not come with any patronizing nonsense about his being a great human teacher. He has not left that open to us. He did not intend to.[26]

Lewis's choice is a false one. We don't have to admit that Jesus was the son of God based on John's portrayal of him. We can simply admit that John created a fictional character based on his own overblown theology. John is yet another example of a theologian who excelled at making things up. Imagination, not revelation.

A Lost Document Behind the Gospels?

The eyewitness hypothesis hits another brick wall when we consider the **Q** document. In the Prologue I mentioned my interest, even as a teenager, in the hypothesis that similarities shared by Matthew and Luke–even to the extent of exact wording–probably meant that both authors used a book of Jesus sayings. It was their source, hence scholars called this document **Q**, from the German word *Quelle*, i.e., source. This has brought comfort to many scholars; there was an earlier document, closer than the gospels to the time of Jesus. Authenticity seemed within grasp!

Well, **Q** may or may not have existed, at least it hasn't turned up yet. There could be another cache of scrolls in a cave somewhere. Or perhaps Luke simply had a copy of Matthew that he copied and modified to suit his needs.[27]

Even if **Q** does turn up, however, we would have to know exactly where it came from for us to be hot on the trail of *contemporary documentation*. As it stands now, the hypothetical **Q** doesn't bring us any closer to knowing the authentic sayings of Jesus, or even verifying that Jesus was real. After all, Jesus' conversation with the devil in Matthew and Luke supposedly comes from Q. Surely no *bona fide* scholar would be reckless enough to suggest that this can be credited to eyewitnesses.

Reading the Gospels 101
Slow, Proceed with Caution

However fascinating (and strong) the case against a real Jesus may be, for the sake of argument I've got no problem saying, "Sure, Jesus existed. Now how do you want to make that case?"

The managers of the Christian brand have to hold onto the gospels for dear life: There *must* to be shreds of evidence in them to underwrite the reality of Jesus. If the Jesus-was-real folks want to paint themselves into this corner, that's fine with me. I'm delighted with the gospels as the playing field. I *want* to stick with the gospels; they're the best tool for showing that the case for a credible Jesus is weak.

Christians who want to hone their skills defending the gospels as history should practice first with the Grimm fairy tales, the stories of Hans Christian Anderson, and fables of Aesop and La Fontaine. If they can turn these into history, the gospels will be a breeze.

Do the First Chapters Succeed as History?
A Close Look at Mark, Matthew, Luke, and John

The remainder of this chapter is a guided tour. There are 98 chapters in the four gospels. Let's a take a close look at just four of them, the first chapter of each gospel. I have a feeling that, with just a little encouragement to read with a critical eye, without rose-colored glasses, fair-minded Christians could see that the gospels fail to deliver history. This is a tip-of-the iceberg glance at the problems that Jesus scholars face as they try to find reliable information about Christianity's central figure.

Remember, we don't know the sources used by any of these authors who wrote so long after the events portrayed, and their theological biases are no secret. So question *everything*: Be critical, apply common sense standards of due diligence. Most of us would be skeptical about the Lincoln story concocted by the enthusiast whom I interviewed earlier in this chapter. But he used exactly the same approach that is followed by the New Testament authors. As you read the gospels, don't let your guard down for a minute.

Mark
Jesus and the Demons

The Proclamation of John the Baptist

1 The beginning of the gospel of Jesus Christ, the Son of God.

2 As it is written in Isaiah the prophet: "Behold, I send My messenger ahead of You, Who will prepare Your way; 3 The voice of one crying in the wilderness, 'Make ready the way of the Lord, Make His paths straight.'"

4 John the Baptist appeared in the wilderness preaching a baptism of repentance for the forgiveness of sins. 5 And all the country of Judea was going out to him, and all the people of Jerusalem; and they were being baptized by him in the Jordan River, confessing their sins. 6 John was clothed with camel's hair and wore a leather belt around his waist, and his diet was locusts and wild honey. 7 And he was preaching, and saying, "After me One is coming who is mightier than I, and I am not fit to stoop down and untie the thong of His sandals. 8 I baptized you with water; but He will baptize you with the Holy Spirit." (NASB)

Wrong about the Old Testament

In verse 2, Mark got the Old Testament quote wrong. This verse is not from Isaiah, but from Malachi. When Matthew copied from Mark, he appears to have noticed this. He dropped the quotation and mentioned no prophet, writing instead, "This is he of whom it is written." Verse 3, however, is based on Isaiah 40:3.

Let me pause here to make an important point, which must be stressed over and over again: The Old Testament has **no** predictions of Jesus of Nazareth, none whatever.[28] There *were* many speculations about a coming hero or messiah in Jewish literature at the time, in the Old Testament and elsewhere. In fact, such expectations were rampant at the time, with many preachers claiming to be messiahs.

"Palestine in the early first century CE was experiencing a rash of messianism," Carrier says."There was an evident clamoring of sects and individuals to announce they had found the messiah."[29] The gospel writers were following common practice to read *their* messiah Jesus back into the Old Testament. They picked verses, often wildly out of context, that they *claimed* point to Jesus. They wanted to make the Jesus story fit the prophecies and expectations, but it was always a stretch. Matthew is the prizewinner for citing Old Testament verses to apply them to Jesus, because he especially was intent on showing the Jewishness of Jesus.

Your neighborhood psychic may claim amazing predictive powers, but her talents fail when you ask for details such as some winning lottery numbers. Old Testament predictions of Jesus? We want details! If Old Testament authors wanted to predict the messiah specifically in the person of Jesus Christ, why didn't they say so? What's the point of being coy or cryptic? Why didn't they write, "the messiah will be Jesus of Nazareth when the Roman oppressors control the land six hundred years from now." *There are no such verses*. Period.

Much is made of the famous Suffering Servant poems in the book of Isaiah as references to Jesus. Yes, the story of Jesus fits, as constructed in hindsight. But we always have to ask: What did the *author of Isaiah* have in mind? If he'd meant a Galilean peasant hundreds of years down the road, if he really was in the business of predicting the future, he could have done a much better job. God could have been a whole lot more precise.

As David Fitzgerald has put it, the gospel writers are good at quote-mining the Old Testament, and it's actually a pathetic, transparent stratagem.

Crowd Counting

Mark reports that everyone in Judah and Jerusalem went to the Jordan to be baptized. We have a right to be skeptical about this. One of the properties of folklore is exaggeration, after all.

For example, we read in Exodus 12:37 that the Israelites leaving Egypt under the command of Moses numbered 600,000–that was just the men. Old Testament scholars must deal with the lack of any evidence whatever–no documents, no engravings, no wall paintings, no shards of pottery from ancient campfires, *nothing*– for the exodus and the wandering for 40 years in the desert. But even those scholars who still think that there was an exodus of some kind know that 600,000 men is an impossibly inflated figure. Mark shows the same sense of drama. Writing at least 40 years after the events he "reports," he says that huge crowds went to John for baptism. The problem is that no contemporary authors in the first century report anything of the kind.

Tensions

It's clear from what we read later in the gospels that there was tension between the disciples of Jesus and the disciples of John. Mark wants to put down Jesus' rival, so he has John say that he is not worthy to untie the thong of Jesus' sandals. Matthew changed the wording so that John confesses that he is not worthy to *carry* Jesus' sandals.

The Baptism of Jesus

> **9** In those days Jesus came from Nazareth in Galilee and was baptized by John in the Jordan. **10** Immediately coming up out of the water, He saw the heavens opening, and the Spirit like a dove descending upon Him; **11** and a voice came out of the heavens: "You are My beloved Son, in You I am well-pleased." (NASB)

Baptism for What?

This text has made a lot of people uneasy. Since John's baptism was for the remission of sins, why would *Jesus*, the perfect son of God, need to be baptized? It looks like Matthew was uneasy with this, so he added words not found in Luke or John. We can be sure that, writing for a Greek-speaking audience, Matthew didn't go back to original sources, more than 50 years after the event. He made this up:

> Then Jesus arrived from Galilee at the Jordan coming to John, to be baptized by him. But John tried to prevent Him, saying, "I have need to be baptized by You, and do You come to me?" But Jesus answering said to him, "Permit it at this time; for in this way it is fitting for us to fulfill all righteousness." Then he permitted Him. (Matt. 3:13-15, NASB)

The author of John's gospel wouldn't have any of this. In his account, Jesus isn't baptized at all. Jesus goes to the Jordan to meet John, who gushes compliments. John says *he* saw the heavens opened and the spirit descending on Jesus, but John omits any mention of Jesus setting foot in the river.

Heavens!

What is a historian supposed to make of the claim that Jesus saw "the heavens torn apart"? Christians commonly read such things casually and shrug them off as typical Bible-talk, but what can it possibly mean that the heavens were torn apart? This is more folklore, as is the voice from heaven: "You are my son, the beloved." It's akin to Mark's report in chapter 9 that the voice of God came from a cloud.

Also, notice that Matthew changes the wording. No longer is it Jesus who sees the heaven torn apart. It becomes a more general event where "the heavens were torn apart," and Matthew reports that the voice from heaven said, "*This* is my son, the beloved," not "*you* are." This declaration is not addressed specifically to Jesus.

Christmas?

Now, here's a biggie. Mark, the first gospel to be written, shows *no awareness whatever* of the virgin birth, wise men coming from the east, shepherds being visited by angels the night Jesus was born. Mark doesn't start his story with Jesus' birth, but with his baptism. There could be a couple of reasons that Mark doesn't describe how Jesus was born:

1. He doesn't tell a birth story because he had never heard the stories that ended up in Matthew and Luke. Most scholars have assumed that this was the case. Indeed, the suspicion is strong that the stories in Matthew and Luke hadn't yet been invented.

2. It's also possible that Mark did know them, but a miraculous birth didn't fit his theology. He may have wanted to push the belief that Jesus was adopted by God at his baptism, and that the baptism itself was required to cleanse Jesus of sin to be qualified. Mark could have been familiar enough with pagan virgin births, and wanted to rule them out.

I said earlier that it's very unlikely that letters flew back and forth among the scattered Christian communities, comparing notes on Jesus stories, and this major discrepancy illustrates the point. And it's not as if Matthew and Luke had been keeping an archive of authentic information that hadn't made the rounds yet. Legends spring up and take on a life of their own.

It's obvious that the early Christians had only skimpy information about their hero, Jesus. He just pops up out of nowhere at about age 30, or so is commonly surmised (the attempt at dating Jesus' birth in Luke is clumsy and inaccurate). His early life is a blank; the Mythicists suggest this is so for the simple reason that there just wasn't anything there. Mark assumed that the announcement of Jesus to the world occurred at the time of his baptism, not before.

The Temptation of Jesus

> **12** And the Spirit immediately drove him out into the wilderness. **13** He was in the wilderness forty days, tempted by Satan; and he **was with the wild beasts; and the angels waited on him.

Forty Days

The "spirit" that descended from heaven "like a dove" when Jesus emerged from the river now drives him into the wilderness. For forty days? Anyone who is looking for reliable historical narrative wants to know who was keeping count. But Mark's agenda was theological. There is a conscious attempt in the New Testament to make Jesus' career parallel aspects of Israel's history. The Israelites wandered in the wilderness for forty years, so Jesus imitates this by being in the wilderness for forty days. He is challenged by one mythical creature, Satan, and cared for by others, the angels.

More Later

Folklore that came along later inflated this story. Matthew and Luke add major expansions. They provide the extensive conversations that Jesus had with the devil. Mark seems to have known nothing about this since he failed to include it. Where did the dialogue between Jesus and the devil come from? It's tough to argue that there was an eyewitness. The dialogue is creative fiction. When we see too much of this, we are allowed to wonder just how much this is the case with the whole Jesus story.

Theologians may insist that there are many levels of spiritual meaning in this Jesus-Satan exchange, i.e., it may be rich in symbolism, metaphor, etc. For someone inside the Christian cult, this may be true. However, those outside are entitled to pull the discussion back to the topic at hand: Are the gospels historical documents? What *actually happened* after Jesus was baptized, if indeed *that* even happened? These two verses about Jesus in the wilderness give us little confidence that Mark had the slightest idea what it means to write history. He passes off fable as fact.

The Beginning of the Galilean Ministry

> **14** Now after John was arrested, Jesus came to Galilee, proclaiming the good news of God, **15** and saying, "The time is fulfilled, and the kingdom of God has come near; repent, and believe in the good news."

In verse 15, we see the introduction of a major New Testament theme: The kingdom of God has come near. In the context of the teaching of Jesus and the apostle Paul, this means the arrival of the "end times" when God's direct rule will descend on the earth. In Greek, *apocalypse* means simply *uncovering*, i.e., the disclosure of God's rule. According to the New Testament, this would be a traumatic event, including widespread suffering and destruction (again, see Mark 13).

Both Matthew and Luke expanded Mark's terse description of John the Baptist's teaching. They add these words to John's message, "Who warned you to flee from the wrath to come?" For John the Baptist, *God is Wrath* overshadowed *God is Love*.

Bart Ehrman describes Jesus as an apocalyptic prophet because of his preaching about the approaching kingdom (the title of his book: *Jesus: Apocalyptic Prophet of the New Millennium*), but John Loftus is less diplomatic when he describes Jesus as "a failed apocalyptic prophet."[30] Both Jesus and Paul believed that the dramatic arrival of God's kingdom would happen "before the present generation passes away," and, of course, ***they were both wrong***.

The words in the Lord's Prayer about the kingdom coming and God's will being done shouldn't be given a watered-down "spiritual" meaning, as is usually done today by Christians who don't want to deal with Jesus getting it wrong. Jesus was probably asking for people to pray for the *prompt* arrival of the kingdom. So when you read this line in verse 15, please be aware that this is no mere passing reference to "the kingdom." Jesus really meant that the time was ripe, with his own arrival signaling that the kingdom was about to dawn. This is cult talk, part of Jesus' delusional thinking we'll cover in Tough Problem IX.

Jesus Calls the First Disciples

> **16** As Jesus passed along the Sea of Galilee, he saw Simon and his brother Andrew casting a net into the sea—for they were fishermen. **17** And Jesus said to them, "Follow me and I will make you fish for people." **18** And immediately they left their nets and followed him. **19** As he went a little farther, he saw James son of Zebedee and his brother John, who were in their boat mending the nets. **20** Immediately he called them; and they left their father Zebedee in the boat with the hired men, and followed him.

Folklore heroes are commonly irresistible, so it's not surprising that we find this theme in the Jesus story. You will notice as you read Mark that one of his favorite words is "immediately." He uses it throughout the gospel to impart a feeling of urgency to the Jesus story. But in this episode, it lessens the credibility of the account. Even as a kid I was skeptical when I read this story, despite the pithy saying of Jesus, "I will make you fishers of men."

And then Simon and Andrew just up and leave, following him. James and John not only left the boat, but their father as well. So much of the story is never filled in. Did these disciples follow Jesus full-time, giving up their livelihoods and never going back to fishing? Matthew would have us believe that the disciples were swallowed by the cult: "Then Peter said in reply, 'Look, we have left everything and followed you. What then will we have?'" (Matt. 19:27) Christians rarely acknowledge that this scene, the gathering of the disciples, smacks of cult behavior. Along comes some charismatic preacher and people drop everything to tag along with him.

In order to maintain much respect for this portrayal of events, it's probably not a good idea to switch to Luke 14:26, "If anyone comes to me and does not hate his father, mother, wife, children, brothers, and sisters, as well as his own life, he can't be my disciple" (RSV). See what I mean about the gospel writers leaving negatives about Jesus in full view? Or more correctly, they didn't seem to regard rejection of family as a bad thing. The father of James and John might have said, "How can I get my sons deprogrammed?" Christians create a lot of problems for themselves when they argue that the gospels are history.

The Man with an Unclean Spirit

> **21** They went to Capernaum; and when the sabbath came, he entered the synagogue and taught. **22** They were astounded at his teaching, for he taught them as one having authority, and not as the scribes. **23** Just then there was in their synagogue a man with an unclean spirit, **24** and he cried out, "What have you to do with us, Jesus of Nazareth? Have you come to destroy us? I know who you are, the Holy One of God." **25** But Jesus rebuked him, saying, "Be silent, and come out of him!" **26** And the unclean spirit, convulsing him and crying with a loud voice, came out of him. **27** They were all amazed, and they kept on asking one another, "What is this? A new teaching—with authority! He commands even the unclean spirits, and they obey him." **28** At once his fame began to spread throughout the surrounding region of Galilee.

For Bible believers, the good news is that there was a synagogue in Capernaum. This leads to the temptation to say, "Aha, Mark got it right, this is historical, here's the synagogue!" The bad news is that the Capernaum synagogue whose ruins still stand today dates from the second century, more than a hundred years after the time of Jesus. Even so, Christians visit the site and feel at least a little awe that "this is where Jesus walked." But there's more bad news; Mark also ushers us here into the superstitious mindset of the first century. If this is history, if this is how Jesus behaved, Christianity is in trouble.

The belief at the time was that the world swarmed with demons that could wreak havoc in human affairs. It was, as the title of Carl Sagan's book suggests, a demon-haunted world. There was a hierarchy in the spiritual world. The swarming demons were, as I mentioned in Tough Problem I, under the sway of the CEO of evil, the devil or Satan. At the other end of spectrum in this spirit-world domain were the ordinary gremlins.

It may be difficult for us citizens of the modern world to appreciate that, for ancient peoples, these were very real and very dangerous powers, not to be trifled with.[31] In this context one of the strangest sayings of Jesus makes sense. In Mark 3:28-29 we read: "Truly I tell you, people will be forgiven for their sins and whatever blasphemies they utter; but whoever blasphemes against the Holy Spirit can never have forgiveness, but is guilty of an eternal sin." You don't want to mess with these powers; even *words* can get you into serious trouble. The full-blown version of this superstition included the practice of *speaking* to demons.

Christians take it for granted that people can speak to a god; that's called prayer. Catholics earnestly believe that they can also speak to dead people; that's called praying to the saints. But most practical, levelheaded, educated people sense that speaking to demons is skating along the thin ice of sanity. Sure, exorcism is fine at the movies, but there's a bit of nervous laughter when we hear that the Vatican employs a staff of exorcists. The Vatican *trains* exorcists, not at Hogwarts, but at the Vatican. The priests who have chosen this specialty are convinced that demons still swarm about us, invade our daily lives, and must be neutralized. These guys haven't caught up to our understanding of mental illness, and that "the evil that lurks in the heart of men" can have many sources other than demons.[32] Mark invites us back into this world, and places Jesus at center stage.

The demons in a deranged man cry out to Jesus and ask if he's come to destroy them (v. 24). They are inhabitants of the spirit world, privy to the "insider information" that Jesus is a special emissary of God. They know he has the power to vanquish them. Jesus speaks a magic spell to defeat the demons, not a very clever one I would have to say: "Be silent, and come out of him." The demon throws one last tantrum and then flees (v. 26).

Perhaps the most plausible detail of this scene is the gullibility of those who were watching, "amazed" (v. 27), and that Jesus' fame about the incident spread (v. 28). Literacy in first century Palestine hovered around five percent, and the same no doubt was true for the capacity to think critically and apply standards of evidence. The gullible can leave a faith healer's tent meeting–or these days, the plush megachurches where the healers ply their trade—and shout hallelujahs about the wonderful cures they've witnessed. It's no surprise that the local yokels who saw Jesus in action would be dumbfounded. There's no reason, however, for **us** to be impressed by stories that were uncritically reported—if "reported" is even the right word here—and grew with the telling over several decades.

Do Christians really want to defend this as history? New Testament scholar Morton Smith wrote a book titled *Jesus: The Magician* because he felt he could make the case that this was how Jesus was perceived. Would Christians really be comfortable with a book called *Jesus: The Exorcist*? My to-do list includes writing a secular commentary on Mark, which I would call *Jesus and The Demons*.

The Jesus in this gospel does not come across as some great moral teacher. Matthew took a step in that direction when he added the Sermon on the Mount, but you have to hunt around in Mark for the gems about moral conduct.[33] In Mark, Jesus' primary message is about the coming kingdom that will bring suffering and anguish to those who aren't among the chosen few, and he has one set-to after another with demons. The gospel of Mark fails as a religious document that we can hold in high esteem.

Jesus Heals Many at Simon's House

> **29** As soon as they left the synagogue, they entered the house of Simon and Andrew, with James and John. **30** Now Simon's mother-in-law was in bed with a fever, and they told him about her at once. **31** He came and took her by the hand and lifted her up. Then the fever left her, and she began to serve them. **32** That evening, at sunset, they brought to him all who were sick or possessed with demons. **33** And the whole city was gathered around the door. **34** And he cured many who were sick with various diseases, and cast out many demons; and he would not permit the demons to speak, because they knew him.

In verse 25, Jesus healed by voice command, but on his visit to the house of Simon and Andrew, he healed Simon's mother-in-law by touch. She was suddenly well enough to get back to her business of serving the men. Word quickly spread that a healer was in the village, and the house was surrounded. Presumable by word and touch Jesus cured people, and his confrontation with demons continued as well. In the first exorcism reported earlier, the demons proclaimed that they knew who Jesus was, and in this episode Jesus explicitly forbids them to speak because they knew him. This is another touch of strangeness, because isn't it the *purpose* of Mark's gospel to make Jesus known to the world?

Well, yes, of course, *we* might say that, but one of Mark's most puzzling ideas was that Jesus was trying **to keep it secret** that he was one who would usher in the kingdom of God. New Testament scholars have puzzled over this "secrecy motif" for decades. Here it is stated explicitly, in Mark 4:10-12:

> When he was alone, those who were around him along with the twelve asked him about the parables. And he said to them, "To you has been given the secret of the kingdom of God, but for those outside, everything comes

in parables; in order that 'they may indeed look, but not perceive, and may indeed listen, but not understand; so that they may not turn again and be forgiven.'"

The parables are usually considered by laypeople today as Jesus' way of teaching helpful lessons, but Mark suggests just the opposite. It makes no sense whatever that Jesus didn't *want* people to mend their ways and be forgiven. In fact, the last couple of lines of the quote are an echo of Isaiah 6:9-10, in which Yahweh tells Isaiah that he doesn't want people to repent until he has brought destruction! Mark might also have slipped in the secrecy motif to explain why Jesus wasn't universally accepted and acclaimed, but this falls flat. Frankly, it might be that Mark just *got it wrong*.

Those who want to defend vv. 29-33 as history have to admit that Jesus was confused at best, deceitful at worst. Do your prefer to insist that we have *bona fide* eyewitness report here—Jesus ordering demons to keep quiet, to keep his secret—or retreat more sensibly to an admission that Mark's creative fiction talents, and his overheated theology, were at work here?[34]

A Preaching Tour in Galilee

35 In the morning, while it was still very dark, he got up and went out to a deserted place, and there he prayed. **36** And Simon and his companions hunted for him. **37** When they found him, they said to him, "Everyone is searching for you." **38** He answered, "Let us go on to the neighboring towns, so that I may proclaim the message there also; for that is what I came out to do." **39** And he went throughout Galilee, proclaiming the message in their synagogues and casting out demons.

Mark contradicts himself right away in this paragraph, i.e., the "secrecy motif" can't be right. After Simon found Jesus praying alone early in the morning, Jesus declares that they should go on to the next towns to proclaim "the message" there, too (v. 38). The message, of course, is that the kingdom of God is almost here. One token of that is his power over the demons. He has come from the spiritual realm, and he has more power than they do.

Mark keeps hammering away at the theme of Jesus' superiority over the demons. It's one way to demonstrate to ordinary people who he is. But, in fact, the religious authorities will later (in Mark 3) make the accusation that Jesus got his exorcism powers from Satan. Jesus replied, in his famous house-divided argument, that Satan would hardly empower him to cast out demons, the beings that served the CEO of evil. We are knee-deep in superstition here.

Jesus Cleanses a Leper

40 A leper came to him begging him, and kneeling he said to him, "If you choose, you can make me clean." **41** Moved with pity, Jesus stretched out his hand and touched him, and said to him, "I do choose. Be made clean!" **42** Immediately the leprosy left him, and he was made clean. **43** After sternly warning him he sent him away at once, **44** saying to him, "See that you say nothing to anyone; but go, show yourself to the priest, and offer for your cleansing what Moses commanded, as a testimony to them." **45** But he went out and began to proclaim it freely, and to spread the word, so that Jesus could no longer go into a town openly, but stayed out in the country; and people came to him from every quarter.

In this episode Jesus heals a leper. The word is ambiguous: A variety of skin diseases could be meant by the Greek word. But the point of the story is that, by touch and words, Jesus cured the man instantly.

There are problems with this text that the ordinary reader may not see. In the literal Greek, verse 43 says Jesus "threw him out" after "severely rebuking him." *What*? He rebuked the leper and gave him the boot? Ehrman notes that translators sometimes tone things down, and he devotes several pages to explaining the problems we're up against just trying to figure out what this text originally said. [35]

At the beginning of verse 41, we read that Jesus was "moved with pity," but a case can be made that the original text of Mark read instead, "Becoming angry, Jesus stretched out his hand." If Jesus was angry, then it makes more sense that Jesus rebuked the man and threw him out. So what was going on here? Matthew and Luke, both of whom copied this story from Mark, didn't have a clue, any more than we do. They both *changed the wording* to remove Jesus' anger. So, once again, we wonder if history has been tampered with, or if there is any history here at all.

Our primary concern, as always in the absence of contemporary documentation, is *what actually happened*, despite the efforts of theologians to divert our attention from that by expounding on the "spiritual" meaning of the story. How and where did this story originate? Christians may be willing to rush to affirm that it happened just as Mark said it did (although Matthew and Luke made alterations): Jesus cured a man instantly. Jesus had that power because God has that power. And we hear, "It's so like you atheists to be doubtful and disrespectful."

But hold on, we're just being curious and cautious (well, maybe ornery as well), and wouldn't it be a good idea if Christians didn't paint themselves into a corner, which is very easy to do here? Christians claim that God's power and compassion are attested by the New Testament stories of Jesus healing. If that's your argument, then you've left the door wide open to a major theological dilemma. We wade into an awkward contradiction, and get tangled up again with the suffering that's part of Tough Problem I.

If Jesus was the great healer that Christians claim, one particular Galilean peasant endowed by God with the power to cure people of diseases by voice and touch, well, God's gesture of compassion here is a pretty weak one.

Just think about the monumental scale of human suffering for millennia, when people had no access to health care, no medications or antiseptics, no painkillers. Heaven waited for thousands of years, as Christopher Hitchens has said so eloquently, with folded arms. Suddenly God allowed this one Galilean to show up to cure people as they crossed his path.

It's not an outrageous question: If God is real and compassionate, why not send an *army* of Galilean peasants with these powers? More to the point, if God can stop microbes in their tracks, why would he require a human being to walk around to touch and talk to people? Why would God require people to ***ask***? If God can cure leprosy, withered hands, fevers, and thousands of other afflictions, why can't he just kick them off the planet once and for all? If, in the beginning, God said, "Let there be light," and the Cosmos sprang into existence, can't he get a handle on disease?

This simple story about Jesus curing a leper should hit us with blunt force: God's power is not matched by his compassion. And even that isn't so infinite after all, if he cured *just one* leper (or even a whole bunch, if we count all the healing episodes in the gospels).

Theology trips over itself here. We are faced with a *choice* in evaluating this story critically: (1) that a man was cured immediately because a holy man touched him, or (2) a story grew in the telling over several decades. It was finally written down 40 or 50 years later, by an author committed to a theological agenda, who–taking Mark as a whole–doesn't impress us as a critical historian. He is a master of fantasy literature. Jesus healing the leper fits that pattern. We have no reason whatever to think that the story can be traced to eyewitness reports–that's a wild guess, a faint hope at best–and there is no contemporary documentation.

Matthew
Keeping Jesus Jewish

This chapter is the opening of the New Testament (with the incorrect ordering of books in our copies of the Bible), one of the famous "virgin birth" accounts (the other is in Luke). However, it's not uncommon for readers to find Matthew's introduction to the Jesus story a little off-putting. It is a long list of names, the ancestors of Jesus. The traditional translations of such lists in the Old Testament used the word "begat," e.g., "Abraham begat Isaac," and many of the diligent faithful have lamented plowing through "the begats" when they tackle the Bible, determined to read it cover-to-cover, so-help-me-god.

It seems such a boring way to begin the story of Jesus. Matthew had his reasons, however, and this approach for launching the story gives it a feel of history, i.e., Matthew is being careful and exact in showing where Jesus came from.

Except that he wasn't. But take a look; find your copy of the New Testament, or do a Google search and read the first 17 verses of Matthew. They are tedious indeed.

The Genealogy of Jesus Christ

Folklore imagination, under the influence of theology, is hard at work here. Anyone who cares to dig into the problems of this list can easily locate the scholarly debate,[36] but you might as well spend your time watching paint dry.

Three points to keep in mind:

1. Matthew simply borrowed from lists in the Old Testament, which are themselves the product of folklore, and he deleted names from the list to keep his pattern of fourteen generations stated in verse 17 (did he really think people wouldn't notice?).

2. Matthew failed to compare notes with Luke (well, it's highly unlikely that they even knew one another), and thus Luke (chapter 3) gives us a

different list of ancestors, causing conservative scholars—for whom the Bible must have no errors—no end of anxiety. Excuses have been offered that fail to convince, e.g., that Luke has listed Mary's ancestors.

3. Matthew's genealogy reflects the belief of many (most?) of the devout in the early church that the messiah had to be a descendant of King David: that would be one of his claims to legitimacy. *Please note this carefully*: There had to be an unbroken bloodline between David and Jesus. That's the whole purpose of including a genealogy.

After listing all the names, Matthew's story finally gets underway.

The Birth of Jesus Christ

18 Now the birth of Jesus Christ took place in this way. When his mother Mary had been betrothed to Joseph, before they came together she was found to be with child from the Holy Spirit. **19** And her husband Joseph, being a just man and unwilling to put her to shame, resolved to divorce her quietly. **20** But as he considered these things, behold, an angel of the Lord appeared to him in a dream, saying, "Joseph, son of David, do not fear to take Mary as your wife, for that which is conceived in her is from the Holy Spirit. **21** She will bear a son, and you shall call his name Jesus, for he will save his people from their sins." **22** All this took place to fulfill what the Lord had spoken by the prophet:

23 "Behold, the virgin shall conceive and bear a son, and they shall call his name Immanuel" (which means, God with us). **24** When Joseph woke from sleep, he did as the angel of the Lord commanded him: he took his wife, **25** but knew her not until she had given birth to a son. And he called his name Jesus.

Matthew should have left well enough alone, but he was swimming against the tide of pagan religions. When he wrote his gospel, Christians were still a tiny minority, and most of the early non-Jewish enthusiasts for the new faith had learned religion at the knees of their pagan parents. They had come to believe that Christ was the key to their salvation, but that didn't mean that all of the pagan ideas they'd grown up with should be chucked.

One of the common ideas in the ancient world was that religious heroes—sons of the gods—were conceived directly by the gods. Virgin birth was an old and comfortable idea. There was probably no conscious decision, "Hey, let's borrow that," but as early Christians attempted to achieve respectability for their new religion, why should their god have an *ordinary* conception? As they cast their eyes over the religious landscape from which they had come, it was only to be expected that some would say, "Anything you can do, I can do better"—or at least as well. Hence Jesus too must have been born of a virgin.

Christian missionaries have always found, much to their chagrin, that new converts commonly create distressing Christian-pagan blends, and tacking on the virgin birth to the cult of Jesus in the earliest days of the faith fits this pattern.

Maybe Matthew himself was unsure about who is right here. Jesus came from the bloodline of King David, not a shabby pedigree, after all. Or he was conceived directly by the spirit of God, arguably an even better pedigree. So Matthew crafted his story to include both schools of thought. Clearly he fails both as a critical thinker and a careful historian.

Catholic theologian Uta Ranke-Heinemann—she's the one who got into hot water with the Vatican for her opinion on the Virgin Birth—refers to this blending of traditions as "a kind of theological schizophrenia." If "Jesus is not a real, authentic son of Joseph," she says, "then neither is he a real, authentic son of David." And if "Joseph is only Jesus' foster father, as the Catholics call him, then David is only Jesus' foster ancestor. The genealogies of Jesus come from a time when Joseph was still considered Jesus' physical father."[37]

In verse 16 Matthew attempted to splice these two traditions together. But the scribes who copied the gospel over the centuries noticed the contradiction, the absurdity of saying that Joseph was the father of a man who had been born of a virgin, and kept rewording verse 16 to try to reconcile the two traditions. Hence there are several different versions of verse 16 in the ancient manuscripts.

Come on, Christians, find the history here!

Creating the Virgin Ex-Nihilo

Ironically, since belief in the Virgin Birth of Jesus is considered by Catholics and evangelicals one that you must hold to qualify as a real Christian, it remained a *minority opinion* in the earliest years of the new faith. As we have seen, Mark ignores Jesus' origins. He launches his gospel with the baptism; that was good enough for him as divine credentialing. Presumably John would have welcomed the Virgin Birth, since he speaks of the divine Word becoming flesh to dwell among us, but he didn't know about it.

The apostle Paul, who was more energetic than anyone else in spreading the message of Christ, seems to have been unaware of it as well. Nor is it mentioned in any of the other New Testament epistles. It stands alone in Matthew and Luke, but eventually gained ascendancy and resulted in the runaway, over-the-top cult of Mary. Otherwise, she too, like her son, would have remained a Galilean peasant. According to the gospels, she was pretty much ignored by her son,[38] but the church has more than made up for that. She became a female divine figure, matching other mother-goddesses in the pagan religions of the ancient world.

Matthew might have had reservations about grafting this pagan element into the Jesus story. We know that he wrote for an audience with strong Jewish sensibilities, and he probably wanted to resist Paul's agenda of lessening Christianity's Jewish component. Paul wanted to minimize the Old Testament law, and he would tell his congregations that they didn't have to become Jews to become Christians. Above all, they could ignore circumcision and dietary laws. Matthew was old school, and puts words on Jesus' lips found nowhere else (chapter 5, in the Sermon on the Mount):

> Do not think that I have come to abolish the Law or the Prophets; I have not come to abolish them but to fulfill them. For truly, I say to you, until heaven and earth pass away, not an iota, not a dot, will pass from the Law until all is accomplished. Therefore whoever relaxes one of the least of these commandments and teaches others to do the same will be called least

in the kingdom of heaven, but whoever does them and teaches them will be called great in the kingdom of heaven. For I tell you, unless your righteousness exceeds that of the scribes and Pharisees, you will never enter the kingdom of heaven.

This flatly contradicts other teaching of Jesus, e.g., about the Sabbath, and we can be sure that Paul would have winced.

On the Hunt for a Pregnant Virgin

The point I want to make here is that Matthew wanted his story to appeal to Christians who were not about to turn their backs on Judaism. That's why he positioned Jesus as an enthusiast for the Old Testament law. He had to recast virgin birth as a Jewish idea, thereby allowing it to appear as less blatantly pagan. One of his techniques for anchoring Jesus to his Jewish roots was to scour the Old Testament for texts that he could apply to Jesus. He does a really bad job of it throughout his gospel, and in his first chapter he makes a colossal blunder.

He seems to have gone hunting through the Old Testament for the word "virgin," and it was his bad luck to come across Isaiah 7:14 in a defective translation. Yes, indeed, there's the word *virgin*, but Matthew was using the Greek version current at the time (the *Septuagint*), which famously mistranslated the word *almah*, which simply means *young woman*. In the original Hebrew text of Isaiah 7:14, there's no virgin in sight, and, in any case, the chapter has no bearing on Jesus. It relates to a political crisis in Jerusalem hundred of years before his time.

I say *famously* mistranslated because his goof was spotted long ago, and has been written about endlessly. Matthew didn't bother to look up the Hebrew original and paid no attention at all to the original context of Isaiah 7, which has *nothing whatever* to do with the prediction of a messiah. If you don't believe me, stop right now and read Isaiah 7. What in the world does it have to do with Matthew's story about Jesus? Nothing, zero, zip.

When Matthew came to verse 7:14 in the Septuagint he must have said, "Wow, this is it! This is the perfect match for Jesus": "A virgin shall conceive and bear a son, and you shall call his name Immanuel." After the last word Matthew *added* an explanation that is not found in Isaiah, "which means, God with us." But sorry, the context of this chapter is far removed from a Galilean peasant preacher who would appear seven hundred years later. It's not a match, not even close–no cigar.

Many Christian translators of Isaiah 7:14 have been guilty of a blatant cover-up of Matthew's mistake. They translate *almah* as *virgin* instead of *young woman*! This is theological bias overriding their integrity as translators: Christians failing the honesty test because they know that they'll be able to get away with it. Ordinary Bible readers will be none the wiser.

They also turn a blind eye to the virgin births in other ancient religions. If relying on willful ignorance is your approach, you'll fail to see that virgin birth *doesn't* make Jesus unique. It makes him part of the herd, pulling him "down" to the level of pagan religions that Christianity supposedly disdains.

The boast, "anything you can do, I can do better," reaches obscene proportions in the way Christians have gone overboard with Matthew's virgin: In time she would be designated Mary, Mother of God, Queen of Heaven. Such titles fit very snugly into pagan pantheons, but Christians who are committed to levelheaded monotheism should flinch at them. When will lay people wise up and slap down theologians who are deaf to their own crazy talk?

We read in vv. 20-21 that an angel delivered a message to Joseph in a dream. Now, of course, it is true that people have dreams and can see and hear extraordinary things in them. But that's not what Matthew reports: He presents it as a fact that "an angel of the Lord appeared to him in a dream." A historian could report with assurance that Joseph had a dream, if she had *contemporary documentation* (for example, Joseph's diary). But a historian cannot report that the *content* of the dream was real, that there was truly an angel who gave him a message. The warning of my therapist friend bears repeating: "Reality is what happens *outside* the patient's head."

Matthew adds a couple of filler sentences about Mary being "with child from the Holy Spirit," a brief backstory to put the virgin conception in context. Joseph wanted to spare her public shame and decided on a quiet divorce (from their engagement). Since virgin birth had been imported from the pagan religions repertory, these sentences are Matthew's novelistic touch.

Thus, on all counts, everything in this 25-verse chapter fails as history. Mythicists score over the Gospels-Are-History team! Of course, mainstream Christian scholars will cry foul about using Matthew 1 in this discussion, because they have admitted for a long time that Matthew's birth narrative is fiction. (Only evangelical scholars have desperately resisted this conclusion.) But it gives us insight into his methodology, his mindset about how to write history: *He just doesn't know how to do it.*

A Brief Stop at the Stable

We're taking a tour of the first chapters of the four gospels, so a digression to Matthew's Chapter 2 (the story of the Wise Men) may seem off course. But I can't resist because this chapter—so familiar, such a fixture of the Christmas season—is a perfect example of folklore overtaking history.

The faithful return to Chapter 2 every December, but they don't read it carefully. They fail to notice what it *doesn't* say. Everybody knows that Jesus was born in a stable. The familiar manger scene is a crèche with shepherds and Wise Men kneeling to adore baby Jesus, surrounded by cattle, a star hovering above. Sad to break it to you, but the "manger scene" is not historical. It's an inference based in a single word, *manger*, created from Christian imagination long after the gospels were written.

As one church was preparing its Christmas nativity pageant with the manger scene, the teachers wondered what role they could give to one hyperactive kid. Well, how could he mess up the part of the innkeeper? He had just one line, "There is no room in the inn," and he delivered it perfectly. However, he felt so sorry for Mary and Joseph as he turned them away that he blurted out, "But you can have *my* room."

Obviously that wasn't Luke's solution. He simply wrote that there was "no place for them at the inn" and had Mary put the newborn child in a manger, a trough for feeding cattle.[39] Meanwhile, we're told in Luke's gospel, shepherds heard from an angel about the birth of Jesus—a lot of drama in the scene: "And suddenly there was with the angel a multitude of the heavenly host praising God." They rushed to Bethlehem and found Jesus in the manger. There is *no mention of a stable*, nor that they took any of their sheep with them. Since Luke mentioned the manger, chances are he did have a stable in mind, although he neglected to mention it, and cattle are usually found in a stable. Voilà; we have the traditional crèche.

Now, what about that star? This is where it gets complicated, and why a careful reading of Matthew 2 can shed some light—*starlight*, in this case—on the issue.

It's clear that Matthew didn't think the Wise Men arrived on the night Jesus was born. He seems to have understood that they had been traveling for some time. They had seen Jesus' star at the time of this birth, and then set out on their journey to Jerusalem. They had not been *following* a star; they had simply seen it as an omen and headed to the holy city. When they got there, Herod was none too pleased that these strangers were on a mission to worship his replacement, a new king of the Jews.

They were told to head to Bethlehem, based on an Old Testament text (another of Matthew's famous quotes). Strangely, it is *then* that they began following the star. That, we know now, would be impossible; those twinkling points of lights do not come to rest over specific places on earth. Matthew, with only the ancients' views on cosmology to go by, imagined that one of did just that."The star goes ahead of them," Robert Price has noted, "like a celestial GPS device, finally stopping over the house of Mary and Joseph."[40] Matthew, of course, had no idea of what a star really is, and how far away they are.

Price suggests that Matthew anticipated the literary genius of J.M. Barie, saying that "no star can pinpoint an individual hovel from high up in space. We are no longer talking about a star, as in the beginning of the story of the Magi. We are talking about Tinkerbell."[41] And once the star has locked the coordinates, what does Matthew report? They go into the *house* and see "*the child* with Mary his mother." Not a stable, but a house; not a newborn babe, but a *paidion*.

The Greek word *paidion* is commonly used for a child the age of a toddler or even older. In Luke's story, the shepherds found in the manger a *brephos*—the Greek word for unborn child or newborn. So, Wise Men mingling with shepherds and cattle in a stable is not what Matthew had in mind, because they arrived long after Jesus had been born. Nor, by the way, does Matthew mention *three* Wise Men; he mentions three gifts. In early Christian art, more Wise Men sometimes are depicted. Folk imagination has created an elaborate mythical tableau of the stable the night Jesus was born.

But that's the least of the mistakes in the broader story. Wise Men arriving from "the East," drawn by an astrological sign, is what we would expect in first century thinking, when meteors or eclipses—happenings in the heavens—were considered good or bad omens. Is that really how God operates, or is it just it how first-century superstition operated? You know the answer.

Historians have long dismissed Herod's negotiations with the Wise Men (also reported in Matthew 2) as utter nonsense: "You go find the new king of the Jews and let me know where he is." None of this is history, not merely because there is no *contemporary documentation*, but because the real Herod would have done no such thing. He wouldn't have trusted these strangers to be his spies. Every element of the story is a literary creation.

And it is bad fiction that doesn't reflect well on God at all and gives us another example of defective theology in the New Testament. Do Christians ever think of the story's implications that Price draws to our attention? You have to ask, he says,

> why the Tinkerbell star first led them to Jerusalem, *the wrong town*–and much worse–to Herod, who only became aware of the birth of a potential rival after the Magi inquired about the newborn King of the Jesus. It was then and only then that Herod resolved to kill Jesus. Why didn't God's celestial homing device lead them directly to Bethlehem in the first place, as it eventually wound up doing anyway? Then Herod would have had no knowledge of the birth and no reason to dispatch a death squad to kill all the baby boys of Bethlehem![42]

The Wise Men ended up in the stable, the story tells us, but nothing of the sort actually happened. Folklore doesn't check facts, it mixes things up, it allows for–it *encourages*–the free reign of human imagination to come up with good stories, and sometimes not-so-good stories. This failure to check facts and the penchant for leaving reality in the dust didn't begin only sometime after the gospels were written. We can suspect that none of the original followers of Jesus, not *one* of the disciples and other peasants in his entourage, were what we would call critical thinkers, people who knew how to put restraints on the stories that spread about Jesus.

Just think what can happen when stories are told and retold by credulous people for decades before they're written down. This is why there is so much fantasy, exaggeration, misinformation, and conflicting material in the gospels, and why the Mythicists wonder if the Jesus stories are even based on a real person. Paul was out there spreading the word about his hallucinations of a risen Christ, without mentioning any details about a real person, and this could have been enough of a framework for the storytellers to build on.[43]

When we see how the elaborate crèche scene emerged from just that *one* word, *manger*, nothing should surprise us.

Luke

Bring on the Angels

Trust Me

> 1 Inasmuch as many have undertaken to compile a narrative of the things which have been accomplished among us, 2 just as they were delivered to us by those who from the beginning were eyewitnesses and ministers of the word, 3 it seemed good to me also, having followed all things closely for some time past, to write an orderly account for you, most excellent The·oph'ilus, 4 that you may know the truth concerning the things of which you have been informed.

Historians might be tempted to say, "Aha, *here* we have something." The author of the gospel–again, no hint about his name or credentials–says that he wants to provide "an orderly account," and he includes that cherished word *eyewitnesses*. We don't know who "most excellent Theophilus" might have been. Since the name means *god-lover*, the author may simply have been indulging in word play. But his motivation is supposedly pure: He is writing his story so that this Theophilus "may know the truth." What more could we want?

It is clear, however, that the author was not an eyewitness himself: All these things about Jesus were "delivered" to the writer (v. 2). The historian's heart sinks. That's not good enough; we need to know his sources. Why should we trust Luke if he was writing 50 years after the fact, perhaps not even residing in Palestine? He no longer had access to eyewitnesses. Luke's motivation was that of all the gospel writers: to win followers to the Jesus movement.

But even so, let's give him the benefit of the doubt and look deeper. Maybe he'll surprise us. He promised history, the "truth about what happened."

Creating the Jesus Story from the Old Testament

Alas, our cautious optimism crashes and burns at the get-go. Luke's first chapter never rises above fantasy. Hey, it's well done, eloquent and charming. Who wouldn't love to see it rendered in stained glass?

As we have seen, Mark had nothing at all so say about Jesus' origin and birth. Matthew only offers his tedious genealogy, the angel's announcement to Joseph that Mary is pregnant, and a few terse comments about Joseph accepting Mary to save her reputation. In his second chapter, after the episode of the Wise Men, he reports that the holy family fled to Egypt to escape Herod.

Luke builds a much more elaborate story, a prequel to the birth of Jesus, told in a whopping 80 verses. And as soon as we begin it, we can tell what Luke is up to.

We saw that Mark modeled the temptation of Jesus in the desert on the Old Testament story of Israel in the desert: 40 days parallels 40 years. Not to be outdone, Luke reaches much more deeply into Israel's past to find a parallel, namely, the story of Abraham and God's promise to him that he would be the father of a great nation.

There was only one catch: Abraham had no children, and his wife Sarah was old, well beyond her childbearing years. But, like the agenda-driven gospel writers, God moves in mysterious ways. He didn't let Sarah's barrenness stand in the way of his promise that Abraham's descendants would outnumber the stars in the sky. Israel's true destiny got underway with the birth of Isaac.

Luke selected this folklore theme to begin his Jesus story, and anyone at the time would have gotten it. Here again we find the story an elderly barren couple, Zechariah (a priest who served in the Jerusalem temple) and Elizabeth. These two are chosen to be the parents of the forerunner to Jesus, John the Baptist. Israel's beginnings can be traced to a barren couple, and the culmination of its history–the beginning of the end–can be credited to the faithfulness of a barren couple.

This is theology through and through. Just in case there might be someone who *didn't* get it, late in the chapter (v. 55), Luke has Mary say that this story is unfolding "according to the promise he made to our ancestors, to Abraham and to his descendants forever."

As is the case with Matthew, Luke didn't know what it meant to write history, despite his posturing. He's not the first writer to mistake *propaganda* for history.

The story is found in Luke 1:5-37. It's too long an excerpt to print here, so please consult your Bible for the text.

———

Of course, Zechariah was shocked to be told that his wife would have a child and voiced his doubt to the angel. He gets a smackdown for being skeptical, for talking back, and is told he won't be able to speak again until the baby is born. The angel predicts a glowing future for their son, omitting any mention that his heroic son would one day be beheaded.

At verse 26 we find that the angel has moved on to visit Mary, to give her the news that she will soon be pregnant by divine intervention. Luke betrays no knowledge whatever of Matthew's famous proof-text, i.e., Isaiah 7:14 ("Behold, a virgin shall conceive"). If he'd had a copy of Matthew in front of him, he might have seen that this quote was simply bizarre, and had no bearing on the matter.

Unlike Zechariah, Mary got a break when she doubts the angel's message. Of course she was nonplussed, since she wasn't married. The angel didn't punish Mary for *her* skepticism, though. Gabriel told her that the holy spirit would do the trick and that her son would be the son of God.

It's at the end of this first half of the chapter that we hear for the first time that Elizabeth is Mary's "kinswoman," and the angel tells her that Elizabeth is six months along on another miraculous pregnancy. Two orders of miracle are going on here: Mary didn't have a husband, and Elizabeth no longer had a functioning womb. Gabriel drops the standard line that Christians have been repeating for two millennia, "with God nothing will be impossible," and departs.

In the second half of the chapter we'll move into a dimension of people relating to people—how refreshing for the historian. In the first half, though, we're in a twilight zone. The dominant player is an angel, which is a major obstacle for any historian, even the most conservative, evangelical scholars. Very few angels, in the entire history of the world, have been spotted in the flesh. Well, let's face it, the actual count stands at *zero*. They are as scarce as spaceship aliens.

Why even belabor this point? Because we're trying to nail down the history quotient in the gospels, and so far things don't look good. Thousands of angels have been depicted in western art, based entirely on imagination, largely because they've been such a common theme in religious fantasy literature. Artists have turned out so many angels because no one has actually seen them. Luke leads us full throttle into this fantasy world. In his two-volume work Luke-Acts, he routinely gives angels roles to play. This earns only demerits from historians.

It would be a stretch to suggest that there were eyewitnesses to these scenes featuring Zechariah and Mary. The text tells us that Zechariah was alone in the temple burning incense when Gabriel appeared to him—no eyewitnesses there—and the crowd outside later assumed that he had seen a vision. Mary is presented as being alone when Gabriel called on her.

Visions are a way of evading the embarrassing truth that angels have never actually been seen. The trick is to get the credulous faithful to believe that the *angels in visions* are real. Angels are a theological device; God was thought to be so high above the human realm that he required messengers to relate to humans.

A nice touch, based on folklore's love of humor, is Gabriel's pettiness in cursing Zechariah to be mute. If I were still a Christian, I wouldn't press this as a way that God treats people. To avoid incriminating God, fess up that it's just fiction. The storyteller got a little confused, by the way, making a silly mistake. In verse 62, deep into the second half, Zechariah asked for a writing tablet to confirm the name of his new son: "And they made signs to his father, inquiring what he would have him called." What? Zechariah wasn't deaf, he was mute. But, even so, if we want to hunt for the slightest scrap of history here, we're going to have to scour the second half of the prequel. Don't get your hopes up.

Now, please turn to Luke 1:39-80 in your Bibles. Again, it's too long an excerpt to print here.

———

Mary visits Elizabeth as soon as she hears that the latter is going to have a baby too, although she doesn't have a clue about the significance of Elizabeth's pregnancy (vv. 39-40). When Elizabeth hears Mary's voice, the baby "leaps" in her womb and she is filled with the holy spirit, presumably the same holy spirit that got Mary pregnant (v. 41). Elizabeth calls Mary "blessed" and even addresses the baby in Mary's womb as "my Lord." She is overawed that the mother of her Lord would come to visit her (v. 43). Elizabeth praises Mary for believing that the words spoken to her by the Lord would come true, although this is precisely what had Mary doubted. Mary recites the famous *Magnificat*, a hymn of praise that has been widely adopted for liturgical purposes, based on Old Testament models.

Since Luke demonstrated his skill as a creative fiction writer in the first half of the prequel, it would be a surprise if he suddenly emerged as an historian in the second half. Why would that happen? Yes, these are people in the second half—the angel has left the stage—but we can be skeptical that Luke has given us history. Even if the characters themselves were truly historical individuals in first century Palestine, we still have to ask the hard, nitty-gritty questions that historians ask. Like this: What were Luke's sources for writing the Mary-Elizabeth episode? Since he was writing perhaps 50 years after the fact, his imagination—given the first half of the prequel—emerges as the prime suspect as his "source."

There's nothing in the story itself to indicate that any eyewitnesses recorded the scene. Remember Ben Witherington's laughable suggestion that Luke interviewed Mary, like some ancient investigative reporter? For Witherington to make that claim stick, he has to do more than just *say* it happened. He'd have to produce–here it is again–*contemporary documentation* to anchor the claim. Except for the fringe evangelical scholars who try with all their might and ingenuity to argue that Luke 1-2 is trustworthy, there are few secular historians or even mainstream religious scholars who have such confidence.

The historian who employs rigorous methods to clear away the clutter, who wants to get to the bottom of things–*what really happened*–cannot avoid the cultural and theological context. Just as Luke idealizes Jesus, he does the same thing in constructing the "holy people" who populate the early Jesus story. They are characters in his drama, and he idealizes them as he writes 50 years later. All along I've described Jesus as a Galilean peasant, and I do not mean this in a derogatory sense. *That's what he was.* We can't be sure that he even knew how to read. Recall that the literacy rate in ancient Palestine was around five percent.

But, for sure, *girls* were never taught to read. The conclusion is inescapable that Mary was illiterate. Thus the historian cannot give any credit at all to the *Magnificat* as a song or poem that Mary could have come up with. It's a feature of the fantasy genre that Luke created. She was teenage peasant at the time, and it is unlikely she would have been familiar with the Old Testament poetry on which the *magnifcat* is modeled. Luke remains stuck outside the groove of the historian; theology guides every detail of the story. He has Elizabeth address the baby in Mary's womb as *her Lord*, and Mary's script includes–as if she knew the theology that Luke would press so feverishly–"from now on all generations will call me blessed."

The heart of the *Magnificat* (vv. 50-53) is the standard theobabble of which the Old Testament authors were so fond, mindless flattery of Yahweh that bears no resemblance to how the world works:

His mercy is for those who fear him
    from generation to generation.
He has shown strength with his arm;
    he has scattered the proud
        in the thoughts of their hearts.
He has brought down the powerful from their thrones,
    and lifted up the lowly;
He has filled the hungry with good things,
    and sent the rich away empty.

Following the description of the circumcision and naming of John, Luke inserts a long poem, which he puts on Zechariah's lips. It celebrates the mighty savior through whom "we would be saved from our enemies and from the hand of all who hate us." Luke remained under the spell of this wrong-headed theology, and he wrote *after* the destruction of Jerusalem in 70 C.E. The mighty savior Jesus saved no one from their enemies or from those who hated them. Sorry, that's just the way history turned out.

Zechariah is sure that his son will be the one to prepare the way of the Lord–in this case, Jesus. The poem ends beautifully with poignant lines that evoke the religious yearning that God will eventually "make everything all better." After all, isn't that why most folks cling to faith?

By the tender mercy of our God,
   the dawn from on high will break upon us,
   to give light to those who sit in darkness
      and in the shadow of death,
   to guide our feet into the way of peace.[44]

The part about the dawn breaking may even be meant to evoke the about-to-dawn kingdom of God that Jesus preached. But John the Baptist, who scorned those who came to him to "flee from the wrath to come," would have had little patience with the "tender mercy of God."

We can be impressed with Luke's mastery at spinning a good story, but it's unlikely that we'll get much history from him. He couldn't wrestle free from the dogma that Israel's story *must* turn out according to an ancient promise made by a tribal deity to a desert-dwelling patriarch. Luke had to tell his story in terms of that expectation, and he re-imagined Jesus in the culminating role.

Jesus was to be the new king, and a triumphant one. That was the point of tracing Jesus back to King David. Of course, the triumphant entry fell flat, all of the hoopla of Palm Sunday notwithstanding, and thus the New Testament sees Jesus in cosmic terms instead of political or military terms. The messiah won't overthrow the Romans, after all, disappointing all those Jewish hopes. No, he will enable the kingdom of God to descend from heaven to earth, "the dawn from on high will break upon us."

Of course, something got derailed. No overthrow took place, and Christianity had to fall back on the claim that Jesus rose from the dead, bringing another kind of victory altogether. This is the story, not the history, that Luke is selling.

John

Jesus on Steroids

When I turn to the gospel of John, I always think of a famous insult that grew out of the bitter feud between Mary McCarthy and Lillian Hellmann, which probably has never been equaled in the history of American letters. McCarthy said of Hellmann, during a TV interview with Dick Cavett in 1980, "Every word she writes is a lie, including *and* and *the*."

Maybe it's not fair to say that *every* word John wrote was a lie, but why is it so tempting to say so? Indeed, Richard Carrier has remarked that John's gospel is "a complete fabrication, of no historical value in discerning the historicity of Jesus."[45] Carrier is blunt in pointing out, for example, that Lazarus is a character invented by John to play the role of Beloved Disciple (wholly unknown in the other three gospels): "John has clearly 'inserted' this figure into these stories he inherited from the Synoptics, and then claimed this new character as his 'source' who saw all these things (Jn. 21:24). In plain terms, that's simply a lie."[46]

As is the case with all theologians, John was confident that he wrote the truth, but his mind was riveted to a twisted extreme theology. More kindly it could be said that John wrote every word "under the influence"; he was inebriated by his exaggerated concept of Christ. The quote, "write drunk, edit sober" has gone viral as a Hemingway witticism, but sleuths have tracked it down to novelist Peter De Vries, one of whose characters (in the 1964 novel *Reuben, Reuben*) says: "Sometimes I write drunk and revise sober, and sometimes I write sober and revise drunk. But you have to have both elements in creation."

John shows his sober side by providing a well-structured gospel, even though it is lopsided (chapters 1-12 cover three years, chapters 13-19 are about one day), but he was drunk on *bad theology*. He went far beyond the tales of Matthew, Mark, and Luke in his portrait of Jesus, which is saying a lot because these earlier three operated with heavy theological biases of their own. John wrote drunk in creating a leading man who was egregiously egotistical. It would be hard to come up with another character, fictional or otherwise, who is so full of himself.

Jesus Helped with the Big Bang?

John saw the story of Jesus starting at Genesis 1:1, "In the beginning, God created." He contends that it was actually Jesus, the Galilean peasant, who created the world: "In the beginning was the Word, and the Word was with God, and the Word was God. He was in the beginning with God. All things came into being through him, and without him not one thing came into being."

Even devout Christians should wish that John had sobered up enough to strike that last sentence. John's account of Jesus might have baffled Matthew, Mark, and Luke. Matthew, as we have seen, traced Jesus' roots back to King David. Mark saw Jesus' 40 days in the wilderness foreshadowed by Israel's forty years of wandering. Luke recalled the Abraham story to draw a parallel, and he even listed Jesus' ancestors going back to Adam (see Luke 3:23-28).

John would have seen these gestures as amateurish provincialism and ignored such limitations. He threw off all restraints. He took the "roots" concept to an unanticipated level, placing Jesus alongside God all the way back when the world was created. John wrote theology with wild abandon and didn't ask anyone to check his work. If he did, and if others approved, then he was part of a cultish Christian enclave that accepted his extremism.

He was so far removed from the original setting of the real Jesus that there was little to hold his theology back. And that's a point in favor of the Mythicists argument: John is a good example of runaway theology creating a mythological Jesus. He would have despised any suggestion that Jesus had been a Galilean peasant; his mythological Jesus was above all that.

Distressingly, for those who care about history—*what actually happened*—John's vision of Jesus is the one that Christians commonly assume is the most authentic. John's gospel became the most popular of the four because it simplistically promises eternal life. All you have to do is latch on to the hero, believe in the Bread of Life, the True Vine, The Way the Truth, and the Life—all cultic codes for Jesus—and you've got it made. John hit on the winning formula. The first verse of his gospel became one of the most famous in the Bible.

The Word Became Flesh

1 In the beginning was the Word, and the Word was with God, and the Word was God. **2** He was in the beginning with God. **3** All things came into being through Him, and apart from Him nothing came into being that has come into being. **4** In Him was life, and the life was the Light of men. **5** The Light shines in the darkness, and the darkness did not comprehend it.

6 There came a man sent from God, whose name was John. **7** He came as a witness, to testify about the Light, so that all might believe through him. **8** He was not the Light, but he came to testify about the Light.

9 There was the true Light which, coming into the world, enlightens every man. **10** He was in the world, and the world was made through Him, and the world did not know Him. **11** He came to His own, and those who were His own did not receive Him. **12** But as many as received Him, to them He gave the right to become children of God, even to those who believe in His name, **13** who were born, not of blood nor of the will of the flesh nor of the will of man, but of God.

14 And the Word became flesh, and dwelt among us, and we saw His glory, glory as of the only begotten from the Father, full of grace and truth. **15** John testified about Him and cried out, saying, "This was He of whom I said, 'He who comes after me has a higher rank than I, for He existed before me.'" **16** For of His fullness we have all received, and grace upon grace. **17** For the Law was given through Moses; grace and truth were realized through Jesus Christ. **18** No one has seen God at any time; the only begotten God who is in the bosom of the Father, He has explained Him. (NASB)

This is a fitting prologue for a gospel that will be long on theology and short on history. We could pose the same question to the author of this gospel that we would pose to any theologian who makes an extraordinary claim: how could he possibly know that a human being born in Palestine *had been present with God* when he created everything? Oh, but, of course, we are expected to grasp that this human hero hadn't become a human *yet*–that's part of the theological scheme.

Alas, verses 1-18 are insider shoptalk that makes theologians swoon (only those within the Christian cult, however), and they have learned from experience that they can get away with it.

At the outset, the hero is an unnamed Word who co-existed with God, but eventually came into the world as "true light." My guess is that these opening sentences of John's gospel, which Christians have heard from the pulpit countless times, are just so much white noise they've become accustomed to. So it's no wonder people don't grasp John's claim here that Jesus helped God create the world. Maybe they don't get it because Jesus Christ is not mentioned until verse 17.

Despite all the theological fluff offered here, there are a couple of negative notes sounded, as a way to introduce themes in the story that is about to unfold: John the Baptist was "not the light" and the main hero was not accepted by his people.

The prologue doesn't introduce the book's main character by name, Bart Ehrman notes. Instead, it "provides a kind of mystical reflection on the 'Word' of God, a being from eternity who was with God and yet was God." Not until the end of it do

> we learn who this "Word" of God was. When the Word became a human being, his name was Jesus Christ. Up to this point, that is, through the first eighteen verses of the book, the ancient reader may not have realized that he or she was reading an introduction to a biography. Rather, the prologue appears to be a philosophical or mystical meditation.[47]

The historian is frustrated at the outset by this "meditation." Our hope is shattered that John's agenda will include recounting *what really happened*. He's an over-the-top hero-worshipper. Does he do any better when it comes to John the Baptist, whom we know from the other gospels?

Justifying John

> **19** This is the testimony of John, when the Jews sent to him priests and Levites from Jerusalem to ask him, "Who are you?" **20** And he confessed and did not deny, but confessed, "I am not the Christ."
>
> **21** They asked him, "What then? Are you Elijah?"
>
> And he said, "I am not."
>
> "Are you the Prophet?"
>
> And he answered, "No."
>
> **22** Then they said to him, "Who are you, so that we may give an answer to those who sent us? What do you say about yourself?"
>
> **23** He said, "I am a voice of one crying in the wilderness, 'Make straight the way of the Lord,' as Isaiah the prophet said."
>
> **24** Now they had been sent from the Pharisees. **25** They asked him, and said to him, "Why then are you baptizing, if you are not the Christ, nor Elijah, nor the Prophet?"
>
> **26** John answered them saying, "I baptize in water, but among you stands One whom you do not know. **27** It is He who comes after me, the thong of whose sandal I am not worthy to untie." **28** These things took place in Bethany beyond the Jordan, where John was baptizing. (NASB)

Some New Testament scholars have drawn comfort from this block of verses. Even the gospel that is widely conceded to be so tainted by theology includes the story of John the Baptist. But the conversation of John the Baptist with these religious emissaries fails to convince for the same reasons that the so-called words of Jesus do. What are the *sources*?

We have no clue about any eyewitnesses who could have recorded the scene. How and when would the conversation have been written down? Even if we want to speculate that a written report was made to the Pharisees (John answers questions sent by their emissaries), it's hard to conceive how the gospel writer would have had access to the reports 60 or 70 years later, well after the destruction of Jerusalem. By all tests that historians employ to *write history*, these verses fail.

The Lamb of God

29 The next day he saw Jesus coming toward him and declared, "Here is the Lamb of God who takes away the sin of the world! **30** This is he of whom I said, 'After me comes a man who ranks ahead of me because he was before me.' **31** I myself did not know him; but I came baptizing with water for this reason, that he might be revealed to Israel."

32 And John testified, "I saw the Spirit descending from heaven like a dove, and it remained on him. **33** I myself did not know him, but the one who sent me to baptize with water said to me, 'He on whom you see the Spirit descend and remain is the one who baptizes with the Holy Spirit.' **34** And I myself have seen and have testified that this is the Son of God."

Now Jesus finally appears. John sees him approaching and pronounces the theological agenda that underwrites this gospel: Jesus is the Lamb of God who takes away the sin of the world.

Tough Problem VIII gives full attention to the bad theology at work here, namely, that God is satisfied by blood spilled in ritual sacrifice, which Christianity kicks up a notch by moving from animal to human sacrifice. There was nothing about blood sacrifice in the opening block of theobabble (vv. 1-18), but Jesus' role as sacrificial lamb is a central concept of this gospel. In fact, John's author *changes the day of the crucifixion* (differing from the other three) so that the death of Jesus takes place at the same time as the sacrifice of lambs in preparation for Passover.

As was mentioned earlier, this author provides another point of contrast: while Jesus visits John the Baptist, he is not baptized by him. The baptism is a central part of the story in Mark, Mark and Luke, but this author deletes it—or was unaware of it. Nor is there a description of the heavens splitting or of a dove descending. In this gospel, John the Baptist *says* that he once saw the spirit descending (but no splitting of heaven), at an unspecified time.

The author of this gospel, as do the others, relegates John to a subservient role. The Baptist confesses that Jesus outranks him, and his role is to help usher in the new age: "I came baptizing with water for this reason, that he might be revealed to Israel." The Baptist confesses that, because he had seen the spirit descending on Jesus, he is able to testify that "this is the son of God." These verses, 29-34, do not help make the case for multiple attestation. At first glance they may seem to do so, but there is no mention of Jesus' baptism. Historians are obliged to see no more here than variations in Jesus folklore.

The First Disciples of Jesus

35 The next day John again was standing with two of his disciples, **36** and as he watched Jesus walk by, he exclaimed, "Look, here is the Lamb of God!"

37 The two disciples heard him say this, and they followed Jesus. **38** When Jesus turned and saw them following, he said to them, "What are you looking for?"

They said to him, "Rabbi" (which translated means Teacher), "where are you staying?"

39 He said to them, "Come and see." They came and saw where he was staying, and they remained with him that day. It was about four o'clock in the afternoon. **40** One of the two who heard John speak and followed him was Andrew, Simon Peter's brother. **41** He first found his brother Simon and said to him, "We have found the Messiah" (which is translated Anointed).

42 He brought Simon to Jesus, who looked at him and said, "You are Simon son of John. You are to be called Cephas" (which is translated Peter).

The author adds another twist here. The Baptist happens to see Jesus walking by and remarks to two of his disciples, "here is the Lamb of God," and they leave John to follow Jesus. That's in marked contrast to the recruiting of disciples in the other gospels. We've not heard before that Jesus won disciples away from John. In Mark, Jesus finds Andrew and Simon fishing by the Sea of Galilee.

If there is any history here, we would require some backstory to take it seriously. Without it, this is simplistic folklore, complete with clichéd script. Andrew finds his brother Simon and tells him, "We have found the Messiah." Based on what? Apparently based on a vision that John the Baptist claimed to have had. I suppose this would work in an age of credulous superstition, and given the huge popularity of the Fourth Gospel, modern believers swallow it as well; they don't grasp that there is just too much *strangeness* here. That Jesus renames Simon as soon as he meets him is part of the same pattern of folklore that ignores common human conventions.

Conservative scholars, bent on preserving the integrity of the Bible, might argue that John and Mark reflect different eyewitnesses, i.e., John's witnesses didn't hear Jesus' comment about "making you fishers of men," and Mark's witnesses didn't catch John's comment that "here is the Lamb of God." But Mark and John wrote their gospels decades apart, maybe even a half-century, and there is no documentation whatever to back the claim that either of them actually had access to eyewitnesses. Nor does John mention that the incident took place anywhere near the Sea of Galilee. In fact, in the next verse, we are told that Jesus decided *to go to Galilee*.

Jesus Calls Philip and Nathanael

43 The next day Jesus decided to go to Galilee. He found Philip and said to him, "Follow me." **44** Now Philip was from Bethsaida, the city of Andrew and Peter.

45 Philip found Nathanael and said to him, "We have found him about whom Moses in the law and also the prophets wrote, Jesus son of Joseph from Nazareth."

46 Nathanael said to him, "Can anything good come out of Nazareth?"

Philip said to him, "Come and see."

47 When Jesus saw Nathanael coming toward him, he said of him, "Here is truly an Israelite in whom there is no deceit!"

48 Nathanael asked him, "Where did you get to know me?"

Jesus answered, "I saw you under the fig tree before Philip called you."

49 Nathanael replied, "Rabbi, you are the Son of God! You are the King of Israel!"

50 Jesus answered, "Do you believe because I told you that I saw you under the fig tree? You will see greater things than these." **51** And he said to him, "Very truly, I tell you, you will see heaven opened and the angels of God ascending and descending upon the Son of Man."

I noted earlier that Jesus is not predicted anywhere in the Old Testament. There are texts that Christians later argued applied to Jesus, and this became the Christian mindset. Hence John can write here that Philip said, "We have found him about whom Moses in the law and also the prophets wrote." Of course, if you say something often and long enough, credulous followers will nod in approval. Even today, most Christians think that Jesus was predicted in the ancient literature."Moses in the law" means the first five books of the Old Testament, and "the prophets" refers to that vast body of writings most famously represented by figures such as Isaiah, Jeremiah, Hosea, and Amos. Jesus of Nazareth is *nowhere* mentioned in any of these writings.

But John is guided solely by his theology and crafts his dialogue accordingly. There is no contemporary documentation. It is exceedingly unlikely that disciples meeting Jesus for the first time would have said any such thing. And note here another confirmation that John knew nothing of the virgin birth: Philip refers to Jesus as the "son of Joseph." Even steeped in his own exaggerated theology, he remained unaware of the virgin birth idea advanced by Matthew and Luke—or he deemed it incorrect and rejected it.

John also gives us here the first glimpse of the arrogant, full-of-himself Jesus that he will present throughout his gospel. The banal exchange with Nathanael about the fig tree concludes (v. 51) with Jesus talking about heaven opening and angels going up and down, upon *him*.

John's problem in a nutshell: He so thoroughly believed his own theobabble, his uber-exalted Christology—Jesus had been there beside God at the time of creation— that he was no longer able to see Jesus as a real person. He could no longer even make a stab at portraying the Galilean peasant Jesus authentically.

By the time the author of the fourth gospel came along, an exaggerated Jesus who was the lifeline to eternal life was imbedded in Christian doctrine. Richard Carrier states the case well: "What Jesus did while on earth was irrelevant to what he could do for you now that he was exalted to the highest throne in heaven, and it was the heavenly Jesus that was sold to the masses, not a mere carpenter from Galilee."[48]

Grasping at Straws
What Would Jesus Do?

Years ago my channel surfing got stopped when I heard the words *oral sex*. It turned out to be a church service, of all things, where it was Q&A time. The pastor was taking questions from the congregation, and a woman asked if oral sex is okay for good Christians to do. Now, while televangelists don't have the smarts when they talk theology, they are survivors in TV land, and they know about strategy and positioning.

If this pastor–a man in this case–had answered, "Don't worry, oral sex is okay," he would've alienated the prudish elements of his congregation, the pornophobic folks who can't stand the idea that people might be having too much fun behind closed doors. If he'd said, "No, oral sex is not okay," he would have earned the contempt of most of his audience, who might also have suspected that he was simply a liar.

So the pastor punted to Jesus. He had a slick answer indeed: "When you are in bed with your husband, be guided by your love for the Lord. Whatever you are about to do, if you can say, 'I do this in the name of Jesus,' then go ahead and do it." He had no way of knowing how much the woman lived in the grip of Christian guilt about sex, but he was off the hook. And he could assume that the woman had a well-tuned image of Jesus. Oral sex probably didn't align with that image, and the pastor could have achieved a secondary goal as well, that of nudging yet one more person into the ranks of the prudish and pornophobic. No doubt he was prepared to say to his own wife, "Sweetie, you know Jesus doesn't mind if we have a good time." Jesus has achieved status as final arbiter.

There is enough good stuff in all those red letters, the very words of Jesus, for people to feel good about a few good rules, and in the 1990s the question "What would Jesus do?" became a favorite mantra among evangelical Christians to encourage and enforce good behavior, as understood by *themselves*, of course. They have Jesus in their corner. A good Christian woman from Mississippi, interviewed on a TV reality show, once said, "I do not believe in homosexuality. I believe it's wrong. It's in the Bible and I believe in the Bible and I love my Jesus."[49] She "loves her Jesus," so *of course* she is against homosexuality.

Hard Choices

In the way they deal with all this, we can put Christians–from their thousands of different denominations–into two main categories. The first kind (a tiny minority) acknowledges that mainstream New Testament scholars have discovered the uncomfortable truth that the real words of Jesus are not retrievable. Well, many won't go that far, but they know that they're in a minefield, and they have to step gingerly to pick out the *real* words of Jesus–or so they think. Christian scholar Jack Nelson-Pallmeyer speaks with refreshing candor when he says, "The Gospels offer competing, incompatible, and irreconcilable portraits of Jesus. We have no good choice but to choose between them."[50]

Of course, this is a deadly admission, because then you have to justify *how you choose*. And it comes down to *what you want Jesus to be like*. This is the way a huge number of Christians operate, and I have no idea if they know they're fooling themselves. I'm pretty sure they don't grasp that they've abandoned a historical approach to the gospels. They live their faith on the basis of a dreamed-up Jesus who never really existed, even if the Galilean peasant was a real person, and that is one of the tough problems that undermines Christianity.

The other kind of Christian, those who have their blinders on, won't hear of talk about problems figuring out what Jesus taught: "Bah humbug! All these Bible scholars can take a hike. The red letters don't lie. *That's what Jesus said.* The Bible is *revelation* after all."[51] Rather than open their minds to honest and serious study of the texts, they are confident that Jesus' teachings are right there for the taking. All you have to do is read the gospels.

These are the folks who become experts in ignoring many of Jesus' teachings, trying to convince themselves and others that Jesus taught things he never did. They've developed a huge arsenal of excuses to evade the clear meaning of words attributed to Jesus. Anyone who argues that the gospels are history has bitten off a lot to chew.

There is overwhelming evidence that the gospels fail as history. Christianity, a faith grounded in claims about a real Jesus who did real things, fails along with them.

Notes

1. Anthony B. Pinn, *Writing God's Obituary: How a Good Methodist Became a Better Atheist* (Prometheus Books, 2014), pp. 92-93.

2. Charles Guignebert, *Jesus* (University Books, 1956), p. 53.

3. As but one example, Luke 14:26, the "hate your family" text.

4. Covered fully with respect to Tough Problem IX.

5. Unlike Jesus, Carrier says "we have over a half a dozen relatively objective historians discussing the history of Alexander the Great." They were "disinterested historical writers employing some of the recognized skills of critical analysis of their day on a wide body of sources they had available that we do not." We can't trust everything they say, Carrier notes, but "we still cannot name even one such person for Jesus." He cites the example of Arrian, "our best historian of Alexander," who, "though he wrote five hundred years later, nevertheless employed an explicit method of using only three eyewitness sources," naming and identifying them, explaining "how he used them to generate a more reliable account," and discussing "their relative merits.

"That alone is quite a great deal more than we have for Jesus," Carrier says, "for whom we have not a single named eyewitness source in any of the accounts of him, much less a discussion of how those sources were used or what their relative merits were." *On the Historicity of Jesus* (Sheffield Phoenix Press Ltd, 2014), pp. 21-22.

6. In his 2007 book, *The End of Biblical Studies* (Prometheus).

7. It is true that most New Testament *manuscripts* that survive were made centuries after the time of Jesus. These are copies of copies of copies of copies of the originals. But the original gospels date from the first century, or a decade or two later at most. For the *intentional* alterations of the texts, see Bart Ehrman's *The Orthodox Corruption of Scripture* (Oxford University Press, 2011).

8. Daniel Dennett and Linda LaScola, *Caught in the Pulpit: Leaving Belief Behind* (Pitchstone Publishing, 2015), p. 29.

9. The red words of Jesus are neatly isolated from the black text, as if to say, "Red is the imprimatur that these are the very words of Jesus." But the red-letter editors can make insane mistakes. In Mark 13, verses 5 to 37 are supposedly Jesus' prediction of the end of the age. He is speaking privately to his disciples, but anyone who is paying attention should be dumbfounded to find these words in verse 14: "Let the reader understand." The *reader*? These words were obviously inserted into the text at a later time. They could not, by any

stretch of the imagination, be part of Jesus' address to the disciples. Yet they are printed in red. What were the editors thinking?

10. John 21:24 is not evidence otherwise: "This is the disciple who is testifying to these things and has written them, and we know that his testimony is true." By the time John's gospel was written, all of the disciples would have been long dead. This verse is in keeping with the robust tradition of attributing authorship to well-known figures, long after those figures had passed from the scene.

11. Ben Witherington, *What Have They Done with Jesus?*, p. 98.

12. I have more to say about this in Tough Problem X.

13. Ben Witherington, *What Have They Done with Jesus?*

14. Well, actually it was, we were just not aware of it. See "Demolishing the historicity of Jesus – A History," by Kenneth Humphreys, published in 2014, http://churchandstate.org.uk/ 2016/05 /demolishing-the-historicity- of-jesus-a-history/.

15. Richard Carrier, *Proving History: Bayes's Theorem and the Quest for the Historical Jesus* (Prometheus Books, 2012), p. 8.

16. I stress *verifiable* because the famous Josephus text that mentions Jesus does not stand up to scrutiny. A strong case has been made that Christian copyists tampered with it.

17. David Fitzgerald came up with the prize-winning title: *Jesus: Mything in Action.*

18. Richard Carrier, *On the Historicity of Jesus: Why We Might Have Reason to Doubt*, pp. 229-34.

19. Carrier at p. 100.

20. Carrier at pp. 57-58.

21. vridar.org/2012/01/25/david-fitzgeralds-next-book-mything-in-action

22. Burton Mack, *Who Wrote the New Testament? The Making of the Christian Myth* (HarperOne, 1996), p. 175.

23. Louis A. Ruprecht, Jr., *This Tragic Gospel: How John Corrupted the Heart of Christianity* (Jossey-Bass, 2008), pp. 13, 180.

24. Peter Brancazio, *The Bible from Cover to Cover: How Modern-Day Scholars Read the Bible* (Unlimited Publishing LLC, 2007), p. 373.

25. Richard Carrier, *Not the Impossible Faith*, p. 166 (emphasis added).

26. C.S. Lewis, *Mere Christianity*, p. 52.

27. See Richard Carrier, *On the Historicity of Jesus*, pp. 269-70, for the case against **Q**, especially footnote 33.

28. A helpful survey of the prophecies claimed, but that fail to do what the gospel writers claim, is Jonathan Erik Sjørdal, *Two Witnesses: Hebrew Texts Changed by the Greek New Testament* (2009). The ancient Christian authors scoured the OT for texts that apply to Jesus, but none actually do—at all. The issue is complex, however. At the time of Jesus there was no standardized Old Testament, and there was a lot of other religious literature, much of it now lost, that the gospel writers could have used.

29. See Richard Carrier, *On the Historicity of Jesus*, pp. 67; see especially pp. 67-81.

30. John Loftus, *The Christian Delusion*, pp. 316-43.

31. It's a big clue that Pope Francis is stuck in the ancient past that he believes in demons; this smiling holy man, who is so widely touted as a breath of fresh air, maintains a staff of exorcists.

32. "The introduction from *The Shadow* radio program 'Who knows what evil lurks in the hearts of men? The Shadow knows!', spoken by actor Frank Readick Jr., has earned a place in the American idiom," Wikipedia [en.wikipedia.org/wiki/The_Shadow].

33. The "moral teachings" that we do find in Mark are commonly ignored or minimized by discomfited Christians, e.g., in Mark 10 we find Jesus' counsel on divorce, so widely ignored,

even in evangelical churches, and his suggestion to a rich man that he sell his possessions and give the money to the poor. Christians have come up with a lot of ways to argue that Jesus really didn't mean what he said—or that such radical advice was meant for that one man only. And in Mark 11:25 Jesus laid down the rule that if you are asking God's forgiveness, you have to first forgive people you might have a grudge against. That is indeed a brilliant moral insight—Jesus gets points for that—but if there is one Jesus guideline that Christians ignore more than any other, this would be it.

34. For more about this as an indictment of Jesus, see Tough Problem IX.

35. See Bart Ehrman, *Misquoting Jesus*, pp. 133-39.

36. A good place to start is the Wikipedia article, Genealogy of Jesus [en.wikipedia.org/wiki/GenealogyofJesus].

37. Uta Ranke-Heinemann, *Putting Away Childish Things*, p. 63.

38. The major exception is the touching scene at the end of John's gospel, i.e., John 19:25-27, in which Jesus—on the cross—directs the beloved disciple to take care of his mother. But like so much of the material in John, we don't know the source for this detail and suspect pure invention. Matthew, Mark and Luke report no such thing.

39. The noun *manger* shares the same roots as the French verb, *manger*, meaning *to eat*.

40. Robert M. Price, *Blaming Jesus for Jehovah: Rethinking the Righteousness of Christianity* (Tellectual Press, 2016), p. 22.

41. Price at pp. 22-23.

42. Price at p. 23.

43. A strong case can be made that Paul's *only* mention of an episode from the gospels, namely the Last Supper, did not derive at all from historical remembrances, but from Paul's theology. If Jesus did exist, and he was the good Jew as portrayed in the gospels, it is unthinkable that he would have urged his disciples to drink his blood, even symbolically. That would require being open to the idea that Jesus willingly adopted ideas from pagan faiths. The sacred meal reflected in the "last supper" probably derives from the pagan milieu that influenced Paul's thinking. More about this in Tough Problem X.

44. Lyrical formatting added, here and in the quote of vv. 50-53.

45. Richard Carrier, *On the Historicity of Jesus*, p. 505.

46. Carrier at p. 500.

47. Bart Ehrman, *The New Testament: A Historical Introduction to the Early Christian Writings* (Oxford University Press, 2015), p. 177.

48. Richard Carrier, *Not the Impossible Faith: Why Christianity Didn't Need a Miracle to Succeed* (2009), p. 79.

49. Interviewed on an episode of the ABC TV show, *What Would You Do?*

50. Jack Nelson-Pallmeyer, *Jesus Against Christianity*, p. 140

51. As pointed out earlier, some modern Bible editors, who should know better but who show no scruples about catering to the ignorance of lay people, print the words of Jesus in red. They are neatly isolated from the black text, as if to say, "Red is the imprimatur that these are the very words of Jesus." The red-letter editors can make insane mistakes. Mark 13:5-37 is supposedly Jesus' prediction of the end of the age. He's speaking privately to his disciples, but anyone who is paying attention should be dumbfounded to find these words in verse 14: "Let the reader understand." The *reader*? These words were obviously inserted into the text at a later time. They could not, by any stretch of the imagination, be part of Jesus' address to the disciples. Yet they're printed in red. What were the editors thinking?

VII

Why the Resurrection Isn't Worth Believing

> If it was the fact, if the dead got out of the grave, why did He not show himself to his
> enemies? Why did He not again visit Pontius Pilate? Why did He not call upon
> Caiaphas, the high priest? Why did He not make another triumphal entry into
> Jerusalem? Why did He not again enter the temple and dispute with the doctors? Why
> didn't He say to the multitude: "Here are the wounds in My feet, and in My hands, and
> in My side. I am the one you endeavored to kill, but Death is My slave." Why didn't
> He? Simply because the thing never happened.
>
> —Robert Green Ingersoll. *Lecture on Orthodoxy.*

Not All Resurrections Are Created Equal

ANYONE WHO READS the New Testament with care can spot the bad resurrections, and even the most devout Christians can sense when they've wandered into dubious Halloween territory. Surely there must be a lot of cold sweat. They've got to muster all their resources to come up with excuses.

Sometimes they just have to roll their eyes and mutter resentments that these verses somehow made it into the New Testament. Surely it is here, above all, that their trust-the-Bible theology is sorely tested. Matthew missed his calling, by about 2000 years: He would have done well making up headlines for supermarket tabloids. Here, for example, is his sensationalistic report on the death and resurrection of Jesus:

> Then Jesus cried again with a loud voice and breathed his last. At that
> moment the curtain of the temple was torn in two, from top to bottom. The
> earth shook, and the rocks were split. The tombs also were opened, and
> many bodies of the saints who had fallen asleep were raised. After his
> resurrection they came out of the tombs and entered the holy city and
> appeared to many. (Matthew 27:50-53).

Matthew doesn't give a head count—was it dozens or hundreds of dead folks who wandered out of their tombs?—but, no matter the number he had in mind, historians wonder why "the many" who saw these lively corpses left no reports of this astounding event. Maybe there was a conspiracy on the part of *non*-Christian observers to cover up the massive bursting of tombs when Jesus died, but if this mass resurrection really happened, why don't any other New Testament authors mention it? It's a pretty spectacular thing to overlook.

Paul is the first author whose writings ended up in the New Testament, and he doesn't seem to have heard this story. An even bigger problem is that Paul hadn't heard about the empty tomb of Jesus either (we'll get to that issue later). The other gospel writers fail to include Matthew's dramatic report about the mass grave exodus: Mark, Luke, and John knew nothing about it. So we are justified in suspecting that Matthew had been eating wild mushrooms, or just gave free reign to his tabloid headline skills.

This tells us something about the superstitions of the time: Matthew felt he could get away with the story because people would take for granted that it was *possible*. After all, a lot of people even today suspect that ghost stories are true. The concept of resurrection was part of the ancient religious mindset.

Which brings us to another of the bad resurrections in the New Testament. In the very first New Testament document to be written, Paul's first letter to the Thessalonians, we hear his prediction of another mass resurrection, more corpses flying out of tombs, this time *literally* flying. In fact, this text is taken a lot more seriously by many modern Christians than Matthew's tabloid episode.

Of course, one of Paul's obsessions was that Jesus would soon return to earth. Jesus was just a few miles overhead in heaven, or even higher, depending on his view of heaven. All the people who had been converted to believe in Jesus, in the wake of Paul's preaching, would be gathered to Jesus when he returned.[1]

But some of the folks in the Thessalonian congregation were worried. What about their dead relatives who had also believed in Jesus? Would they be left out? Not to worry; Paul assures them that their dear departed will be included, declaring

> by the word of the Lord, that we who are alive, who are left until the coming of the Lord, will by no means precede those who have died. For the Lord himself, with a cry of command, with the archangel's call and with the sound of God's trumpet, will descend from heaven, and the dead in Christ will rise first. Then we who are alive, who are left, will be caught up in the clouds together with them to meet the Lord in the air; and so we will be with the Lord forever. (1 Thess. 4:15-17)

Musical accompaniment for the night of the living dead: Now that's a nice touch.

I know, I know, this is crazy cult talk: newly alive corpses floating up to the clouds to meet Jesus. Even Christians who are big fans of the apostle Paul might get uneasy driving by the town cemetery and imagining some of those burial plots bursting open with their dead relatives, leaping to the clouds to "meet Jesus in the air."

I assure you I'm not making this up. This text is in the very first New Testament document to be written: It's about as *authentically Christian* as you can get. It comes not from some fringe character but the apostle Paul, one of the primary architects of the Christian faith. It's another illustration of the over-the-top superstitious outlook of ordinary folks in the first century. There is one saving grace, though: We'll see later in this chapter that Paul probably intended these to be *spiritual* bodies, a distinction that seems lost on most Christians today.

Not all the Bible's resurrections are quite so creepy. Among the "minor" resurrections scattered in the gospels and Acts, the one that probably comes to mind as the standout is the raising of Lazarus by Jesus, described in John 11.

Jesus received word that his friend Lazarus was ill. Could he help out here with his healing powers? But, no, he declares that "this illness does not lead to death, rather it is for God's glory, so that the Son of God may be glorified through it" (v. 4). John's heavy-handed theology is already obvious.

Even after Jesus got the message about his ailing friend, he deliberately put off going see Lazarus for two days. The author of the gospel is heightening the drama with this detail, and then presents Jesus in a bit of an argument with his disciples. Jesus had said (v. 11) that Lazarus had "fallen asleep," which the disciples had taken literally, hence they say "if he has fallen asleep, he will be all right" (v. 12). John's theological agenda is now clear with vv. 14-15: "Then Jesus told them plainly, 'Lazarus is dead. For your sake I am glad I was not there, so that you may believe.'"

Since Jesus himself would end up being dead for only about a day and a half, John wants his readers to know that the miracle that Jesus pulls off here is indeed special: Lazarus had been in the tomb for *four* days.[2] In v. 39, Lazarus' sister Martha warns Jesus that "there is already a stench because he has been dead for four days," or as the King James translation bluntly puts it, "he stinketh."

This is a voice-activated resurrection: Jesus "cried with a loud voice, 'Lazarus, come out!' The dead man came out, his hands and feet bound with strips of cloth, and his face wrapped in a cloth." It is clearly the point of these details that the body that was put into the tomb is the same body that came out four days later. John will also make much the same point in his story of Doubting Thomas: The body of the newly alive Jesus is the same one that had wounds in his hands and his side. This is John's concept of resurrection, which is important to bear in mind for consideration later.

Up from the Grave He Arose

What do Christians today commonly mean by *resurrection*? What do they think happened to Jesus? I suspect that they assume that Jesus revived on the Sunday after his crucifixion. His body in the tomb came alive again, he walked out, departed the scene, and later visited his disciples. This is firmly embedded in the popular imagination especially because of vivid scenes in the gospels of Luke and John. In Luke, the resurrected Jesus shows up for a chat on the road to Emmaus and later eats a boiled fish. John has Jesus invite Thomas to touch his hands and the sword wound in his side–a wound reported, by the way, only in John's gospel.

The miracle of it all for Christians today, the part that makes it worth believing, is that the dead body of Jesus was suddenly alive again. This goes far beyond resuscitation, in which a person who is *almost* dead is brought back from the edge in the nick of time. The human brain dies if it has been deprived of oxygen for more than a few minutes; then the situation is hopeless. Resuscitation is not an option if there has been no respiration, no circulation of the blood, for many hours.

The reason that burial in the ancient world took place the day that a person died was that microbes begin their work on dead flesh immediately. Thus the resurrection of Jesus "on the third day," the re-igniting of life in his body, ranks as one of God's miracles. All the damage done by the organs ceasing to operate is overcome. Imagine, as the ancient gospel writers could not have, how much miracle work would've been involved reconstructing cells and complex cell structures that already had decomposed into mush.

Most Christians will probably proclaim with enthusiasm that this is exactly what happened, and this is exactly what it is important to *believe* happened. It is, by far, God's greatest miracle, the Easter event that marked a turning point in world history, celebrated in an old hymn that I recall from my childhood:

> **L**ow in the grave He lay,
>   Jesus my Savior,
>   Waiting the coming day,
>   Jesus my Lord!

> **U**p from the grave He arose,
>   With a mighty triumph o'er his foes,
>   He arose a Victor from the dark domain,
>   And he lives forever, with His saints to reign.
>   He arose! He arose!
>   Hallelujah! Christ arose!

> **V**ainly they watch His bed,
>   Jesus my Savior,
>   Vainly they seal the dead,
>   Jesus my Lord!

> **D**eath cannot keep his prey,
>   Jesus my Savior;
>   He tore the bars away,
>   Jesus my Lord![3]

When we sang these words we had no doubt that the body of Jesus was miraculously alive again.

Many liberal Christians, trying to bring their faith into alignment with a scientific understanding of the world, and willing to dispense with naïve miracles, have settled for interpreting Jesus' resurrection metaphorically. Of course, conservative Christians—entirely within their rights, it would seem to me—ridicule such wishy-washy compromise and skepticism. But resurrection understood metaphorically is probably not the least of their worries. What if, according to the New Testament itself, the body of Jesus that was put in the tomb actually didn't have *anything to do with* the resurrected body of Jesus?

Most Christians would be nonplussed at the suggestion. Isn't that just another liberal ploy to wiggle out of believing that Jesus really truly rose from the dead? But not so fast. Don't all New Testament verses about Jesus' resurrection have to be considered? We will shortly explore Paul's take on the resurrection, and the case can be made that Paul had a different idea about it, i.e., his view is at odds with what we find in the gospels.

It Ain't Easy Being Brought Back to Life

Let's pose a few questions to Christians who are adamant that the body of Jesus really truly sprang back to life. There are major problems to overcome.

What Happens Next?

In a murder mystery by Agatha Christie or Arthur Conan Doyle, the hero detective might be told upon arriving at a crime scene, "We've got a dead body on our hands." But for Christians who are overcome with joy that Jesus walked out of the tomb and is alive and well, the opposite problem soon becomes obvious: "We have a *living* body on our hands." How do they deal with the newly alive body of Jesus? He supposedly made a few appearances, but then what? "Well, he ascended into heaven," is the quick answer, and the first chapter of the Book of Acts says that the ascension of Jesus up to heaven took place 40 days later.

But we all know that this is a *lie*. It just won't do for Christians, at least those who see the problem, to insult our intelligence by saying that the ascension is just a metaphor. It was *not understood that way* by the original author. At best, we might generously call the story creative fiction or an outburst of religious fantasy; maybe the man who wrote the story, in full naiveté, took it seriously. Nevertheless *it is a lie*: The body of Jesus did not leave Planet Earth.

We all know that heaven is not some destination just a few miles overhead. Whoever wrote this story accepted the common notion that the Earth is a flat, solid, immovable structure resting beneath the realm of heaven. For the resurrection to be true, the shape of the Earth doesn't matter; its location and movement are irrelevant. But it's impossible to insert *the ascension* into the context of our current knowledge of the Earth as a planet that rotates and itself orbits the Sun, which in turn orbits the galactic center. Whatever your religious beliefs, says British scholar A.N. Wilson, you must know that "a man ascending vertically from the Mount of Olives, by whatever means of miraculous propulsion, would pass into orbit."[4]

Do Christians really want to go this route? Assume for a moment that the ascension of Jesus happened as described. He disappeared into the clouds and, although the witnesses below didn't know it, the living body of Jesus just kept going, up, up, up into orbit. Even Christians with the hardest skulls can sense that this is silly. And then they come up against an alarming forced-choice situation:

- The body of Jesus ascended up through the clouds and beyond, as described in the New Testament, and thus remains in orbit to this day. Remarkably, however, it has escaped detection, even in our time when NASA routinely monitors hundreds of thousands of pieces of space junk much smaller than a human body, *or*,

- The resurrected living body of Jesus remained on Earth, and, at some point, *he died again*. Who cannot be 100 percent certain that is actually what happened?[5]

By ending the story of Jesus so fancifully, by saying that he floated up out of sight forever, the New Testament is guilty of a cover-up. The storytellers declined to tell us what actually happened to Jesus. The Mythicists are not surprised, and we are entitled to wonder: Just how much of the entire Jesus story is a hoax? The folks who insist that the body of Jesus, the brutally crucified body that was put in a tomb, sprang back to life, must deal with these tough choices and legitimate suspicions.

Couldn't God Get the Story Straight?

In July 1969 when American astronauts landed on the Moon for the first time, President Nixon was not at a loss for words in bragging about the accomplishment. He announced that it was "the greatest week in the history of the world since Creation." This was long before Republican presidents had to pretend to be suitably pious—it wouldn't have worked for Nixon anyway—and evangelicals were stunned. They cleared their throats loudly, and Billy Graham, who had the president's ear, pointed out his error. He explained that Holy Week—Good Friday and Easter—outranked the moon landing; human technology was no match for God's most magnificent miracle. How could anything outrank the salvation of all mankind accomplished by the death and resurrection of Jesus?

But this exaggerated importance of Easter morning inevitably raises the crucial question: What exactly *did* happen during Holy Week, on Easter morning? We must ask this because the gospels differ in their depiction of events. They simply *don't agree* on what took place at the tomb. If this is most important event in world history, *why is it so poorly attested?* Why is there so much muddle and confusion? We have seen earlier that the gospels were written decades after the supposed events, we have no contemporary documentation, and we have no basis whatever for supposing that the stories are based on eyewitness accounts.

Evangelical scholars have worked overtime trying to reconcile the differences in the four empty tomb stories, and one of their tactics is the suggestion that the gospels capture different eyewitness accounts. We all know that eyewitnesses can disagree on how an event has unfolded. Or rather, they are looking at events from different perspectives. But this won't do; there are glaring differences. Jesus emerging alive from the tomb is supposed to be the most important event in human history. How could God have inspired conflicting stories about it?

By the way, the scholarly literature on the resurrection/empty tomb stories is vast beyond imagining—books, articles, journals, doctoral dissertations . . . thousands of Bible specialists trying to sort out the discrepancies and contractions, hoping to detect and glean tiny fragments of history that these stories may preserve. The anthology, *The Empty Tomb: Jesus Beyond the Grave*, includes massive notes and bibliography to guide those who are curious enough to dig beyond the surface in this arcane scholarly realm.[6]

Here are the basic details of the empty tomb stories that emerge from a quick read of the relevant chapters of the four New Testament gospels.

Mark 16: At dawn, three women arrive at the tomb: Mary Magdalene, Mary the mother of James, and Salome. Before arriving, they'd wondered who they might find to roll the large stone from the tomb entrance, but on arrival they find that it has already been removed. They enter and find a young man sitting there, dressed in white. He tells them that Jesus has been raised and they should tell Peter and the disciples that Jesus will meet them in Galilee. They flee terrified, and—here is the abrupt ending of Mark that has bothered so many—tell no one.

Matthew 28: Only this gosepl reports, in chapter 27, that Pilate had ordered guards placed at the tomb. Then, before dawn on Easter morning, two women arrive at the tomb, Mary Magdalene and "the other Mary." During an earthquake, an angel from heaven (who looked like lightning, dressed in a garment white as snow) rolls away the stone and sits on it. The guards faint. The angel tells the women that Jesus has been raised, and orders them to go tell the disciples. But they ran smack into Jesus, who tells them to let the disciples know he will be in Galilee.

Luke 24: Mary Magdalene, Joanna, the mother of James, and other unnamed women arrive at the tomb. They find the stone removed, enter and see not a corpse but two men dressed in dazzling clothing. This scares them and they bow to the ground. The men tell them that Jesus has been raised, as Jesus had said would happen. They return to tell "the eleven" and others, who consider their report "an idle tale." In some manuscripts there is an additional verse, i.e., Peter ran to the tomb and was puzzled that it was empty.

John 20: Mary Magdalene alone goes to the tomb while it's still dark and finds the stone rolled away. She goes to tell Peter and another disciple, "the one whom Jesus loved," that the body of Jesus is missing, both of whom run to the tomb. The latter reaches the tomb first, but when Peter catches up, he enters the tomb and is followed by the other, who "believes" because they found the burial clothes. These two head home, but Mary remains weeping at the entrance. She then sees two angels in the tomb who ask why she's crying. When she turns around, she sees Jesus, but mistakes him for the gardener. She recognizes him when he addresses her by name and tells her to go to the disciples with the news that he is about to ascend to be with his father, which she does.

Conservative Christian scholars labor diligently, and implausibly, to create a storyline that accommodates all of these contradictions and inconsistencies. Meanwhile, secular historians shrug their shoulders. Why bother?

They know it's not worth the effort. They recognize what's going on with these documents written decades after the "event": a layering of legend and folklore. It was a process that proceeded as gospels continued to be written.

Bart Ehrman points out how Christian spin-meisters got really carried away in the Gospel of Peter, which was written even decades later, perhaps 150-200 C.E. According to this gospel, "Jesus comes out of the tomb as tall as a mountain, supported by two angels, nearly as tall themselves." Behind them, "from the tomb, there emerges the cross, which has a conversation with God in heaven, assuring him that the message of salvation has now gone to those in the underworld."[7] The story had grown quite a bit in the telling.

The empty tomb stories fail to advance the case for Jesus' resurrection. And guess who is probably one of the strongest allies of those who are skeptical of these accounts? The apostle Paul! He is *obsessed* with the resurrection of Jesus, a theme that he drives home relentlessly, yet he fails to mention an empty tomb in any of his letters. Wouldn't that be the most important aspect of the Jesus story for him to recall? He'd have shouted it from the rooftops.

Paul's Letter to the Galatians

The Smoking Gun

We will get to the full weirdness of Paul later (Tough Problem X), but let's take a quick look at his famous rant to the churches in Galatia, and its implication for the tale of the empty tomb.

Paul's only experience of the risen Jesus was through visions and revelations (i.e., hallucinations). These he considered of such superior quality that he deserved to be ranked with the disciples who knew and followed Jesus. (Paul, of course, never did.)

It's impossible to know the original setting and circumstances of his revelation experiences, despite the dramatic accounts in the Book of Acts. The famous "road to Damascus" episode is recounted three times in Acts, written maybe 40 or 50 years after the "event," but Paul makes no mention of it in his letters. That raises suspicions.

Historians know that Paul's letters must be given greater weight than stories created a half-century later. His letters are the closest witness we have to what the earliest Christians believed; Paul's failure to mention the empty tomb and the dramatic Damascus Road conversion are curious omissions indeed.

In his letter to the Galatians he brags about keeping his distance from the original disciples. Even if the Damascus Road conversion is fiction, there can be no doubt that Paul's hallucinations turned him into a passionate follower of the risen Christ. But we have to wonder about his mental state. Wouldn't it have been a natural impulse for him to rush back to Jerusalem or Galilee looking for the disciples, to learn as much as he could have about Jesus? But no, he wasn't interested. Apparently, his private revelations were all he needed.

He begins his letter to the Galatians by stressing his direct pipeline to God: "Paul, an apostle, sent neither by human commission nor from human authorities, but through Jesus Christ and God the father, who raised him from the dead." Later in the first chapter (vv.15-20), he is blunt about his independent status.

God had set him apart before he was born, Paul says, calling Paul through his grace. Not a very modest start. Then, when it pleased God to reveal his Son to him so he "might proclaim him among the Gentiles," Paul "did not confer with any human being," nor did he "go up to Jerusalem to those where already apostles before" him, those lousy bastards. No, "he went away at once into Arabia" with a nonstop return ticket back to Damascus. Then, *after three years*, he "did go up to Jerusalem to visit Cephas [Peter] and stayed with him fifteen days." You can almost see him scowling a bit as he grudgingly admits that detail. But, he hastens to add, "I did not see any other apostle except James the Lord's brother."[8] That's it! Other than that, it's all from me! "In what I am writing to you, before God, I do not lie!"

Scholars of Christian origins, as well as secular historians, would dearly love to know what Paul and Peter talked about for a full fifteen days. No record survives, though—no contemporary documentation at all—to fill us in on the information and insights exchanged.

But how could Paul have come away from those two weeks with Peter and not hear about the empty tomb on Easter morning? According to both Luke (at least in the version with the extra verse, 24:12) and John, Peter had dashed off to the tomb. Matthew reports that Peter soon heard about it from the women. Why does Paul write so passionately about the resurrected Jesus and yet not mention the empty tomb? There would seem to be four possibilities:

1. It just slipped Paul's mind. That seems so unlikely, given his strong belief in the resurrection. Wouldn't he have felt that the empty tomb was a true "Aha" event to prove his belief?

2. Paul indeed heard it from Peter, but didn't believe it and hence didn't care to repeat the story.

3. The stories of the empty tomb had *not been invented yet.* There was no Easter morning tomb drama at all for Peter to tell Paul about: These stories emerged only later when the gospels were written. Secular historians see nothing shocking about this option. The gospels are full of fantasy and legend, and the fantasy elements of the empty tomb stories themselves are obvious.

4. Paul had no use whatever for resurrection of a body that had gone into the ground—or, in this case, a tomb. The body that had died was no longer of any use; the physical body was *not* what was resurrected.

Galatians is the smoking gun: We know from this letter that Paul spent time with Peter, and inevitably–unavoidably–would have heard about the empty tomb from Peter *if it were a true story.* The reason an empty tomb reference is missing in Paul's letters–overwhelmingly, it seems to me–is that the gospel writers had not yet spun their tales. I will have more to say below about Paul's concept of a spiritual resurrection, in which the body that dies plays no part.

We should note, by the way, that although Paul's Letter to the Galatians does qualify as contemporary documentation, it represents only *his* side of the story. Paul says that he "stayed with Peter" for fifteen days, but we also know from other texts that the two didn't get along very well. So did they really hang out all that much during those fifteen days? It's too bad we don't have a record of the visit from Peter's perspective. But if *anything* about their hero Jesus had been discussed, surely the startling events of Easter morning would have been included.

The Dubious Value of a Forty-Day Resurrection

I've mentioned the famous quip from Steve Jobs that even the people who expect to go to heaven don't want to have to die to get there. I would add that most people who expect to go to heaven don't imagine that they will *take their bodies* with them.

For the most part, modern Christians are comfortable with the soul vs. body dichotomy: The soul is housed in the body, but once the flesh wears out, the soul takes flight. Your soul–this supposed divine spark that makes you *you*–goes to heaven to somehow merge with God and enjoy the company of Jesus. Most folks now sense that heaven really isn't "up there"–there's no place for human bodies to go.

Of course there are the fringe Christians–the true fundies and followers of nut case cults–who look forward to "the rapture." They take Paul at his word in 1 Thessalonians that those "saved in Christ" will float up to meet Jesus in the clouds. But in my experience, most Christians are troubled by such silliness. It just doesn't make much sense and reeks of cult craziness. No thank you, we won't be taking our bodies with us to heaven. There is no sense in which our bodies will be rebooted; that smacks too much of zombies and Frankenstein.

So what, then, is the point of the body of Jesus getting rebooted? How does that relate to individual human beings getting to go to heaven? How in the world would it guarantee that? Maybe, at a stretch, it might seem to work if people really did believe that the body of Jesus ascended to heaven. Then it will happen to ordinary folks as well? No, there is just too much strangeness hobbling these concepts. How would the rebooted body of Jesus relate to *our souls* shuffling off this mortal coil and reaching their final destinations?

I mentioned in the Prologue that one of my seminary professors wondered out loud about the value of a forty-day resurrection–what good is it?–because he knew very well that Jesus didn't float up to space, to remain in orbit until the day of the rapture. Jesus died again and was buried again. Period. So what has been proved or demonstrated by the regeneration of his flesh for a few weeks?

The New Testament isn't even of one mind about the length of time that Jesus was alive again. We get the figure of forty days from the first chapter of Acts, but the gospels of Mark and John seem to have a much shorter time in mind before the ascension. Of course, that's irrelevant. Forty days or four days, it makes no difference. Jesus didn't float up anywhere, so if his body came alive again, he *died again* at some point. He was dead and buried. His body being alive again for a short period is simply ghoulish, and imparts no deep "spiritual meaning" whatever.

There seems to be deep confusion here in the struggle to figure out how human souls co-exist with our fleshy selves, and then eventually escape to be with God.

Confusion As Well About the Resurrected Body of Jesus

The layering of legend and fantasy in the empty tomb stories is matched by confusion about the characteristics of Jesus' alive-again body. Of course, let's face it: As much as stories of zombies and the walking dead have fascinated humans, no one *in real life* has ever bumped into a rebooted human body. (We're talking about those who have been in the grave for a while, cold and *dead,* as opposed to legions of folks who have claimed NDEs.)

So the storytellers rely on imagination, which supplies the details: Newly alive humans may have an unusual, unexpected aspect, and can do neat tricks. And it should be no surprise that the gospel writers assumed the resurrected Jesus could do remarkable things indeed.

Mark 16:9-20

Here, in Mark's forged ending, Jesus is said to have appeared three times before ascending: to Mary Magdalene (nobody believed her), then to two of the disciples as they walked in the country (nobody believed them), and finally to the eleven as they were gathered at a table. Jesus scolded them for not believing, after which he went up to heaven and sat down at God's right hand. One tantalizing detail: In verse 12, we read that he appeared to the two disciples alone "in another form."

Matthew 28

As Mary Magdalene and "the other Mary" were rushing to tell the disciples, they ran into Jesus. They grabbed his feet and worshiped him. Later, on a mountain in Galilee the disciples saw Jesus and worshiped him, although we are told that some doubted.

A later liturgical formula got placed on Jesus' lips: "All authority in heaven and on earth has been given to me. Go therefore and make disciples of all nations, baptizing them in the name of the Father and the Son and of the Holy Spirit" (28:18-19). (What serious historian could give any credit whatever to words supposedly uttered by a resurrected corpse?) Matthew neglects to mention any ascension of Jesus to heaven.

Luke 24

This is a different story that appears only in Luke, although it might have been based on a verse in Mark's forged ending, i.e., v. 12. Jesus, we are told, appeared to two of his followers who "were walking into the country." After Peter left the empty tomb wondering what had happened, the scene shifts to a road a few miles from Jerusalem.

There, two men were walking to the village of Emmaus and Jesus came along beside them. But they didn't recognize him. (The resurrected Jesus must not have looked like his former self.) They described the tragic end of their Lord to this stranger. Jesus lectured them on the meaning of the events, and accompanied them to their destination in Emmaus. He broke bread with them, they suddenly recognized him, and he vanished. His body had become one that could morph into a recognizable form and then—poof!—go away.

The two men returned immediately to Jerusalem to find the disciples. They described their experience and—poof again!—Jesus suddenly appeared in their midst. To prove that he is no ghost, Jesus said, "Look at my hands and my feet. See that it is I myself. Touch me and see. For a ghost does not have flesh and bones as you see that I have" (Luke 24:39). He even ate a piece of boiled fish to drive home the point. After giving them his lecture about the meaning of his death, Jesus led them to Bethany where he blessed them, then "withdrew from them and was carried up to heaven."

Careless pseudo-historian that he was, Luke forgot all about this when he wrote the first chapter of his sequel, The Book of Acts. (Or perhaps some unknown redactor meddled with the text.) All of the events above happened on Easter day in both Luke and Acts, but Jesus seems to have had a round-trip ticket to heaven.

In Acts 1:3, we read that "he presented himself alive to them by many convincing proofs, appearing to them over the course of forty days." The disciples quizzed him about when he would "restore the kingdom to Israel," but he evaded the question, more or less with, "How the hell should I know?" Then, "as they were watching," he got "lifted up, and a cloud took him out of their sight." Suddenly two men in white robes appeared and ordered them to stop standing about gawking. They returned to Jerusalem.

The author emphasizes that Jesus still has his original body: There was flesh and bones, and he ate a meal. Yet he had the capacity to appear and disappear. And this writer knew nothing of Matthew's story that Jesus appeared to the disciples on a mountain in Galilee.

John 20-21

John has Jesus present himself first to Mary Magdalene. He must have looked very different because she mistook him for the gardener. If you've taken Jesus away, she says to Gardener-Jesus, "tell me where you have laid him, and I will take him away." Only when Jesus addressed her by name did she recognize him, and he warned her, "Do not hold on to me because I have not yet ascended to the father." (What sense does *that* make?) She followed his order to go tell the disciples.

These two chapters provide the most extensive resurrection narratives. The disciples were behind locked doors ("for fear of the Jews"), yet Jesus suddenly appeared among them. We might wonder if John thought Jesus had ghostly qualities, but then we read that Jesus *breathed* on the disciples, saying "receive the holy spirit."

As it happens, Thomas was missing on this occasion. (Robert M. Price likes to point out the absurdity of a disciple, amply forewarned, not hanging around to meet the *resurrected Son of God*."What was Thomas doing, going out for pizza?") A week later, John tells us, Jesus "came and stood among them" again, although the doors were again locked. He invited Thomas, who didn't believe that Jesus had appeared to the others the first time, to touch his hands and sword wound. In Caravaggio's rendering of this scene, which appears on the cover of this book, Thomas poked his finger right into the wound.

One of the strangest chapters in the New Testament is John 21. Jesus showed up when the disciples had gone fishing early in the morning on the Sea of Tiberius (Galilee), but they didn't recognize him. Since they hadn't caught any fish, he instructed them to cast their net on the other side of the boat. Then they brought in a huge haul, 153 large fish to be exact. Only then did "the disciple whom Jesus loved" recognize him. Jesus invited them to come have breakfast.

A bizarre exchange ensued, in which Jesus asked Peter three times if he loves him, predicting that, when he gets old, someone "will fasten a belt around you and take you where you do not want to go" (v.18). The cryptic verse 19 adds, "He said this to indicate the kind of death he would have to glorify God." Well, Peter's curiosity was piqued: What would happen to the disciple whom Jesus loved? *None of your business* is the gist of Jesus' reply. Perhaps these verses were tacked on to the end of the gospel to shed light on the ultimate fate that befell Peter and the beloved disciple.

Although Jesus had earlier told Mary Magdalene (when she mistook him for the gardener) that he "had not yet ascended," this gospel does not report an ascension at its conclusion.

The later writings are not entirely clear on what to make of the resurrected body of Jesus. It seemed capable of passing through locked doors, yet was corporeal enough to eat, speak, and point to its wounds.

The purpose of this excursion has been get a grasp of what early Christians *thought* had happened, not to determine what really did. The legends of the empty tomb and Jesus sightings build on one another. Mark was the first, with more elaboration as the other gospels pick up the story. With no contemporary documentation, there's no way to anchor these accounts historically. Nothing but speculation and wishful thinking traces them back to any eyewitnesses.

Remember, the very earliest Christian documents, the epistles of the New Testament—especially those of Paul—reflect *no knowledge whatever* of any of these "events." The legends sprouted with Mark's seedling and grew more details as Matthew, Luke, and John reworked the story to suit their individual theologies. As we will see, Paul's concept of resurrection didn't even need Jesus to walk out of a tomb.

Jesus and Who Else?

Bunnies and eggs figure prominently in our celebrations of the coming of spring; they are symbols of new and abundant life. But they've got nothing to do with Jesus, right?

Think again. The very word *Lent* derives from a Germanic root that means "to lengthen," a reference to days getting longer as winter moderates. It's no accident that the resurrection of Jesus was thought to be a springtime event: a god coming back to life. From time immemorial, people assumed that the renewal of plant and animal life was connected to the resurrection—the reinvigoration or rejuvenation, at least—of the deities who were responsible for crops and fertility. After enduring months of bleak winter, people yearn for the return of new life and are grateful to the gods for making it happen.

The study of comparative religion can do wonders for jolting people out of religious parochialism and silliness. A former Facebook friend once posted gleefully one Easter morning, "He is risen!" But there are any number of gods of which this can be claimed. Christianity is *chock full* of borrowed ideas. As I mentioned in an earlier chapter, John Loftus has challenged Christians to apply the "outsider test of faith" to Christianity. If you can cut down another religion, are you sure your own faith can pass the test you use to falsify others?

If lots of other gods were believed to come back to life, what's so special about Jesus? If you're going to crow about *your* god rising from the dead, you need to be confident about disqualifying the other resurrections. Otherwise, ho hum, all these other rising gods set the example for Jesus (or more, accurately, those writing about him) to follow. Guess what: Your dance partners are other pagan faiths! You're dealing with stock-in-trade mythologies from the ancient world.

We saw in the last chapter that Jesus fits right in with other heroes on the Rank-Raglan hero scheme. I quoted Richard Carrier there, and this is his take on resurrection specifically.

> Many dying-and-rising gods predate Christianity, as we often know this from *pre*-Christian sources. Many effected their deaths and resurrections in different ways (the differences being moot to the point that they nevertheless died and rose back to life), and some even "returned to life on earth by being raised from the dead" in essentially the same way as Jesus did (who, after all did not stay on earth any more than they did). Whether one kind of resurrection or the other, these gods include Osiris, Dionysus, Romulus, Hercules, Asclepius, Zalmoxis, Inanna, and Adonis-Tammuz.[9]

For centuries, Christianity enjoyed a monopoly on resurrection, because the primacy of the New Testament was unquestioned and unchallenged until the 19th century. A handful of earlier skeptical voices like Diderot, Voltaire, and Jefferson come to mind, but few people thought to question the accounts of the empty tomb. In addition, the literature of the ancient world, with so many accounts of other gods, their exploits and resurrections, was not widely known outside academic circles.

But the more Christianity is studied in its ancient context, the more we see that it emerged as one of many cults that thrived at the time of its birth. There are hardly any original concepts in the New Testament. Even the teachings of Jesus, or those attributed to him if he is indeed a mythical character, are derivative. Chances are the early Jesus cult would have faded from the scene had it not been for the fanaticism of the apostle Paul and others who espoused a version of Christianity that, for all practical purposes, left the real Jesus of Nazareth—if there was one—in the dust.

Meeting Jesus in the Clouds

Corpses Not Welcome

Remember Paul's assurance to the Thessalonians (1 Thess. 4:16) that their dead relatives would rise from their graves to meet Jesus in the clouds? He knew what happened to corpses: Prior to the common practice of embalment, bodies were buried quickly because decomposition began immediately. Hence there were strong taboos about coming into contact with a dead body.

A body that has been in the ground for any length of time is unspeakably revolting. Hence there were taboos even against walking on graves. So when we read the verses in 1 Thessalonians about folks emerging from their graves to meet Jesus in the sky, we may shudder in disgust because *we misunderstand Paul's thinking*. He wasn't all that clear about it himself there. But he offered more detail, as we shall see shortly, in 1 Corinthians 15.

Now, Paul was a nasty piece of work; that's what Tough Problem X is about. On at least one level, though, I don't think he was stupid. Paul did not think that it was some horrible rotting flesh that would come out of the ground. He figured there was a *spiritual* body. So to grasp resurrection as Paul understood it, in contrast to the stories found in the gospels, it is important to read his epistles with some care.

Of course, Paul's take on resurrection may be misunderstood because Christians commonly don't read the epistles. There's not much excitement in these documents; readers yawn their way through them. I guess they can be forgiven: There are no cool stories in the epistles about Jesus walking out of a tomb or showing his wounded side and hands to his disciples.

Why Pay Attention to Paul?

It's one of the ironies of Christian origins that we can glimpse Jesus only through prisms created by writers decades after his death, based, at best, on second-hand information. Another irony is that the man who promoted Christianity with more vigor than anyone else never even *met* Jesus. There is no documentation, no hint at all, that Jesus and Paul crossed paths. Of course, that's one reason Paul never tells any stories about Jesus. Since the gospels hadn't been written yet, he didn't have them to around to "look up stuff." Since we know the gospels, it would appear that we know more about Jesus *than Paul did.*

So what good is Paul, then, this also-ran who never even met Jesus in person and in fact had persecuted the first Jesus followers? Well, Paul would have sworn on a stack of Bibles, so to speak, that he had encounters with Jesus *even better* than meeting Jesus in person walking around in Palestine. His visionary or mystical encounters with Jesus were extremely real, and trumped anything that the original disciples had known.

Of course, such encounters of people with gods have been claimed for millennia— what else is new? But eventually Christian authors would come along who had to say more than "he had a private religious experience." Hence tales were spun of Paul's dramatic encounter with Jesus on the road to Damascus: He had been knocked to the ground (as Caravaggio painted the scene, Paul was flat on his back beside his horse), and there was blinding light and a booming voice from the sky.

Despite such theatrics (an effort to help people visualize it), Jesus for Paul was strictly and only a spiritual entity. For the apostle born out of due time (1 Cor. 15:8), the on-going miracle—the one that turned his life around completely—was that Jesus still lived in the celestial realm and paid him visits. Although life had been snuffed out of a body on a cross, Jesus' life and his existence endured. Jesus, as a person who had walked the earth, was dead and buried. He was gone for good. It couldn't have mattered less to Paul if the body of Jesus rotted away in a tomb.

Hence he *never claimed* that Jesus appeared to him *bodily.* We have no way of knowing what prompted the vivid hallucinations in which Jesus was so real to Paul, temporal lobe epilepsy or something else. But they convinced him, as nothing else ever had before, that the Pharisees were correct about resurrection, not the Sadducees who rejected it.

Paul was confident that his mystical encounters and conversations with Jesus were just as valid as those enjoyed by the original disciples hanging out with Jesus.

This was the substance of Paul's delusion—at least so I say, using that blunt word, as have countless others who don't trust "data" derived from mystical encounters. But during the last 2,000 years, Christian theologians have taken Paul at his word, and that's why they pay attention to his writings. That's why his Letter to the Romans has been studied probably more than any other document in Western history.

As I will discuss later in Tough Problem X, Christian scholars, theologians, and preachers have made a specialty of turning a blind eye to Paul's strangeness. The colossal Christian blind spot about this deeply flawed person is difficult to wrap our minds around. However, anyone who is deeply curious about Christian origins, who wants to grasp what *early Christianity* was like, must plunge right in and do a full immersion in Paul's writing. Yawning your way through the epistles is just part of Christian discipline, if you want to get at Christian truth as it was "in the beginning."

And on the topic of the resurrection, what Paul actually meant by a *spiritual body,* there are a few key texts to consider that allow us to see that he, in fact, had no use for an empty tomb.

Made of Celestial Stuff

The Spiritual Body

If Jesus really *did* exist, if there are echoes of his authentic teaching in the gospels, it would appear that he was a delusional apocalypticist. He believed that the kingdom of God was about to arrive, and not in some watered-down metaphorical sense. It was on the verge of being very real and dramatic, during his own time. Governments would be no more, and rulers would be removed from their seats of power. God and Jesus would be in charge after sinners had been purged and destroyed, and the righteous remnant would enjoy the bliss of God's company in the new kingdom.

The apostle Paul was a dyed-in-the-wool apocalypticist as well. We can be certain of this from Paul's own letters. It's impossible to be quite so sure about Jesus because his message got filtered through, and distorted by, the various gospel writers.

Because the coming kingdom of God was one of Paul's primary obsessions—he was confident he would live to see it up close and personal—we can be sure that he gave it a lot of thought: What would it really *be* like, with God and the surviving righteous Christians calling the shots and running the world? We get a glimpse of his warped fantasy life when he gave advice to the Corinthians about lawsuits among Christians, who were called "saints" in the argot of the early church. He felt that it was a scandal for Christians to take one another to court. Their anticipated roles in the upcoming kingdom made any resort to civil courts seem absurd:

> Does any one of you, when he has a case against his neighbor, dare to go to law before the unrighteous and not before the saints? Or do you not know that the saints will judge the world? If the world is judged by you, are you not competent to constitute the smallest law courts? Do you not know that we will judge angels? How much more matters of this life? So if you have law courts dealing with matters of this life, do you appoint them as judges who are of no account in the church? (1 Cor. 6:1-4, NASB)

Yes, you read that right: After Jesus has come back and God's kingdom has been put in place, Christians–those whom he addresses in the letter–will be in a position to judge *angels*. For the illiterate lower classes that fell under the spell of Paul's pie-in-the-sky message, this was heady stuff. This text could rank as "Exhibit A" in making the case that Paul was off-the-wall delusional.

This also helps make the case that Paul could lie awake nights thinking about many of the details of the coming kingdom. Since no one was ever going to die, he must have pondered what our bodies would look like, decade after decade, century after century. When we're in our teens or twenties, we might be proud of our bodily prowess, but we usually have less to celebrate when we drift into our forties, fifties, and beyond–and this was before people had any medical care at all. Would I want to be stuck with this body *forever*? Such concepts of time–decades and centuries–dissolve in the contemplation of eternity, but even so, how would *flesh* endure forever and ever?

I mentioned earlier that Paul could not possibly have meant that it would be rotting flesh that would be propelled from graves to meet Jesus in the clouds. And Paul addresses this very issue. Human flesh as we know it will be a thing of the past when Jesus gets back and brings God's kingdom with him.

Twinkling Eyes and Trumpets

As we struggle through the tedium of the epistles, it's common for our eyes to glaze over and miss crucial details in Paul's writing. For those who fight tooth and nail to defend the empty tomb stories, a body bouncing back to life, 1 Corinthians 15 provides a sobering corrective, an **Aha** moment about Paul's thinking–and why an empty tomb meant nothing to him:

> But someone will ask, "How are the dead raised? With what kind of body
> do they come?" Fool! What you sow does not come to life unless it dies.
> And as for what you sow, you do not sow the body that is to be, but a bare
> seed, perhaps of wheat or of some other grain (vv. 35-37).

Talking about "sowing" a body belies the ancient ignorance of atoms and molecules, genetics and DNA. Paul struggled to explain how flesh would be transformed, and since the heavenly realm was about to be lowered to earth, or vice versa, he could speak of *heavenly* bodies.

> Not all flesh is alike, but there is one flesh for human beings, another for
> animals, another for birds, and another for fish. There are both heavenly
> bodies and earthly bodies, but the glory of the heavenly is one thing, and
> that of the earthly is another. There is one glory of the sun, and another
> glory of the moon, and another glory of the stars; indeed, star differs from
> star in glory (vv. 39-41).

And then comes his big distinction between the earthly and the heavenly."What is sown is perishable, what is raised is imperishable. It is sown in dishonor, it is raised in glory. It is sown in weakness, it is raised in power. It is sown a physical body, it is raised a spiritual body. If there is a physical body, there is also a spiritual body" (vv.42-44). A few verses later, he states explicitly that "flesh and blood cannot inherit the kingdom of God, nor does the perishable inherit the imperishable" (v.50).

In light of that last sentence alone, it's hard to imagine Paul tolerating the suggestion that the corpse of Jesus walked out of a tomb and later floated up to heaven. And as would be the custom of thousands of theologians in the centuries that followed, he throws the cloak of mystery over a belief that is indefensible by logic and common sense. Listen, he says, "I will tell you a mystery! We will not all die, but we will all be changed" (v.51).

We now arrive at one of the most well-known passages of Paul's writings. It's one of the most beloved, because of its setting in Handel's *Messiah*. The transformation will happen *in a moment*, he says,

> in the twinkling of an eye, at the last trumpet. For the trumpet will sound, and the dead will be raised imperishable, and we will be changed. For this perishable body must put on imperishability, and this mortal body must put on immortality. When this perishable body puts on imperishability, and this mortal body puts on immortality (vv. 52-54).

Again Paul mentions the trumpet that he promised to the Thessalonians–the whole thing was orchestrated in his fantasy–but here he adds that all those bodies flying out of the graves aren't really the corpses that were put in the ground: The dead will be raised *imperishable*. These are made of different stuff. These are new spiritual bodies. The corpses remain to rot, just as Paul no doubt assumed that the body of Jesus remained to rot, wherever it had been placed.

Richard Carrier's massive chapter (125 pages), "The Spiritual Body of Christ and the Legend of the Empty Tomb,"[10] is a *tour de force* analysis of the Pauline language and the subtleties of Paul's thought in grappling with the *form* in which humans will endure forever in God's kingdom. Paul's view, Carrier says, was that flesh and blood "goes away, to corruption and decay. Period. Flesh does not receive immortality. It cannot receive it. That is why there must be a new, different body, one capable of immortality. And the only stuff in the universe like that is the stuff of heaven."[11]

And here's the resurrection rub: Paul, Carrier continues, "could not possibly have believed that the risen Jesus was composed of flesh and blood." He said "such things are perishable, and they cannot enter heaven, so they cannot have any place in the resurrection." And he contradicts Luke by saying "that the risen Christ *is* a spirit." Nor, says Carrier,

> can Christ's resurrection-body have had blemishes like wounds, since that contradicts Paul's teaching that the raised body is glorious, indestructible, and not made of flesh. Nor can Jesus have eaten fish, since, as Paul says earlier, the raised body will not have a stomach, nor any need of food.

Thus, Carrier concludes, we can "reject all the Gospel material emphasizing the physicality of Christ's resurrection as polemical invention."[12] What a *coup de grace* he deals to the common Christian assumptions about the supposed unity and inerrancy of Scripture! Paul and the gospels clearly are *not* in agreement about the nature of the resurrection. Paul would be standing in the pews shouting down today's preachers as they read their Easter Morning texts (from the gospels, of course) about that empty tomb.

It's important to remember that Paul encountered Jesus *only* in his visions and meditations, in his hallucinations credited as revelations. He understood Jesus as a celestial, heavenly being, and he demonstrated extraordinarily limited curiosity–if any at all–about Jesus the real person. In fact, the Mythicists build their case partially on the possibility that Paul's celestial Jesus was historicized by spinners of legend who sought later to create an earthly Jesus as well.

Of course, any reader of Paul today should come to a full stop at the term "spiritual body." What the hell is that supposed to mean? It's theobabble. But Paul was a *bona fide* theologian, a master at making things up as he went along. His mind was locked onto the idea that the world would soon be transformed, remade in the image of divine perfection, so he must have come up with a new version of the flesh that humans are blessed (and cursed) with. But, if so, he kept it to himself.

For hundreds of years, pious Bible readers have adored Paul and remained in awe of his "deep spiritual insights." What is a spiritual body? Damned if they know, but Paul said he was telling them a mystery, and that's the primary comfort commodity of religion. Nonsense prevails, business as usual.

But Seeing Is Believing

The faithful are rarely content, however, with "believing in things unseen." After all, God once showed up *in person*, as his own son. He sent Jesus into the world so that the reality of God would become tangible: The Word became flesh and dwelt among us! People want to touch and see, an impulse that clutters churches with paintings and sculpture. Even incense has been added to the mix, from time immemorial, to satisfy the sense of smell: Divinity must even have an aroma.

Paul did his best to spin a fine web of theobabble about spiritual bodies, but we can suspect that there was a collective shrug about that among the faithful. Most folks probably felt that Doubting Thomas wasn't too far out of line in wanting to touch the body of Jesus. A spiritual body doesn't make nearly as good a story for those Easter morning services, Paul or no Paul. Revived flesh with nail holes still visible is about as compelling as anything could be. So it's no surprise that fantasy stories about Jesus making personal appearances were circulating by the time the gospels were written, after Paul had disappeared from the scene.

The gospel stories won in the court of public opinion: women finding an empty tomb, an angel rolling away the stone, Thomas poking his finger in the sword wound, Jesus showing up for breakfast on the beach. These are the scenes have become common in church art, none more compelling than Caravaggio's rendering of Thomas staring at Jesus' wound and inserting his finger. Paul's spiritual body came in a distant second.

Most Christians today would be puzzled at the suggestion that it wasn't the corpse of Jesus that woke up on Easter morning. Gosh, isn't *that* the miracle of it all? A spiritual body just doesn't cut it, and even substantial scholars sense that it's cheating, another stab at the liberal excuse, "Well, you can't take that literally."

Jesus scholar A.N. Wilson wants Jesus himself alive again. He "often heard clergymen say that Christ did not rise from the dead, but that it made sense (often "a very real sense") to speak of him being "alive" in the hearts and minds of his disciples." That didn't make sense to him."I do not see how one *can* be a Christian if one does not believe Christ rose from the dead, and that in an objective and absolute sense,"[13] which rules out settling for a spiritual body.

Perhaps God's resurrection of Jesus was a unilaterally beneficent gesture, a gift of forgiveness and salvation to all mankind? Nope, think again. Examine that concept as rationally as you can: It manifests shallow magical thinking on a couple levels.

First, a Galilean peasant gets executed, and in some form or fashion, comes back to life, and this reinfusion of life is the event by which God could allow himself to forgive people for sinning. Richard Dawkins has famously said that the idea is "barking mad." Serious thinkers have wondered for ages why an all-powerful God would need such a hair-brained scheme. Why not *just forgive* people?

It gets worse. Paul added another layer of magic, and this is the major catch that excludes most members of the human race. In order for it actually to work, individuals have to *believe* that God set this up; they must embrace the dogma enthusiastically. Paul is specific about it in Romans 10:9-10: If (and *only* if) "you confess with your lips that Jesus is Lord and believe in your heart that God raised him from the dead, you will be saved. For one believes with the heart and so is justified, and one confesses with the mouth and so is saved."

This core of the New Testament message is simply inane, and yet the devout have bought both of these clumps of magic for a couple of thousand years. Who could be surprised if, with a few of the names changed, these schemes and formulas ended up on the syllabus at Hogwarts? They could very well be part of its graduate course in magic, divination, and the dark arts.

What Made Paul Snap?

Anyone who has read the gospels knows that Jesus got into one tangle after another with the Pharisees, one of the many Jewish factions at the time. We know from Paul's letter to the Philippians and from the Book of Acts that Paul was himself a Pharisee. So if those run-ins of Jesus with the Pharisees are indeed an authentic glimmer of history, we shouldn't be surprised that Paul was a persecutor of the early Jesus cult. But why his abrupt about-face?

We read in Acts 23 that the Pharisees locked horns with the Sadducees about the resurrection of the dead:

When Paul noticed that some were Sadducees and others were Pharisees, he called out in the council, "Brothers, I am a Pharisee, a son of Pharisees. I am on trial concerning the hope of the resurrection of the dead." When he said this, a dissension began between the Pharisees and the Sadducees, and the assembly was divided. The Sadducees say that there is no resurrection, or angel, or spirit; but the Pharisees acknowledge all three (23:6-8).

Perhaps resurrection of the dead was an idea that Paul did embrace as a Pharisee—in theory. It was one of the standard doctrines that Paul would have included in his checklists of beliefs. Then, one day, it suddenly became very real. There was that earth-shattering, soul-searing moment when he encountered the still-alive Jesus, whose life had not been snuffed out on the cross after all. This changed Paul's life utterly, about as close as anyone can come to having a personality transplant. We can grant this even if the dramatic Road to Damascus version of events is a tall tale.

Of course we are not obliged to concede that his encounter with Jesus was anything other than his private fantasy. Plenty of people have screamed their fantasies at full volume to convince the world that gods have confided in them, which is exactly what Paul ended up doing. We always should remain grounded by that comment of my therapist friend, mentioned earlier: "Reality is what happens *outside* the patient's head." If we fall into the trap of saying, "Yes, of course, how can we doubt it?" to all of the revelations that have been claimed over the millennia, we would have thousands of religions to choose from . . . but, wait a minute, that's what we *do* have. Revelations, meditations, hallucinations—these habits and diversions of piety provide data about the roiling of the human brain. They fall far short of explaining how the cosmos works.

Debunking the Resurrection without Science

Please notice that I have not strayed into science during this discussion. Scientifically astute skeptics might be tempted to brush aside all I have said about the body of Jesus coming back to life, "Well, we know that resurrection is impossible." This approach, however, gives Christians a "gotcha" moment: "Aha, you doubters are just falling prey to a worldview that excludes miracles. But we know that God can perform miracles whenever he wants." Then we're driven back to the hopeless standoff that has stymied dialogue for centuries: Yes, God can; No, God can't.

A.N. Wilson, a faith-sympathetic Jesus scholar, cannot be accused of rigid scientism. Yet he voices the sentiment of most educated students of religion when he calls the gospel resurrection story "palpably and obviously untrue—bodies do not, in our *kosmos*, resurrect themselves."[14] I would have no trouble resting my case on that, and that alone.

I have not chosen that route, however, because I don't have to; the Bible is self-incriminating. For abundant reasons, from the sloppy and derivative account of the empty tomb to Paul's theobabble about a "spiritual" resurrcection, We can see that the resurrection claim for Jesus, *as most of the faithful understand it today,* is utterly bankrupt.

Christianity, a mystery religion that adopted the once-common theme of a dying-and-rising god, is now a walking theological corpse with a ghoulish fantasy at its heart.

Notes

1. See Richard Carrier, *On The Historicity of Jesus: Why We Might Have Reason to Doubt*, pp. 178-180, for details about first century cosmologies.

2. "On the third day" does not mean that Jesus was dead for three days. He died on Friday (day 1), was in the tomb all day Saturday (day 2), and rose on Sunday (day 3). So it was lights-out for Jesus for maybe 36 hours.

3. *Up From the Grave He Arose*, Robert Lowry, 1826-1899.

4. A.N. Wilson, *Jesus*, p. 3.

5. There is *another* choice, for those who are willing to give up the idea that resurrection means that the body of Jesus came back to life; we look at this option later in the chapter.

6. Robert M. Price & Jeffrey Jay Lowder, eds. (Prometheus Books, 2005).

7. huffingtonpost.com/bart-d-ehrman/didnt-make-the-bible_b_905076.html, 20 September 2011.

8. Was James the *actual* brother of Jesus? Does Paul's mention of this "brother" bolster the case that Jesus was a real person (i.e., not fictional)? It's complicated; see Richard Carrier, *On the Historicity of Jesus*, pp. 586-92.

9. Richard Carrier, "How Not to Defend Historicity." In Frank R. Zindler & Robert M. Price, eds., *Bart Ehrman and the Quest of the Historical Jesus* (American Atheist Press, 2013), Kindle loc. 1522.

10. Richard Carrier, "The Spiritual Body of Christ and the Legend of the Empty Tomb." In Robert M. Price & Jeffrey Jay Lowder, eds., *The Empty Tomb: Jesus Beyond the Grave* (Prometheus Books, 2005), pp. 105-231.

11. Ibid., p. 134.

12. Ibid., p. 135.

13. A.N. Wilson, *How Can We Know*, pp. 68-69.

14. A.N. Wilson, *Jesus: A Life* (W.W. Norton & Co., 1992), p. 66.

VIII

Just say NO to Human Sacrifice and Cannibalism

> I would never want to be a member of a group whose symbol was a man nailed to two pieces of wood.
>
> —George Carlin

The Sanctity of Killing Animals

THE BIBLE is right there, in its modest black binding, on each of our night tables beside the bed—or so the pious would have us believe. It's right there at church in pride of place on the altar, in posh white leather binding with gold edges. An icon, a talisman. In those courtrooms where separation of church and state hasn't yet caught on, it is a guarantor of honesty as witnesses raise their right hands to swear to tell the truth, the whole truth. All this as a consequence of the Bible's status as the very Word of God.

Yet there within its pages, overlooked by most, smothered by stories suitable for stained-glass windows and coloring books, lurks a strange religion—several of them, actually. Curious folks who make the effort to read the Bible cover to cover—a *considerable* effort, they soon find out—discover the weirdness soon enough. Any piety that motivated them to get through the entire Bible may not survive the journey.

I suspect that the Old Testament doesn't get a lot of traffic other than isolated tall tales—Joseph and his amazing technicolor dreamcoat, Moses parting the Red Sea, Samson getting a haircut, David killing Goliath—because there is just too much stomach-churning tedium in its pages, rooted deeply in ancient religious practice. The details about animal sacrifice, for example, don't hold a lot of appeal these days, and are usually a great puzzlement: Why is this stuff in the Bible at all? How did chopping up living creatures come to be at the heart of religious practice?

Animal sacrifice had its origins in the human quest to get on the good side of divine powers. How do you get a god to stop being mad at you? Or, to put it a little less personally: How do you avert the anger of a god, or the gods, in general? It was the most natural thing in the world for our distant ancestors to assume that all the lightning and storms, floods and droughts, earthquakes and volcanoes, and diseases and deformities were evidence that the gods were angry. (By no means has this idea gone out of fashion.) It's no surprise that appeasing the gods became an obsession, and very early in our history humans decided that giving gifts to the gods might get them to calm down.

Now, what do you get for the God who has everything? Clearly one of the most precious things we possess is *life itself*, so sacrificing living things seemed a common sense approach. Human sacrifice has occasionally been practiced, but animal sacrifice turned out to be more practical and, as less sadistic people eventually realized, more humane. (Those who have respect for animals understandably find it a dreadful, deplorable idea with no shred of humaneness at all.)

In the early millennia of human civilization, after raising cattle was discovered to be easier than hunting wild animals, wealth came to be measured in cattle and livestock. Those with the largest herds had power and prestige. And with goats, sheep, and cows in plentiful supply, they became animals of choice for making sacrifices to the gods. It was concluded as well that the gifts should be of high quality. It wasn't a good idea to bring inferior goods to the altar or temple. Hence there are chapters in the Bible specifying the animals that will qualify for sacrifice, with excruciating detail on how they are to be slaughtered and chopped up.

Holy Torah!
No, Not Really

The first five books of the Bible are the highly revered *Torah* or *Pentateuch*, supposedly the pinnacle of God's revelation. But in the Torah we encounter the strange religion that I mentioned at the outset. There's a big dose of weirdness at the opening of the third book, Leviticus. Since I'm fairly confident you've not read it recently, let's look at the opening nine verses. Believe it or not, the foundations of New Testament theology are right here.

Yahweh summons Moses and tells him to give instructions to the congregation about making burnt offerings from their herd. It must be an unblemished male, brought to the entrance of the tent of meeting:

> You shall lay your hand on the head of the burnt offering, and it shall be acceptable in your behalf as atonement for you. The bull shall be slaughtered before the LORD; and Aaron's sons the priests shall offer the blood, dashing the blood against all sides of the altar that is at the entrance of the tent of meeting. The burnt offering shall be flayed and cut up into its parts. The sons of the priest Aaron shall put fire on the altar and arrange wood on the fire. Aaron's sons the priests shall arrange the parts, with the head and the suet, on the wood that is on the fire on the altar; but its entrails and its legs shall be washed with water. Then the priest shall turn the whole into smoke on the altar as a burnt offering, an offering by fire of pleasing odor to the LORD. (Lev. 1:4-9).

From our perspective there's nothing rational about this, but the ancients saw the world differently. The gods hovered in the realm of the clouds and beyond. Since humans loved the smell of burning animal fat, it would have been logical to share this pleasure with the gods. Hence the author of Leviticus wrote with a straight face about a "pleasing odor to the LORD." God was close enough overhead, apparently, to get a whiff.

The role of blood also may have been significant. It would be many millennia before people figured out exactly what blood is, but the earliest humans knew that it was the stuff of life. Surely it was a common experience to see humans and animals bleed to death: When the blood was gone, life was gone. And since life was precious, what better gift to offer to the gods? In the passage above, notice the handling of blood especially, with Aaron's sons dashing it against the sides of the altar.

The Moral Monster on the Prowl

These words of Leviticus are direct orders from God, the savage tribal god that roams so much of the Old Testament. Blood played a role in one of his most heinous acts, when the Israelites were about to flee Egypt. To avoid having their firstborn slaughtered by Yahweh on the hunt for Egyptian children, the Israelites were to sacrifice an unblemished yearling lamb.

> They shall take some of the blood and put it on the two doorposts and the lintel of the houses in which they eat it. They shall eat the lamb that same night; they shall eat it roasted over the fire with unleavened bread and bitter herbs . . . . It is the passover of the LORD. For I will pass through the land of Egypt that night, and I will strike down every firstborn in the land of Egypt, both human beings and animals; on all the gods of Egypt I will execute judgments: I am the LORD. The blood shall be a sign for you on the houses where you live: when I see the blood, I will pass over you, and no plague shall destroy you when I strike the land of Egypt. (Exod. 12:7-8, 11-13)

It is jarring to try to reconcile this story with the concept of God that theologians espouse today. This old god had to *see* blood smeared on the doorposts to know where the Israelites lived? And he planned to snuff out all the firstborn in Egypt, of animals as well as people? It seems that killing swaths of people and animals was his clever way of making the point that "I am the LORD."

Why do people fail to see the creepiness of marking the doorposts with blood? Why not chalk or charcoal—or Post-It Notes?

Pope Blood on Tour

Yes, I'm Serious

I suspect that the blood obsession still haunts the religious psyche when I read that a vial of Pope John Paul II's blood toured the U.S. in 2014, to be *venerated* by the faithful (not *worshipped*, church officials insisted), especially in the wake of John Paul's canonization. Apparently, during one of the pope's many illnesses, one nurse was savvy enough to spirit away a vial of his blood—no dummy she. A pope relic was a big prize; there were Catholic hearts to be set aflutter and coffers to be filled.

Relics are big business. A saint body part is the best relic, and what could be more prized than a piece of Jesus' body? We are told specifically in the New Testament that one piece of his body was cut off; more than a few churches have claimed to possess Jesus' foreskin. We trust, of course, that there could have been only one. I wonder why anyone would want to venerate a part of Jesus that they deny he ever made full use of.

Second best is an item owned by the saint; third best, something touched by the holy person. I have also seen somber women dressed in black in dark cathedrals touching the frames of saint pictures and muttering prayers, as if to pick up a flow of holy energy. Relic adoration is one most bizarre aspects of Catholic piety, religious sentiment gone entirely off the rails.

Highly tuned Christian myopia accounts for the inability to see the crassness of all this. And the implications: The pathetic, desperate attempt to grasp holiness at close range, with the eyes if not by touch, suggests perhaps a hint of skepticism or even latent atheism. Are the pious trying to ward off disbelief? God is so distant and invisible, but a fragment of a saint puts God almost within reach, made to seem *real*. So the pope's blood goes on tour.

Modern Christians Wouldn't Want to Be There

Once animal sacrifice became entrenched as a way to "get right with God," the practice turned into a major industry, thriving in Jesus' time. Sacrifices took place in the tent of meeting, if the Mosaic folklore about a nomadic people is to be credited at all. But the sacrifice industry in first century Palestine was housed in the Jerusalem Temple. The fabled Temple of King Solomon had been destroyed by the Babylonian invaders in 586 B.C.E., but the restored Temple, magnificently enhanced by King Herod, dominated Jerusalem. There are many references in the gospels to Jesus' activities in and around the Temple.

Now just try to imagine what went on there, with hundreds of people arriving at the Temple every day to offer sacrifices to appease God for their sins. We read in Mark 1:44 that Jesus ordered the leper whom he had cured, "See that you say nothing to anyone; but go, show yourself to the priest, and offer for your cleansing what Moses commanded." This man would have had to purchase a dove or two to be burned on the altar. If you grew up a Jew, the Temple was one major focus of your life. It would be impossible to imagine getting along without the Temple and its bureaucracy of priests who ran the show.

There is little doubt that most of us would have been grossed out by a stroll through the Temple. Reza Aslan vividly describes the scene, with priests crammed into the Temple "to ensure that the fires of sacrifice are kept aflame day and night":

> The stink of carnage is impossible to ignore. It clings to the skin, the hair, becoming a noisome burden you will not soon shake off. The priests burn incense to ward off the fetor and disease, but the mixture of myrrh and cinnamon, saffron and frankincense cannot mask the insufferable stench of the slaughter.

A priest slits an animal's throat, and an "assistant collects the blood in a bowl to sprinkle on the four horned corners of the altar, while the priest carefully disembowels and dismembers the carcass." Then "the entrails and fatty tissue are torn out of the corpse, carried up a ramp to the altar, and placed directly atop the eternal fire."[1]

Bear in mind that it was *God himself* who thought all of this was a good idea–so the Bible says. Put yourself in that ancient situation: the hordes of priests–you would not want to know any of them–the fires, the blood, gore and foul odors. Now try to deny that this biblically mandated practice is some pretty strange religion.

This sacrifice-based religion prevailed for hundreds of years in Jerusalem, but it came to an end a few decades after the death of Jesus. Rome eventually got fed up with Jewish uprisings and laid siege to the city, which fell in 70 C.E. The Temple was destroyed, and this strange religion succumbed with it. Judaism began a long transition from blood-soaked priests to rabbis wearing fur hats.

Religion Can Grow Up

There were dissenters, though. Even as an atheist I can concede that some spiritual musings are better than others, and eventually it dawned on a few people that butchering and burning animals was a foul practice, and not good religion. Surely, they thought, God doesn't hanker for the smell of burning animal fat. A few spiritual thinkers sensed that religion needed to rise above such nonsense.

We glimpse this insight in the preaching of those who envisioned a *greater* god who cared about how people treat one another. The prophet Hosea in the 8th century B.C.E. felt sure that God wanted something better: "For I desire steadfast love and not sacrifice, the knowledge of God, rather than burnt offerings" (Hos. 6:6). Isaiah had Yahweh ask, "What to me is the multitude of your sacrifices?" I've had enough, he says, "of burnt offerings of rams and the fat of fed beasts; I do not delight in the blood of bulls, or of lambs, or of he-goats" (Isa. 1:11, RSV).

But these dissenters were no match for organized religion. A massive temple—have you noticed that priests and ministers always want to *build*?—requires a bureaucracy to run it, which in turn means massive cash flow. Once you've got buy-in from the gullible public, which has always been awed by temples, cathedrals and sprawling megachurches, you've got it made.

Hosea and Isaiah's ideas about better religion gained no traction, and the cult of sacrifice resumed in the 5th century B.C.E. when the Solomon's Temple got patched back together after the return of the Jewish elite from exile. This Second Temple stood until the Roman obliteration in 70 C.E.

Did Jesus agree with Hosea and Isaiah? Was it his intention to set Judaism on a better course? Given his apparent expectation that the "end of the age" was near, probably not. It's hard for us to understand his act of civil disobedience, the so-called "cleansing of the Temple." What was that about? Was he against sacrifice itself? Maybe, but the gospel accounts are not helpful.

In Mark's version (11:15-17), Jesus "entered the temple and began to drive out those who were selling and those who were buying in the temple." He "overturned the tables of the money changers and the seats of those who sold doves; and he would not allow anyone to carry anything through the temple." Then there's Jesus' famous statement to the money changers: "Is it not written, 'My house shall be called a house of prayer for all the nations'? But you have made it a den of robbers."

We could take this to mean that Jesus was opposed to sacrifice. The money changers were there for worshippers to get rid of their Roman money. They needed the Temple coinage to buy animals for the burnt offerings. And Jesus aimed his wrath at those who sold doves. But, strangely enough, Jesus didn't quote the Hosea or

Isaiah verses cited above, but instead Isaiah 56:7, "for my house shall be called a house of prayer for all peoples."

But of course, the Jerusalem Temple was never open to all people. Beyond certain points, Gentiles and women were forbidden, and the line immediately before this (also Isaiah 56:7) *endorses* sacrifice, saying "their burnt offerings and their sacrifices will be accepted on my altar." We suspect that Mark is inventing when he says that Jesus "would not allow anyone to carry anything through the temple." This shows the novelist's naiveté. Mark had probably never seen the Temple and he had no grasp of how large it had been. When Matthew and Luke copied this story, they deleted this line–it was just too farfetched."Den of robbers" is also a borrowed line, from Jeremiah 7:11.

Mark is creating his Jesus-script from Old Testament fragments. The animal sellers and moneychangers weren't robbing anyone. People got their money's worth. It is impossible to pierce this fog to know what Jesus thought about sacrifice.

John give a strange account of the incident, the least likely to represent what actually happened. He seems not to have known what the Temple was for or how large it was. His Jesus seems surprised to find "people selling cattle, sheep, and doves, and the moneychangers seated at their tables":

> Making a whip of cords, he drove all of them out of the temple, both the sheep and the cattle. He also poured out the coins of the moneychangers and overturned their tables. He told those who were selling the doves, "Take these things out of here! Stop making my Father's house a marketplace!" (John 2:14-16)

Why u mad, bro? The Temple's industry was animal sacrifice, so *of course* it was a marketplace, and had been for centuries. In Mark's gospel, Jesus ordered the man he'd healed to make his Temple sacrifice.

Then John's account takes an even stranger turn. Jesus suggests that if the Temple were destroyed again, he would rebuild it again in three days. John adds a heavy-handed explanation for this: "But he was speaking of the temple of his body. After he was raised from the dead, his disciples remembered that he had said this" (John 2:21-22). We shouldn't be surprised that the narrative sags under John's ponderous theology.

Christians like to think that Jesus made a mess in the Temple as a bold act of civil disobedience against the corrupt religion of the time. We know there were deep resentments against the Temple system that sucked in vast sums of money. It was run by the privileged elite. But still, for the masses of people, it was a permanent fixture of their piety. Jesus may have created a minor fuss in the Temple when he lost his temper, but one man with a whip would have caused little more than a ripple.

What really happened and what Jesus thought he was doing are impossible to figure now, since the gospels came along so much later. We have no way of knowing how much the story was garbled, misremembered, or misunderstood–or created out of whole cloth–by the gospel writers.

Restoring the Temple
One More Time

Chances are you've never lost sleep over this passing of the Temple into oblivion: A grotesque religion was dead and gone. Of course, Judaism itself survived–the much better aspects of it. There were factions of Judaism at the time that despised the Temple and its cult; they too said *good riddance.*

The story is far from over, however. There are Jews today who take the Old Testament orders for sacrifice in dead earnest. God meant it then when he spoke in Leviticus, and he means it now, still today. And it won't do to set up a new temple just anywhere. You could build the most spectacular temple ever in Brooklyn, Vermont, or London, but it wouldn't do. According to the most retrograde orthodox Jews, the temple must be restored in Jerusalem, right where it was, because that is precisely where God wants it. Hope springs eternal for these folks, because Israel itself was reborn in 1948, and, thanks to the 1967 Six Day War, Jerusalem is now under Israeli control. Let the rebuilding of the Temple begin! It's doubtful that many modern Israelis want any such thing.

But, say the die-hard fanatics, surely it was God who brought about the rebirth of Israel in 1948 and the Six Day War in 1967. So in his own good time, God will see to it that the Temple will rise again.

So the die-hards are getting ready. The new Temple will need qualified priests, and it is here that the full craziness perhaps begins. Since priests suitable for Temple service must be undefiled, ritually pure, they must have had no contact with dead bodies or even graves. Thus classes of priest-trainees, boys recruited for the privilege, are being raised in compounds constructed to prevent them from *ever walking on the ground.* In a place like Palestine, which has been inhabited for millennia, *any* ground you step on could once have been a grave, hence this precaution.

Let's kick the craziness up a few more notches. In the fourth book of the Torah, we find the stipulation that purification can be accomplished only by a priest being sprinkled with water that has been mixed with the ashes of a *red* heifer. Why in the world a red heifer? And again, the excruciating details: "Then the heifer shall be burned . . . its skin, its flesh, and its blood, with its dung, shall be burned. The priest shall take cedarwood, hyssop, and crimson material, and throw them into the fire in which the heifer is burning" (Num. 19:5-6). Since red heifers are very scarce–there can't be any gray or black hairs on the beast–this is a major worry for those who are preparing to get a new Temple up and running. All of this silliness, bear in mind, is to prepare priests who qualify to resume animal sacrifices. Again, because that's what *God still wants.*

Seriously, a red heifer? If there is anything that would qualify as a dumb idea, this is it. Could there be a more stunning example of religion gone totally off the rails? Well, yes, actually there is.

Opposites Attract
Against All Odds

Certain brands of fanatic American evangelists also want to see the Temple rebuilt, as a precondition for Jesus' return: They want to hasten or at least enable the Apocalypse. So they're all in favor of helping ultra-orthodox Jewish fanatics get ready to run the new Temple. They know, of course, that the Chosen People will all be killed at the Apocalypse for failure to accept Jesus as the messiah. Them's the breaks.

Crazy religion makes strange bedfellows. The kooky Americans have helped finance a Pentecostal cattle breeder from Mississippi, Clyde Lott, who can supply red heifer embryos to the Jews committed to this project. Plenty of frozen embryos on hand in Israel will help ensure that nothing can go wrong: There will be enough red heifers to burn for ashes to mix with water for the purification of Temple priests. Catholic holy water has met its match in this holy cow water.[2]

I have to assume that most of the pious people who scan through Leviticus and Numbers 19 realize that this is strange religion, and they balk: "Well, this has nothing to do with me." They might even wonder why such chapters can't be sliced out of the Bible. Isn't it time to have a streamlined Bible? People cherry pick anyway–in their minds most of the Bible is already on the cutting room floor–so why not appoint an official church commission to pick out the decent parts? Why waste all that paper on hundreds of pages of worthless dross? I've argued earlier that most of the Bible simply isn't worth reading, and the crassness and stupidity of animal sacrifice should be obvious to all.

So what if the Temple was destroyed in 70 C.E. Just let it go. The very earliest Christians, who considered their faith in Jesus as "Judaism with a twist," kept going to the Temple and assumed that the laws of the Torah were still binding. But with time, their influence diminished, especially as Paul was successful with his mission to make Christianity less Jewish (e.g., no more dietary laws, no more circumcision). Indeed, once Jerusalem had been sacked and the Temple destroyed in 70 C.E., there were probably very few of the original Jesus followers left. As we have seen, the gospels were written after these cataclysmic events, and that's one reason there's so much fiction, so little history in the gospels: The eyewitnesses to Jesus–if he was real–already were long gone.

The Temple and institutionalized blood sacrifice got stuffed into the clutter of the past. Believers who are repulsed by Leviticus and Numbers can breathe a sigh of relief. Right?

Leviticus
A Distant Mirror for Christianity

No, actually, things are not that simple. It turned out to be very hard for pious folks of the ancient world to get blood sacrifice out of their system, and we find that animal sacrifice is deeply imbedded in the Christian psyche. The faithful may frown: "What *are* you talking about?"–but it's the elephant in the room that Christians can't see, and it's an even bigger and uglier elephant than devout Christians suppose. Christian have crossed an ominous line indeed because they believe that God *upped the ante*. God was no longer satisfied with doves, sheep, goats, and heifers. The New Testament moves us into the ominous world of *human* sacrifice.

That lilting verse, with seemingly such an elegant, elevated sentiment, John 3:16, is the favorite of so many Christians, but without awareness of its full implications: "God so loved the world that he gave his only begotten son." Gave him *for what*? We all know the end of the story: to be killed on the cross, to be sacrificed to enable God's forgiveness. In John 1:19, we read explicitly, on the lips of John the Baptist: "Behold the Lamb of God who takes away the sin of the world," echoing the thought in Leviticus 16 that a lamb driven from the camp of the Israelites carried away their sins with it.

The author of John's gospel was determined to make it clear that this was Jesus' role, but to bear sins by *dying* instead of disappearing into the wilderness. John even changed the day of the crucifixion. The Synoptic gospels recount that Jesus died the day after Passover–the Last Supper was the Passover meal. But John places the crucifixion the day before Passover, in fact at the *very hour* that the Passover lambs were being slaughtered.

Thus John makes it abundantly clear that this is one of the messages of the New Testament: Jesus is the *human sacrifice* that is now part of God's scheme. The Epistle to the Hebrews probably is read less than even the epistles of Paul, but it's a standout document in the Christian canon. It likely comes from the first century, is written in superior Greek, and may even pre-date the gospels. The author was on much the same page as the author of John's gospel, because he thought of Jesus strictly in celestial terms.

There is no earthly Jesus, no Galilean peasant, in Hebrews. Its author was familiar with the Temple sacrificial rituals. His aim seems to have been to convince a Jewish audience that Jesus was all that they had hoped for. He drew parallels to the Temple rituals, perhaps precisely because the Temple *had* disappeared; Jesus had been the sacrifice made once and for all. The writer is fully up to the task of churning out theobabble:

> But when Christ came as a high priest of the good things that have come, then through the greater and perfect tent (not made with hands, that is, not of this creation), he entered once for all into the Holy Place, not with the blood of goats and calves, but with his own blood, thus obtaining eternal redemption. For if the blood of goats and bulls, with the sprinkling of the ashes of a heifer, sanctifies those who have been defiled so that their flesh is purified, how much more will the blood of Christ, who through the eternal Spirit offered himself without blemish to God, purify our conscience from dead works to worship the living God! (Heb. 9:11-14)

Recalling the good old days of the temple, with all that sprinkling of blood, on "both the scroll itself and all the people," the "blood of the covenant that God has ordained," the writer reminds his readers of their Old Testament roots: "Indeed, under the law almost everything is purified with blood, and *without the shedding of blood there is no forgiveness of sins*" (Heb. 9:19-22, emphasis added). So he drives home the point about Jesus, the human sacrifice:

> But as it is, he has appeared once for all at the end of the age to remove sin by the sacrifice of himself. And just as it is appointed for mortals to die once, and after that the judgment, so Christ, having been offered once to bear the sins of many, will appear a second time, not to deal with sin, but to save those who are eagerly waiting for him (Heb. 9:26b-28).

Paul Clinches It

While the Epistle to the Hebrews might be called one of the obscure books of the New Testament, Paul's Letter to the Romans is anything but. It bears repeating, as I often do, that Romans is one of the charter documents of the Christian faith. It set the course for Christian theology for the next thousand years, and has provoked endless commentary and debate. Countless theologians and preachers have tried to outdo one another singing its praises.

It's actually a dreadful book, but I will admit that Paul did an amazing job of getting Christians off the hook: He lifted the burden of the Torah. Based on his arguments in Romans and his other letters, Christian might as well go ahead and slice gobs of pages out of the Old Testament. Paul knew Judaism was widely admired in the ancient world, but the Old Testament law, those endless pages of useless rules and rituals, was a yoke that few could bear. Admirers of Judaism balked at circumcision and the arcane dietary laws. Paul's flash of insight, what he felt sure was God's message to him personally, was that Christ was a key for sweeping all of this aside.

It would have been great if Paul could've just stopped at the simple thought that Jesus represented a supreme gesture of divine love. I suspect that's how many Christians today, who have never even tried to plow through the book of Romans, look at Jesus: **God = love = Jesus**, end of story.

But Paul was, to his very marrow, a Jew who understood the Old Testament law as God's supreme plan to keep humans in line. Except that it had never actually worked out that way. So Jesus Christ was God's Plan B. But Paul reduced Jesus, the celestial Jesus who alone mattered to him, to a magical formula. Believers no longer had to obsess about all those Old Testament laws, once Jesus-as-magic-formula was in place. He explains this in Romans 3:21 (NASB):

> But now apart from the Law the righteousness of God has been manifested, being witnessed by the Law and the Prophets, even the righteousness of God through faith in Jesus Christ for all those who believe . . .

Yes, God was righteous once upon a time because he gave the law, the very complex and burdensome law, for people to follow. But now God has revealed that the law has been set aside. As far as Paul was concerned, even the most pious and generous people didn't really measure up to God's standards. Here the full, twisted magic-formula theology of Paul is stated in a nutshell:

> [F]or there is no distinction; for all have sinned and fall short of the glory of God, being justified as a gift by His grace through the redemption which is in Christ Jesus; whom God displayed publicly as a propitiation in His blood through faith. This was to demonstrate His righteousness, because in the forbearance of God He passed over the sins previously committed; for the demonstration, I say, of His righteousness at the present time, so that He would be just and the justifier of the one who has faith in Jesus. (Rom. 3:22-26, NASB)

Notice what he says here: You don't have to measure up to all those laws. (By the third century C.E. the rabbis had decided there were 613 of them.) God is not going to hold your failure against you, because he *forgives you as a gift*. His grace, his generosity, his just being so darned nice, allows this gift.

But, and this is a huge *but*, the mechanism that enables this grace to unfold is a *human sacrifice*: a sacrifice of atonement through Jesus' blood. In Joseph Daleiden's critique of Christianity he sums up the horror of it all: It "doesn't make any sense that to atone for man's wickedness God willed his Son put to death. The theologians try to tell us that only this murder . . . of a god will expiate humankind's wicked nature."[3]

Here's the final catch as well: It is effective only *through faith*. None of this will fall into place on your behalf unless you believe it, and the human sacrifice is the lynchpin of this malignant arrangement. So God isn't so darned nice after all. As was mentioned earlier in the discussion of resurrection, it's a mad scheme. It could only have emerged from a tortured, troubled mind. If God is all-loving and all-powerful, then it should be a piece of cake for him to forgive people, but Paul couldn't leave well enough alone; he gerrymandered the plot of God's salvation. He was the Rube Goldberg of theology. Paul may or may not have been the writer of Ephesians–the scholarly jury it still out on that–but if not, then another author who forged in his name echoed the same sentiment: "Therefore be imitators of God, as beloved children and live in love, as Christ loved us and gave himself up for us, a fragrant offering and sacrifice to God" (Eph. 5:1-2, NIV).

The Old Testament Brush with Human Sacrifice

The Old Testament, for all its matter-of-fact embrace of animal sacrifice, which is revolting enough, escaped the temptation to add human sacrifice to the mix. There are a few oblique references to it, in a few texts that reflect disapproval. It's too bad that Christian theology didn't pay more attention to them.

In Genesis 22, we find the story of Abraham's near-sacrifice of his son Isaac. He is ordered by God to kill his son for a burnt offering, and I must say that the story is a masterpiece of the folk genre. The innocence of Isaac is brilliantly evoked:

> Isaac said to his father Abraham, "Father!" And he said, "Here I am, my son." He said, "The fire and the wood are here, but where is the lamb for a

burnt offering?" Abraham said, "God himself will provide the lamb for a burnt offering, my son." So the two of them walked on together (Gen. 22:7-8).

As we all know, at the very last moment, an angel of the Lord intervened: Abraham had passed the test of blindly following divine orders, and the boy was spared.

Paul oozed his praise for Abraham as an example of superior faith (Rom. 4:1-3). Pious theologians, following his example, have approvingly exploited this story for centuries. The non-pious have seen the far more sinister implications of this kind of religious servitude, but my point in drawing attention to it here is that God didn't, after all, want human sacrifice. Even the moral monster Yahweh balked. Christians, take notice.

Another story of human sacrifice is found in Judges 11. We read that Jephthat, "the son of a prostitute and a mighty warrior," made a vow to God that if he was successful in battle against the Ammonites, "then whoever comes out of the doors of my house to meet me, when I return victorious from the Ammonites, shall be the Lord's, to be offered up by me as a burnt offering." A mighty warrior, maybe, but not a very bright bulb. Obviously folklore is setting us up here. When Jephthat is sighted at a distance returning home after the victory, it is his daughter, his only child, who comes running to greet him, "with timbrels and with dancing." Yes, he's upset, and he breaks the news to her that she will be a burnt offering because of his promise to God. She was allowed to go on retreat for a couple of months to "bewail her virginity," then Jephthah fulfilled his oath.

This was probably the most disturbing Bible story for me as a kid. It just didn't make sense. What was *wrong* with these people—and with this God? Jephthah could have put on sackcloth and ashes and prayed to Yahweh for a thousand hours to apologize for breaking his vow. What was wrong with God for not suggesting this solution for a broken vow? (Of course, as a kid I didn't entertain that heretical thought.) And if an angel of the Lord had intervened to save Isaac, where was the angel when Jephthah was about to light the fire under his daughter? No, none of it makes sense. And I am reasonably confident that gazillions of Bible readers have felt that same way as I did about this gruesome story. Even its original author, I'm sure, meant it as a terrible tale.

The lesson here to Christians: Human sacrifice is a thoroughly bad idea, and the Old Testament does not offer imprimatur for sacrificing humans to get right with God. Yet the New Testament rushes precisely in this direction.

It's so easy to become immune to the clear meaning of the New Testament account of a human sacrifice. Christian minds have become numb to the appalling dogma that they take with a shrug. They go along with Mark's Jesus quote: "For the Son of Man came not to be served but to serve, and to give his life a ransom for many" (10:45).

Certainly many religions and cultures, scattered the world over, have embraced human sacrifice at one time or another. All of them we hope have gotten over it. How might that have happened? How did the revulsion finally set in? At some point, sensitive, thoughtful people said, "Okay, this is revolting."

As we have seen, theologians revel in mystery. But to me, the biggest mystery of all is that most Christians have not yet become nauseous about the butchery at the heart of their faith.

They believe that God caved in on human sacrifice and selected a Galilean peasant for the experiment. Did God say to himself, "Let's see if I'll feel good enough to forgive people if Jesus gets tortured to death"? The theologians of the New Testament saw nothing horrid about this. Their successors even thought up the name *Good Friday* for the day he died. One voice of protest I've heard is that of Christian writer Jack Nelson-Pallmeyer: "Is Jesus the 'Son' of a bloodthirsty deity who can only be appeased through the violent sacrifice of God's only offspring?"[4]

Most of the religions on the planet finally turned their backs on such savagery, but the New Testament preserves it, like a severed limb soaking in formaldahyde. For centuries, theologians have perfected their skills as spin-doctors to make human sacrifice look like something else, *anything* else. They pile on slick interpretations, metaphors, superficial superlatives–the full arsenal of theobabble. But who can't see through it?

In a speech at the queen of Catholic universities, Sam Harris did not mince words: "I hate to break it to you here at Notre Dame, but Christianity is a cult of human sacrifice . . . it celebrates a single human sacrifice as though it were effective."[5] How can the justifications and rationalizations possibly be worth it? In the interest of sane religion, *just let it go*. As well as slicing out gobs of Old Testament pages, Christians should also take the razor to the New Testament.

By embracing human sacrifice, Christian have taken pagan dance partners, as I indicated was the case with resurrection. They're in very bad company.

Décor by Quentin Tarantino

It's a cause for despair–at least for decent folks looking on from the outside–that for many Christians the torture death of Jesus must never be minimized. The more blood the better. Seemingly *that* brings more bang for the buck: God meant Jesus to be a human sacrifice, so there can be no skimping.

For the lacerated Jesus in his film, *The Passion of the Christ,* Mel Gibson drew on a robust tradition of bleeding. The images that have emerged in Christian art are horrific: nails through Jesus' hands, his body sagging on the cross, thorns piercing his brow producing beads of blood, the sword thrust in his side. People who have grown up within the cult of atonement through bloodshed, who have become numb to this ghastly stuff, apparently see nothing wrong with it, and indeed experience it as a window onto spiritual truth.

Outsiders prefer that Christians think again. Psychologist Phil Zuckerman has recounted his daughter's encounter with a church that could have come out of the blood-drenched imagination of Quentin Tarantino. They visited a California mission, a lovely place with "beautiful landscaping, old buildings, indigenous flowers, a trickling fountain." But when they walked inside, his daughter

> lost it. The space was full of crucified Jesuses. Every wall, from floor to ceiling, was adorned with wooden and plaster sculptures of Jesus on the cross: bloody, cut, and crying in pain. Some were very life-like, others more impressionistic. But all exhibited a tortured man in agony. My daughter had no context to understand it; she had no idea what Christianity was all about and had never been exposed to this most famous killing in history. She just saw what it objectively was: a large torture chamber. And she burst into tears and ran out.

They went outside and he wondered how he, a secular parent, could "explain such gore to a five year old."

> Um, well, you see . . . there are millions of people who think that we are all born evil and that there is an all-powerful God who wants to punish us forever in hell—but then he had his only son tortured and killed so that we could be saved from eternal torture. Get it?

Besides being "baldly untrue," Zuckerman rightly calls it all "totally, horrible, absurdly sadistic and counter-intuitive and wicked."[6] There is no rational context that can justify this brand of piety, and the kid saw that it was grotesque.

We can wonder as well how much damage is done to those who grow up in that grim shadow. Novelist Stephen King, no stranger to gore and terror, was taken aback by what he encountered in one Catholic home. Back in his days as a schoolteacher, one of his students, whom he calls Sondra, was withdrawn, somber and friendless.

> One day her mother hired me to move some furniture. Dominating the trailer's living room was a nearly life-sized crucified Jesus, eyes turned up, mouth turned down, blood dribbling from beneath the crown of thorns on his head. He was naked except for a rag twisted around his hips and loins. Above this bit of breechclout were the hallowed belly and the jutting ribs of a concentration-camp inmate. It occurred to me that Sondra had grown up beneath the agonal gaze of this dying god, and doing so had undoubtedly played a part in making her what she was when I knew her: a timid and homely outcast who went scuttling through the halls of Lisbon High like a frightened mouse.
>
> "That's Jesus Christ, my Lord and Savior," Sondra's mother said, following my gaze."Have *you* been saved, Steve?" I hastened to tell her that I was saved as saved could be, although I didn't think you could ever be good enough to have *that* version of Jesus intervene on your behalf. The pain had driven him out of his mind. You could see it on his face. If *that* guy came back, he probably wouldn't be in a saving mood.[7]

The faithful heap on additional stupidities. They mindlessly equate Jesus' suffering with the suffering of the world, though the world's suffering continues unabated.

Christian mystics have gotten off on contemplation of Jesus' agony and suffering. The gory tableau is an insult to decency. It is truly bad theology.

Bowing Out Gracefully

Can't Christians rise above all this? Is their faith supposed to be a genre of horror film? After all, there is far better mythology about dying heroes to swoon over: Elijah was taken to heaven by a chariot of fire; Mohammed was escorted there on a winged horse. Moses had a dignified end:

> So Moses the servant of the LORD died there in the land of Moab, according to the word of the LORD. And He buried him in the valley in the land of Moab, opposite Beth-peor; but no man knows his burial place to this day. Although Moses was one hundred and twenty years old when he died, his eye was not dim, nor his vigor abated. (Deut. 34:5-7, NASB)

What would be wrong with a simple martyr's death for Jesus? If there is a glimmer of historical truth in the gospel accounts of his crucifixion by the Romans (we can't really be sure), it would be a good enough story that Jesus, the holy man, died an unjust and undeserved death. He could be mourned and worshipped for that alone, as is the case with many Christian martyrs.

The Christian mythmakers who spun the stories chose their myths poorly. They were possessed by a macabre understanding of God. Thus at the heart of Christianity we find not only the ghoulish belief in resurrection, but the abhorrent dogma that a man died because God's bloodlust included human blood.

But Wait, the Story Gets Worse

We know the myth we're stuck with. We find the most familiar version of it in the so-called Apostles Creed: Jesus "suffered under Pontius Pilate; was crucified, dead and buried; he descended into hell; the third day he rose again from the dead, he ascended into heaven, and sits at the right hand of God the Father Almighty." And he's planning to come back. Jesus might have believed this himself—again, the gospel accounts can't be trusted—but Paul certainly did.

In the meantime, while we're waiting, Jesus didn't want folks to forget that he had taken a bullet for them. One of the beliefs of the primitive church was that Jesus wanted his followers to occasionally eat a meal commemorating his sacrifice. We all know the story of the Last Supper:

> For I received from the Lord that which I also delivered to you, that the Lord Jesus in the night in which He was betrayed took bread; and when He had given thanks, He broke it and said, "This is My body, which is for you; do this in remembrance of Me." In the same way He took the cup also after supper, saying, "This cup is the new covenant in My blood; do this, as often as you drink it, in remembrance of Me." For as often as you eat this bread

and drink the cup, you proclaim the Lord's death until He comes. (1 Cor. 11:23-26, NASB)

This is, in fact, appalling. And the story gets worse: Christians were expected to eat bread and drink wine as tokens of *Jesus' body and blood*. At this point, our instincts as historians should kick in. Let's get to the bottom of this. Where did this tall tale come from? Jews were famous for their taboos against eating or drinking blood: Few things would have been more abhorrent. Would Jesus really have asked his followers to do this? It would have been very much out of character.

Most Christians are probably familiar with the accounts of the Last Supper in Matthew, Mark, and Luke, but the quote above is the scene as recalled by Paul in his first letter to the Corinthians. As I explained earlier, our skepticism is high when we read stories in the gospels because they are *late* documents–decades, often several decades, after the fact–certainly later than Paul's letters.

So we snap to attention when we see Paul confirming an event recorded later by the gospel writers. In fact, this is big news, because it's the *only* event from the life of Jesus in the gospels that Paul seems to have been aware of. So, isn't this that rare commodity that historians crave, contemporary documentation? The later gospel accounts fail miserably in this regard: They display no reliance on contemporary documentation, such as eyewitness accounts or objective transcriptions of Jesus' words at the Last Supper. There is nothing to allay the historian's suspicions that, in the gospels, the words of Jesus on the last night of his life were just made up, created out of novelistic imagination.

Paul's letter is contemporary documentation in the sense that it tells us what he was thinking when he wrote it in the late 50's, maybe 25 years after the death of Jesus. But is it certainly *not* contemporary documentation for the Last Supper, since he wrote it so long after the supposed event. So where did Paul get this information, these words of Jesus about what to eat and drink in his memory? Grasping at straws, we might say, **Aha**, those 15 days that Paul spent with Peter (part of Tough Problem VII), after he had purposely stayed away from Jerusalem for three years. That's when he found out what Jesus said at the Last Supper.

But, truthfully, that seems awfully far-fetched as well. We already have been shocked that Paul came away from that 15-day visit knowing nothing about Jesus that he cared to write about later. In all his letters, he says zero about the life of Jesus: no parables, no encounters with demons, none of the miracles (walking on water, changing water into wine), none of Jesus' teachings or healing. So how likely is it that the exact script of the Last Supper, as reported in 1 Corinthians, is based on anything Peter might have told him? It's a stretch, to say the least.

And in fact our hearts sink–the historian cringes–when we read the text carefully. Paul doesn't say, "This is what Peter told me," but instead: "For I received from the Lord what I also handed on to you, that the Lord Jesus on the night when he was betrayed." How did he "receive it from the Lord"? Paul had private revelations or visions of Jesus, and shares the results of these with his followers. So we come to a dead stop in our efforts to work out what happened the night of the Last Supper. We are entitled to wonder if the gospel script of the Last Supper *originated* with Paul, cooked up in his imagination (= visions), and this is the tradition that eventually ended up in the gospels.

The 'Hood that Paul Called Home

Jesus was a Galilean Jew whom we can expect shared the taboos about eating blood. Paul was a Jew as well, but his Judaism might have been compromised. He grew up in the city of Tarsus, and had probably been exposed to a range of religious ideas and practices. Scholar A.N. Wilson sheds light on Paul's environment:

> Like any great port, Tarsus had a mixed population. The ancient writers speak of Tarseans as pirates, seafarers and worshippers of Mithras. It was probably Pompey's soldiers, in their Eastern campaigns, who first introduced this cult to the Roman people. It became especially popular in the army, most of whom, in the first century, were Asiatics. Archaeologists show that Tarsus was a centre of keen Mithraic worship until the downfall of the Empire. The most distinctive feature of Mithraic worship is that the initiates either drank the blood of the sacred bull or drank a chalice of wine as a symbolic representation of the blood.

> If Paul's parents were Jewish, they would have been disgusted at the idea of the cult of Mithras, since the drinking of blood is one of the most fundamental taboos in Jewish life. But for those who practiced the religion of Mithras, it was commemorative of the life-principle itself. From the bull slain by Herakles, for example, flowed not merely blood but life, corn, plenteousness. It symbolized springing up of new life beyond the grave.

> The cult owes much to the dying and rising gods–the Syrian Adonis, the Babylonian Thammuz, the Egyptian Osiris. Every autumn in Tarsus the boy Paul would have seen the great funeral pyre at which the god was ritually burnt. The central mystery of the ritual was that the withering heat of the summer sun had brought the god to his death but that he would rise to life again in the spring, at about the time when the Jews were celebrating the Passover.[8]

This information should prompt yet another **Aha** moment. I've often said that Christian origins are messy, and that almost all of the ideas in the New Testament are imported: There's nothing new under the Christian sun.

None of this proves that Paul lifted the Christian Eucharist from the cult of Mithra, but we can see the mix of ideas that may have influenced him. There's an awful lot that looks familiar! And there were those in the ancient church who squirmed about these possible connections. Michael Grant finds resemblances to the Eucharist in the "sacramental repasts of the pagan mystery religions." Admittedly, if we knew enough, he says, we'd find that "these apparently pagan features were incorporated in the Christian ritual through the mediation of contemporary Jewish thought." But "the similarities were unmistakable, and proved a thorn the flesh of the propagandists of Christianity, who felt compelled to explain them away as tricks of the Devil."[9]

Christians love their Jesus, but they're probably not so sure about Paul; his letters, despite their occasional Hallmark moments, are a chore. He proved to be a champion Christian soldier, but giving him credit as founder goes too far. But the fond hope of keeping Paul in second place might not stand up to close scrutiny. Hyam Maccoby, one of the leading Jewish scholars of Christianity, states the case bluntly:

> To admit that Paul was the creator of the Eucharist would be to admit that Paul, not Jesus, was the founder of Christianity. It means that the central sacrament and mystery of Christianity, which marks it off as a separate religion from Judaism, was not instituted by Jesus. Nor are the ideas underlying this sacrament–the incorporation of the worshippers in the body of the divine Christ by the process of eating the god–part of Jesus' religious outlook: indeed, he would have found such ideas repugnant, though not unfamiliar, for they were a well-known aspect of paganism . . .[10]

Note the last thought carefully: The primary idea that lurks behind the sacrament, the eating of the god, would have been repugnant to Jesus the Galilean peasant. *That*, above all, stands in the way of taking the script for the Last Supper seriously, as words that Jesus would have uttered.

Scholars have argued for centuries about the messy origins of Christianity–the strange mixture of borrowed ideas and where they came from–and we can be sure they will continue to do so, as long as there are academic institutions willing to pay their salaries. But rank-and-file believers will continue to ignore this angst and curiosity, and suck up the mindless orthodoxies that the churches have taught for centuries. They want nothing to complicate their safe passage to heaven. Human sacrifice, sugar-coated with florid theology, will do just fine.

Oh No, It Gets Even Worse

When I was a kid, my favorite Sunday rolled around four times a year. Maybe we knew the word *Eucharist*, but we just called it *communion Sunday*. It was my favorite because the sermon would always be shorter. Everyone in the congregation had to go to the altar to receive communion. We knelt at the railing for the minister to come along with the bread and grape juice. Since all this coming and going cut into the sermon time, the preacher couldn't be as expansive as he usually was.

Everyone in those Methodist pews knew that the bread and grape juice *symbolized* the body and blood of Jesus. I don't know how old I was when I discovered that the Catholics had a different take on it. But it never dawned on us that pretending to eat the body and drink the blood of somebody–*anybody*–was macabre. Certainly we had no grasp that the practice had ancient cultic roots. It was something the New Testament told us to do. In fact, Jesus told us to do it. Nor do I recall how old I was when I found out that the Catholic understanding of communion includes *transubstantiation*.

I continue to be awed that Catholic theologians can reach the depths of sheer silliness that transubstantiation requires. An entrenched idea may seem to fray around the edges, so the theologians sew on patches and do the darning. One brief digression to illustrate the point: It dawned on Catholic thinkers that the sinlessness of Jesus was jeopardized through his mother's lineage. That is, no original sin could have been passed down to the Savior through his father's side because he didn't have a father.

But Jesus had not been delivered by a divine stork; Mary was a key component in his arrival, and she was human. Inescapably, she would have been a carrier of original sin. So Jesus was tainted; by the implications of their own demented theology, Catholics sensed that vital dogma was in trouble. Never fear: The intrepid conjurers huddled and worked it out how Mary had been born without original sin. That is, she had been conceived in the usual way, but by a clever miracle, the transmission of original sin was blocked by God's touch. Mary's conception had been clean of original sin. It had been an *Immaculate Conception*.[11]

Of course, nobody smacked these card sharks on the head and yelled, "What do you guys think we are, crazy?" And nothing is crazier than transubstantiation. This is the belief that, during the Mass, the bread and wine actually *become* the body and blood of Jesus. In fact, this is known as the Miracle of the Mass. At the point of Consecration—when the priest lifts the chalice and the wafer above his head—commonly a bell rings to signify that the miracle has happened. No matter that the bread and wine look the same, they are in fact *literally* the body and blood of Jesus. Thus Christians—well, Catholics at least—are in the business of eating real flesh and blood. In fact, early Christians, who gathered privately in homes, and whose rituals were not understood by outsiders, were accused of cannibalism because they reportedly ate the human form of their god. This was a natural mistake if they were overheard to say, "Take, eat, this my body." Transubstantiation means that the ritual really *is* cannibalism. Theology and practice took a catastrophic turn for the worse.

In the Protestant church, we were quite content to have the bread and grape juice be symbolic. And when we examine the words of Jesus at the Last Supper, in the gospels or in 1 Corinthians 11, it's hard to escape the conclusion that he—that is, the leading character in this fantasy narrative—meant them symbolically as well: Do this in remembrance of me. More or less, "This is a gesture to keep me in mind."

Is John's Bad Theology to Blame Again?

What possibly could have been the motivation for inventing transubstantiation? Isn't symbolism enough? Why not leave well enough alone? Perhaps, from the perspective of the theologians in charge, it's always a good idea to pump up the quotient of magic to wow the pew creatures. It does make for good ceremony. But, again, theology may have been driven to extremes by relentless logic.

Now, I confess, I really have no interest in digging into the history of transubstantiation—what a useless piece of malarkey—any more than I would like to spend a day watching grass grow. But I have a hunch about the scripture and theology that enticed priests to think it up.

It's always been a curiosity that John's version of the Last Supper omits mention of the Eucharist. There's no reference to breaking bread and drinking wine in remembrance of Jesus. Instead, during John's Last Supper (chapter 13), Jesus washed the feet of the disciples. But earlier in the gospel, in chapter 6, we find a passage that trumps considerably Jesus' words at the Last Supper in the Synoptic gospels. In fact, Jesus' words in chapter 6 are graphic, and, frankly, disturbing. This comes close to being religion at its worst:

> Then the Jews began to argue with one another, saying, "How can this man give us His flesh to eat?" So Jesus said to them, "Truly, truly, I say to you, unless you eat the flesh of the Son of Man and drink His blood, you have no life in yourselves. He who eats My flesh and drinks My blood has eternal life, and I will raise him up on the last day. For My flesh is true food, and My blood is true drink. He who eats My flesh and drinks My blood abides in Me, and I in him. As the living Father sent Me, and I live because of the Father, so he who eats Me, he also will live because of Me. This is the bread which came down out of heaven; not as the fathers ate and died; he who eats this bread will live forever." (John 6:52-58, NASB).

So, how is it possible to *eat Jesus* if he gone away to heaven. And who knows how long it will take him to come back? Eating his flesh and blood is essential for obtaining eternal life. He is very specific about it. Very disturbing indeed.

So, eating symbolic bread and wine just won't do; it must be literally so. Just as theologians were driven by the relentless logic of original sin to concoct the Immaculate Conception, so the logic of the "whoever eats me" in John 6 may have driven them to imagine a miracle that turns ordinary bread and wine into "the flesh of the Son of Man." And it happens during every Mass. At the Methodist Church we did communion four times a year, but the Catholics did it every Sunday, several times in fact.

Frequency keeps the magic intact.

A Tale of Two Sinks

But really, do people take it all that seriously? I hope that a lot of good Catholics roll their eyes and give it a *wink-wink* when the subject comes up. Priests, however, tend to be a serious bunch, and it's no joke to them; they are custodians of this detritus. The hocus pocus is their bread and butter.

This was brought home to me, long ago and far away, when I participated in an ecumenical service as a pastor. Occasionally all the churches in town put on a show of false and forced camaraderie by worshipping together, and we rotated from church to church. When it was the Catholic Church's turn to host, we were all getting into costume in a room behind the sanctuary.

In the small kitchen area there were two sinks. One of them was obviously for washing dishes, such items as chalices and plates. But there was a smaller sink next to it."Why two sinks?" I was naïve enough to ask, immersed as I was in Protestant ignorance. I was told that the small sink did not drain into the city sewer system; its drainpipe simply went through the wall and issued onto the lawn outside.

But why? Because it would be a desecration for the blood of Christ to be poured down the sink into the city sewer: The wine *really had become* the blood of Christ during the Mass. If there was any blood left over, it was more fitting for it to be poured into the soil outside the church. This was the sink for Jesus' blood, providing a more honorable disposal. I would find out later, after a bit more exposure to Catholic ceremony, that the priest commonly holds a bowl or plate beneath the wafer as he passes it to the communicant. God forbid that this real fragment of Jesus' real body should fall on the floor. But what would be the harm in that, if the leftover wine/blood ends up on the lawn?[12]

Catholics have also told me that they were coached never to chew the wafer; that would be disrespectful to the body of Christ. Just let the wafer soften in your mouth, then swallow it. Let me get this straight: The leftover blood cannot be poured into the city sewer, but after gently swallowing the wafer, your body turns it into shit, which ends up in the city sewer. The theologians need to huddle again and work out *de-transubstantiation*: the reverse miracle of turning the flesh of Jesus *back* into unmasticated bread once it hits the stomach and points south. Is it any wonder that H.L. Mencken could refer to "the intellectual horror of transubstantiation"?[13]

I came away from that ecumenical service enlightened, but from the standpoint of holding onto "rational" religion, this was far too much information.

A Handy Salvation Chart

Let's quickly review the salient points of Tough Problem VIII:

Core Theology of the Christian Faith

Article of Faith	What It Really Is
Bodily resurrection of Jesus	Ghoulish superstition
Human sacrifice	Repellent barbarism
Eating Jesus' flesh and blood symbolically	Macabre cult stuff: weird
Eating Jesus' flesh and blood, literally	Really macabre cult stuff: disturbing, freakish, *Hannibal Lecter.*

Who Needs It?

It's not uncommon to hear people claim that they're not into *organized* religion. They do believe in God and Jesus, but there's too much about the churches that turn them off: the buildings to maintain, bureaucracies and predatory priests, the nosy busybody factor, the never-ending appeals for money. And not everyone can stomach the ritual; some folks have sensibilities that are offended by all the barbarity and nonsense. They may not say much about it. They just stay away.

I suspect that, when push comes to shove, many compassionate Christians would just as soon brush aside convoluted doctrine and rigmarole, and attend to the business of *being good people*. While some Christians are hung up on John 3:16—you gotta *believe* the right things—others sense that you get to heaven by doing good and being a decent human being: After all, that's what St. Peter's big ledger book at the Pearly Gates is all about. Do you have enough stuff in the positive column? Have you been naughty or nice? Preachers and priests may hem and haw about this—they will obsess about their theological grids and metrics—but people gifted with common sense know instinctively that good behavior is the real test.

So, away with all the stuff that doesn't matter, the absurd runaway theology and superstitions, and get back to the basics: Let's just be "Jesus" Christians. And who cares about all the scholarly arguments about Jesus and the gospels? Most folks just roll their eyes if anyone suggests that the gospels aren't reliable. We should be able to find out how to be real Jesus Christians by reading what he said. Pay attention to all those red letters. Take Jesus at his word.

That's what we'll do next.

Notes

1. Reza Aslan, *Zealot: The Life and Times of Jesus of Nazareth*, pp. 4-6.
2. For this story, see especially the article by Lawrence Wright, *The New Yorker*, July 20, 1998, "Letter from Jerusalem: Forcing the End," but a Google search yields a lot of recent information on the red heifer project.
3. Joseph L. Daleiden, *The Final Superstition*, p. 186.
4. Jack Nelson-Pallmeyer, *Jesus Against Christianity*, p. 141.
5. Transcribed from speech given 4 May 2012. YouTube, youtube.com/watch?v=hv8zdGmc_Vg.
6. Dr. Phil Zuckerman, "Does Christianity Harm Children?," Website: *The Secular Life* (4 August 2014).
7. Stephen King, *On Writing: A Memoir of the Craft* (Pocket Books, 2001), pp. 78-79.
8. A.N. Wilson, *Paul: The Mind of the Apostle*, pp. 25-26.
9. Michael Grant, *Saint Paul*, p. 126.
10. Hyam Maccoby, *The Mythmaker: Paul and the Invention of Christianity* (HarperCollins, 1987), p. 113.
11. Note to Catholics (but not to Protestants, who couldn't care less) who are commonly ignorant of their own faith: the Dogma of the Immaculate Conception, which was promulgated by the Vatican in 1854 after centuries of contemplation, has nothing whatever to do with the virgin birth of Jesus.
12. I would find out much later that the sink is called a *sacrarium* or *piscina* (the former sounds better), and that wine left over from the Eucharist is supposed to be consumed, and not poured down the separate drain. The sink was originally intended for the disposal of baptismal and holy water and holy oils. But when cheap wine is used in the sacrament—the priest doesn't want to drink the leftovers!—he usually turns to the sink. Hence my original lesson in the purpose of the sink was based on common usage.
13. H.L. Mencken, *Treatise on the Gods*, p. 56.

IX

What a Friend We Don't Have in Jesus

> It was reserved for one who said, "Love your enemies," to tear asunder the veil between time and eternity and fix the horrified gaze of men upon the gulfs of eternal fire.
>
> —Robert Green Ingersoll, *Lecture on Orthodoxy.*

The Gospel Goes Downhill

IMAGINE THIS: A new preacher arrives in town. He has deep pockets, excessive charisma, and a Joel Osteen smile, with a plastic wife to match. Billboards and TV spots stir up interest in the grand opening of his Tower of Plenty megachurch. The new reverend has recruited 250 locals for the choir and the buzz spreads. He buys Costco's full supply of mammoth flat-screen TVs. This guy knows show business.

The first service is a sellout. With all those TVs, he is larger than life—much larger—as he sweeps across the carpeted half-acre stage in his perfectly sculpted Wall Street suit. No surprise, his message is pure prosperity gospel: For more than half an hour he exudes confidence that God wants you to have life and have it abundantly.

But suddenly—is this a sour note?—what is he saying? All 4,000 butts squirm in their seats, and the smiles fade. All worked up now, the preacher has gone off-message; he has let down his guard. Until now, the folks have loved his massive ego, but the Osteen persona has faded. His toothy "ain't salvation great?" smile has morphed into the evil grimace of Jack Nicholson's version of the Joker in *Batman*.

He has been shouting these words:

> Whoever comes to me and does not hate father and mother, wife and children, brothers and sisters, yes, and even life itself, cannot be my disciple. Do not think that I have come to bring peace to the earth; I have not come to bring peace, but a sword. For I have come to set a man against his father, and a daughter against her mother, and a daughter-in-law against her mother-in-law; and one's foes will be members of one's own household. Whoever loves father or mother more than me is not worthy of me; and whoever loves son or daughter more than me is not worthy of me.

Some folks have a high tolerance for sleazy evangelists, but it *is* possible to go too far. It takes less than a half hour for the massive auditorium to empty. This guy forgot that, if the agenda is to get folks to idolize the *preacher*, to the exclusion of everything else, it rarely works to put your craziness on full display.

This is one of the stunning mysteries of Christianity, a faith that revels in mystery: The words above are from *Jesus*, as found in Matthew 10 and Luke 14. How has this major world religion succeeded despite the alarming megalomania of Jesus? The preacher from Galilee sounds like the typical cult fanatic.

I don't imagine these verses are included in any rotation of scriptures to be read aloud in church. We can be sure that preachers have skipped over them countless times while hunting for Bible verses to preach about. They wince and cringe when they glance over them: "Oh no, that won't do."

I don't think I need to write anything more in this chapter: Jesus is *so* overrated. Most of us would unfriend him; I rest my case.

Just kidding. There's actually a lot more to say; Christian ignorance and denial about Jesus are a scandal. The verses above are just a start.

Jesus needs to be censored quite a bit, a task that gets the assistance of timid Bible translators. If you want to find out how sneaky some of them can be, do a search of Luke 14:26 at Biblegateway.com. On the drop-down menu of the versions of the Bible available (there are dozens, as surely befits the *one* true Word of God) and take a look at how the verse gets manipulated and softened.

Just as preachers have balked at these verses, I'm sure that laypeople have been shocked as well. How could Jesus have said this? *Did* he say it?

We aren't going to wrestle with the issue of authenticity anymore; that was part of Tough Problem VI. Instead, for our Tough Problem IX about Jesus, we'll stick with the lay person's favored assumption: If it's in the gospels, Jesus said it.

Let's Try a Shell Game

The favorite dodge when heartburn-inducing passages of the Bible are quoted for their shock value is that they have been "taken out of context." But in just what context would this teaching be okay? The context in Luke 14 is straightforward; we read that large crowds of people were following him when he launched into this tirade about what he expected of his followers. These are other texts in which Jesus approvingly quotes Old Testament law about honoring father and mother, but he would not be the first–or the last–preacher to praise a treasured moral code while missing the mark in his own life.

Another dodge is that "Jesus really didn't mean that"–as if the embarrassed believer is enough of an expert on ancient languages to have any basis for that guess. Scholar Hector Avalos takes aim at this excuse and obliterates it in a 40-page chapter, "Hateful Jesus: Luke 14:26," in his book *The Bad Jesus*.[1] Avalos examines the text with devastating precision and demonstrates that "hate your father and mother" means exactly what it says.

So Christian squirming and dissembling continue. In the Contemporary English Version, the verse gets softened: "You cannot be my disciple, unless you love me more than you love your father and mother, your wife and children, and your brothers and sisters. You cannot come with me unless you love me more than you love your own life." These translators have simply excised that unpleasant word "hate," giving Jesus a love-me-more approach.

This is simply dishonest, and is it even less offensive, really? How can any self-respecting translator, theologian, or preacher assume that making this change–a lie, covering up the word *hate*–fixes the problem? Does this make Jesus any better? Most of us today would cross the street to avoid being accosted by a Bible-waving fanatic shouting, "You gotta love me more than you love your dad and mom."

Maybe This Verse Is Just a Mistake . . . or Not?

In fact, some scholars might concede that the hate-your-family verses are hard to rule out as real Jesus words. They use what's called "the criterion of embarrassment." That is, if there is something hard to swallow, it *would* have been clipped out unless the gospel writers had reason to believe that it was authentic. Who were *they* to censor Jesus? So, even though it's embarrassing, since Jesus said it, they had to include it.

I think the "criterion of embarrassment" fails on two counts. This failure could be a comfort to Christians who hope that Jesus just wouldn't have said anything so blatantly obnoxious. But it also removes a major apologist prop for the authenticity of the Bible. Here are the problems with the criterion of embarrassment:

1. Matthew and Luke, writing decades after the fact, could hardly have been worried that eyewitnesses (long dead by then) were about to check their work. They didn't feel compelled to leave something in for fear of someone faulting them for not getting the script right. We know how much they made stuff up, all over the place.

2. The hate-your-family verses may not have been the least bit embarrassing to Matthew and Luke. These authors belonged to the Jesus cult; they were writing to convince the world that Jesus was the son of God. They wanted to bring fiercely loyal followers to the church, those who would not be dissuaded by hostile family members. In the diverse marketplace of religions at the time, it was a dog-eat-dog, cult-eat-cult world. There was nothing bizarre at all about looking for folks who would be willing to leave family behind.

Of course, Jesus' level of callousness doesn't fly with Christians today, especially those who brag about family values.[2] But there it is: Hate-your-family is parked in plain view in the New Testament. Whether it actually can be traced back to Jesus himself is largely irrelevant. The gospel writers wanted their readers to believe Jesus was "speaking in character" when he said it.

Trouble at Home

"I really want to smack that kid," one of my New Testament professors once said."That kid" was the twelve-year old Jesus described in Luke 2:41-51. In this famous story, Mary and Joseph had taken him with them to Jerusalem for Passover, and when they left town to return home they assumed (à la *Home Alone*?) that he was somewhere in their group of travelers, presumably extended family and neighbors.

But Jesus had stayed in Jerusalem to discuss religion with the elders in the Temple. His distraught parents returned to hunt for him, and finally found him:

> When his parents saw him they were astonished; and his mother said to him, "Child, why have you treated us like this? Look, your father and I have been searching for you in great anxiety."

> He said to them, "Why were you searching for me? Did you not know that I must be about my Father's business?" But they did not understand what he said to them. (Luke 2:48-50)

A lot of mothers would have boxed his ears and said, "Don't talk back to me, young man!" However, the distraught Mary calms down and resumes pondering: "His mother treasured all these things in her heart" (v.51). That, after Luke says she and Joseph didn't understand what he was saying.

And that makes no sense, either, in light of Luke's earlier story–only a chapter earlier!–that Mary had been told the grand news about her son by an angel, and that there, too, she "treasured all these words and pondered them in her heart" (Luke 2:19). So why would she be puzzled and surprised?

Luke tries to smooth out this rough patch, sensing perhaps that Jesus came off as too much of a smart aleck. Then, he adds, Jesus "went down with them and came to Nazareth, and was obedient to them" (v. 51).

Later in the gospels, Jesus' family still doesn't have a clue about his mission and ministry. In Mark 3:21 we read, "When his family heard it, they went out to restrain him, for people were saying, 'He has gone out of his mind.'" Jesus got so caught up in his obsession with the Kingdom of God that there was a disconnect with his family, as we can glean from other scenes in the gospels as well.

In John 7:6 we find this tidbit: "For not even his brothers believed in him." What? Hadn't Mary told them who their older brother was? That should have stopped sibling rivalry in its tracks. And shouldn't Jesus have been in awe of his mother–at least as much in awe as Catholics are today?

The traditional Hail Mary prayer, based on Luke 1:42, includes these words, "blessed art thou amongst women, and blessed is the fruit of thy womb, Jesus." Yet does Jesus himself endorse this sentiment? Not when a "woman in the crowd raised her voice and said to him, 'Blessed is the womb that bore you and the breasts that nursed you!'" Better toss out that Mary statue, lady: "But he said, 'Blessed rather are those who hear the word of God and obey it!'" (Luke 11:27-28)

And we find this episode in Matthew 12:46-50 (copied from Mark 3:31-35):

> While he was still speaking to the crowds, his mother and his brothers were standing outside, wanting to speak to him. Someone told him, "Look, your mother and your brothers are standing outside, wanting to speak to you." But to the one who had told him this, Jesus replied, "Who is my mother, and who are my brothers?" And pointing to his disciples, he said, "Here are my mother and my brothers! For whoever does the will of my Father in heaven is my brother and sister and mother."

This doesn't seem to be so much out of character for a preacher who expected his followers to hate their families.

It's no surprise, of course, that Bible translators often try to put the best possible spin on alarming texts, even when they're not trying to soften the actual wording.

Here's the heading the New Revised Standard version puts above these verses: "The True Kindred of Jesus." It could just as well be "Jesus Rebuffs His Family."

As is clear from his rude retorts to some prospective followers, family just didn't count for much:

> As they were going along the road, someone said to him, "I will follow you wherever you go."
>
> And Jesus said to him, "Foxes have holes, and birds of the air have nests; but the Son of Man has nowhere to lay his head." To another he said, "Follow me."
>
> But he said, "Lord, first let me go and bury my father."
>
> But Jesus said to him, "Let the dead bury their own dead; but as for you, go and proclaim the kingdom of God."
>
> Another said, "I will follow you, Lord; but let me first say farewell to those at my home."
>
> Jesus said to him, "No one who puts a hand to the plow and looks back is fit for the kingdom of God." (Luke 9:57-62)[3]

If you want to follow Jesus, you can't take time to bury your father or even say goodbye to your family? The family-values Christians who love their Jesus search the gospels in vain for fragments of teachings that actually champion the *value* of family.

The only texts that depict Jesus even talking to his mother, other than as a twelve-year old brat in the Temple, are found in John 2 and 19. The first is at wedding of Cana, to which Jesus and his mother and disciples had been invited.

> When the wine gave out, the mother of Jesus said to him, "They have no wine." And Jesus said to her, "Woman, what concern is that to you and to me? My hour has not yet come." His mother said to the servants, "Do whatever he tells you." (John 2:3-5)

The other is when Jesus was hanging on the cross with his mother, his mother's sister, and Mary Magdalene standing nearby:

> When Jesus saw his mother and the disciple whom he loved standing beside her, he said to his mother, "Woman, here is your son." Then he said to the disciple, "Here is your mother." And from that hour the disciple took her into his own home. (John 19:26-27)

This touching scene gives us the only glimpse of warmth on the part of Jesus toward his mother. Even if these two episodes are authentic—highly improbable in the gospel of John—they provide very little for us to go on in trying to build the case that Jesus was a family-friendly guy.

Calendar Crisis

It's awfully hard to get Christians to *pay attention,* to evaluate anything credited to Jesus with open-minded honesty. Their particular way of looking at him is firmly fixed already, whether its the awesome muscular judge depicted on the wall of the Sistine Chapel or the "meek and mild" Jesus that prevailed in Victorian imagery.

Jesus has accrued many titles: Son of God, Son of Man, Redeemer, Savior, King of Kings, Messiah, Suffering Servant, Friend ("What a Friend We Have in Jesus"). Thanks to George Frederic Handel's setting of Isaiah 9:6, some of the titles applied to Jesus by the church (*mis*interpreting Isaiah 9:6) are familiar to most of us: "and his name shall be called Wonderful Counselor, Mighty God, Everlasting Father, Prince of Peace." Ironically, the New Testament itself never applies this text to Jesus.

Another title, far less complimentary, has gained currency in the last century as scholars have looked rigorously at all the words credited to Jesus: *Apocalyptic Prophet*, which means, basically, a preacher who proclaims that "the end is near." For the gospel writers, that also meant the return of Jesus to rule in glory.[4] The term doesn't have such a familiar ring because most levelheaded Christians, I suspect, find *apocalypticism* eccentric–and they really aren't counting on Jesus coming back. Sure, they hear it in the creeds and in New Testament readings, but this is just so much ritual white noise.

But a substantial minority of Christians really do believe that Jesus will return, and soon. According to Pew research reported in 2010, a whopping 41 percent of Americans think Jesus will come back by 2050: Jesus said it, and he meant it.

We have to wonder, however, why those who are so eager to see Jesus come back– that expectation is planted right there in the gospels and Paul's letters–haven't read the fine print in those awkward, undermining verses that have escaped notice or are glossed over. Jesus said that the "end of the age"–the coming of the kingdom–would happen "before this generation passes away." Full stop. There's nothing ambiguous about that. Paul frantically preached his message about Christ, an urgent one because he also believed Jesus would be back soon, in time for him to savor the moment. There's nothing ambiguous about that either. Something is wrong: epic fail for these predictions.

Let's take Jesus at his word and just admit it: He was *wrong*, as was Paul. Those who are expecting Jesus to reappear before 2050 have conceded that we must ignore some of the things Jesus said, because "before 2050" was **not** what Jesus had in mind–if you take him at his word.

The prayer that Jesus taught people to pray included the words "thy kingdom come": He seems to have assumed it was just around the corner. But the folks who keep looking at the sky, hoping to glimpse Jesus, from now until 2050, can't bring themselves to acknowledge that Jesus was wrong about his return trip. They tacitly admit, as they are forced to, that he was wrong, *really* wrong, about the timing. The problem for them: Admitting out loud that he was wrong about the timing leaves them just a baby step away from fessing up that the prediction itself was rooted in delusional thinking.

Wrong Doesn't Mean Bad

Now, it's actually easy to show how Jesus was wrong about other things as well, but we can cut him some slack. Even if you want to argue that the Galilean peasant was the son of God, that doesn't mean that he was all-knowing. In the form of a human being (for a few years, at least), he could make mistakes. Maybe it was only in the sweet by-and-by, after he'd gone up to heaven to sit at God's right hand that he shared in omniscience.

Now, that doesn't line up with the Trinity doctrine, i.e., Jesus was, from the very beginning, an *undifferentiated part of God* along with the Father and the Holy Ghost—but that's so silly I won't even bother going into it. You can write your own Tough Problem XI all about the Trinity if you like.

So, trinitarian nonsense aside, maybe we really can't fault Jesus of Nazareth, the carpenter's son, for not knowing all the amazing things about nature that we've learned since Copernicus, Newton, Darwin, Pasteur, Einstein and Hubble. God himself presumably knew them long before any of these illustrious thinkers figured them out, but Jesus the man, trekking around Palestine in the first century, did not.

I can't agree with strident atheists who ridicule Jesus for not knowing that the Earth orbits the sun, that demons can't be transferred into pigs or that blindness can't be cured by smearing diseased eyes with mud and spit. Truly, Jesus was a citizen of his time and participated fully in the superstitions of the day.

However—let me digress a moment here—we must not pretend that we can skip the Enlightenment and just adopt the superstitions of the first century. Just because we can understand why Jesus could have believed something foolish doesn't mean that *we* should. That leads to a blind obsession with Jesus, a boundless Jesus-idolatry. It's especially chilling when we encounter such wrongheadedness at the highest levels of government, now, in the 21st century.

The medieval Catholicism of Justice Antonin Scalia was well known, but even so, who can be prepared for his simple-minded understanding of the New Testament? Here's what Scalia had to say in an interview with *New York Magazine*:

> In the Gospels, the devil is doing all sorts of things. He's making pigs run off cliffs, he's possessing people and whatnot. And that doesn't happen very much anymore . . . . It's because he's smart . . . you're looking at me as though I'm weird. My god! Are you so out of touch with most of America, most of which believes in the devil? I mean, Jesus Christ believed in the devil! It's in the Gospels! You travel in circles that are so, so removed from mainstream America that you are appalled that anybody would believe in the devil! Most of mankind has believed in the devil, for all of history. Many more intelligent people than you or me have believed in the devil.[5]

You can shout all you want, "Jesus Christ believed in the devil! It's in the Gospels!", but that's no way to stand up for Jesus. Just admit that Jesus believed in devils and demons. Cut him some slack. What else could we have expected of a Galilean peasant? It was a wildly superstitious age: "Catching someone's disease would have meant catching someone's sin. In a world crawling with demons, it would have meant getting the devil on your back."[6]

There are much bigger problems in Jesus' thought to overcome. He believed things about God that many of us today, Christians included, would find repugnant. It's the flaws in Jesus' thinking that are disturbing, not what he could be excused for not knowing, once you let go of the silly notion that he was part of an invisible three-headed God.

Being Wrong Is Not as Bad as Being Vindictive

Which brings us back to the apocalyptic prophet. Some folks might be tempted to say "Oh well, Jesus just got the timing wrong. The idea of bringing the Kingdom of God to earth is still a good idea—whenever it might happen—and won't it be glorious?"

Well, no. Again, folks, please read the fine print, which isn't fine at all, in any sense of the word. The coming of the kingdom is not a swell idea, unless you're pretty sure you're a part of God's elect, a very exclusive club. According to Jesus, it will be grim indeed for everyone else. Read the details in Mark 13, all those sinister red-letter words of Jesus. This is nasty get-even theology. When the kingdom arrives,

> the one on the housetop must not go down or enter the house to take anything away; the one in the field must not turn back to get a coat. Woe to those who are pregnant and to those who are nursing infants in those days! Pray that it may not be in winter. For in those days there will be suffering, such as has not been from the beginning of the creation that God created until now, no, and never will be. (Mark 13:15-19)

Suffering, "such as has not been from the beginning of the creation." In Matthew, Jesus adds more grim detail, comparing his glorious arrival with the story of Noah and the flood—God's greatest act of genocide, ever—and that's saying a lot:

> For as the days of Noah were, so will be the coming of the Son of Man. For as in those days before the flood they were eating and drinking, marrying and giving in marriage, until the day Noah entered the ark, and they knew nothing until the flood came and swept them all away, so too will be the coming of the Son of Man. (Matt. 24:37-39)

Are you sure this is what you want? This is the kingdom that Jesus taught people to pray for, and it is not sweetness and light. Jesus sets the tone here for the thousands of vindictive Christian preachers who would follow, terrorizing people into submission with threats of banishment and punishment.

Apocalyptic preachers are bad news. Sometimes humor has been used to relieve the gloom of this pathetic theology: "Jesus is coming. Look busy."

Compassion Compromised and Cancelled

When Christians are in a good mood and want to show Jesus in the most positive light, they fondly point to the magnificent sentiments that we find in Matthew 25:34-40. It's an eloquent appeal to the imperatives of compassion:

> Then the King will say to those on His right, "Come, you who are blessed of My Father, inherit the kingdom prepared for you from the foundation of the world. For I was hungry, and you gave Me something to eat; I was thirsty, and you gave Me something to drink; I was a stranger, and you invited Me in; naked, and you clothed Me; I was sick, and you visited Me; I was in prison, and you came to Me."

> Then the righteous will answer Him, "Lord, when did we see You hungry, and feed You, or thirsty, and give You something to drink? And when did we see You a stranger, and invite You in, or naked, and clothe You? When did we see You sick, or in prison, and come to You?"

> The King will answer and say to them, "Truly I say to you, to the extent that you did it to one of these brothers of Mine, even the least of them, you did it to Me." (NASB)

Presumably, "the least of them" means the humble and poor, those who don't have any weight to throw around. They commonly lack food, drink, clothing, and friends. They can end up on the wrong side of the law. Back then, and now, it was all too common to ignore the plight of the destitute and disadvantaged. And the message here is clear: The way you treat these people is the way you treat Jesus. How cool is that!

These verses are high-impact preaching at its best, in the tradition of the Old Testament prophets who condemned neglect and abuse of poor people at the bottom of the social order. They must go in the "well done!" column of the great things that Jesus said.

But it's not that simple. Sensitive Christians could only wish that Jesus had said these words in a different context. Standing alone, these verses would work admirably for a heartwarming Sunday morning homily. But let's not follow the Christians in doing for this passage what they often accuse Bible critics of doing, taking scripture out of context.

These seven verses are part of a warning about eternal punishment that is the primary thrust of Matthew 25. It is a vile, sinister piece of scripture that ruins these lovely words. It's common for Christians to quote just these few verses to make Jesus look good, but that amounts to censoring Jesus. Matthew 25 is actually one of the major clues that Jesus expected the kingdom of God to arrive in the immediate future—and it would be a devastating event for all but a few.

I cannot stress enough the importance of reading this chapter, *all* of it, carefully, before ruling out my suggestion that Jesus is overrated. His words here are an indictment.

The Three Chunks of Matthew 25
Brace Yourself

Verses 1-13
Getting Ready for the Groom's Arrival

Matthew 25 starts, innocently enough, with the Parable of the Ten Bridesmaids, or as the King James Version correctly translates it, "virgins." Half of them were wise, half were foolish. Not surprisingly, among teenage boys in Sunday school, this text has prompted a lot of snickering about foolish virgins. Or so I remember.

However, we did take the message seriously. This parable was taken as a lesson about always being prepared, the importance of planning ahead. But it's not quite that pedestrian. The bridesmaids were charged with providing light, via oil lamps, for the wedding banquet, and they were awaiting the arrival of the bridegroom. This is code for the arrival of Jesus when he returns to earth (elsewhere also Jesus refers himself as the bridegroom, e.g. Matthew 9:15). Five of the bridesmaids have brought along an extra bottle of oil for their lamps, but five did not. When the bridegroom finally shows up, the negligent five must rush out to buy more oil.

When they return, they're out of luck. The doors to the banquet hall have been closed: "Later the other bridesmaids came also, saying, 'Lord, lord, open to us.'"

Did the bridegroom in Jesus' parable smile beatifically, open the door, and say, "No problem, better late than never!" Nope. He replied, "Truly I tell you, I do not know you." So, Jesus warned, "Keep awake therefore, for you know neither the day nor the hour" (Matt. 25:11-13). What a guy.

The chapter goes downhill from here.

Verses 14-30
Capitalist Fervor

Now we come to the Parable of the Talents. This one baffled me as a common-sense kid who'd been taught to be careful and practical. I could see that those five bridesmaids were screw-ups, though their bridegroom sure didn't cut them any slack. But the man who stars in Jesus' Talent Show was a cruel and greedy jerk.

While he's away on a journey he entrusts money (the domination was a *talent*, a large sum) to three of his slaves. Two of them make investments that double the money, but the third is cautious and buries the money for safekeeping. This incurs the wrath of his master. When I say that the chapter is vile, this is one reason why:

> Then you ought to have invested my money with the bankers, and on my return I would have received what was my own with interest. So take the talent from him, and give it to the one with the ten talents. For to all those who have, more will be given, and they will have an abundance; but from those who have nothing, even what they have will be taken away. As for this worthless slave, throw him into the outer darkness, where there will be weeping and gnashing of teeth. (Matt. 25:27-30)

This could be one of the favorite texts of the prosperity-gospel preachers: "For to all those who have, more will be given, and they will have an abundance; but from those who have nothing, even what they have will be taken away." It's bad enough that Jesus would say "from those who have nothing, even what they have will be taken away," but the truly horrid verse is the last one: "As for this worthless slave, throw him into the outer darkness, where there will be weeping and gnashing of teeth."

I can hear the retort of apologists scrambling to the defense: "Oh, but this is not Jesus speaking, it's a character in one of his parables." Well, Jesus presents this character as the *one who is right*. There are probably shelves full of doctoral dissertations on this section of Matthew 25 alone, attempting to save Jesus from being as nasty and mean-spirited as he sounds here.

These verses aren't very nice, and they certainly don't align well with the message about helping the downtrodden that we find in the oft-quoted feel-good verses, 34-40. This poor slave, who was cautious with his master's money, is sent off to grim punishment in outer darkness where he will weep and gnash his teeth in torment, or at least disappointment.

How can this not be a major violation of decency and fair play? If Jesus intended to portray the master in this story as a role model, I wonder what his idea of an unfair villain would look like.

Verses 31-46
The Muscled-Up Jesus

Now we come to the awesome muscular Jesus of the Sistine Chapel, judge and final arbiter. We see the setting of those famous nice words, vv. 34-40, but the sinister context is in full view:

> When the Son of Man comes in his glory, and all the angels with him, then he will sit on the throne of his glory. All the nations will be gathered before him, and he will separate people one from another as a shepherd separates the sheep from the goats, and he will put the sheep at his right hand and the goats at the left. (Matt. 25:31-33)

Those on the left are the folks who failed to show compassion; they didn't feed the hungry, clothe the naked, visit those in prison. Their negligence is catastrophic: "You that are accursed, depart from me into the eternal fire prepared for the devil and his angels" (v. 41)."Truly I tell you, just as you did not do it to one of the least of these, you did not do it to me ... and these will go away into eternal punishment, but the righteous into eternal life" (vv.45-46). This represents confused theology on at least one count, and possibly two, depending on how highly you rate the theology of the apostle Paul and John, the gospel writer.

Yes, This Is Terrible Theology

Of course, we might sometimes want to make the case that eternal punishment is fitting for serial killers and tyrants, for priests who rape kids, even for the legions of grinning millionaire frauds in their megachurches. But only in our angriest moments.

The level of our rage and disgust must always be tempered when we decide their punishments. Martin Luther King is famous for his claim that "the moral arc of the universe bends toward justice," and if that is so, *eternal* punishment is never an option. Theologians and preachers who relish punishment that *never, ever* ends are in dire need of anger management therapy: "Cruel and unusual" doesn't even begin to cover their twisted revenge solution.

Notice that this text doesn't target killers, tyrants, evil priests, or religious frauds. The judge in Matthew, none other than Jesus himself, aims his wrath at people who have not lived up to standards of compassion. This text would have us believe that the sins of apathy and indifference merit eternal punishment. As journalist Jeffrey Tayler has put it, Jesus "was at times a heartless prophet of doom for the sinners he supposedly loved, commanding those who failed to give comfort to the poor to 'depart . . . ye cursed, into everlasting fire, prepared for the devil and his angels.'"[7]

Also, Confused Theology

Paul and John felt that the key to salvation–getting into that small pool of folks who will be with Jesus as he reigns forever–was *belief in Jesus*. Period. As Paul puts it so bluntly in Romans 10:9, "if you confess with your lips that Jesus is Lord and believe in your heart that God raised him from the dead, you will be saved." Paul, and perhaps John as well, would have not discounted doing good deeds, but that was not the key to it. Indeed they would have argued passionately that believing in Jesus would result in saintly behavior–being a good person and acting compassionately–as a fruit of faith. History has shown that tree to be a pretty barren one.

And we cannot help notice the starkly different theology that Matthew 25 presents. Jesus says, just as bluntly as Paul states his theology, that being sorted to the right instead of to the left on Judgment Day–eternal life instead of eternal punishment–depends entirely on how good you've been, in particular on how good you've been to the poor and disadvantaged. It would be hard to find a more glaring Bible contradiction, or a more significant one in terms of Christian theology.

And Even Self-Contradictory Theology
Cruel Punishment for Cruelty?

Matthew 25 begs the question for us: How could the theology of Jesus be bad here, since he is so hung up on compassion as the key to salvation? I suspect that many Christians would come down on the side of being a good person as the real basis for getting to heaven. So, by that standard, this is indeed good theology, but it sends people to eternal punishment for failing to be compassionate. That's pretty severe punishment, a far cry from compassion, for apathy and indifference. Who could pass muster? Most people aren't as compassionate as they should be: Jesus the compassion advocate would have an awful lot of us marched off to eternal fire.

Don't be fooled by that block of verses in Matthew 25 that get all the good press. When we look at the whole context of the chapter, we see Jesus as a pretty awful muscular judge.

Christians will point to other passages in the gospels that show Jesus' compassion. He saved an adulteress from being stoned by Tea Partyers: "Let anyone who is without sin throw the first stone" (John 8). Can there be any recommendation for compassion better than his Parable of the Good Samaritan in Luke 10:25-37? Jesus even used hyperbole to emphasize the importance of compassion, as we find in Matthew 18:21-22:

> Then Peter came to Him and said, "Lord, how often shall my brother sin against me, and I forgive him? As many as seven times?"
>
> Jesus said to him, "I do not say to you seven times, but seventy times seven" (RSV).

So Christians may feel confident that Jesus was a good guy, after all.

Well, how do we resolve the disparity? I can remind Christians that this text about forgiving seventy times seventy is used to introduce the Parable of the Unforgiving Servant, which ends grimly indeed. Jesus begins by saying that "the kingdom of heaven is like a certain king who wanted to settle accounts with his servants." The king forgives a massive debt owed to him by a servant, but the servant refuses to do likewise for a fellow servant. When the king finds out he is furious."Should you not also have had compassion on your fellow servant, just as I had pity on you?" The king delivers the servant "to the torturers until he should pay all that was due to him."

Torturers? That's pretty extreme. Who cannot be shocked when Jesus then says that is what his "heavenly Father also will do to you if each of you, from his heart, does not forgive his brother his trespasses." So the heavenly Father is up for torture? As was the case in Matthew 25, the penalty for the failure of compassion is disproportionately and hypocritically severe.

No Love Wasted on Gentiles

I am suspicious of acutely religious folks who gush fountains about love but then turn out to restrict their love severely in practice. Like Jesus, for example, in this incident that's always been a bit of an embarrassment for compassionate-Jesus fans:

> Jesus went away from there, and withdrew into the district of Tyre and Sidon. And a Canaanite woman from that region came out and began to cry out, saying, "Have mercy on me, Lord, Son of David; my daughter is cruelly demon-possessed."
>
> But He did not answer her a word. And His disciples came and implored Him, saying, "Send her away, because she keeps shouting at us."
>
> But He answered and said, "I was sent only to the lost sheep of the house of Israel."
>
> But she came and began to bow down before Him, saying, "Lord, help me!"
>
> And He answered and said, "It is not good to take the children's bread and throw it to the dogs."

> But she said, "Yes, Lord; but even the dogs feed on the crumbs which fall from their masters' table."
>
> Then Jesus said to her, "O woman, your faith is great; it shall be done for you as you wish." And her daughter was healed at once. (Matt. 15:21-28, NASB)

How can this possibly reflect well on Jesus? He relented only when she begged him on her knees. Matthew found this story in Mark 7 and altered the wording, but both of them preserve Jesus' reference to Gentiles as *dogs* outside the scope of his message, which was aimed only at the Jews. Since Matthew was catering to a Jewish audience, this story would have pleased his readers.

In light of this text, we can be skeptical about the words of the resurrected Jesus at the very end of the gospel: "Go therefore and make disciples of all nations, baptizing them in the name of the Father and of the Son and of the Holy Spirit (Matt. 28:19). Very inclusive, but that's not how he felt when he was being rude to the Gentile woman who asked for help. Did Jesus change his mind after he was resurrected?

Despite our working assumption that the red-letter text is from Jesus, I also can't help but mention the likelihood that somebody inserted Matthew 28:19 to smooth out the rough edges of his conversation with the Canaanite woman. And we have to pause skeptically at the words, "baptizing them in the name of the Father and of the Son and of the Holy Spirit." This sounds very much like a liturgical formula that would have come into existence by the time Matthew wrote his gospel, but would not have been uttered by Jesus himself.

Eternal Fire

Epic Fail as a Moral Concept

The gospels would have us believe that John the Baptist was the warm-up act for Jesus. John attracted large crowds ("there went out to him all the country of Judea," Mark 1:5, RSV), and he positioned himself as the one who was "making straight the way of the Lord." John was perhaps cynical about the motives of those who flocked to him, saying, "You brood of vipers, who warned you to flee from the wrath to come?" (Luke 3:7, NASB)

This verse, believe it or not, sets the tone for much of what we find in the gospels, and in keeping with the theme of wrath, notice what John says Jesus will do:

> John answered and said to them all, "As for me, I baptize you with water; but One is coming who is mightier than I, and I am not fit to untie the thong of His sandals; He will baptize you with the Holy Spirit and fire. His winnowing fork is in His hand to thoroughly clear His threshing floor, and to gather the wheat into His barn; but He will burn up the chaff with unquenchable fire." (Luke 3:16-17, NASB)

Just as slavery has fallen out of favor, so has the idea of hell and eternal punishment among sensitive, compassionate thinkers. Hell and eternal punishment fall into the category of the *cruel and unusual*. Pain and torture that go on *forever* can't be part of sound theology. Superior morality excludes revenge, from God or anyone else, and I suspect that most ethicists have recognized that revenge is poisonous. On the practical level alone, it serves no purpose.

Nowadays, our sense of morality is *superior to that of the God and Jesus of the Bible.*

Remember Martin Luther King's claim that the "moral arc of the universe bends toward justice"? Of course, that's preacher talk: eloquent, even magnificent, but devoid of meaning. People are fooled because it sounds so darned nice. Martin Luther King could get a lot of mileage out of it–and more power to him–in his battle against racist Christians. A better, less theological, less poetic way of stating the point is that humans have developed a keener sense of justice through the millennia. For example, two hundred years ago, there was little widespread revulsion against slavery, but sensibilities have changed because humans figured out that slavery is cruel, demeaning and morally reprehensible.

God "getting even forever" has no place in a universe whose moral arc is bending toward justice. And just who is the Manager of the Cosmos getting even with? You and me and all mortals–as Robert Price has said, "ephemeral non-entities like us"– who are trying to make it in a world not known for fairness.[8] We can shout back at God, as we are always tempted to do at bullies: "Pick on someone your own size!"

As is the case with human sacrifice, revenge demeans theology. In the centuries before Jesus, Jewish theology absorbed pagan ideas about eternal punishment. It seemed like a good idea at the time to explain how God would make up for the suffering of the chosen people, and for the seemingly endless success of evildoers *in this life*. But this is "get even" theology, pure and simple, and Jesus seems to have bought it, as so many of his sayings attest. If this is true, he espoused a deeply flawed concept of God. So, alas, if you want to delete hell from your theology, you'll find Jesus blocking the way. How *the hell* can we give him points as a serious thinker?

Taking His Ball and Going Home

There are other times when Jesus seems, inexplicably, to give a shrug to pettiness and cruelty that would appall compassionate people. We read in Matthew 10 that he gathered the twelve disciples to send them out to preach the news about the coming kingdom of heaven. They were authorized to work miracles as tokens of the new age that was about to dawn: "Heal the sick, raise the dead, cleanse lepers, cast out demons." Jesus ordered them to visit towns and villages in Israel only ("Go nowhere among the Gentiles, and enter no town of the Samaritans," v. 5), but he anticipated that some people would give the disciples the brushoff.

Understandably, itinerate preachers mooching off the land aren't always given a warm welcome, no matter the country or century. But Jesus won't cut anybody any slack if they show the cold shoulder: "If anyone will not welcome you or listen to your words, shake off the dust from your feet as you leave that house or town. Truly I tell you, it will be more tolerable for the land of Sodom and Gomorrah on the day of judgment than for that town" (Matt. 10:14-15). Remember that Sodom and Gomorrah were burned to the ground. This is Jesus the Great Moral Teacher?

Sometimes he shows some very warped priorities. People are doing terrible things to each other, yet here's what Jesus thinks is the worst thing you could possibly do: "Truly I tell you, people will be forgiven for their sins and whatever blasphemies they utter; but whoever blasphemes against the Holy Spirit can never have forgiveness, but is guilty of an eternal sin" (Mark 3:28-29). *Seriously?* Matthew actually intensified the wording when he copied Mark, saying "whoever speaks against the Holy Spirit will not be forgiven, either in this age or in the age to come (Matt. 12:32). This is the babble of a cult fanatic.

Another example of Jesus in a bad mood: Believers have always struggled with the story of Jesus cursing the out-of-season fig tree for—of all things—not having ripe figs. This usually strikes readers as a display of bad temper.[9] Jesus inexplicably uses his power to curse the tree as an illustration of superior faith; we read one his worst teachings:

> Have faith in God. Truly I tell you, if you say to this mountain, "Be taken up and thrown into the sea," and if you do not doubt in your heart, but believe that what you say will come to pass, it will be done for you. So I tell you, whatever you ask for in prayer, believe that you have received it, and it will be yours. (Mark 11:22-24)

How can anyone take this drivel seriously? "Well, Jesus was speaking metaphorically. You can't take this literally," may be the common evasion to soften the absurdity of these verses. But it is one crappy metaphor. If faith is supposed to be a source of comfort, this works *against* that goal: How many people throughout the Christian era have beaten themselves up for not having the level of faith that Jesus expected?

Countless devout Christians have prayed with all their might to prevent bad things from happening. But, alas, their faith wasn't up to the task. Cult leaders rarely see the damage that their teachings can bring."Shame on them," we want to say, and shame on Jesus, too, for prodding his followers to have faith that can move mountains when they know full well that the mountains will stay put.

The Sermon on the Mount

I once had a workplace encounter about this most famous of Jesus' sermons. One of the games played in corporate America is the checking of references; employers want to talk to people who have known and worked with prospective new hires. It's a game because the candidates provide the names of people they've coached to say good things about them. For many years I was involved in the game. It was my job to qualify applicants for admission to an advanced certification program.

I commonly asked, "On a scale of one to ten, how would you rate this candidate as a manager, motivator, team player, public speaker, etc." I heard a lot of "tens," but on one occasion the top grade in all categories was "nine." The man explained, "I don't give tens. I wouldn't even give the Sermon on the Mount a ten." My response was a chuckle, "Wow, you're tough."

What I *wanted* to say was, "How right you are, the Sermon on the Mount is far below a ten," but, of course, wearing my business hat at that moment, I held my tongue. But this guy's refusal to give a ten is based on assumption that *of course it deserves a ten*. The Sermon on the Mount is supposedly the highest statement of morals and ethics imaginable. Jesus' reputation as a great moral teacher derives from a few of his magnificent parables (e.g., The Good Samaritan), but primarily on the high ratings usually given to the Sermon on the Mount. It's the Gold Standard.

For the typical Christian, I suspect a word-for-word study of the 121-verse text of the Sermon, *without* the knowledge that their hero Jesus was the speaker, would induce a lot of hemming and hawing, dissent and disagreement.[10] A lot of Christians would reject, even ridicule, what I consider its best parts. They would brush aside as nonsense the verses that non-Christian observers also dismiss as ridiculous. There's some really bad advice in the Sermon on the Mount.

Some Good Stuff

There are a few gems in the Sermon. Let's look at them first.

> **Matthew 5:23-24:** "Therefore if you bring your gift to the altar, and there remember that your brother has something against you, leave your gift there before the altar, and go your way. First be reconciled to your brother, and then come and offer your gift" (NKJV).

Your worship of God can't be genuine if you remain un-reconciled with others.

> **Matthew 6:5-7:** "And when you pray, you shall not be like the hypocrites. For they love to pray standing in the synagogues and on the corners of the streets, that they may be seen by men. Assuredly, I say to you, they have their reward. But you, when you pray, go into your room, and when you have shut your door, pray to your Father who is in the secret place; and your Father who sees in secret will reward you openly. And when you pray, do not use vain repetitions as the heathen do. For they think that they will be heard for their many words" (NKJV).

Don't make a public display of your piety. Prayer should be private.

> **Matthew 7:1-5:** "Judge not, that you be not judged. For with what judgment you judge, you will be judged; and with the measure you use, it will be measured back to you. And why do you look at the speck in your brother's eye, but do not consider the plank in your own eye? Or how can you say to your brother, 'Let me remove the speck from your eye'; and look, a plank is in your own eye? Hypocrite! First remove the plank from your own eye, and then you will see clearly to remove the speck from your brother's eye" (NKJV).

Since we all have our faults and failings, we're not entitled to judge others.

Unfortunately, since Jesus went to his eternal reward, his followers have specialized in ignoring these top-notch ethical teachings, which is a puzzle to those of us who keep an eye on Christians. What's the point of having a Bible, after all, if you're just going to say, "No thank you, these rules aren't for me"?

There are so many different brands of Christianity because Christians can't get along. They refuse to reconcile, they judge severely, and they make elaborate public displays of their piety. In our own era, it would seem that televangelists and the egomaniacs who run megachurches have convinced themselves that Jesus' contempt for ostentatious worship can be given a wink.

Every Little Thing Gonna Be All Right
Jesus Channeling Bob Marley

The Sermon on the Mount usually gets so much good press because it opens with the famous Beatitudes, which lend themselves to embroidery and Hallmark cards. They can be used to make the case that Jesus was a good guy because they seemingly offer comfort to those who need it most. Christians who want to gush over the Beatitudes need to look at Luke's version of them, too, since he changed Matthew's wording. For example, Matthew's "Blessed are the poor in spirit" becomes Luke's "Blessed are the poor."

But countless sermons have been preached about the Beatitudes, chewing on such differences and drawing many different lessons. Go ahead and relish the Beatitudes; other aspects of the Sermon on the Mount deserve far more scrutiny.

A lot of verses can be discounted because they're so far removed from the realities of everyday life and the way ordinary people get along in the world. The heart of Matthew 6 is perhaps the worst section of the Sermon. There may be general agreement about its poetic merits—some of these words end up on greeting cards—but *no one* outside of monastic orders would dream of taking these words seriously. It is not advice for *everyman* to "not store up for yourselves treasures on earth, where moth and rust consume and where thieves break in and steal" (Matt. 6:19-21, RSV), or to "not worry about your life, what you will eat or what you will drink, or about your body, what you will wear. But strive first for the kingdom of God and his righteousness, and all these things will be given to you as well." (Matt. 6:31-33).

We know that this just does not happen. It's a formula for resigning from life and being a free-spirit moocher. And that last sentence shows its roots in cult fanaticism.

Every Christian with a pension plan who conscientiously builds up treasure on earth, who gets up and goes to work every day to keep a roof overhead and food on the table knows that these verses are shallow nonsense. No, we are not provided with food, just like God feeds birds. No, we don't get decent clothing because lilies are beautiful. I don't know *any* Christian who operates on this basis. These verses in the Sermon are famous, and I suppose, hold a certain idealistic appeal. They have served for centuries as pulpit drivel. But they are wrongheaded and Jesus was wrong to preach them.

Of course, there have been extremist Christians who have tried to put such abandonment of responsibility into practice. The result has been silly, slovenly behavior passed off as piety. In the fifth century, Saint Simeon Stylites the Elder decided to focus only on God by sitting on top of a pole in Aleppo, Syria for 37 years. I guess he sat there "striving first for the kingdom of God"—no ambition or drive—and not worrying about clothing and food. Maybe Jesus would have approved, but most

Christians would consider this eccentric selfishness. Even the most fervent evangelicals who love their Jesus would not dream of sending their kids off to college recommending slothful holiness.

"Oh, well, Jesus was so holy, it made sense to him," might be one excuse, but these verses detract from his reputation as a great moral teacher. Yes, over-indulgence in material things can be discouraged, but Jesus speaks here as an extremist with lightweight intellectual credentials.

We can be sure that none of the peasants following him around took him all that seriously. They couldn't have survived in that harsh environment if they had followed his advice.

Now, More Bad News

Jesus' advice that folks should "strive first for the kingdom of God" instead of worrying about food and clothing is a mark of religious zealotry, and he shows his hand as a Javert near the beginning of the Sermon on the Mount. In Victor Hugo's *Les Miserables*, Inspector Javert is a tiresome, sinister, detestable character because of his obsession about the law; even the smallest infraction must be punished with unwavering zeal. Was Jesus the role model? His words here are strident:

> Do not think that I have come to abolish the law or the prophets; I have come not to abolish but to fulfill. For truly I tell you, until heaven and earth pass away, not one letter, not one stroke of a letter, will pass from the law until all is accomplished. Therefore, whoever breaks one of the least of these commandments, and teaches others to do the same, will be called least in the kingdom of heaven; but whoever does them and teaches them will be called great in the kingdom of heaven. For I tell you, unless your righteousness exceeds that of the scribes and Pharisees, you will never enter the kingdom of heaven. (Matt. 5:17-20, ESV).

Are these the real words of Jesus? That's our premise in this chapter—and I'll follow where that leads in a moment—but it's more likely that this text, found only here in Matthew, was meant to counter the faction in the early church that wanted to downplay the Old Testament law.

Yes, the apostle Paul insisted, Jesus was the fulfillment of the law. But as far as he was concerned, Jesus had erased the law's importance as well; it had become irrelevant. Matthew 5:17-20 is a smack at the liberalism reflected in Acts 10:9-16, Peter's vision about food, which is a flat repudiation of Old Testament dietary laws. These laws were so important in the time of Jesus that Jews were forbidden to share the same table with Gentiles. So there is a way to get Jesus off the hook here and make him less the role model for Javert: Just admit that he didn't say these words endorsing the law so fervently. They are Matthew's propaganda.

If these are the real words of Jesus, it's more difficult to make the case that he was a good guy. Small minds latch on to unchanging laws from the past—God said it once upon a time, so it's true forever—without considering how times and circumstances change. Morally sensitive people can see that a few of the Ten Commandments have not stood the test of time, so we cannot hold any ethical teacher in high esteem who isn't willing to bend and adjust.

Well, in a sense—not to his credit, unfortunately—Jesus *was* willing to modify: He made the law even more severe and unreasonable. How in the world can these sayings in the Sermon on the Mount (from Matt. 5:21-22, 27-30, NASB) be considered an improvement?

> You have heard that the ancients were told, "You shall not commit murder" and "Whoever commits murder shall be liable to the court." But I say to you that everyone who is angry with his brother shall be guilty before the court; and whoever says to his brother, "You good-for-nothing," shall be guilty before the supreme court; and whoever says, "You fool," shall be guilty enough to go into the fiery hell.

> You have heard that it was said, "You shall not commit adultery"; but I say to you that everyone who looks at a woman with lust for her has already committed adultery with her in his heart. If your right eye makes you stumble, tear it out and throw it from you; for it is better for you to lose one of the parts of your body, than for your whole body to be thrown into hell. If your right hand makes you stumble, cut it off and throw it from you; for it is better for you to lose one of the parts of your body, than for your whole body to go into hell.

If most Christians, through over-familiarity, didn't automatically recognize these as Jesus sayings, they might regard them as the ranting of a crazy street preacher. Anger and lust, or just saying "you fool," are enough to get you packed off to hell?

Christian apologists have argued that Jesus was speaking metaphorically when he suggested plucking out eyes and cutting off right hands if they cause you to sin, although the anti-masturbation lobby has no doubt gleefully embraced these verses. I know of only one distinguished Christian who took Jesus literally. The early theologian Origen (who died in the 3rd century) supposedly, following Jesus literally, cut off his testicles to avoid banishment to hell. The story cannot be verified, but we can verify that Jesus' amputation metaphor is despicable, and the theology is just as bad.

Here is something decent people know: Everyone who has evil thoughts gets points for not acting on those thoughts. It's called maturity, self-restraint, successful socialization, common sense, being a good person—whatever. But, no, Jesus teaches, no points are earned! Evil thoughts are just as bad as evil actions.

How much torment these verses have provoked! Thoughts flow impulsively like water, and once an evil thought has popped into your head—a burst of lust, for example—you're toast. This is disgraceful teaching and bad theology.[11]

Subverting Marriage Realities

Jesus also gets major demerits for hardening the Old Testament teaching about divorce, thereby bringing incalculable anguish during the ensuing centuries. Many billions of people have gone into marriages for a wide variety of reasons, e.g., convenience, lust, desperation, family obligations and alliances, pregnancy—sometimes even love. It dawns on a lot of people, months or years into a marriage: "Well, this was a mistake."

Jesus is guilty of a grievous logical fallacy in his pronouncement on divorce. Why do men and women get married? Jesus sees the "natural order" as God's idea, and said this to the Pharisees:

> Have you not read that the one who made them at the beginning "made them male and female," and said, "For this reason a man shall leave his father and mother and be joined to his wife, and the two shall become one flesh"? So they are no longer two, but one flesh. Therefore what God has joined together, let no one separate. (Matt. 19:4-6)

Nothing wrong with the idea that God arranged for men and women to hook up, but it doesn't follow at all that God has actually *arranged* all marriages, picking each woman for each man, ever since humans began cohabitating.

It is shortsighted, destructive and dangerous to argue that God's law and intent are violated when couples don't get along after all. Yet Jesus does just that in Mark 10. He condemns divorce, culminating in the famous verse 9: "Therefore what God has joined together, let no one separate." Did Jesus *really* think that it's God who makes all the matches, so many of which are disastrous?

Which brings us back to Jesus' remark on the topic in the Sermon on the Mount:

> It was also said, "Whoever divorces his wife, let him give her a certificate of divorce." But I say to you that anyone who divorces his wife, except on the ground of unchastity, causes her to commit adultery; and whoever marries a divorced woman commits adultery. (Matt. 5:31-32)

In Mark and Luke we do not find the words "except on the ground of unchastity." Somehow, in a small mercy, Matthew saw fit to add that modification.

Let it be noted, by the way, Christians have shown far more common sense than Jesus on this matter: They *do* get divorced, as much as their non-Christian neighbors. They've figured out that the layer of theology imposed on marriage ("what God has joined together"), is irrelevant and impossible to sustain in reality. *They know that Jesus was wrong.* This is one of his failures as a moral teacher.

The Catholic church has maintained a level of rigidity on divorce that defies all logic and compassion, based on Jesus' bad counsel on the matter. Yet the church has, for money, figured out ways to help couples escape matrimonial bonds. Don't we all have our favorite stories of shrewd Catholic maneuvering? Mine is about the man who, for enough cash, after more than 20 years of marriage and three children, was able to buy an annulment. The church, it would seem, is not opposed to laying up treasure on earth.

Speaking of Ignored Jesus Rules . . .

The Sermon on the Mount includes a few other mandates that most Christians don't take seriously, that they would, in fact, shout down emphatically. I have mentioned these earlier, but they fall so far off the chart of high ethical standards that they deserve a word here as well. These are the commands to turn the other cheek and give whatever is asked (Matt. 5:38-42), and not ask to get back what's been taken from you (Luke 6:30).

"Turn the other cheek," and "go the second mile" have become clichés, or at least comfortable aphorisms, and perhaps many people don't connect the dots; they don't even know that Jesus is the source. We can cheer that Jesus, who elsewhere has no trouble with vindictiveness, here repudiates retaliation (an eye for an eye, which is wrong on so many levels), but there are commands in these verses that are problematic, and it's hard to see how they rank as helpful moral concepts.

"Do not resist an evildoer" is simply inexplicable as a viable ethical principle. How could any great moral teacher advise that? If we are raised as moral beings with a sense of right and wrong, we know that there are many evils to be challenged and vanquished; that's the moral thing to do. Some Christians may object that "turn the other cheek" was the basis for the non-violent protests of Gandhi and Martin Luther King—thus being "Christlike." But not so fast: Gandhi and King used "turn the other cheek" precisely *to resist evildoers.* The command not to resist is simplistic—was Jesus misquoted?—but as this saying stands, it is morally inept.

Come on, Christians, just admit that even the most decent people balk at these suggestions. Christians throughout the ages have found many ways to be generous, and even the most generous would hesitate to do *any* of these five things.

Was Jesus indulging in hyperbole? Maybe, but it's also possible that his head was in the clouds. He was giving bad, impractical advice. We don't know of any context that might make it seem like anything but nonsense. Lacking that, these extreme generosity tips don't give us much assurance that he was a bright guy.

Morality can be lofty, but it also has to be down to earth. Folks have to be able to say, "Yes, that sounds like a good idea. It may be tough, but I can see myself doing it." Refusing to say *No* to any and all borrowers doesn't make you a generous moral person; it makes you as easy mark.

In this part of the Sermon, Jesus also commands people to love their enemies. He waxes poetic about his listeners being children of the Father in heaven, with a reward for doing more than just greeting their brothers:

> You have heard that it was said, "You shall love your neighbor and hate your enemy." But I say to you, Love your enemies and pray for those who persecute you, so that you may be children of your Father in heaven; for he makes his sun rise on the evil and on the good, and sends rain on the righteous and on the unrighteous. For if you love those who love you, what reward do you have? Do not even the tax collectors do the same? And if you greet only your brothers, what more are you doing than others? Do not even the Gentiles do the same? (Matt. 5:43-47).

I suspect that most Christians throughout the centuries have given this a shrug, "Well, that's Jesus for you," knowing that love for enemies in virtually impossible to achieve and sustain. It's naïve idealism that reflects little understanding of human hurts and anger. Praying for those who persecute you is more realistic, and Jesus seems to say that this kind of generosity of spirit qualifies one as a "child of the Father in heaven," because God himself is generous to evil and unrighteous people. He gives them sunshine and rain too, just as he does for good and righteous people.

But I'm not sure this line of argument is all that compelling as a reason to love one's enemies, and Jesus puts in a zinger at the end: He makes a jab at the Gentiles, saying they love only their own. This makes us wonder: Just who was his audience for the Sermon on the Mount?

There is some uncertainty about that. At the beginning of Matthew 5, we get the impression Jesus delivered it privately to his disciples, away from the public on some hilltop. Yet at the ending, we read that "the crowds were amazed at his teaching." From this slap at the Gentiles, should we infer that his message was only for Jews? After all, in Matthew 10, Jesus ordered his disciples not to go among the Gentiles.

Matthew 5, with its collection of rules and commandments that Christians have been quite content to blatantly ignore, ends with the ultimate absurdity: "Be perfect, therefore, as your heavenly Father is perfect" (v. 48). Those who are deeply into the Christian cult, feeling obligated to *ooh* and *aah* about everything Jesus said, assume that this commandment is the ultimate moral counsel. It is undoubtedly Matthew's reinforcement of Jesus' statement a bit earlier in the chapter, "For I tell you, unless your righteousness exceeds that of the scribes and Pharisees, you will never enter the kingdom of heaven" (v. 30).

Well, ordinary people (including a lot of ordinary Christians, I'm pretty sure) know that this is flippant advice. If you're not locked into believing that Jesus really said it, then it's better for Jesus' reputation to assume that Matthew, writing for his Jewish audience, was trying to counter the teachings of Paul and put these words onto the lips of Jesus. Paul's despair over the impossibility of perfection–exceeding the righteousness of the scribes and Pharisees was out of the question–would make it hard for him to grasp Jesus as a morality guru. For Paul, Jesus was not a lawgiver providing the rules for getting right with God, but a mystical, magical savior: By dying and rising he had accomplished everything that Matthew assumed came from following the law.

Where Was Jesus' Head?

One Way to Make Sense of It

"You have to take that with a grain of salt," is a softer, gentler approach that Christians may use, trying to excuse Jesus for his utterly impractical advice. This isn't as harsh (or heretical) as admitting that Jesus was wrong. But if Christians scrutinize all of those red-letter words of Jesus carefully, and don't try to sugarcoat his primary obsession–get ready ASAP for the coming Kingdom–some of his advice makes more sense, given his expectations. Christian cherry pickers have managed, over the centuries, to tone down their *apocalyptic prophet*. But his nasty message about the imminent end of the age remains in all those verses that the cherry pickers skip over.

One sweet and sentimental verse in the Sermon on the Mount that has always had a hollow ring to it may shed light on Jesus' seeming passivity. Can you name a time in human history when the following verse has been true? "Blessed are the meek, for they will inherit the earth" (Matt. 5:5). I sure can't, unless you count an early grave in the earth. Alan Jay Lerner penned a lyric that expresses the common cynicism about this claim: "It's not the earth the meek inherit, it's the dirt."[12] Why would Jesus say this? He lived at a time when the Jews were acutely aware that the powerful Romans ruled with an iron hand. How would the meek come out on top?

Maybe Jesus' apocalyptic delusion was that God would finally put his foot down and topple the arrogant. Over and over we hear from Jesus that the end of the age, the kingdom of God, is near. One of many examples: "For the Son of Man is to come with his angels in the glory of his Father, and then he will repay everyone for what has been done. Truly I tell you, there are some standing here who will not taste death before they see the Son of Man coming in his kingdom" (Matt. 16:27-28).

Just as had been the case with his pal John the Baptist, and would be the case with the apostle Paul, Jesus had no doubt that the end was near. It was urgent that people be ready, and the transition–*finally*, the arrival of the Kingdom of God on earth–meant that the old order would be overthrown. Jesus would reign with the angels. In one text that gives us insight into Paul's delusional thought, the latter even promised people that they would sit in judgment on angels (1 Cor. 6:3).

The New World Order

With this glorious state of affairs just around the corner, old practices could be set aside. When Peter complained about leaving everything and following him, Jesus promised big things ahead for his followers: They "will also sit on twelve thrones, judging the twelve tribes of Israel. And everyone who has left houses or brothers or sisters or father or mother or children or fields, for my name's sake, will receive a hundredfold, and will inherit eternal life" (Matt. 19:28-29).

Hence it's no surprise that the meek will inherit the earth: At the renewal of all things, Jesus added, "many who are first will be last, and the last will be first" (v. 30). The lowly masses, those generally despised and held in contempt, will be the winners."Jesus said to them, "Truly I tell you, the tax collectors and the prostitutes are going into the kingdom of God ahead of you" (Matt. 21:31).

If you're trying to hold on to Jesus as a real person in first century Palestine, and to the gospels as authentic documents, it's reasonable to argue that Jesus was *not* laying down ethical principles for people to follow for centuries to come. He assumed that history was about to end. Christianity? *He had no idea there would be any such thing*, that history would keep rolling along and a world religion was just getting started in his name.

He was giving ethical principles *for the interim* before the end time, to help people qualify for the Kingdom that was just around the corner. He would soon be on his throne, with the apostles ruling along with him. With this in mind, some of the Jesus sayings fall into place:

- God's reign was coming soon, with Jesus in charge. So what would be the point of laying up treasures?

- With the Kingdom just over the horizon, Jesus appears to have been in a recruiting mode, trying to find the select few who would mend their ways. Hence he dispatched the disciples on the mission to spread the word. His advice to them about food and clothing was the same as that in the Sermon in the Mount: Don't take money, a bag, or a spare tunic.

- God was soon to settle accounts, and he would take care of getting even. So don't bother to resist evildoers; go ahead and let people strike you on both cheeks.

- God's great "getting even" would be traumatic, which makes some sense of Jesus' rant (Matt. 10:34-39) about bringing not peace but a sword, setting family members against each other, and forsaking one's own life.

The problem, of course, is that all that is nonsense, and creepy in the extreme. The "coming of the Kingdom" hasn't happened, and only those who are remarkably detached from reality hold out hope for it now. Even those Christians who think Jesus will return before 2050 probably don't grasp the full bloody scope of it all–as Jesus himself depicts it. It was at the core of Jesus' message. Even if he was a fictional character, it's at the core of his fictional message. Oops.

Running Out of Steam

Matthew 7 is the most disappointing of the Sermon's three chapters. It does begin with the five verses in which Jesus prohibits judging, which is a standout teaching. (But was Jesus himself exempt from this rule? In Matthew 23, he was unsparing in his scathing judgment of religious leaders.) And in verse 12 we find one version of the Golden Rule, "In everything do to others as you would have them do to you." But Matthew 7 is mostly a clutter of aphorisms that fall far short of being great moral teaching, though they do seem to fit Jesus' severe vision of the coming kingdom:

- Do not give what is holy to dogs, and do not throw pearls before swine.

- Ask, and it will be given you. Even though you are evil, you know how to give good gifts to your children. How much more will your Father who is in heaven give good gifts to those who ask him!

- Enter God's kingdom through the narrow gate. The gate is large and the road is wide that lead to death and hell. Many people go that way. But the gate is small and the road is narrow that lead to life. Only a few people find it.

- Watch out for false prophets. They come to you pretending to be sheep. But on the inside they are hungry wolves. You can tell what they really are by what they do.

- Not everyone who says to Jesus, "Lord, Lord," will enter the kingdom of heaven. Entry is only for those who do what his Father in heaven wants.

Jesus brings the sermon to a close with an appeal, a warning, that is fairly typical of religious fanatics:

> So then, everyone who hears my words and puts them into practice is like a wise man. He builds his house on the rock. The rain comes down. The water rises. The winds blow and beat against that house. But it does not fall. It is built on the rock. But everyone who hears my words and does not put them into practice is like a foolish man. (Matt. 7:24-27)

I suppose someone trying to teach great ethical principles might want to stack the deck in his favor. But too much of those words in the Sermon are just inferior dreck geared toward Jesus' shortsighted and wrong-headed theology about the end times. The story of the House Built on the Rock has always been a favorite with the faithful. It makes good sense. But the teachings in the Sermon on the Mount fail, for the most part, to qualify as anything like solid rock.

I've Got a Secret!

Surely the parables of Jesus run a close second, behind the Sermon on the Mount, as crowd pleasers. We get to hear about the Good Samaritan, the Prodigal Son, and the Good Shepherd. Jesus is presented over and over in the gospels as preaching to the crowds, having compassion on them, reaching out to them with the good news of the Kingdom of God. He used parables to get his message across.

Except that he didn't.

The parables, as Jesus explained privately to his disciples, were a technique to *prevent* people from understanding. So Jesus was fooling people? How can that be? Christians might look at you as if you're crazy if you point this out to them. It's true, though, from Jesus' own words in Matthew, Mark, and Luke. (We can leave John out of this discussion because there are no parables in that gospel.)

Mark 4:10-12 says, "When he was alone, those who were around him along with the twelve asked him about the parables." His response: "To you has been given the secret of the kingdom of God, but for those outside, everything comes in parables; in order that 'they may indeed look, but not perceive, and may indeed listen, but not understand; so that they may not turn again and be forgiven.'"

The version in Matthew 13:10-17 has the disciples coming and asking him, "Why do you speak to them in parables?" His answer, a long-winded one this time:

> To you it has been given to know the secrets of the kingdom of heaven, but to them it has not been given. For to those who have, more will be given, and they will have an abundance; but from those who have nothing, even what they have will be taken away. The reason I speak to them in parables is that "seeing they do not perceive, and hearing they do not listen, nor do they understand." With them indeed is fulfilled the prophecy of Isaiah that says: "You will indeed listen, but never understand, and you will indeed look, but never perceive. For this people's heart has grown dull, and their ears are hard of hearing, and they have shut their eyes; so that they might

not look with their eyes, and listen with their ears, and understand with their heart and turn—and I would heal them."

When Matthew copied from Mark, he added a touch more severity, and brought in the Old Testament to back it up. Jesus wasn't about to let anyone get off easy.

In Luke 8:9-10, his disciples ask him what the parable meant. He says, "To you it has been given to know the secrets of the kingdom of God; but to others I speak in parables, so that 'looking they may not perceive, and listening they may not understand.'" Luke adds Matthew's tough line a bit later in the chapter: "Then pay attention to how you listen; for to those who have, more will be given; and from those who do not have, even what they seem to have will be taken away" (v. 18).

Since Matthew, Mark, and Luke report these words of Jesus, it can't be a matter of just one gospel writer getting things wrong. Of course, Matthew and Luke copied from Mark and made their own adjustments, but they must have felt that Mark had it right. These three gospel writers had no way of knowing that their documents would one day be bound together, and that makes it very easy for us to detect their doctoring of the texts. They changed things as they saw fit. There is so much uneven, contradictory stuff in the gospels, especially when John is added to the mix, that the careful reader has to wonder, "Why couldn't these guys get their story straight?"

Well, they wrote independently, without contemporary documentation, and gave their imaginations free rein. They really could not have imagined one thing, however: Someday lots of people would do fact-checking on what they said. Nor did any of the gospel writers seem to know that there *were* contemporary historians who wrote extensively about first-century Palestine, yet failed to mention Jesus *at all.*

Good Christian folks who bristle at the idea of the gospels being wrong about anything, who feel compelled to stick with the red-letter text as a transcript of what was said by the Son of God, have a sinister Jesus on their hands in these verses. He did *not* want people to repent and be saved from "the wrath to come." It should be equally troubling to them that the gospel writers were okay with this cult-leader portrayal of a Jesus who told his secrets only to insiders.

The Evil Twin

Jesus in John's Gospel

By now, you know how I feel about John's gospel. Tough Problem VI was partly about why it cannot be trusted. But, oh the irony: It is the gospel that people seem to cherish the most. For feel-good religion, how can you beat, "Do not let your hearts be troubled. Believe in God, believe also in me"? (John 14:1) There are so many grand and lofty verses, "God so loved the world, that he gave his only son, yada, yada, yada," and John overflows with promises of eternal life. That's the bottom line for so many folks, getting to escape death and be coddled forever in the everlasting arms. John's gospel offers the best free ticket ever.

But maybe I'm being too hasty in my contempt for the Fourth Gospel. What more could I ask for in falsifying Christianity? John is a goldmine to make the case that Jesus is overrated; in almost every chapter we come across deal-breaking texts. So if

Christians want to keep a firm grip on John's gospel, that's all the more reason it deserves our special attention here.

I would remind Christians, however, that they have the option of going along with a broad consensus of New Testament scholars—outside evangelical academia, that is—who concede that the Jesus of this gospel is largely the product of overheated theological imagination. It's not really about Jesus of Nazareth, since it is the latest of the four gospels. There's only a slim chance it preserves any genuine historical remembrances."History" was of very little concern to its author, whose profession was theologian and propagandist. The colossal Jesus monologues are his invention, but Christians have taken for granted that they can and should be taken at face value. They fail to grasp that it's really not such a good idea to do so.

We've already seen how egregiously egotistical the Jesus of this hallowed hagiography is. It turns out, for readers who manage to wade through those colossal monologues, that he is also a crashing bore.[13] But Christians remain under the spell. How else can we explain those placards at sports events: "John 3:16"? So let's stick with Jesus *verbatim* in John's gospel.

Are you sure you don't want to turn back?

Negligent Homicide

My biggest problem with Jesus in John's gospel, one I sensed in my distant youth as a critical Bible student, is that he simply isn't *real*. Jesus here is an artificial, contrived figure—a tediously written, poorly developed character in an inferior novel. But if we grant that John got it right, that this is what Jesus was really like, then the case can be made that our exaggerated hero was sometimes a real jerk.

This becomes obvious when we read John 11 without rose-colored glasses. We've glanced briefly at this story (Tough Problem VII), but it's worth another look here. How can even the most pious Jesus fans not be taken aback by the story of Lazarus in this chapter? This is one of the most famous episodes in the gospels, with one of the most stupendous miracles. Yet Matthew, Mark and Luke, writing much earlier, somehow never got wind of it. The shortest verse in the Bible (at least in most English versions) is here, verse 35: "Jesus wept," and of course, this gets a lot of mileage as proof of Jesus' compassion.

But that's not quite the whole story: Jesus knew that Lazarus was sick—he received a message from Lazarus' sister—but delayed going to his bedside. He let him die so that he could pull a stupendous stunt to boost his own reputation and get people to believe! John makes this explicit in verses 14-15: "Then Jesus told them plainly, 'Lazarus is dead. For your sake I am glad I was not there, so that you may believe. But let us go to him.'" He's *glad* he wasn't there? Please, if you're going to take this story at face value, then admit that this is obnoxious behavior.

And, in fact, Martha, Lazarus' sister, gets in a zinger, upbraiding Jesus for his neglect. If you'd been here, Lord, he'd be alive. Sure, yes, I believe you're "the Messiah, the Son of God, the one coming into the world" (11:20-27).

When Mary arrived on the scene, she also complained, (v. 32): "Lord, if you had been here, my brother would not have died." Maybe even John himself sensed that

Jesus had been callous in not showing up sooner, and thus makes a point of telling his readers how upset Jesus was that Martha and Mary were distraught: "When Jesus therefore saw her weeping, and the Jews also weeping which came with her, he groaned in the spirit, and was troubled. And said, 'Where have ye laid him?' They said unto him, 'Lord, come and see.' Jesus wept" (11:33-35, KJV).

This was a voice-activated resurrection (11:43-45): Jesus "cried with a loud voice, "Lazarus, come out!" The dead man came out, his hands and feet bound with strips of cloth, and his face wrapped in a cloth. Jesus said to them, 'Unbind him, and let him go.'" We are not told if Lazarus was as annoyed as Martha and Mary had been that Jesus had let him die.

When this story is taken at face value, Jesus is a seriously compromised hero. The story is much less of a burden if we acknowledge that it is theology-soaked fiction: The only reason that John includes the story is to give Jesus a dramatic occasion for pronouncing, "I am the resurrection and the life. Those who believe in me, even though they die, will live, and everyone who lives and believes in me will never die."

Don't forget that this is the gimmick of the Fourth Gospel: the promise, made repeatedly, that the faithful will get out of dying if they *just believe*.

Always the Center of Attention

From time immemorial, countless religious charlatans–from major messianic pretenders to run-of-the mill cranks–have claimed to be sons of God, and they have sounded a lot like the leading man of the Fourth Gospel.

But people who are *truly* pious, humble and devoted to helping others, don't talk like this. If indeed this is the way Jesus presented himself, he falls off the charts as someone worthy of worship. John had adopted a hugely exaggerated theology about Jesus, and made his Jesus speak accordingly, against all odds that the Galilean peasant would even have *known how* to talk like this.

Here is the huge ego on display. Take it at face value if you will–argue that this is Jesus *verbatim*–and he is, well, just *unreal*. He is himself a forgery.

- "I have said this to you, so that in me you may have peace. In the world you face persecution. But take courage; I have conquered the world!" (16:33).

- "If you believed Moses, you would believe me, for he wrote about me" (5:46).

- "Jesus said to him, 'I am the way, and the truth, and the life. No one comes to the Father except through me'" (14:6).

- "No one has ascended into heaven except the one who descended from heaven, the Son of Man. And just as Moses lifted up the serpent in the wilderness, so must the Son of Man be lifted up, that whoever believes in him may have eternal life" (3:13-15).

- "Jesus said to her, 'Everyone who drinks of this water will be thirsty again, but those who drink of the water that I will give them will never be thirsty. The water that I will give will become in them a spring of water gushing up to eternal life'" (4:13-14).

- "The Father judges no one but has given all judgment to the Son, so that all may honor the Son just as they honor the Father. Anyone who does not honor the Son does not honor the Father who sent him. Very truly, I tell you, anyone who hears my word and believes him who sent me has eternal life, and does not come under judgment, but has passed from death to life" (5:22-24).

- "The works that the Father has given me to complete, the very works that I am doing, testify on my behalf that the Father has sent me" (5:36).

- "For I have come down from heaven, not to do my own will but the will of him who sent me. And this is the will of him who sent me, that I should lose nothing of all that he has given me, but raise it up on the last day. For this is the will of my Father, that everyone who looks on the Son and believes in him should have eternal life, and I will raise him up on the last day" (6:38-40).

- "And Jesus cried out and said, 'Whoever believes in me, believes not in me but in him who sent me. And whoever sees me sees him who sent me. I have come into the world as light, so that whoever believes in me may not remain in darkness'" (12:44-46, ESV).

- "My sheep hear my voice. I know them, and they follow me. I give them eternal life, and they will never perish. No one will snatch them out of my hand. What my Father has given me is greater than all else, and no one can snatch it out of the Father's hand. The Father and I are one" (10:27-30).

Ten of these over-the-top, full-of-himself quotes are enough to make the point. There are many more scattered throughout John's gospel.

As I mentioned earlier, C.S. Lewis, that most beloved of Christian apologists, thought he had nailed the truth of Christianity by pointing out that this level of bragging could have been made only by a lunatic *or* by someone who truly was the son of God. Since Lewis's brain was welded shut by Christian dogma, he assumed that *lunatic* was simply out of the question.

Sadly, Lewis had little use for critical Biblical study, though it was thriving during his lifetime: It's what allows us to see that John's Jesus is contrived. Hence, for Lewis, there was nothing offensive about the egregiously egotistical Jesus. Of course a *bona fide* son of God was entitled to talk like that!

But those who are not spellbound by the Jesus cult, those who are startled by John's exaggerated Jesus after reading Matthew, Mark, and Luke, can argue that being the son of God is not a good enough excuse for the outrageous rhetoric. Jesus' claims *are simply not true*, and when push comes to shove, most reasonable Christians I know would hesitate to argue otherwise.

By any reasonable standard, the great swaths of Jesus preaching in John are also just bad theology. Nobody has the inside track to eternal life or any right to package, promote, and sell it. The offer of "everlasting life" in the much-loved John 3:16 is just cheap gimmickry.

Good grief, selling the afterlife has been big business in religion for millennia. As has been the case with so many theologians and preachers, John thought he'd hit on the winning formula, and he pressed the theme relentlessly in his gospel. He keeps hammering eternal life through Jesus. But bad theology pursued with such a heavy hand is especially obnoxious. By world standards–that is, from the sweeping perspective of comparative religion–John was an unremarkable theologian who promoted an unremarkable leading man.

The Sinister Edge

"Amazing Grace, how sweet the sound, that saved a wretch like me; I once was lost but now am found, was blind, but now I see." Decent well-adjusted people should disrespect religions that invite people to disrespect themselves. Self-loathing, self-describing oneself as a wretch, is unhealthy and destructive. Nasty religion trades on this, and thus decent people should bristle at the words of Jesus in John 12:25: "Those who love their life lose it, and those who hate their life in this world will keep it for eternal life." There's that word again, *hate*, in fact, the same Greek word that Jesus used when he counseled hatred toward family members.

Jesus does enough of this dysfunctional talk to suspect that, for all his preaching about love, he didn't live up to the standards of decency that Christians commonly assume. In John 9, we find the extended story of Jesus the magician healing a blind man using mud and spit–again there is too much of the Harry Potter touch here. At the end (v. 39), Jesus says: "For judgment I came into this world, that those who do not see may see, and those who see may become blind."

Why don't more Christians see how weird this is? And don't forget the flip side of John 3:16: Eternal life is reserved for those who believe in Jesus, but those who don't are out of luck; the eternal life club is an exclusive one. Christians usually look so puzzled when we point out that this is bad theology: John and his Jesus would assign most humans to oblivion, and it serves them right for being sinners.

Evangelical scholar Benjamin Witherington makes a most remarkable confession about the writer who precedes John by several decades. He speaks with far more candor than most of his niche-market believers would welcome:

> Mark, our earliest gospel, is both stark and dark. It presents a mysterious Jesus operating in an apocalyptic scenario and mode. For example, Jesus is depicted as doing regular battle with the powers of darkness. Jesus the exorcist is in fact on display from the very first miracle story in Mark, in the first chapter.[14]

Yes, *exorcist*. More Harry Potter. There is very little moral teaching in Mark as Jesus arm-wrestles with demons and predicts the horrendous end of the world as the

Kingdom of God dawns. The gospels that follow do add moral teaching (although John is skimpy on that score) and some humanizing touches–different tones and accents are added–but God's battle with the powers of darkness through Jesus remains a central theme.

Why and how do the powers of darkness even exist if God is all-powerful? That conundrum hobbles Western monotheism and diminishes the gospels. And it means that these charter documents of the Christian faith have bequeathed generous helpings of bad theology to Western thought.

The Crackpot Factor

If we can just keep the first-century context of Christianity in mind, the world in which the faith sprang to life, it would us help keep matters in perspective, and put the brakes on Jesus adoration. Richard Carrier offers this insight into what was happening then in Palestine, namely, "a rash of messianism":

> There was an evident clamoring of sects and individuals to announce that they had found the messiah. It is therefore no oddity or accident that this is exactly when Christianity arose. It was yet another messiah cult in the midst of a fad for just such cults. That it among them would alone survive and spread can therefore be the product of natural selection: so many variations of the same theme were being tried, odds are that one of them would by chance be successful, hitting all the right notes and dodging all the right bullets. The lucky winner in the contest just happened to be Christianity.[15]

One of the common themes was deliverance from on high: God would intervene to put a stop to the humiliation of the Chosen People, and–no surprise–the particular messiah-figure doing the talking would play a starring role. Of course, they were all wrong. The humiliation of the Chosen People was never reversed, and in fact reached its culmination with the obliteration of the Jerusalem Temple in 70 CE.

But before history delivered this bitter dose of reality, the messiah preachers kept right on making their claims to anyone who would listen. I'll be back, Jesus promised the high priest in Mark 14:62, and with power and clouds of heaven. It was essentially a repeat of his warning in the dreadful apocalypse described in Mark 13. But this messiah's promise never came to pass. The high priest never did get a glimpse of Jesus seated at the right hand of power and coming on the clouds.

It's hardly a surprise that the disciples bought into the delusions of their leader. A couple of them put in a request: Let us sit at your side when you come back in your glory, they asked. He replied that they didn't know what they were asking for (Mark 10:35-40). It seems that Jesus already knew the seating arrangement in the coming kingdom, and although these two disciples didn't get exactly what they wanted, his band of followers would be pretty well set after all:

> Jesus said to them, "Truly I tell you, at the renewal of all things, when the
> Son of Man is seated on the throne of his glory, you who have followed me

will also sit on twelve thrones, judging the twelve tribes of Israel." (Matt.
19:28)

Messiahs commonly have only a thin grasp of what the real world has in store. At the
time of Jesus' arrest in Gethsemane, he rebuked a colleague who had pulled a sword
to defend him: "Do you think I cannot call on my Father, and he will at once put at
my disposal more than twelve legions of angels?" (Matt. 26:53, NIV)

I'm going to make the wild guess that a lot of people who "love their Jesus" have
been won over by *other* texts that allow a warm and fuzzy feeling. He had compassion
for the harassed and helpless sheep (Mathew 9:36), said that the one without sin
should cast the first stone (John 8:7), and invited the little children to come to him
(Matt. 19:14). Viewed in that light, the "kingdom of heaven" can have an innocuous
flavor rather than something tainted by cult strangeness.

But *cult strangeness* is precisely what we're neck deep into with the Jesus sayings
about the pecking order and seating arrangements in heaven, as well as the angel
militia, that he seemed so confident about.

No fair crying "metaphor" here, by the way. That's a modern ruse to blunt the
impact of these crackpot musings. We know the thought-world from which Jesus
came, the rampant messianic fever at the time, and there is no reason whatever to
suppose that Jesus wasn't describing reality as *he perceived it*, that he meant exactly
what he said. Once again, I can stress that it is irrelevant whether Jesus himself
harbored such delusions about himself. Whether Jesus was a myth or not doesn't
really matter.

The gospel writers saw fit to depict Jesus this way because they bought into
messiah theologies that dominated Jewish thought in the first century.

Figuring Out Jesus
A Final Word on How to Do That

"Well, I don't believe that!" a woman once protested when I pointed out Jesus
expected his followers to hate their families. She had the good sense to overrule
Jesus, because she loved her religion and *her* concept of Jesus. Whether she could
have articulated it or not, she had come firmly down *against* the idea that the Jesus
sayings in the gospels can be trusted. As we have seen throughout this chapter,
trusting Jesus sayings is disastrous for healthy Christianity and good theology. She
had developed *her own idea of Jesus*, and she wanted to stick with it.

And there's the rub: Where do you get your own idea of Jesus? The problem is
that there are hundreds of different ideas about who Jesus was, what he was like and
taught. As Bart Ehrman has said, people freely create "the ideal Jesus of their
imagination." If you admit–God forbid–that the gospels writers got some of the story
wrong, then you are forced to pick and choose, based on your own instincts and
sensibilities. Laypeople and preachers have been doing it for centuries.

Scholars have done a lot of posturing and pretend to be more sophisticated about
it, weighing (what they wrongly consider) evidence and probabilities. They think
they've worked out sound criteria for jettisoning some of Jesus' sayings while keeping

others. This all sounds very reasonable, but it's proved to be a bias-based exercise that doesn't work. Highly educated scholars, just like untutored laypeople, see in Jesus what they want to see.

That has left the field of Jesus scholarship in turmoil. After decades of producing erudite studies, there is no consensus whatever on which "Jesus sayings" can confidently be traced back to him. It's very hard to see how the sayings of Jesus could have been preserved. Nor has there been anything approaching consensus on who Jesus was, and what he was like. In a sense, Christianity has been left stranded, because its central figure is a mystery man, dwelling in obscurity because the gospels have smothered history with theology: When you read the gospels you're not seeing what you *think* you're seeing.

And, of course, denial about the problem, along with all the Christian overconfidence about Jesus, is tiresome and inappropriate. Christians ignore or are simply unaware of the gigantic scholarly effort that has gone into the "Jesus problem." This effort has gone under the umbrella term, "The Quest for the Historical Jesus," and the quest has stumbled through one failure after another for decades, as scholars grasp for a methodology that might prove workable.

One of the top Jesus scholars on the planet–indeed, I have no trouble saying ***the*** top scholar–is atheist Richard Carrier, who (as we saw with Tough Problem VII) is resetting the course of Jesus studies. Christians should be beating a path to Carrier's door to get their hands on his books, if they want to get to the bottom of the Jesus problem–if they want to understand why there is a Jesus problem. But they don't, and they won't. They prefer to stay cozied up to the Jesus that they have conjured in their imaginations.

Jesus Might Be Outclassed by the Competition

It's not hard to show that many Christians don't take some of their own precious theology very seriously. New Testament scholar Bart Ehrman drives home the point with a story about his experience in the classroom. He teaches at the University of North Carolina at Chapel Hill, and is fond of catching his students off guard by asking them a series of questions at the outset:

> How many of you in here would agree with the proposition that the Bible is the inspired Word of God (PHOOM! Almost everyone raises their hands)
>
> OK, great: Now, how many of you have read the Harry Potter series? (PHOOM! Again, almost everyone raises their hand).
>
> And now, how many of you have read the entire Bible? (This time: scattered hands, here and there, throughout the auditorium.)

He'd have a laugh, remind the students that they're the ones who think the Bible is God's inspired word, and then leave them with this zinger: "I can see why you might want to read a book by J.K. Rowling. But if God wrote a book–wouldn't you want to see what he had to say?"[16]

I won't belabor the point here that the Bible gathers dust in most Christian homes. It's Ehrman's mention of Harry Potter that can help us get to the heart of the matter.

I've made several references in this book to Biblical ideas and spells that seem to be very much on a par with the magic of Harry Potter and his pals. But hey, all those college students in conservative North Carolina vote with their reading habits: They prefer to read stories about Harry Potter, *instead of* stories about Jesus. We've heard forever the Christian hype that the gospels are "the greatest story ever told"–well, at least since the 1965 movie about Jesus with that title. Jesus is such a gigantic figure, so why wouldn't his story be the greatest ever?

Except that it isn't. His shortcomings that I have pointed out in this chapter, some of them really awful, make that clear. There's so much in the gospels that drag us down, and that the apologists work hard to excuse and overcome. I'd be willing to bet big money that the 1965 film doesn't include the Jesus quote about hating your family or any other of the embarrassing, chilling things that are credited to him. As we have seen, Yes, there are good items in the Jesus story, but they are seriously undermined by the bad items.

Does Jesus actually hold up well when he is compared with Harry Potter? At least one scholar has drawn attention to the disparity:

> Harry Potter is popular in a way that Jesus is not. Harry Potter's movies have made billions, while Mel Gibson's *The Passion of the Christ* (2004) was disturbing, bloody and ultimately unsatisfying, riddled with the unresolved complexities in a system where the all powerful and all-knowing God has to trick or deceive his creation, Satan. Harry's popularity is crucial–he is the gospel of our time; the best selling story. Yes, he is a repacking of the Jesus story, but one that eclipses that story completely. While we can sift through Harry and trace back to Jesus, why would we? Harry is a much more humane, in depth, vibrant character than the Jesus of the gospels, infinitely easier to identify with, champion, and even love.[17]

Indeed, if we were to compare Jesus with any number of superior heroes in world history, he would, on balance, be considered second or third rate. You don't have to agree with Jewish, Islamic or atheist critics of Christianity to figure that out. The four gospels are enough to make the case, as Robert Price points out, that "the precious gospel of gentle Jesus meek and mild fails to mask an unimaginably cruel message of doom and damnation for most of the human race."[18]

How Have They Been Able to Get Away with It?

The story of Jesus–who he really was as he wandered around Palestine for a few months–died with him. Even the apostle Paul, who spread his version of Christianity with such zeal, didn't know the story of Jesus.[19] Well, if he did, he omitted any mention of it in his letters that survive in the New Testament. Jesus gained traction as a divine being in large part because Paul was sure that Jesus' resurrection had enabled the magic formula for gaining eternal life. That was all he needed to know. And that was the great appeal of Christianity that won converts; other preachers besides Paul were spreading the same message. There were probably many co-inventors of the faith.

The gospels came along decades later, with what seems like great detail about Jesus' preaching and healing activity, but with distressing paucity of information about his life. The gospels actually had a pretty short shelf life. They may have been read aloud in churches in the years after they were first written, but then they disappeared into the rarefied world of Christian scholars and ecclesiastical authorities. Thus all of the negatives about Jesus, the flaws in his preaching and personality, which the gospels unwittingly preserve, remained out of sight, for centuries.

You can get away with a lot when that happens. After all, the message of the church was not about the Galilean peasant, his faults and foibles, as eventually recounted in the gospels. It was about salvation to be attained through belief in the resurrected Christ, for the most part, Paul's magical formula.

In our era of easy access to the gospels, you can find any verse you want in seconds via Google, and we all know what a great job the Gideons have done, it is hard to grasp that, *for more than 1,500 years*, no ordinary Christian could get his hands on a Bible, and wouldn't have been able to read it if she had. In fact, church authorities resisted, tooth and nail, the translation of the Bible from Greek and Latin into the languages of the people: The mysteries of faith were a closely guarded secret, and they didn't want the uneducated masses rummaging around in the sacred texts. The King James Version in English was one of the major breakthroughs on this front in 1611. By this time, obviously, Christianity was the dominant religion of the West, with sixteen hundred years of momentum. It was quite a head start for convincing the people in the pews that Jesus was the perfect son of God, the best human being that had ever lived. Who in his right mind was about to start nitpicking the gospels?

The phenomenon of critical Bible study is a relatively recent development in the Christian West. It's only in the last hundred and fifty years or so that serious scholars—even the devout ones—have approached the gospel portraits of Jesus with curiosity and skepticism instead of mindless adoration. When that is done, the negatives about Jesus stand out in bold relief, but then denial becomes the *modus operandi*; the cherry pickers step gingerly around the bad texts.

After all, they know that Jesus is their Lord and Savior, warts and all. But, of course, there can't really be any warts. Nothing can be allowed to impair Jesus' lord-and-savior status. Legions of Christian apologists earn their livings making up excuses, explaining why the bad Jesus texts don't mean what they seem to mean, nuancing the translations, falling back on metaphor and hyperbole to disguise the goofs and blemishes. These cover-ups should be eschewed by scholars and preachers who claim, by virtue of their religious scruples, to have cornered the market on integrity.

The negatives about Jesus are in full view and are unambiguous. But the denial goes on. How else to account for the countless Christians who insist that they "love their Jesus" and earnestly want to know what Jesus would do, *and* are confident that they know enough to tell others exactly what Jesus would do?

After all, isn't Jesus their pal? Rub shoulders with too many Americans, and this cloying piety bubbles to the surface. With his boots on the ground in pious Middle America, even author Stephen King, who specializes in scary stuff, was afraid to unleash Christian piety:

> I taught writing for a year at the University of Maine in Orono and had one class loaded with athletes and cheerleaders. They liked informal essays, greeting them like the old high school friends that they were. I spent one whole semester fighting the urge to ask them to write two pages of well-turned prose on the subject of "If Jesus were my teammate." What held me back was the sure and terrible knowledge that most of them would take to the task with enthusiasm. Some might actually weep while in the throes of composition.[20]

This level of emotional investment in Jesus remains in place because of massive Christian ignorance and myopia about the Bible. The preachers who have perfected cherry picking continue to advocate that Jesus is a hero *sans pareil*, and that's good enough for the faithful who flock to the megachurches every Sunday. It's very hard to break the spell of stained glass portraits and 2,000 years of Christ-the-Savior propaganda. The claim sticks that he was a good guy, indeed the best guy ever.

The Solution to Erasing This Colossal Misunderstanding?

The solution falls far short of being radical or scandalous. The Christians who pack the pews—athletes and cheerleaders included—must face the gospels squarely, committed to genuine due diligence, unarmed with arsenals of excuses. No skipping the loads of troublesome verses. Then they can evaluate Jesus as candidly as any other flawed moral teacher would be, and escort him off the pedestal.

How cool it would be if Christians could *discover* the gospels, with all the rough terrain in sharp focus, unblinded by pious convention. To do that, they must be willing to say **hush** for a while to the legions of apologists. The time for fairy tales is over.

Notes

1. Hector Avalos, *The Bad Jesus: The Ethics of New Testament Ethics* (Sheffield Phoenix Press), pp. 50-89.

2. A notable exception: Jehovah's Witnesses who shun their "disfellowshipped" family members. They of course will claim that it's done out of love, but the shunned apostates feel very differently.

3. As elsewhere in this book, dialogue in my quotations of Bible passages has been split into separate paragraphs to make it easier to follow.

4. A compelling book on this view of Jesus is Bart Ehrman's *Jesus: Apocalyptic Prophet of the New Millennium* (Oxford University Press, 2001).

5. Quoted in Jennifer Senior, "In Conversation: Antonin Scalia," *New York Magazine*, 6 October 2013.

6. Scott Korb, *Life in Year One: What the World Was Like in First-Century Palestine* (Riverhead Books, 2011), p. 118.

7. http://brane-space.blogspot.com/2014/01/is-jeffrey-tayler-correct-in-his.html

8. Robert M. Price, *Blaming Jesus for Jehovah*, p. 100.

9. This episode has stumped observers for ages, but Dennis MacDonald has provided a possible source. We don't know who Mark was, of course, but MacDonald suggests that he was influenced by Greek literature. In *The Homeric Epics and the Gospel of Mark* he calls the gospel a *novel* that reflects Homeric parallels. There is a story about Odysseus learning a lesson, not from a fig tree, but an oak tree. MacDonald places the texts side by side: "In both columns a tree provides information concerning the return of a hero" (p. 113).

10. He probably wasn't the speaker at all, of course. Matthew created a fictional setting for this famous event. Telling us that Jesus went onto a mountain to preach the Sermon is a nod toward Moses on Mt. Sinai: Jesus is the new lawgiver. (Curiously, when Luke presents a shortened version of the Sermon, he says it was delivered at a "level" place–go figure.)

    The Sermon on the Mount, says Carrier, "is a well-crafted work that cannot have come from some illiterate Galilean. In fact, we know it originated in Greek, not Hebrew or Aramaic, because it relies on the Septuagint text of the Bible for all its features and allusions. It has "a complex literary structure that can only have come from a writer, not an everyday speaker," relying "extensively on the Greek text of Deuteronomy and Leviticus especially, and in key places on other texts." Carrier cites the part about turning the other cheek etc. (Matt. 5:38-42) as an example, saying it was "redacted from the Greek text of Isa. 50:6-9," doesn't contain Jesus' words, and "reflects needs and interests that would have arisen after the apostles began preaching the faith and organizing communities and struggling to keep them in the fold." *On the Historicity of Jesus*, pp. 465-66.

11. Notice, by the way, the wording of Matthew 5:28: "But I say to you that everyone who looks at a woman with lust..." It was just assumed, by Jesus or the gospel writers, that his preaching was for men, straight ones at that.

12. For the 1960 musical *Camelot*.

13. I acknowledge that "crashing bore" was once said about another god as well, by comedienne Anna Russell in her description of the head god Wotan in Wagner's Ring Cycle of operas. She said of another character, Albrecht, that he was "excessively unattractive"–and that too is not far off the mark with respect to the Jesus of John's gospel.

14. Ben Witherington III, *What Have They Done with Jesus? Beyond Strange Theories and Bad History–Why We Can Trust the Bible*, p. 119.

15. Richard Carrier, *On the Historicity of Jesus*, p. 67.

16. From Bart Ehrman's blog, 24 October 2014.

17. Derek Murphy, *Jesus Potter Harry Christ: The Fascinating Parallels Between Two of the World's Most Popular Literary Characters*, pp. 417-18.

18. Price, *Blaming Jesus for Jehovah*, p. 120.

19. Only John's gospel permits a calculation of three years for Jesus' ministry. In Mark's gospel, it seems to last just a few weeks.

20. Stephen King, *On Writing: A Memoir of the Craft*, p. 131.

X
Bad News Paul, a Delusional Cult Fanatic

> We have to admit that Paul was no martyr and was not even notably truthful; he was
> first and foremost a survivor. Despite his undoubted belief on the genuineness of his
> vision at Damascus and subsequent visions, he was in some respects unscrupulous,
> especially when he felt that the Lord's cause required a policy of deception.
>
> —Hyam Maccoby, *The Mythmaker: Paul and the Invention of Christianity*

The Greed of Faith
A Run-up to the Smack-down of Paul

THERE IS a New Testament story in Acts 5 that is especially devoid of moral substance
and bereft of any redeeming value. The ugly protagonist of the story–the heavy–is
Peter. Yes, *that* Peter, the Rock upon which Jesus would build his church. According
to Catholic piety, Peter was the first pope. Pretty high on the holiness scale, but, as it
turns out, pretty low on the scale of human decency.

Acts 5 presents a time when the church was proudly communistic: All members
pooled their goods and cash so that everyone would have enough to get by. One
couple, Ananias and Sapphira, were okay with giving their fair share but balked at
turning over everything to the church. Ananias sold a field, with his wife's consent,
but "kept back some of the proceeds."

It seems that Peter could read people pretty well, and he was ready with his own
theological spin on their deception:

> "Ananias," Peter asked, "Why has Satan filled your heart to lie to the Holy
> Spirit and to keep back part of the proceeds of the land? . . . How is it that
> you have contrived this deed in your heart? You did not lie to us but to
> God!" Now when Ananias heard these words, he fell down and died. And
> great fear seized all who heard of it. The young men came and wrapped up
> his body, then carried him out and buried him. (Acts 5:3-6)

Instant death, for lying! It gets worse:

> After an interval of about three hours his wife came in, not knowing what
> had happened. Peter said to her, "Tell me whether you and your husband
> sold the land for such and such a price."
>
> And she said, "Yes, that was the price."
>
> Then Peter said to her, "How is it that you have agreed together to put the
> Spirit of the Lord to the test? Look, the feet of those who have buried your
> husband are at the door, and they will carry you out." Immediately she fell
> down at his feet and died. When the young men came in they found her
> dead, so they carried her out and buried her beside her husband. And great
> fear seized the whole church and all who heard of these things. (Acts
> 5:7-10)

There's no hint that Peter felt the least twinge of remorse, either for scaring the couple to death or for terrorizing the church. The author of Acts included this story because he apparently felt no remorse either. He was an advocate for the Christ cult and was just as zealous for uncompromising commitment. Ironhanded Peter was the good guy.

Maybe Peter could pull it off for a while with Ananias and Sapphira dead and the church terrorized, but the time has long since passed when preachers could demand all your money. The greed of faith has diminished only slightly, though. Some denominations still get away with 10 percent tithing, and they all seem obsessed with buildings and property, bureaucracies and priesthoods, requiring vast sums of money. Those in authority, following in Peter's footsteps, always have their hands out, and have commonly used the fear of the Lord to extract as much as possible.

We Also Own Your Enthusiasm and Morality

Faith is greedy with regard to emotional investment as well. In Luke 10:27, we read the standard decree of Jesus: "You shall love the Lord your God with all your heart, and with all your soul, and with all your strength, and with all your mind." I suspect that most Christians have a hard time identifying with this. *All, all, all, all.* This chant is part of the white noise theobabble they commonly hear from the pulpit.

Paul put it another way in his letter to the Galatians, but he watered down nothing: "I have been crucified with Christ. It is no longer I who live, but Christ who lives in me" (Gal 2:19) and "Those who belong to Christ Jesus have crucified the flesh with its passions and desires" (Gal. 5:24). Even the pious who say their nightly prayers have a hard time embracing the extremism of Jesus and Paul, with multiple loyalties to families, jobs, education, and their own interests and hobbies. *All* of your heart, strength and mind are focused on God? The passions of the flesh have been crucified?

I don't think so; *they* don't think so. Maybe that's why super pious people who join holy orders are commonly held in awe and considered so holy: They claim to do what ordinary mortals can't do (and really don't even want to do). Of course, the church settles for far less, but the greed of faith hasn't disappeared. It usually insists that this bar is high as well: Jesus wants as much as possible of your fervent devotion.

Faith is also greedy in protecting its turf. It claims that it has a monopoly on *meaning*: Only a religious orientation can provide purpose and a reason to live. Mahalia Jackson wouldn't have it any other way: "Without God, I could do nothing, Oh Lord, Without God, You know all my life would fail."[1]

Faith is confident that it owns morality as well, that it's the only guide for good behavior. TV celebrity Steve Harvey, a twice-divorced adulterer who easily qualifies as one of the nation's high profile hypocrites, has famously said that he doesn't want to associate with atheists because "they have no moral barometer." The champions of faith, even those who don't know the difference between a compass and a barometer, would have us believe that religious belief is the only grounding for human decency: "This is *our* domain."

The pontificators insist that humanity would be morally adrift without God setting the rules. Faith is greedy to be the one and only anchor. But the God of the Bible–both the Old and New Testaments–is a moral monster, as so many critics have pointed out as apologists try to evade and excuse the obvious. Secular ethicists, beginning at least with the ancient Greeks, have done well in working out the grounding of morality without the help of gods.

It is a scandal that Christians remain oblivious to the robust secular deliberations on morality, and so readily retreat to the mindless posturing that good behavior derives only from divine decree. They have an uphill battle to sustain the arguments for their "morality greed." It is unjustifiable on any grounds.

The Greed That Surpasseth All Understanding

Once we have the gift of life, we are very reluctant to let it go. We think it'd be great to live forever, but after a bit of thought we realize there are no alternatives to death. No matter how much we panic at the prospect of it.

Perhaps on other planets there may be intelligent creatures that live for thousands of years. They might not age as we do, but surely they too face eventual oblivion. Heaven seems to be an easy answer to our death angst, a very popular one. Yet it breaks down on close examination. As Christopher Hitchens has asked, why would anyone welcome an eternity praising Jesus as an alternative to oblivion? The idea is hard to sustain.

As our awareness of the Cosmos has expanded, the truth has sunk in that *everything* dies: vast chunks of matter as well as living organisms. Microbes, redwoods, lions and tigers and bears–they all die, oh my. Gibraltar will crumble, every mountain will tumble; planets will melt or burst into flame as their stars expand or explode.

It seems that the Universe itself will die. There have commonly been two models: The one that current evidence favors has it expand forever and become cold, lightless, and lifeless. Or it may collapse back on itself–the Big Crunch, when all the atoms in you and me and everything else will once again be squeezed into a singularity, billions of years after the Big Bang.

Well before the impermanence the entire Cosmos was understood, there were wise folks who knew that human awareness is a fleeting thing–that's just the way it is. The author of Isaiah 40 recorded his reflections, confident that the only thing that could defy decay was God's word:

> All flesh is grass, and all the goodliness thereof is as the flower of the field: The grass withereth, the flower fadeth: because the spirit of the Lord bloweth upon it: surely the people is grass. The grass withereth, the flower fadeth: but the word of our God shall stand forever. (Isaiah 40:6-8, KJV)

Some humans can shrug and say, "C'est la vie," tossing off the human revulsion at the very idea that they will be snuffed out. But others ache to see mother again in heaven. (That myth has certainly been oversold.) They shrink in horror of the fate that awaits us by virtue of our participation in the Cosmos.

"Lucky to Be Alive" Isn't Lucky Enough

It's been common to try to find a way out of death, and thus we end up embracing the ultimate foolishness. Surely, on this planet, religion has thrived to help assuage the fear of death. Earlier I mentioned the barb that "religion was born when the first con man met the first fool," and one of the first products that the con man offered was escape from death. In all fairness, however, not all the con men pushed this product. The religious thinkers who gave us the Old Testament had no concept of heaven whatever. There was no "eternal reward." Following God's law was its own reward, then you died. Period.

The Old Testament told tales of people who had lived for hundreds of years, with first prize going to Methuselah, whom folklore granted 969 years. The assumption might have been that people who lived in the distant past, nearer the time of God's burst of creative energy, enjoyed a vitality that has since diminished. But now we mere mortals are stuck with a few decades at best. Yet we balk at being thankful and content with that. We refuse to properly savor our brief gift of awareness.

In his role as evolutionary biologist, Richard Dawkins reminds us of our good fortune to be here for even a little while.

> We are going to die, and that makes us the lucky ones. Most people are never going to die because they are never going to be born. The potential people who could have been here in my place but who will in fact never see the light of day outnumber the sand grains of Arabia. Certainly those unborn ghosts include greater poets than Keats, scientists greater than Newton. We know this because the set of possible people allowed by our DNA so massively exceeds the set of actual people. In the teeth of these stupefying odds it is you and I, in our ordinariness, that are here. We privileged few, who won the lottery of birth against all odds, how dare we whine at our inevitable return to that prior state from which the vast majority have never stirred?[2]

And whine we do, although in our calmer moments we might take Dawkins's point, "How cool is that," and revel in the privilege of having lived at all.

But fear of death and our deep distress that bad behavior goes unpunished were a challenge that theology eventually felt compelled to overcome. By the time Jesus had come along, after Judaism had moved beyond the stark when-you're-dead-you're-dead theology of the Old Testament, belief in an afterlife had gained traction.

There was perhaps a lot of floundering—after all, it's a guessing game—trying to imagine how "living forever" would come to pass and what it would be like. As we saw in our glance at John 11 (Tough Problem IX), Lazarus' sister Mary was sure that her brother would come to life again on the day of resurrection. Jesus and Paul seem to have felt that the Kingdom of heaven was a new regime that would be lowered to Earth from God's realm overhead. All those who had repented in time were eligible, and thus could avoid being snuffed out.

Christopher Hitchens is no doubt right that "religious faith . . . will never die out, or at least not until we get over our fear of death."[3] I prefer the cynical punch offered by a Facebook friend: "As long as people are afraid of death, they will continue to embrace religion. What a bunch of pussies."[4] And this is the greediest greed: Our little share of life–being here for a blip in eternity–isn't enough, dammit. We want it to go on forever.

Terror in the face of death has probably created more pussies than anything else in human history. The con men have the answer. They rise to the occasion to offer the way out, the escape from oblivion.

And one of the heroes of the New Testament has few equals in the flimflam business.

Bad News Paul
The Ultimate Con Man

Gospel is the translation of the Greek word *euangelion*, which means *good news*. Hence, in the context of the New Testament, evangelism meant to announce or spread the good news about Jesus Christ. The authors of the four gospels–Matthew, Mark, Luke, and John, whoever they were–are commonly called the evangelists, though, as we saw in the last chapter, much of the news they spread about Jesus wasn't all that good. The apostle Paul, however, carried a sour message punctuated with few redeeming features. He is Bad News Paul, and in his wake we find a colossal theological mess.

For all his bravado, I suspect that Paul, preaching so frantically about how to be saved, was running at least a little scared. My guess is that he was inordinately terrified of death, and almost sure he'd found a way to get out of it. He was going to be among the select few who would get to meet Jesus as he descended through the clouds, to be part of God's kingdom forever.

Of course, it didn't work out that way; he died like everyone else. The New Testament is silent about how. Acts ends with Paul under house arrest in Rome.

It's strange that the author of Acts couldn't have come up with something more. After all, he demonstrated consummate skill in filling his book with fabrication and fantasy (and the gospel of Luke before that). So we're left wondering about Paul's demise. I like to think that, as Paul was about to be executed with a blade poised above his head (that's one of the legends), or as he was about to slip away on his deathbed, he wondered, "Gee, what went wrong? How come Jesus never showed up?"

For all his confidence during so many years of tireless preaching–that incessant pleading for others to give themselves totally to Jesus Christ–was there a whisper of doubt? Were there moments of running scared? He wrote this in his letter to the Philippians:

> I want to know Christ and the power of his resurrection and the sharing of his sufferings by becoming like him in his death, if somehow I may attain the resurrection from the dead. Not that I have already obtained this or

> have already reached the goal; but I press on to make it my own, because Christ Jesus has made me his own. Beloved, I do not consider that I have made it my own; but this one thing I do: forgetting what lies behind and straining forward to what lies ahead, I press on toward the goal for the prize of the heavenly call of God in Christ Jesus. (3:10-14)

Boy, he's pathetically desperate for that heavenly goal. Maybe one way to overcome his uncertainty was to press on pressing on, grasping for his prize. As his letters in the New Testament show so clearly, he was like a machine, obsessed with Jesus Christ.

It's puzzling that there is no hint in the Acts that Paul was a prolific letter writer. One of the reasons he had a major impact on the development of Christianity, and on Western thought, was that his letters ended up in the New Testament. In them he never mentions the dramatic story of his conversion that we find three times in Acts (chapters 9, 22, and 26). Paul has such a great reputation because the author of Acts was the best publicist Paul could have wished for.

Because of this reputation, some religious scholars argue that Paul was the inventor of Christianity. There are reasons to make this guess, but it's not that simple: He was *one* of the inventors. He has a high profile because his letters are among the charter documents of the Christian faith. And just as Paul pressed on pressing on, Christians have pressed on in the faith because of Paul's obsession.

The Bully Saint

Yet Paul is a profoundly unattractive character, a presumptive hero with disheartening defects. Classical scholar Michael Grant, some of whose comments about Paul I've already cited regarding Tough Problem III, bends over backwards to be fair to Paul. But it's hard to escape the obvious. Paul letters, he says, "display a startling mixture of conciliatory friendliness and harsh, bitter, inexorable bullying." For Grant, Paul "is the very opposite of a tranquil, serene personality. Always pursuing, always pursued, he is the victim of violent, manic-depressive alternations of moods."[5]

In explaining his selection of Phillipians 4:8 to read at his father's funeral, Christopher Hitchens said it shines "out from the wasteland of rant and complaint and nonsense and bullying which surrounds it."[6]

It's a scandal that Paul is a star in the Christian firmament, that the term "saint" accrued to his name. Anyone who is curious about Paul's great reputation, who wants to get to the bottom of things, should take the Book of Acts with a grain of salt and read Paul's letters very carefully. They're not easy reading, so most good Christians don't bother. Thus they miss all of the exquisite material for disqualifying Paul as a hero: His letters provide all the testimony we need to knock him off the pedestal.

Am I being too harsh here? Was Paul really a con man?

It's perhaps worse than that. Most con men know they're pushing bunkum, but there's not a whisper of a doubt that Paul believed the trash he peddled about winning eternal life. Paul was a delusional cult fanatic.

Chipping Away at Sainthood

The Turnoffs

Paul's Big Blind Spot

Jesus of Nazareth

Are there any Christians who assume that Paul was one of Jesus' disciples? Given the depth of Christian ignorance about the faith, nothing would surprise me. But surely Paul's dramatic conversion on the road to Damascus, an event almost everyone can associate with Paul, is a major clue that originally he was not part of the Christian movement. In fact, he persecuted Christians with fervor. He was on his way to Damascus to put an end to their foolishness.

Christians realize that Paul originally wanted to eradicate the Christian movement, and then did a stunning about-face, but it might come as a surprise to them that Paul had not met Jesus. As far as we know, Paul had never even seen Jesus or heard him preach. There's been speculation, though, that he couldn't have been so opposed to the Jesus movement without having heard Jesus preach. Indeed, perhaps such encounters had sparked his animosity. After all, the gospels tell us that Jesus was always tangling with religious authorities, and maybe Paul was one of them. Since we are told that Jesus attracted huge crowds all over the place, how could Paul and Jesus not have crossed paths?

Remember, however, that the gospel accounts of the wildly popular Jesus cannot be trusted. No first century historians report massive throngs of people following a Galilean peasant preacher. And however tempting it may be to speculate that Paul had known Jesus, there is no evidence—no documentation—to support the speculation. If Paul had been one of the religious leaders picking on Jesus, why do the gospel writers fail to mention that? Paul doesn't show up until Acts 8, well after Jesus' demise.

We can say with certainty that Paul does not mention any such encounter in his letters, and he is mysteriously silent about the life and preaching of Jesus of Nazareth. *That* would be hard to explain if Paul had seen Jesus in the flesh. This silence has always bothered scholars who wish that Jesus and Paul had at least run into each other, and it should bother lay people who are the least bit curious about Christian origins.

It's not lost on the Mythicists—those who argue that Jesus is a fictional character—that it is impossible to glean any information about a real man named Jesus from Paul's letters. You will hunt in vain through them—Romans, 1 Corinthians, 2 Corinthians, and the shorter ones—Philippians, Galatians, Philemon and 1 Thessalonians—for any details about Jesus.[7]

None of Jesus' preaching, parables, miracles, healings are mentioned. We hear nothing about him walking on water, turning water into wine, or raising Lazarus. Paul doesn't seem to have gotten wind of any of these stories and traditions.

His lack of interest in Jesus is startling. The only exception to this is the script of the Last Supper, and we saw in Tough Problem VIII how highly unlikely it is that Paul's "words of Jesus" on that occasion are authentic.

So here's one of the big conundrums as we tackle the problem of Paul: There is a profound disconnect between Paul's thought and the *real person* Jesus (at least as we encounter him in the gospels), though they shared the certainty that Jesus would come back to Earth soon. Paul was under the spell, almost literally we could say, of a *theological concept* of the Christ figure. In fact, he did not love Jesus; he betrays little knowledge of him. This is what I mean by his having a blind spot. What he loved was the risen, resurrected Christ.

This is so very odd; Paul was a contemporary of Jesus who seems to never have bumped into him, yet there were swarms of people whom Paul could have tapped for information about Jesus after he had, literally, seen the light (Acts 9, 22, 26). He avoided the circle of Jesus' first followers, staying away from the disciples. As we have seen in the discussion of Galatians (Tough Problem VII), Paul did not go to Galilee to find the disciples after his conversion; that didn't happen for three years. And when he did meet Peter eventually, he *avoided contact* with others who had known Jesus.

So why would he choose to stay out of the loop? Because, oddly enough, he *wanted it that way.*

Paul was convinced that he knew the truth about a heavenly Christ figure–not *Jesus*, Christ–and wanted to stand firm in his own understanding. He thought that his own experience of the risen Christ was all the validation he needed. It surely had been traumatic. It may or may not have been the dramatic Damascus Road encounter described in Acts, but the impact on his person and personality had been profound.

We get the closest description of the event in 1 Corinthians 15, in a text that should get a prize for its blend of humility and bragging. Paul offers a chronology of Christ sightings to the disciples and others. He reports:

> Last of all, as to one untimely born, he appeared also to me. For I am the least of the apostles, unfit to be called an apostle, because I persecuted the church of God. But by the grace of God I am what I am, and his grace toward me has not been in vain. On the contrary, I worked harder than any of them–though it was not I, but the grace of God that is with me. Whether then it was I or they, so we proclaim and so you have come to believe (1 Cor. 15:8-11).

One untimely born? Scholars have wondered about this imagery; it is based on the Greek term for *abortion*, a birth that is poorly timed. Perhaps Paul is saying that, in not having known Jesus, he was as unfortunate as someone who had *not* been a contemporary of Jesus. He was obviously chagrined that he had persecuted the earliest Jesus followers, but after God's grace had put him on the right track ("by God's grace I am what I am"), he "worked harder than any of them"! But, typically for the obsessive Paul, he had to give God credit for that as well.

There may be an element of truth in his claim that he worked harder than anyone else, which is why some commentators give Paul so much credit for inventing Christianity.

It's a Vision Thing

So, Christ appeared to Paul. What form did that take? As we saw in the discussion of resurrection (Tough Problem VII), Paul did not think that the physical body of Jesus had escaped from a tomb. Presumably, Jesus' spiritual body was with God in heaven above, awaiting return.

Paul's give and take with the Risen Christ was via visions. Christians may very well embrace visions as a valid way to know God, so why not give Paul the benefit of the doubt? But this means coming to terms with the blunt truth that Paul knew Christ *only* through visions.

When Christians accept the "vision thing," they're walking into a trap. As was discussed regarding Tough Problem II, if you're going to give the thumbs up to Paul's visions, saying, Yes, he really had chats with a dead man, then why don't Protestants give thumbs up to the thousands of Virgin Mary visions that Catholics have claimed? How can they rule out the visions by which Joseph Smith breathed life into Mormonism? It sounds pretty phony to say, "But Paul was on our team, so we know that his visions were real." Visions are a dangerous, shaky foundation.

Of course, Christians will protest that the Risen Christ was not a *dead* man. That's the whole point, one of their fundamental dogmas! They're trapped in dogma, however, with a claim about Jesus that has never been verified, one that most of the other religions of the world regard with as much skepticism as atheists do. But still, if you want to embrace the idea that Paul was getting messages from a living dead man, be careful. If you insist that Paul was talking to a (disembodied) spiritual being–in his case Jesus, who was somewhere in the sky waiting for the right moment to come back to Earth–how is that any more plausible or dignified than getting information from dead people via séances?

"No, that's not the way it was. Jesus was with Paul in spirit," believers protest, prattling on about the spiritual realm. Spiritual reality, spiritual truth, spiritualism, spirituality–why should we trust these slippery claims? If your neighbor claims to be talking to her dead grandmother in dreams, don't you roll your eyes? Yet we're supposed to take seriously that dead Jesus talked to Paul? Isn't that worth an eye-roll? Atheists want to know where you draw the line, before wandering over the line into the land of psychics and mediums. Absolutely we are entitled to say to Christians, "You're putting us on."

Christians themselves have felt the need to make spiritual contacts and visions seem more real, more concrete. Hence the creative fiction writers got to work, and vivid stories were conjured. In Acts, the Holy Spirit is a master at special effects. This was long before people realized that "spirit" working on physical matter was problematic. How exactly would that work?

> When the day of Pentecost had come, they were all together in one place. And suddenly from heaven there came a sound like the rush of a violent wind, and it filled the entire house where they were sitting. Divided tongues, as of fire, appeared among them, and a tongue rested on each of them. All of them were filled with the Holy Spirit and began to speak in other languages, as the Spirit gave them ability (Acts 2:1-4).

In the murky realm of chattering spirits, how can Christians be sure that Paul was really hearing Jesus, instead of getting input from his imagination? Even if you concede that it was a mix of both, then you also have to concede that some of what Paul tells us could be fantasy and fiction, or ideas that seeped into his consciousness from pagan religions. When we look carefully at his description of the Last Supper, we can be especially suspicious. As I've pointed out earlier, Jesus asking his followers to drink his blood, even symbolically, strikes us as alarming pagan intrusion.

Paul didn't have any gospel scrolls to consult about what happened in that famous upper room. And he made a point not to mingle with the disciples. So where did he find out about the Last Supper? He tells us: He heard about it from Jesus! But how? Could it be that, when the meal was over, Jesus sneaked out, somehow found Paul—whom he'd never met—and gave him a blow-by-blow description of the Last Supper? Of course, no such clandestine meeting, farfetched in the extreme, is mentioned in the gospels, and no, that's not what Paul meant. Here's what we read in 1 Corinthians 11:23-24 (emphasis added):

> *For I received from the Lord* what I also handed on to you, that the Lord Jesus on the night when he was betrayed took a loaf of bread, and when he had given thanks, he broke it and said, "This is my body that is for you."

The receiving from the Lord was the voice of Jesus in his head. Perhaps a voice that he imagined coming from the sky, if you trust the Damascus Road accounts. Paul told this story to the Corinthians, so he no doubt repeated it many times in the churches he visited. Thus it could have become part of church liturgy used in worship. If this is the case, it's no surprise that it ended up as part of Mark's version of the Last Supper, to be copied in Matthew and Luke. So Paul's revelation morphed into "a true incident" in Jesus' life. The Mythicists certainly aren't surprised, and they suspect the entire Jesus story came into being in much the same way.

Paul testifies repeatedly in his writings that he knows this or that because he got it from the Lord. In his nasty letter to the Galatians (1:11-12), he shows no hint of humility or uncertainty:

> For I want you to know, brothers, that the gospel that was proclaimed by me is not of human origin; for I did not receive it from a human source, nor was I taught it, but I received it through a revelation of Jesus Christ.

Indeed he claims divine authority for his wackiest ideas. As I mentioned earlier (Tough Problem VII), Paul assured the Thessalonians that their dead relatives, transformed into "spiritual bodies," would float from their graves to meet Jesus in the clouds.

Any curious and even mildly skeptical reader would ask: *How does Paul know that?* Where does he get this information about how events will unfold when Jesus returns? Maybe he saw too many zombie movies? We can rule that out, but we can't rule out the vivid turmoil in his head–his tortured visions. He was sure that Jesus had been speaking to him, declaring "**by the word of the Lord**, that we who are alive, who are left until the coming of the Lord, will by no means precede those who have died" (1 Thess. 4:15).

What shall we call this–revelation, imagination, hallucination? This is the dilemma, the *embarrassment*, that Christianity faces. Paul is its greatest hero, its most fervent missionary, the most prolific theologian who helped *create* Christianity and shaped Christian thought more profoundly than anyone else; few texts have had as much impact as his Letter to the Romans. Yet he was guided by his personal visions to the exclusion of almost everything else.[8]

A Rogue Apostle

The original disciples were probably vexed about this upstart Pharisee who had suddenly "got religion." This intruder had come out of nowhere to claim equal status with the original disciples, which was, no doubt, a great shock.

What were they saying behind Paul's back? They'd been scared to death of him because he had once been hell-bent on destroying the first Christians. In Acts (9:1-2), we can glimpse the Paul they knew. He even had gone by a different name:

> Meanwhile Saul, still breathing threats and murder against the disciples of the Lord, went to the high priest and asked him for letters to the synagogues at Damascus, so that if he found any who belonged to the Way, men or women, he might bring them bound to Jerusalem.

Not even after his conversion did he show any interest in getting back to Galilee to make apologies to the disciples and find out as much as he could about Jesus. He had snapped. He was now exuberantly pro-Christ, but he still preferred to remain outside the loop. In Galatians 1:15-17, remember, he proudly recounted his independence from the disciples. He was a rogue apostle, a loose cannon. In every sense of the term, he had gone off the reservation.

The Book of Acts, written decades later, would have us believe that Paul was less of a rogue. There we catch the author of Acts in a lie, a *big* lie. It says Paul, soon after his sudden conversion, had preached his new faith so enthusiastically that he angered the Jews in Damascus. He had to escape by being lowered in a basket through a hole in the city wall. And here's the lie:

> When he had come to Jerusalem, he attempted to join the disciples; and they were all afraid of him, for they did not believe that he was a disciple.

But Barnabas took him, brought him to the apostles, and described for them how on the road he had seen the Lord, who had spoken to him, and how in Damascus he had spoken boldly in the name of Jesus. So he went in and out among them in Jerusalem, speaking boldly in the name of the Lord. (Acts 9:26-29)

But his statement in Galatians tells us that this is precisely what Paul did *not* do. He didn't blend. He didn't *want* to blend: "I did not confer with any human being," he'd said. It was only decades later that the author of Acts created an idealized version of events, absolutely unaware that Paul had told the truth in his letter to the Galatians.

The guy who came up with the stories in Acts would have us believe that Paul had achieved hero status in his own lifetime. Maybe so, maybe not: "Clearly, the author of Acts was not writing actual history but revisionist history. Which we call pseudohistory. He simply made things up, with little real care for historical accuracy or fact."[9]

One of the best examples of this is Acts 15, a description of the so-called Jerusalem conference of Christian leaders. Paul showed up to make the case that circumcision was no longer relevant in the scheme of salvation, and should be dropped as a membership requirement; penis mutilation certainly didn't play well in the campaign to win Gentiles for Christ. Acts 15 reads like a press release by Paul's agent. Though there was "much debate," Paul prevailed and was sent off the victor and called "our beloved Paul"! That seems to be laying it on a bit thick.

And what was the author of Acts thinking when he began the very next chapter with his report that Paul circumcised Timothy "because of the Jews" before taking him along on his missionary travels? That makes no sense whatever. It's hard to imagine that Timothy was all that keen on the idea: "Sure boss, let's do this."

It's also in Galatians that Paul reveals he did not mix well with the original Jesus crowd, who still believed that Jews and Gentiles should not share the same table. The truth of the gospel, in Paul's view, was that dietary laws were no longer relevant–no more than circumcision was. Certainly an admirable sentiment, mandated by Paul's theology that belief in Christ was all that mattered. But it was an issue that set him apart from those who were still very much attached to their Jewish heritage:

But when Cephas [Peter] came to Antioch, I opposed him to his face, because he stood self-condemned . . . when I saw that they were not acting consistently with the truth of the gospel, I said to Cephas before them all, "If you, though a Jew, live like a Gentile and not like a Jew, how can you compel the Gentiles to live like Jews? (Gal. 2:11, 14)

This is in keeping with Paul's habit of denigrating the competition wherever he encountered it. He reacted sharply to others who also preached about Christ. It's amazing that there is so much dirty laundry in Paul's letters–which ended up as holy scripture![10] He wrote this to the Corinthians:

But I am afraid that as the serpent deceived Eve by its cunning, your thoughts will be led astray from a sincere and pure devotion to Christ. For if someone comes and proclaims another Jesus than the one we proclaimed, or if you receive a different spirit from the one you received, or a different gospel from the one you accepted, you submit to it readily enough. I think that I am not in the least inferior to these super-apostles. I may be untrained in speech, but not in knowledge; certainly in every way and in all things we have made this evident to you. (2 Cor. 11:3-6)

And what I do I will also continue to do, in order to deny an opportunity to those who want an opportunity to be recognized as our equals in what they boast about. For such boasters are false apostles, deceitful workers, disguising themselves as apostles of Christ. And no wonder! Even Satan disguises himself as an angel of light. (11:12-14)

Other apostles are "Satan in disguise?" The nastiness here is who Paul really was.

Yes, he was a visionary. But not in the sense that he saw great things ahead for the betterment of this world; he had contempt for that notion. It was in the sense that there were *visions* bouncing around inside his head. There was a divine man speaking to him from beyond the grave."I see dead people" is one way to win friends and influence people, but it should be distrusted–profoundly.

The elephant in the Christian room for centuries has been Paul's emotional volatility and instability, and theologians have made it an art form to nuance his craziness as profundity. They ooze nonsense about his "spiritual genius."

A Seriously Troubled Soul

Paul needed help. For all his jabbering about belonging to Jesus and God, he needed a Dear Abby to bare his soul to. Inappropriately, he blurted out his dysfunction to the congregation at Rome, which he had not yet visited. Was he lying on his therapist's couch as he dictated these words?

For we know that the Law is spiritual, but I am of flesh, sold into bondage to sin. For what I am doing, I do not understand; for I am not practicing what I would like to do, but I am doing the very thing I hate. But if I do the very thing I do not want to do, I agree with the Law, confessing that the Law is good. So now, no longer am I the one doing it, but sin which dwells in me. For I know that nothing good dwells in me, that is, in my flesh; for the willing is present in me, but the doing of the good is not. For the good that I want, I do not do, but I practice the very evil that I do not want. But if I am doing the very thing I do not want, I am no longer the one doing it, but sin which dwells in me. (Rom. 7:14-20, NASB)

Note that last part about the sin that *dwells within*. Sin was one of the *dramatis personae* in the play that was Paul's life, and it controlled all the action. Only grabbing onto Christ–embracing the magic faith formula–could get him out of this quagmire of failure. And this, in Paul's view, was the grim circumstance of all humans. In Romans 5:12, he explains the origin of our misery, namely Adam: "Therefore, just as sin came into the world through one man, and death came through sin, and so death spread to all." Why? Because, he says, "all have sinned."

In Romans 3:10-18, Paul pours it on. He explains just how rotten we are in these nine verses, into which he sweeps fragments from a few psalms and Isaiah. As it is written, he says,

> There is no one who is righteous, not even one;
>   there is no one who has understanding,
>   there is no one who seeks God.
>
> All have turned aside, together they have become worthless;
>   there is no one who shows kindness,
>   there is not even one.
>
> Their throats are opened graves;
>   they use their tongues to deceive.
>
> The venom of vipers is under their lips.
>   Their mouths are full of cursing and bitterness.
>   Their feet are swift to shed blood;
>   ruin and misery are in their paths,
>   and the way of peace they have not known.
>   There is no fear of God before their eyes.[11]

In Paul's view, this was the human condition, and he was sure that only the amazing grace provided by belief in Christ could save the wretched souls, i.e., those who wised up in time. He was confident that God was mad at the world; wrath was the default divine mood. Paul was imprisoned by his own pessimism. "To say that he was self-contradictory is an understatement," says A.N. Wilson. "He was a man who was fighting himself and quarreling with himself all the time; and he managed to project the warfare in his own breast on to the Cosmos itself."[12]

These days if we have friends and family with such damaged self-worth, who have internalized the sick message that "sin dwells within me," we get them into therapy and onto medications. We consider it our duty to help them restore a sense of wholeness and wellbeing so they can function in the world. Paul lived before such interventions were even possible. Christianity has suffered immeasurably because Paul's depression-saturated theology ended up as scripture.

Now that it's achieved that status, theologians in the Christian camp have been duty-bound to tout Paul as an exemplar of spiritual genius. The results are disheartening. Just one example is the fawning of C.H. Dodd, a prominent New Testament scholars of the 20th century. He began his 1932 book on Paul with this declaration: "The Epistle to the Romans is the first great work of Christian theology." It is so obviously not.

There are other texts that confirm our suspicions about Paul's mental stability. He drops details about his religious "gifts" that should stun sane Christians–at least make them sit up and take notice, and have doubts about taking him seriously. I heartily recommend that Christians read 1 Corinthians 14 with a critical and open mind.

From time to time, we see videos of religious dervishes "speaking in tongues," carried away, hysterically jabbering nonsense with bystanders in awe that these folks are channeling Jesus or the holy spirit. The Book of Acts bravely tries to put the best possible spin on this practice:

> When the day of Pentecost had come, they were all together in one place. And suddenly there came from heaven a noise like a violent rushing wind, and it filled the whole house where they were sitting. And there appeared to them tongues as of fire distributing themselves, and they rested on each one of them. And they were all filled with the Holy Spirit and began to speak with other tongues, as the Spirit was giving them utterance.
>
> Now there were Jews living in Jerusalem, devout men from every nation under heaven. And when this sound occurred, the crowd came together, and were bewildered because each one of them was hearing them speak in his own language. (Acts 2:1-6, NASB)

It is clear from 1 Corinthians 14 that Paul was addressing something else entirely. Those who had the gift of "tongues" were not speaking other languages. They were mumbling gibberish that came from the holy spirit, which no one understood, though a few supposedly had the gift of interpreting it.

So that's what church was like in Paul's day. If we are in a generous frame of mind, we simply confess that this is primitive religion running at full tilt. Less generously, we call the whooping, hollering, and yelling mindless hysteria. But here's the stunner: *Paul was a gibberish kind of guy.* Seeing him in action this way, how many folks really would call him a "spiritual genius"?

He did at least see some need for restraint. Here's his warning in 1 Corinthians 14:18-19, accompanied by a big dose of egotism:

> I thank God that I speak in tongues more than all of you; nevertheless, in church I would rather speak five words with my mind, in order to instruct others also, than ten thousand words in a tongue.

Apologists who want to push Paul as a spiritual genius should include this in the mix, along with his certainty that he had conversations with Jesus. As we discussed early on (Tough Problem II), his visions could very well have been a byproduct of frontal lobe epilepsy. The vision thing, and other aspects of his religious fervor, are far more of a turn-off than a turn-on.

Jesus Will Be Here . . . Any Minute Now

If there had been a Kook of the Year Award given in 2011, it might have gone to Harold Camping. Although trained as an engineer, Camping had enjoyed a long career in the prediction business, as a radio evangelist. Here's the straight scoop, from Wikipedia, about his fifteen minutes of fame:

> Camping predicted that Jesus Christ would return to Earth on May 21, 2011, whereupon the saved would be taken up to heaven in the rapture, and

that there would follow five months of fire, brimstone and plagues on Earth, with millions of people dying each day, culminating on October 21, 2011, with the final destruction of the world. He had previously predicted that Judgment Day would occur on or about September 6, 1994. His prediction for May 21, 2011, was widely reported, in part because of a large-scale publicity campaign by Family Radio, and it prompted ridicule from atheist organizations and rebuttals from Christian organizations. After May 21 passed without the predicted incidents, Camping said he believed that a "spiritual" judgment had occurred on that date, and that the physical Rapture would occur on October 21, 2011, simultaneously with the final destruction of the universe by God.[13]

Notice that Christian organizations joined in the rebuttal. Most Christians, even of the evangelical persuasion, shook their heads and wagged their fingers at Camping, glaring with folded arms: "He's giving us a bad name!"

Oh really? Well, true enough, Camping was giving the faith a bad name, but it gives me great pleasure to report he had help from the apostle Paul. Who, in turn, was standing on the shoulders of end-of-the world ranters who had preceded him, namely, John the Baptist and Jesus of Nazareth. The Book of Revelation, bringing up the rear of the New Testament, probably written decades after Paul's time, offers spectacular imagery of the end time. Harold Camping's doomsday message was about as New Testament as you can possibly get!

It's not as if Paul's expectation of Jesus' return was a minor theme, allowing Christians to brush it off as some trivial aberration. Paul was hyperactive in his efforts to bring his "good news" to as many people as possible so they could be saved "from the wrath to come," which might show up any day. Even when he offered his pathetic advice on marriage to the Corinthians (more about this shortly), he was looking over his shoulder for Jesus to arrive:

> Because of the present crisis, I think that it is good for a man to remain as he is. Are you pledged to a woman? Do not seek to be released. Are you free from such a commitment? Do not look for a wife. But if you do marry, you have not sinned; and if a virgin marries, she has not sinned. But those who marry will face many troubles in this life, and I want to spare you this. What I mean, brothers, is that the time is short. From now on those who have wives should live as if they do not; those who mourn, as if they did not; those who are happy, as if they were not; those who buy something, as if it were not theirs to keep; those who use the things of the world, as if not engrossed in them. For this world in its present form is passing away. (1 Cor. 7:26-31, NIV)

Yes, you read that right: "If you're happy, snap out of it!" Some of Paul's sayings have ended up on greeting cards and Christian memes, e.g., "Love is patient and kind," but I'm fairly certain that the folks dedicated to tidying up Paul's reputation would like to bury these verses, e.g."From now on those who have wives should live as if they do not." Maybe this could go on Wedding Anniversary cards sold in Christian bookstores!

Paul was not a happy person. The minor and major details of his message bubbled over from a burning conviction that the world would soon be transformed and only those who were saved would survive the horrific arrival of Jesus to rule the Kingdom of God on Earth. He didn't just have the timing wrong; the entire concept is tortured and misguided. It is bad theology that emerged in the centuries preceding the Common Era. The thinking of John the Baptist was poisoned by it, as was the thinking of Jesus and Paul.

One of the most common things I hear from commonsense Christians is that they "don't accept all that doctrine," because it's too brutal. They find it hard to embrace the idea that the problems of history have such simplistic solutions; that Jesus is hovering somewhere to return to make things better, and that most of humanity–those who have not heard the "good news"–will be massacred to mark the occasion.

But the New Testament is saturated with this bad theology. The decent Christians, wanting to distance themselves from carnage theology, nonetheless commonly say, "I just want to follow the teaching of Jesus."

But atheists can hold their feet to the fire: "Oh really, Jesus is your man? The one who said that you have to hate your family to be one of his disciples?" As we saw in the last chapter, there are as many reasons to reject Jesus as there are to reject Paul.

So Jesus Comes Floating Back

Then What?

Paul's obsession with Christ and his imminent return cast a deep, dysfunctional shadow over much of what he taught. He was determined to escape death, and he had the mechanism all worked out, with precision. Nothing else mattered.

He was so submerged in Christ that he looked at the world as if from under water. Hence so much of what he writes is distorted, and even the scholars who specialize in Paul–to say nothing of ordinary readers–find themselves bothered and bored by his rambling letters and twisted theology. Even his first readers found his letters wearisome, as he reveals in one of his moments of candor: "I do not want to seem as though I am trying to frighten you with my letters. For they say, 'His letters are weighty and strong, but his bodily presence is weak, and his speech contemptible'" (2 Cor. 10:9-10).

While Paul may have figured out the escape from death, he doesn't paint the picture of what the future held for those who were saved, once Jesus descended through the clouds and the glorious Kingdom of God was in place. He doesn't venture a guess about what would happen to the *vast litter of dead bodies*, millions of them, in the wake of God's cleansing wrath. We do not know how Paul had the furniture arranged in the blissful eternity under Jesus' rule.

He assured the Corinthians that they would get in, expressing certainty "that the one who raised the Lord Jesus will raise us also with Jesus, and will bring us with you into his presence" (2 Cor. 4:14). He apparently thought it would be just swell, compared to our dreary earthly existence: "For this slight momentary affliction is preparing us for an eternal weight of glory beyond all measure" (v. 17). Did he even know what "weight of glory" might entail?

Imagine the lucky few who are escorted into this ill-defined realm of glory. They remain alert and aware, fully invested with their full faculties so they can appreciate this wonderful gift. Then, it's praising God endlessly–just getting started after trillions of years. They'd need to have a very high level of tolerance for boredom to endure all that praising God endlessly. All normal and noble human pursuits would be cancelled and nullified.

Eternal life in the presence of Jesus: How could that even be interesting?

Split Personality

It's too bad that Paul didn't live long enough to collect royalties on his lovely "love" sentiments. Paul's good reputation has an enormous head start because of 1 Corinthians 13, the Hymn to Love, as it has become known. Everybody knows this text. Do a Google search for "Hymn to Love" and it pops right up. It shares top honors–how cool is this–with links to the 1949 song *Hymne à l'amour* written in memory of Edith Piaf's lover Marcel Cerdan.

This chapter is among the most cherished in the Bible; it is commonly read, ironically enough, during wedding ceremonies. It opens like this: "If I speak in the tongues of mortals and of angels, but do not have love, I am a noisy gong or a clanging cymbal." The resounding conclusion is, "And now faith, hope, and love abide, these three; and the greatest of these is love." And in between: "Love is patient and kind; love is not jealous or boastful." See, everybody knows it.

Christian hackles might have gone up earlier when I stated that Paul was wrong about almost everything. Isn't this just evidence of my snarky atheism? How can he have been wrong when he speaks so eloquently about love? Can't I give him credit for that? But it's really not easy to do that, because Paul gushed about love *only* when he spoke about the Christian in-group.

The context of Paul's celebration of love in 1 Corinthians 13 is a long passage advising church members how to behave. It is not hard to figure out, from the detail that Paul goes into, that congregations in those days–as remains the case to this day!–struggle with factions that quarrel and jockey for power and position.

Hence Paul was at his elegant best in extolling love as a way to overcome church pettiness and politics. But, wait a minute, isn't there a whiff of hypocrisy here? Recall that Paul didn't hesitate to rail against those who followed Christ as understood by other preachers. He became his usual severe self, displaying nasty mean-spiritedness. And those who fell outside the Jesus cult were disqualified from the love that was supposedly part of the deal of being "true disciples of Jesus."

The love that Paul advocated so urgently in 1 Corinthians 13 was about love that *humans* should strive for. Paul was not describing God's love for the world. Remember those words of Jesus about the arrival of the kingdom of God? Those who didn't have God's seal of approval–maybe like the ink stamp on your hand proving you've paid to get into a club–were out of luck. According to Jesus, it would be grim. Where's the love here? Paul didn't know about the preaching of Jesus, but he would've lapped up these words of the Galilean fanatic about the sudden end, just like the days of Noah when the flood came and swept everybody away (Matt. 24:37-39).

Paul was counting on that very thing: sweeping away all the unsaved. This doesn't sound very much like "love is patient and kind" to me. He labeled the luckless masses "those who are perishing." The fortunate saved ones (including himself, naturally) he called "the aroma of Christ," with the gospel "veiled" to "those who are perishing" (2 Cor. 4:3). So, for all his talk about love, and the Christian pleading that we should give him credit for it, the answer is no, not really.

This comes out in the frighteningly bad theology that he voiced so openly in the Letter to the Romans. Whenever I hear Paul described as a "spiritual genius," I wonder if his idolaters have read and really understood the first chapter of Romans. Paul's failure at anger management–his ugly vindictiveness–should repel decent, compassionate readers. Boy, did he hate sinners, and his contempt for homosexuals (more about that shortly) touched off this tirade:

> And since they did not see fit to acknowledge God, God gave them up to a debased mind and to things that should not be done. They were filled with every kind of wickedness, evil, covetousness, malice. Full of envy, murder, strife, deceit, craftiness, they are gossips, slanderers, God-haters, insolent, haughty, boastful, inventors of evil, rebellious toward parents, foolish, faithless, heartless, ruthless. They know God's decree, that those who practice such things deserve to die–yet they not only do them but even applaud others who practice them. (Rom. 1:28-32)

By any reasonable standard, there are only two items on Paul's list that merit the death penalty, i.e., murder and inventing evil–the latter depending on the specific evil that has been "invented."

Yet he offers sweeping condemnation of those who are guilty of envy, deceit, craftiness, gossip, rebellion against parents, and foolishness: *They deserve to die.* By God's decree, no less. Christians confidently claim that the angry God of the Old Testament retired from the field as the loving God of the New Testament won the battle of the gods. They are sadly mistaken, because they don't bother to read the Bible from which their ideas about God supposedly derive.

Jesus foresaw unprecedented human suffering–worse than Noah's flood–when he returned, and Paul was ready with death sentences for most of the people he saw around him living flawed and imperfect lives."God is love" has always been the common chant about the perspective of the New Testament, but that's not the case at all."God is wrath" was the ruling sentiment for Paul:

> For the wrath of God is revealed from heaven against all ungodliness and wickedness of those who by their wickedness suppress the truth. (Rom. 1:18)

> But by your hard and impenitent heart you are storing up wrath for yourself on the day of wrath, when God's righteous judgment will be revealed. (Rom. 2:5)

While for those who are self-seeking and who obey not the truth but wickedness, there will be wrath and fury. (Rom. 2:8)

The Anti-Marriage Counselor

These days, if you want to get married in a church, many pastors require a course in premarital counseling, to reduce the level of blindness–going into marriage–that love causes. This is premarital training, which, throughout the ages, has been as scarce as pre-parental training. It's often said that a new baby doesn't come with an instruction manual, although Dr. Spock pretty much changed that (no, not *that* Spock: Dr. Benjamin Spock, 1903-1998, author of the best-selling *Baby and Child Care*). And now the books on marriage success have piled up as well, which is all to the good.

But the apostle Paul would not have been on board with this. No pastor who specializes in premarital counseling can recommend Paul as a source of guidance. Of course, since the end time was near, Paul had little use for marriage. What was the point?

He was not married, and he hoped that people could follow his example. Sex was probably a turnoff for him; he could get along quite well without it: "It is well for a man not to touch a woman" (1 Cor. 7:1).[14] He conceded, begrudgingly, that people get horny, so the high water mark of his marital advice was this gem: "For it is better to marry than to be aflame with passion." The King James Version, as usual, puts it more quaintly: "[L]et them marry: for it is better to marry than to burn" (1 Cor. 7:9).

Most people go into marriage relishing the prospect of full-throttled passion, ready to have as much sex as their hearts desire–in bed, on the kitchen table or at the beach. No pastor who offers marital counseling would discourage that. (Well, some might frown on doing it at the beach.) But Paul would have cringed; he doesn't seem to have had much fun in his life, in bed or out of it. Christ was the prize he sought, and he kept his eye on the prize."But put on the Lord Jesus Christ, and make no provision for the flesh, to satisfy its desires" (Rom. 13:14).

Flaunting Weak Theology

"How can you doubt God? Just look at the world around you." Countless theists have said this to doubters, as if to say, "Case closed!" The natural world, so the argument goes, makes God obvious. Paul was not the first one to espouse this shallow theology, but he certainly popularized it; he anchored it firmly in Christian thought and thus gave permission to countless Christians to use it.

Here is one of the texts that secures his status as a clumsy, tiresome, sinister thinker. God has wrath in store for everyone on the planet who doesn't shape up the way Paul thinks they should–and nature itself is proof of this. This is not the work of "spiritual genius":

> For the wrath of God is revealed from heaven against all ungodliness and wickedness of those who by their wickedness suppress the truth. For what can be known about God is plain to them, because God has shown it to them. Ever since the creation of the world his eternal power and divine

nature, invisible though they are, have been understood and seen through the things he has made. So they are without excuse; for though they knew God, they did not honor him as God or give thanks to him, but they became futile in their thinking, and their senseless minds were darkened. (Rom. 1:18-21)

In fact, of course, God's eternal power and goodness *cannot* be inferred from the things he has made. Paul failed to grasp that this is weak, sophomoric theology: At most, an unknown, undefined creative force could be inferred. Paul himself was certain of many things about God (he wrote about them extensively), precisely because they are *not* obvious from nature, e.g., that God is wrathful, loving to a *few people*, joined at the hip to Christ and the holy spirit. Paul spent a hell of a lot of time and energy preaching about these divine attributes.

In Romans, Paul is looking to explain why God is permanently in a bad mood, so he makes the argument here (he spins it) that people should have been able to figure out God by just looking around at the world. Since this doesn't dawn on them, however, God has all this wrath in store.

Well, it's hard to jump to specific theological conclusions just by looking around at the world. Any theologian today, with the advantage of almost 2,000 years of debate to refine arguments for God, knows that the we-can-see-god-in-nature argument must be used with extreme caution. With so much calamity and suffering delivered by nature, its message about God is a very mixed one.

How in the world could C.H. Dodd say that Romans is the first great work of Christian theology?

Proof That God Elected Obama . . . Twice

Paul once got out of a scrape—he was about to be flogged—by claiming that he was a Roman citizen. The commander who was about to administer the punishment was astonished, but took his word for it. The incident is reported in Acts 22:22-30, but Paul does not mention his citizenship in any of his letters.

Well, maybe there is, in Romans 13, a hint of it, in a text that has caused no end of embarrassment. Romans is a bad book, and the 13th chapter is one of the low points. Paul tells everyone to "be subject to the governing authorities," condemning anyone who rebels as doing so "against what God has instituted." Rulers, he fawns, "hold no terror for those who do right, but for those who do wrong." So submit to them, "not only because of possible punishment but also as a matter of conscience."

Perhaps this excessive pro-government eulogy reflects Paul's citizenship—he was just being loyal—but it is possible as well that he was trying to defuse suspicion about the upstart Christian movement. Had his letter, on its way to Rome, fallen into the wrong hands and been read by the authorities, they would have been pleased to know that they had God's approval, and smile on the groveling Christians.

What more could authoritarian rulers want to justify their dictatorships? This text has always been despised by those who favor democracy and the accountability of rulers. It is difficult for conservative we-hate-Obama Christians to remain in Paul's corner on this issue.

Paul had no interest whatever in theories of good government. He expected all governments to be abolished as soon as Christ returned to establish the Kingdom of God. And when Christians fail to understand that he was governed by this obsession, it is easy for them to misunderstand other Pauline texts that seem compatible with democracy.

He is often given credit, incorrectly, for egalitarian sympathies. Was he a Jeffersonian long before Jefferson proclaimed that all men are created equal? He does say that

> in Christ Jesus you are all children of God through faith. As many of you as were baptized into Christ have clothed yourselves with Christ. There is no longer Jew or Greek, there is no longer slave or free, there is no longer male and female; for all of you are one in Christ Jesus. And if you belong to Christ, then you are Abraham's offspring, heirs according to the promise. (Gal. 3:26-29)

But this is no statement of some governmental ideal, or a recommendation for equal treatment under Roman law. While we can say that common human distinctions made no difference in the community of those who belonged to Christ, Richard Carrier makes it clear that Paul's thinking was very much inside his delusional box, not outside of it,

> not asserting a political concept, but a very prejudicial theology, where only those who "have been baptized into Christ" are equals (for only they, as he says, "united in Christ"). And not only that, but they are equals only in the sense that they all share the same "promise" in the afterlife, not in the sense that they share the same legal rights.[15]

Christians have made Paul out as friend of democracy that springs—somehow—from the love of Christ. In 2 Corinthians 3, he argues that belief in Christ means that the burden of the Old Testament law has been lifted, and he concludes with the eloquent pronouncement that, "where the Spirit of the Lord is, there is liberty" (v.17).

I was familiar with this verse long before I knew much about Paul, because it was on the masthead of *The Indianapolis Star*, a newspaper that I saw every day as a kid. The quote seemed a perfect blend Christian earnestness and love of personal freedom, which never would have entered Paul's thinking.

This bears repeating: Paul was expecting the return of Jesus in the near future. So he was not following in the footsteps of Solon to affirm theories of sound government. Nor was he a predecessor of John Locke or Jefferson. He could not have cared less about these matters. Paul's thought was simplistic: Leaders are ordained by God, period. But governments were irrelevant. Paul even had contempt for the judicial system. He ridiculed members of the church for taking one another to court. Since they would soon be judging the angels above, couldn't they come to terms out of court? (See 1 Cor. 3:6.) How can the word *delusional* not come to mind?

Finally, before we leave Paul's fulsome praise of government authorities, here's a stunner: Paul's wording, in his enthusiastic endorsement of rulers (Rom. 13:1-5), undermines confidence in the gospels.

Did Paul have a massive brain freeze? As Raphael Lataster has pointed out, Paul seems to have forgotten what the rulers did to Jesus![16] Or, perhaps he never even knew the story. Many times I've noted how much Paul didn't know about Jesus, and that seems to have included the crucifixion stories so familiar to us. Paul shows no awareness of the trial and crucifixion at the hands of the Romans: Now the Romans are the good guys! Paul didn't seem to have learned about the empty tomb during his visit with Peter, nor much about the crucifixion and the role that Romans had in that.

The Killing of Curiosity
Untold Damage to Western Thought

The two personalities that dominate the New Testament are Jesus and Paul, with Peter coming in a distant third. In the gospels, Peter, supposedly the rock foundation of the church, is not an admirable figure: He never seemed to "get" Jesus (who once ordered him, "Get thee behind me, Satan") and, when push came to shove, denied knowing him. Peter figures in the first half of the Book of Acts—where he seems to have his act together—then vanishes from history, or from *Acts*, at least, which fails to qualify as history. According to fanciful Catholic tradition, Peter somehow ended up in Rome.

Paul stands head and shoulders above the roster of apostles named in the gospels because he wrote letters, and these survived and ended up as standout documents in the New Testament.[17] Wouldn't it be terrific if we could find some humanity-affirming theology in his work? After all, you've got it made when your letters are given the rank of inspired Holy Scripture—no matter how carelessly you tossed them off.

Ironically, Paul's profile today is higher than it was when he was alive; his impact in the long term was substantial. It is an overstatement to claim that Paul invented Christianity, though, because it is clear that there were other preachers out there spreading the word about the new cult. We know this because Paul railed against them, and cautioned people not to listen to other preachers.

Somehow, the Jesus cult had spread considerably before Paul hallucinated his way into the new movement. He was on his way to Damascus to track down Christians who were already there, after all, and the congregation in Rome had taken root without his help. A lot of creative minds probably worked to nurture the Christ myth. Four gospels were eventually fabricated to tell the story, not counting the ones that didn't make it into the New Testament. But Paul's letters were canonized, long after he had passed from the scene, and he ended up winning the contest as "most influential Christian" of the ancient world.

Did he help create humanity-affirming theology? Tragically, in his letters there is no hint whatever of curiosity about the world or appreciation of anything other than the rewards of belonging to Christ. The beauties and blessings of life merit no mention at all there. They contain no hint whatever that Paul had any interest in education, art, architecture, human creativity, or exploration of the natural world and the heavens above.

Ancient curiosities seem not to have rubbed off on him. Well before his time, Aristarchus of Samos, Eratosthenes, and Hipparchus of Nicaea had been measuring the sky and trying to work out the mechanics of planetary movement. The only reason Paul looked up was to spot Jesus coming back. He was a maniac for Christ. Western civilization paid a heavy price for his single-minded devotion to a tacky magic formula for evading death.

Paul ridiculed wisdom and use of the mind, causing incalculable damage. In large part, the darkness of the dark ages is rooted right here:

> Where is the one who is wise? Where is the scribe? Where is the debater of this age? Has not God made foolish the wisdom of the world? For since, in the wisdom of God, the world did not know God through wisdom, God decided, through the foolishness of our proclamation, to save those who believe. For Jews demand signs and Greeks desire wisdom, but we proclaim Christ crucified, a stumbling block to Jews and foolishness to Gentiles, but to those who are the called, both Jews and Greeks, Christ the power of God and the wisdom of God. For God's foolishness is wiser than human wisdom, and God's weakness is stronger than human strength. (1 Cor. 1:20-25)

With these words embedded in sacred scripture, it would be an uphill battle to value excellence of the mind; Paul can take much of the blame for how Christianity came to be defined. Richard Carrier has painted a grim picture of the Dark Ages that reigned in Europe after the fall of the Roman Empire.[18] No, Christianity did not cause the fall, but it was there to fill in the vacuum, and did its best to smother and cancel the achievements of Greek and Roman culture.

When the fresh air of the Renaissance finally blew across Europe, we can suspect that even some deeply pious folks had gotten bored waiting for Jesus to return. It had remained part of the unalterable dogma because it was right there in the sacred text: Paul's obsession in black and white. But serious thinkers, whose curiosity about the world and thirst for knowledge and beauty could not be suppressed, finally couldn't take Paul seriously any longer.

The Poison of Anti-Semitism

For many centuries, it was taken for granted in the Christian West that anti-Semitism is justified ("The Jews killed Christ"), and it is one of Christianity's most profound embarrassments that anti-Semitism is deeply rooted in the New Testament itself. John's gospel portrays Jews as villains, those who hounded Jesus to his grave. But there is an especially horrifying passage in Paul's first letter to the Thessalonians. Some scholars have suggested, knowing how proud Paul was of being a Jew, that this doesn't sound like him. Are these verses an interpolation?

> For you, brothers, became imitators of the churches of God in Christ Jesus that are in Judea, for you suffered the same things from your own

compatriots as they did from the Jews, who killed both the Lord Jesus and the prophets, and drove us out; they displease God and oppose everyone by hindering us from speaking to the Gentiles so that they may be saved. Thus they have constantly been filling up the measure of their sins; but God's wrath has overtaken them at last. (1 Thess. 2:14-16)

If the Book of Acts can be trusted, admittedly a big "if," we know that Paul was not hindered from speaking to the Gentiles about Christ. In fact, he was authorized to do so, and given the blessing of the Jerusalem church. So either Paul was having a bad day, or these words were inserted into the text by a hateful copyist who didn't know that Paul had not been hampered; the chapter flows perfectly well without it.[19]

But the damage was done, whether the words came from Paul or from a copyist: The Jews "have constantly been filling up the measure of their sins; but God's wrath has overtaken them at last." These sentiments were assumed to be Paul's, and throughout the centuries Christians have been all too willing to function as instruments of God's wrath overtaking the Jews. The Holocaust is the culmination of hatred against the Jews in the Christian West.

Women Loving Women, Men Loving Men

If there is anyone we could nominate as "least likely to understand human sexuality," it would be Paul. We have already seen that he wished everyone could remain single as he was; that it was not good for a man to touch a woman; that he saw marriage as a means to cool sexual passion. It's not an outrageous guess that Paul suffered from considerable libido dysfunction.

As is not uncommon when that is the case, he seems to have thought too much about what went on in other people's bedrooms. He heaped invective on those who acted on their sexual impulses. These gems (emphasis added) are all from Romans 1, in the context of the revulsion Paul felt about homosexual behavior:

> **God gave them** up in the lusts of their hearts to impurity, to the degrading of their bodies among themselves . . .

> **God gave them up** to degrading passions . . .

> **God gave them up** to a debased mind and to things that should not be done . . .

Of course, we could have expected that, if Paul believed the Leviticus texts (18:22 and 20:13) that it as an abomination for men to have sex with men.

Paul is disgusted, and he assumes that God feels the same way as he does. Of course, that's a common mistake theologians make: My feelings reflect God's feelings. Chances are, of course, that the ancient priests who wrote Leviticus had as little understanding of human sexuality as Paul did. They probably were repulsed at the idea of a man "playing the role of a woman," i.e., for them, being submissive during sex. Any hint of a man acting like a woman would have been abhorrent.

Paul assumed that his visceral reaction was the only proper one. Here is the full blast of his gut response:

> For this reason God gave them up to degrading passions. Their women exchanged natural intercourse for unnatural, and in the same way also the men, giving up natural intercourse with women, were consumed with passion for one another. Men committed shameless acts with men and received in their own persons the due penalty for their error. (Rom. 1:26-28)

One of the most common reactions to homosexuality across the world is that it is *unnatural*. That is the basis for Paul's vehemence here. But surely–and this is a question that we can ask even today–how does "going against nature" justify the revulsion? There's something else going on here that prompts Paul to use words like *degrading* and *shameless*.

Which brings us back to Paul's lack of understanding of human sexuality. We can cut him some slack here, because human sexuality has been the subject of real study only in modern times. It's been a long, slow, painful slog to get people to realize that such scholarship has been done. It is exceeding frustrating that churches balk on gay rights and hide behind the call for "more study." When I left the Methodist ministry in the 1970s we commonly heard, "We need to study this some more," and that is still heard today, even though homosexuality has been studied to death.

In 1973, the American Psychiatric Association removed homosexuality from the *Diagnostic and Statistical Manual of Mental Disorders*. There was an outcry from old school therapists who made their livings trying to cure homosexuals, but now there is a collective shrug. No one had been able to demonstrate that homosexuality is a pathology, that it can be treated, much less "cured." And the argument that it is unnatural has no meaning, since same-sex attraction has been consistently observed as a part of nature.

Unfortunately, those who are repulsed by homosexuality–who take *unnatural* as a clinching argument–just assume that Paul is an authority. His opinions are thrown about as if they should matter; they are commonly heard in the debate today. This is another example of damage done by one of Paul's rants. Why do religious people take him seriously on *anything* to do with sex? He was wrong about heterosexuality! He was so wrong about so much–about marriage, about Jesus coming back, about government, about church members getting to sit in judgment of angels.

A Delusional Cult Fanatic?

Yes, Delusional–or a Reasonable Facsimile Thereof

Of course people can believe crazy things without being delusional. Religions are chock full of foolish dogmas because people are gullible and have not been trained to think critically. From an early age, they may have been subjected to brainwashing–otherwise known as Sunday school or catechism–where critical thinking skills are not encouraged.

Am I being unkind? No: The sole purpose of Sunday school and catechism is to pass on dogma undiluted, and most of it certainly qualifies as foolish. People are not taught about standards of evidence, that due diligence should be applied to supernatural claims. Hence it has been easy for religious marketers throughout the world to build an impressive catalogue of beliefs over the millennia, from the banal to the crazy.

But at what point are we entitled to use the word *delusional*? Is talking to dead people delusional? A widow in one of my parishes confessed to me that, alone in the evenings, she would stare at the photo of her dead husband and scold him for dying, for leaving her alone. My guess is that she was not delusional; she knew that she was not really communicating with him.

When Catholics pray to their saints, they may truly believe that the saint is paying attention, but this pious behavior has been encoded in their brains by years of exposure to Catholic custom. It's just the thing to do. They may even believe that it really works, but I would hesitate to say that praying to saints is delusional.

We have reason to believe, however, that Paul had gone over the edge in his fantasy life. From what he reports in his letters–maybe we can say he was too candid–*delusional* does not seem too strong a word. He thought he was enhancing his stature and credibility by being so candid, and his followers were probably suitably wowed. Almost any preacher could say almost anything about the spiritual world with lots of people willing to give the thumbs-up. His audiences in the first century were impressed when Paul talked about his heavenly journeys.

But today, what are we to make of Paul's statement in 2 Corinthians 12?

> It is necessary to boast; nothing is to be gained by it, but I will go on to visions and revelations of the Lord. I know a person in Christ who fourteen years ago was caught up to the third heaven–whether in the body or out of the body I do not know; God knows. And I know that such a person– whether in the body or out of the body I do not know; God knows–was caught up into Paradise and heard things that are not to be told, that no mortal is permitted to repeat. On behalf of such a one I will boast, but on my own behalf I will not boast, except of my weaknesses. But if I wish to boast, I will not be a fool, for I will be speaking the truth. But I refrain from it, so that no one may think better of me than what is seen in me or heard from me, even considering the exceptional character of the revelations. (2 Cor. 12:1-7)

It has always been a bit of a puzzlement that Paul speaks in the third person here; isn't this his own experience? He protests that he doesn't want to boast, but the person he mentions was "caught up into Paradise and heard things that are not to be told, that no mortal is permitted to repeat." Paul was, at the very least, the confidant of the person who "heard things not to be told," and Paul claimed repeatedly that he had heard things straight from Lord. As we have seen in our discussion of the script of the Last Supper, Paul reports that he heard it from the Lord. He was sure that

Jesus was talking to him. I suspect that this is far more delusional than praying to a saint.

Paul is not standing in front of us. We can't interview him, so it's hard to make a diagnosis two millennia after he walked the Earth. But he told his niche market that he heard voices from the beyond. It's hard to make the case that this is *not* delusional behavior.

What a mess. Christian theology is deeply rooted in the "information" that emerged from Paul's hallucinations.

The Little Cult That Could

When I'm in a confrontational mood, I point out that Christianity is the cult that won. It started out as a teeny tiny sect within Judaism, and remained a small minority religion for well more than two centuries. Its slow crawl from obscurity–indeed its survival–is nothing remarkable in that context, something Richard Carrier abundantly demonstrates in a book titled *Not the Impossible Faith: Why Christian Didn't Need a Miracle to Succeed* (2009). By quite a few accidents of history, Christianity eventually became the state religion of the remnant of the Roman Empire. In other words, *it won*. And its particular set of foolish dogmas became the core of mainstream belief. Its reputation for craziness receded, lost in the fog of respectability.

Of course, doesn't everyone know that cults believe crazy things? Does Christianity fail this test? Here's a streamlined version of the Christian message:

> A Galilean peasant preacher was chosen by God to be his son–whether at his conception, birth, baptism or resurrection, there is disagreement–and God required his son to be executed to enable forgiveness of sins. After Jesus' resurrection he ascended into heaven to await his return to earth, at which time most of humanity will be massacred. However those who believe that Jesus rose from the dead will escape the slaughter and have eternal life. While Jesus is away in heaven, his faithful followers routinely eat facsimiles of his body and blood.

Every word of this summary is based on New Testament teachings, and the quotient of magic, the quotient of *weird*, is high. And we see this especially in the Apostles Creed, which has puzzled secular observers forever. It shockingly skips over the life of Jesus–his teaching and deeds–to peddle the blend of fairy tale and magic:

> I believe in God, the Father almighty, Creator of heaven and earth, and in Jesus Christ, his only Son, our Lord, who was conceived by the Holy Spirit, born of the Virgin Mary, suffered under Pontius Pilate, was crucified, died and was buried; he descended into hell; on the third day he rose again from the dead; he ascended into heaven, and is seated at the right hand of God the Father almighty . . .

This version of Christianity has undergone countless modifications over the centuries, especially as more enlightened believers have come to see the crudeness and silliness of so much of it–even the untenability of it all. But Paul was there at the creation and played a major role in defining "Bible-based" Christianity. It would be hard to "out-cult" the faith that Paul championed so feverishly.

Christian Scholars Can't Get Enough

Just as The Sermon on the Mount has been vastly overpraised, so too has Paul's Letter to the Romans; Christian theologians have been obsessed with it. Ben Witherington's 400-page analysis of Romans includes an *18-page* bibliography of scholarly works on it, a list he says "could go on for miles."[20] Evangelical scholar Douglas Moo published a 1,000-page commentary on Romans, one of a series, the *New International Commentary on the New Testament,* "loyal to the Scriptures as the infallible Word of God."[21] A *thousand pages* on the sixteen chapters of Romans? Lay people would scratch their heads at this colossal waste of time and energy—if they ever got wind of it—and wonder what all the fuss is about.

Paul's mediocre theology has been taken much too seriously. Wouldn't you think that his spectacular error about Jesus coming back soon would have been a tip-off that he was a crank, incapable of crawling out of a deep hole of magical thinking? "Lose yourself in adoration of a resurrected man, and you will have a seat in Paradise," is essentially his message. I don't even know what a "spiritual genius" would look like, but surely this isn't it.

The Fanatic
You Wouldn't Want to Know Him

Albert Schweitzer famously once said—to the shocked silence of New Testament scholars—that, if all the myth and fiction could be stripped away, the Jesus of history would not be an attractive character. Of course, uncovering the unattractive Paul is not difficult. Part of the mystery of Jesus is that he never wrote anything, but Paul left a substantial paper trail.

The Book of Acts cannot be trusted, but Paul's letters come from the man himself. When Christians dig beyond his occasional sweet sayings in his writings—the "good stuff" you're supposed to find in The Good Book—it's not a very pretty picture. We can see his irascibility, for example, in his belittling of the Galatians, so it's no surprise that Paul just wasn't that likeable. Even he admits that he knows what people say behind his back: "his bodily presence is weak, and his speech contemptible" (2 Cor. 10:11).

His intensity and intransigence were a major turnoff. Even one of Paul's greatest fans, evangelical scholar Ben Witherington, is candid, saying he has "little doubt that most moderns, even most modern Western Christians, would have been taken aback by Paul. We would have seen him, both before and probably also after his conversation, as a fanatic. We would also likely have seen him as too driven and too single-minded—a person without a life apart from his missionary work."[22]

I'm thrilled that Witherington gives us permission to use the word *fanatic* in describing Paul! We can see that by reading his letters. The opening of 1 Corinthians is typical, sounding like teenage hero worship. Paul was a Jesus groupie:

> Paul, called to be an apostle of Christ Jesus by the will of God, and our brother Sosthenes, to the church of God that is in Corinth, to those who are sanctified in Christ Jesus, called to be saints, together with all those who in every place call on the name of our Lord Jesus Christ, both their Lord and ours: Grace to you and peace from God our Father and the Lord Jesus Christ. (1 Cor. 1:1-3)

And Witherington is right about Paul's lack of work-life balance. Paul had no life whatever outside his missionary work. He had no wife, no family,[23] and he gave himself no time for kicking back and enjoying life. He was humorless, possessed, and obsessed to reach as many people as possible, to save them from the general slaughter when Jesus returned:

> I am talking like a madman—I am a better one: with far greater labors, far more imprisonments, with countless floggings, and often near death. Five times I have received from the Jews the forty lashes minus one. Three times I was beaten with rods. Once I received a stoning. Three times I was shipwrecked; for a night and a day I was adrift at sea; on frequent journeys, in danger from rivers, danger from bandits, danger from my own people, danger from Gentiles, danger in the city, danger in the wilderness, danger at sea, danger from false brothers, in toil and hardship, through many a sleepless night, hungry and thirsty, often without food, cold and naked. And, besides other things, I am under daily pressure because of my anxiety for all the churches. (2 Cor. 11:23-28)

This guy needs to lighten up and get a life. Who asked *him* to be so driven? No one, actually, least of all the original followers of Jesus. His passion sprang from his hallucinations, and his imagination was stoked by a potent mixture of Jewish and pagan mythologies. All designed, pathetically, to engineer escape from death.

It's too bad that all of his energy and bravery, which he clearly had in abundance, couldn't have been channeled to face life and death honestly—and with a good deal more good cheer! The world would be a much better, safer place without delusional cult fanatics.

Fear Not

Paul told the Corinthians that he didn't want to frighten them with his letters, but Christians should be afraid . . . very afraid. I urge the faithful: Please read every paragraph of Paul's letters as if your spiritual well-being depended on it, and be prepared, boldly and bravely, to cast a veto.

My own veto comes in the form of a put-down that I owe to the clever screenwriter Mark Andrus, creator of *As Good As It Gets*. In this film we follow the transformation of Melvin Udall (Jack Nicholson), a neurotic, obsessive-compulsive misogynistic writer of romance novels. Melvin possesses no religious sensibilities and does not suffer fools gladly.

His neighbor's housekeeper asks him to check in on the neighbor, who is recovering from an assault: "Open his curtains for him so he can see God's beautiful work, and he'll know that even things like this happen for the best." Pious Christian drivel. Melvin snaps back, "Where do they teach you to talk like this? . . . Sell crazy someplace else, we're all stocked up here."

As I have said repeatedly, if Christians were to read the gospels critically, unapologetically and without rose-colored glasses, they would find the heavy-handed fantasy factor quite depressing. It's an uphill battle to isolate strains of "healthy" religion in the accounts of Jesus. Now, after undergoing the strain of finding positive things about Jesus, it's probably not a good move to turn right away to Paul's letters, because in these the heavy-handed fantasy factor is out of control.

If these worn-out Christians were to hear gems of Paul's tortured theology from a wild-eyed preacher at their front door—Paul would have loved *that* job—they would tell him to get lost."Sell crazy someplace else, we're all stocked up here."

The very smart Thomas Jefferson wouldn't have bought the crazy. He was turned off by so much in the gospels, and literally cut out the stuff that bothers rational, decent people. Theologians and preachers have not shown such courage in dealing with Paul. Instead, they have idolized him and put the best possible spin on his egregious display of crazy. They should have used their scissors too, leaving a litter of Paul slices on seminary floors, with only one or two pages of his letters intact.

Actually, I wouldn't even be that generous. Notwithstanding his few feel-good platitudes, my edited version of the New Testament would omit Paul entirely.

Notes

1. Lyric by B. Brown.

2. Richard Dawkins, *Unweaving the Rainbow: Science, Delusion and the Appetite for Wonder* (Mariner Books, 2000), p. 1.

3. Christopher Hitchens, *God Is Not Great*, p. 12.

4. Daron Brown, Facebook, 30 October 2014.

5. Michael Grant, *Saint Paul* (Phoenix Press, 2000), pp. 22-23.

6. Hitchens at p. 12.

7. There are other letters attributed to Paul, but there is substantial scholarly opinion that the following are not authentic: Ephesians, 1 Timothy, 2 Timothy, Titus—and maybe Colossians, 2 Thessalonians. Bart Ehrman has been blunt that we should be honest in calling the letters what they are, namely, forgeries. Traditionalists wince at this word, even though they agree that Paul probably was not the author. Instead they say that the forged letters were written by Paul's disciples, or written by followers in the "school of Paul." Thus we can see that spin matters as much to theologians as it does to politicians.

8. What were the influences that stoked his imagination? There was a lot of ferment in both pagan and Jewish thought in Paul's time. Religious imagination in general had produced a wide range of literature; there were concepts and ideas in the air that he could have soaked

up. See especially, John J. Collins, *The Apocalyptic Imagination: An Introduction to the Jewish Matrix of Christianity* (Eerdmans, 2016).

9. Richard Carrier, *On the Historicity of Jesus*, p. 363. A good primer on the problems of the Book of Acts is Richard I. Pervo's *The Mystery of Acts: Unraveling Its Story* (Polebridge Press, 2008).

10. See Galatians 2:1-6 especially.

11. Lyrical formatting added.

12. A.N. Wilson, *Jesus: A Life*, p. 23

13. Wikipedia, Harold Camping [en.wikipedia.org/wiki/Harold_Camping] (accessed 9 Nov 2014).

14. In all fairness to Paul, however, "sins of the flesh" included a lot more than sex: "Now the works of the flesh are obvious: fornication, impurity, licentiousness, idolatry, sorcery, enmities, strife, jealousy, anger, quarrels, dissensions, factions, envy, drunkenness, carousing, and things like these. I am warning you, as I warned you before: those who do such things will not inherit the kingdom of God" (Gal. 5:19-21).

15. Richard Carrier, "Christianity and the Rise of American Democracy," in John Loftus, ed., *Christianity Is Not Great: How Faith Fails* (Prometheus Books, 2014), p. 188.

16. Raphael Lataster, *There Was No Jesus, There Is No God* (2013), p. 93.

17. Yes, there are epistles credited to Peter and John, but scholars have major doubts about their authenticity. They failed to have the same impact as Paul's writings.

18. Richard Carrier, "The Dark Ages," in John Loftus, ed., *Christianity Is Not Great: How Faith Fails* (Prometheus Books, 2014), pp. 209-21.

19. Richard Carrier makes the argument that this text is an interpolation: richardcarrier.blogspot.com/2011/06/pauline-interpolations.html

20. Ben Witherington III, *Paul's Letter to the Romans: A Socio-Rhetorical Commentary* (Eerdmans, 2004), p. xvii.

21. Eerdmans, 1996.

22. Ben Witherington III, *What Have They Done with Jesus? Beyond Strange Theories and Bad History–Why We Can Trust the Bible* (HarperOne, 2007), pp. 235-36.

23. In Acts 23:16, however, there is a surprising reference to Paul's nephew.

Conclusion
The Falsification of Christianity

> With no evidence for an afterlife, we should recognize the true value of our current lives as our one and only shot at happiness. Wasting it on unfounded claims and ancient myths is an absolute tragedy.
>
> —Armin Navabi

A Major Modern Falsification

ON THE EVENING of 30 October 1938, CBS Radio's *The Mercury Theatre,* broadcast a dramatization of H.G. Wells's novel *War of the Worlds.* The program was presented in the form of news bulletins, and many listeners became terrified: It sounded, for all the world, like a Martian invasion was under way.

Panic was so widespread that it made the front page of the *New York Times.* The broadcast had begun with this chilling declaration:

> We know now that in the early years of the twentieth century this world was being watched closely by intelligences greater than man's and yet as mortal as his own. We know now that as human beings busied themselves about their various concerns they were scrutinized and studied, perhaps almost as narrowly as a man with a microscope might scrutinize the transient creatures that swarm and multiply in a drop of water.

Why did the ominous words about the world being watched sound plausible? So plausible that an *alien invasion* even seemed possible? Well, the world had been prepared for this scenario, at least in part, by the imagination and lifework of Percival Lowell.

Lowell was a Bostonian aristocrat who enjoyed a distinguished career as a specialist on Japanese culture. For the last 25 years of his life, though, he indulged his fascination with Mars. He built a telescope in Arizona to study Mars, and made detailed drawings of our nearest neighbor in the solar system. He was sure he saw extensive canals, and he imagined that an ancient and advanced Martian civilization was engaged in a massive engineering project to redistribute water from the Martian polar caps. He was not shy in broadcasting his conclusions, and the lore about very smart Martians grew in the popular imagination. In fact, H.G. Wells himself was at least partially inspired by Lowell's work.

Today, of course, Mars has been studied more than any other planet in the solar system. Throughout the 20th century telescopes and photography improved, and dozens of probes have been sent to Mars. Every square kilometer of its surface has been mapped, and our robots have been crawling over the barren landscape for more than a decade. Indeed, the terrain is fascinating, but we now know that there are no canals. There is no life at all. Lowell had been seeing things, perhaps imperfections in the telescope lens or atmospheric aberrations, but he had been dead wrong. The ancient and advanced Martian civilization *has been falsified.* It existed only in Lowell's imagination, and got wiped out by real information.

There is one other major falsification I'd like to mention, one far more momentous. In 1920, astronomers Harlow Shapley and Heber Curtis held a famous debate at the National Academy of Sciences about the size of the universe. Shapley argued that the Milky Way Galaxy *was* the universe–the whole universe. Curtis maintained, on the other hand, that the many fuzzy patches of light in the night sky were not evolving solar systems inside the Milky Way (Shapley's position), but instead were other galaxies far beyond.

Our local galaxy[1]

Just three years later, astronomer Edwin Hubble proved that one of those fuzzy patches of light is a galaxy well beyond our own. It's the closest one to us, the Andromeda Galaxy. Hence, our home galaxy, grand though it may be, is just *one* colossal swarm of stars in the vastness of space teeming with billions of other colossal swarms. Because of Hubble's very patient observations using the 100-inch telescope on Mount Wilson, Shapley's position had been falsified. He had been dead wrong. His "small" universe got wiped out by information, too.

Christianity Has Been Falsified
Wiped Out by Information

Are theological concepts just as vulnerable? Can it be proved that gods do not exist, in particular the *grand fromage* creator deity that Western theists insist is the "one true god"? Conclusive proof would be hard to come by, but reasonable people can be satisfied by arguments based on probabilities. Just how likely is it, for example, that there is an all-powerful, all-knowing master deity who pays attention to each one of us? In Tough Problem IV, we saw why this is not very likely at all. The contradictions that theists live with, in the headstrong embrace of their grand spirit-in-charge, are staggering and inexplicable: They cannot be resolved.

Christian blogger Matt Herndon, who loves following Jesus, speaks with candor about dense theology that trips over itself. He had been shocked to discover that one of his seminary teachers, a professor F. LeRon Shultz, had abandoned the Christian ship:

> Essentially, Shultz decided that Christianity–and theism in general–are too incoherent to be believed. Certain theological matters that believers claim to not understand because they are unknowable mysteries are, Shultz concluded, unknowable because they don't actually make sense.[2]

Secular thinkers have been impatient with theism for this reason, for ages–well, at least since the Enlightenment. But what about unequivocally falsifying and disqualifying Christianity, one particular religious brand–as opposed to theism? Now *that* is a done deal.

Of course, this statement is met with wails of indignation from the Christian camp."How can you possibly say that?" Well, I can say it because the Ten Tough Problems I've covered in detail leave Christianity in shambles. Hey, be my guest: Try to wade through the apologetic literature cranked out endlessly by paid Christian defenders. Much of it is tedious sophistry, some of it is clever and slick, argued earnestly. But nobody can get away with forever rationalizing and championing fallen mythologies. We could just as easily put the apologists to the task of defending the theologies of Thor, Neptune, Isis and Osiris; I know they could rise to the occasion. Whether it's Christ or Poseidon, you are in for a high quotient of brain hurt if you try to follow the tiresome arguments of apologists.

Or we may hear wails of indignation based on Christianity's success: "There are more than two billion Christians. Are they all wrong?" That, of course, is the wrong tack to take. Yes, it has been successful, but so have all of the failed religions of the past, for a while and to varying degrees. In the history of the human species, billions of people have believed in thousands of religions/gods that have been falsified. Christianity stands in this long tradition. How could it not? It is naïve, even childish, to suppose that the religion you were born into—or chose—just happens to be the religion that is right. The idolizing of Jesus, the making so much of a first century Galilean peasant, will end up on the scrap heap of history too.

Get *over* it.

In these chapters, I've presented my approach to the falsification of Christianity in detail. I suspect that Christianity is fatally wounded by any one of these Ten Tough Problems. Taken together, the case is overwhelming: This major world religion is hopelessly broken, and has been from the very beginning.

Christianity has been successful because due diligence is never encouraged as a virtue of faith."Don't ask so many questions" is the *modus operandi*. Priests, ministers and theologians don't want people poking around, peering into the fissures or touching crumbling facades. And most lay people, it seems to me, are willing to keep their minds closed: Their faith is all that wards off an honest embrace of mortality. Their faith is a comfort zone, and they react with knee jerks to the suggestion that there are ten tough problems. *They don't want to hear it*, and they don't want to face the problems head on.

There are two books just a click away on Amazon with the title, *Why I Am Not a Christian*—one by Bertrand Russell and the other by Richard Carrier. Neither has found an enthusiastic Christian readership. Christians don't want to see what happens when serious thinkers go nosing about in the murky underworld of their theology.

Do Christians long for that era when serious thinkers were *not allowed* to go nosing about? Victor Stenger recalls the time when critical thought was forbidden by the church. At the very beginning of the scientific revolution, there was no "clean break between science and religion."

> All of the great pioneers of science—Copernicus, Galileo, Kepler and Newton—were believers, although they hardly had a choice in the matter.

Open non-belief was nonexistent at the time. Except for Galileo, these greats incorporated their beliefs into their science. Galileo was the only one of the founders of the science who tried to separate science from religion.[3]

Christianity has been considerably discomfited by the loss of such control, and has been forced to welcome diversity in the marketplace of religious ideas. Liberal Christians especially know that it is bad manners to point their fingers at Judaism or Islam and bluntly declare, as was done for centuries, "We're right. You're wrong,"

The forced ecumenism is accompanied by choruses of complaints about today's rampant secularism. Yet there seems to be little awareness of how severely the faith has been blindsided by the recent eruption of atheist writing. This pen-mightier-than-the-sword assault has never happened to this extent in the history of the world. Ever. We're living it right now, and atheist books continue to roll off the presses.

Since Christians are, as I have so often pointed out, an incurious bunch, especially about their own faith, they have remained mostly oblivious to this assault. The falsification of Christianity has gone unnoticed by them. The faithful don't realize that their cherished notions have been left in shambles. It's a bit like clinging to the belief that the Sun orbits the Earth. We all know that this concept was falsified a long time go. It, too, got wiped out by information. Christian dogma has about as much merit as the Earth-centered solar system.

Of course, there are the apologists who have mounted valiant counteroffensives, e.g., William Lane Craig, Lee Strobel, Gary Habermas, Donald Johnson, Alister McGrath, Alvin Plantinga, John Haught, and Barry Whitney, all of whom defend *their own versions* of the faith. Why are we not surprised? A lot is at stake, the least of which is the truth of ancient dogma.

If nothing else, Christianity is a monumental, fractured, hungry bureaucracy that has been in the process of bloat for centuries. It employs hundreds of thousands of clergy; its real estate and investment portfolios are vast. It would be in big trouble if people really did stop believing in droves. Beneath the monumental structure are collections of beliefs—different cults, different factions—that must be buttressed at all costs.

It's no surprise whatever that most of the apologists are employed by seminaries and schools of theology owned by denominations. They're paid to come up with answers. Apologists are specialists at circling the wagons.

A Religion that Could Have Been

Now here's a thought experiment to bring home the truth about the perennial apologist enterprise. What if Percival Lowell's enthusiasm about Martian canal builders had spawned a religion? We know from the history of human gullibility that it doesn't take much to get people to bow down and worship something new. People used to think that Mars itself was a god. So a cult could have emerged—let's call it *Marcanalism*—about a pantheon of clever Martian gods who reengineered a planet, and with whom humans could communicate telepathically. Human imagination could have filled in hundreds of details about the Martian gods.

Just one exceptionally zealous human claiming to discover encrypted golden plates once buried in a New York meadow by Martian explorers could have attracted millions of followers in no time, with temples and bureaucracies, priests and squeaky-clean door-to-door missionaries to promote the new one-true-religion. The Marcanal elders could have lifted a lot from the Mormon playbook!

Everything was going just swell until really smart engineers on Earth built bigger telescopes to peer at Mars and sent robot rovers to snoop around its desolate plains, finding not so much as a weed. It turns out that there are no canals or Martian engineers, no Martians or any life at all. The place is barren and dead, but with enough atmosphere to whip up blinding dust storms. The busy earth-bound engineers have continued their probing and suspect that, aeons ago, water may have flowed. Their search for life on the Red Planet, even microbial Martians, continues.

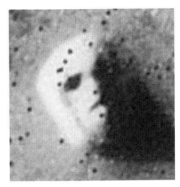

The Viking I "Face on Mars": A matter of perspective.[4]

But the earth-bound Marcanalists are not about to take all of this denial and negativity lying down. They *know* that their Martian deities are real. They testify passionately to the personal relationships they have with these deities who reside just one orbit away. It's insulting to say that they have been imagining everything. All the outside skeptics—those who don't appreciate the subtlety and beauty of true Marcanalism, and the personal rewards of the faith—just don't get it.

And, of course, there are highly trained Marcanalist apologists who do a mighty job of explaining why Marcanalism isn't a bunch of hooey. Why, all those canals that Percival Lowell saw have since been buried by colossal sandstorms! The Martian engineer-saints have taken refuge in vast underground caverns out of sight from prying telescopes and rovers! The Marcanalist apologists even claim that their faith has deep roots in the Roman worship of Mars. Ordinary Romans prayed to the same deities modern Marcanalists do.

Naturally, there has been a massive cover-up of the truth by NASA. Occasionally NASA slips up and leaves the evidence for Marcanalism in full view: The famous "face mountain" photo clearly shows a remnant of the engineering glory that once was. A walking figure can be spotted in another. Just look closely at thousands of Mars photos: Numbers and letters can be seen etched on stones. *Of course*, NASA scoffs at these phenomena. But if it can fake a Moon landing, it can fake or slant the evidence to falsify Marcanalism.

Christian and Marcanal Apologists

Birds of a Feather

The marching orders from all ecclesiastical authorities is precisely the same: Build the case—against all odds and evidence—that the one-true-faith remains intact, immune to all assaults from science, reason, and common sense.

Christian apologists are recruited from the ranks of true believers who are heavily invested emotionally and whose thinking will never budge. They sing from the same choir book: "No, No, No–We're not wrong!" They'd rather put their hands in a fire than fess up that cherished dogmas have been falsified. Indeed, their brains are so wired that they *cannot do so.* Hence they qualify perfectly as apologists. They will never waver. It's postman piety: "Neither snow nor rain nor heat nor gloom of night stays these couriers from the swift completion of their appointed rounds."

In this book, I've quoted C.S. Lewis, Lee Strobel, Barry Whitney, William Lane Craig, and John Haught. By all means, read the works of these and other apologists and marvel at their sophistry and theological gerrymandering. Christian pastors, whose faith may be more vulnerable that they care to admit, take some comfort from the arguments offered by these writers: It's a good idea to remain in the comfort zone.

Lay people who have gotten wind of the atheist assault may feel that atheists have been put into their place by the clever apologists. But the folks in the pew also fail to engage in serious poking and probing.

Evade and Bluff to Win

One evasive tactic of apologists is the claim that religion can't be measured by the same standards we apply to science. Sure, the claim of canals on Mars could be falsified, but no amount of "more data" can falsify God because spiritual truths cannot be determined by data. This is a slick maneuver by theologians to set the rules in such a way that theology is exempt from testability. The feelings of people *in their hearts* for God, Jesus, the saints, etc. are true and unassailable.

We are asked to believe that God is the most colossal force in the universe, yet none of his actions can be measured and tested. If you believe, *then* you can detect God. If we really had "an inner sense telling us about an unobservable reality that matters to us and influences our lives," said Victor Stenger, "then we should be able to observe the effects of that reality by scientific means." But, so far, we "see no proof that the feelings people experience when they perceive themselves to be in touch with the supernatural correspond to anything outside their heads."[5]

Theologians ignore this obvious fact, or they accept "evidence" that really doesn't measure up ("God cured my mother's cancer"). They rest on the assurance that their God is safe and cannot be refuted. But Christian apologists are very much in the business of refuting faith with evidence.

They do it all the time when they argue with passion and eloquence that Judaism isn't true. They can show, based on their own collection of facts, how Judaism falls short and why Islam is a dangerous aberration. And Mormonism? Well, it's not hard to show what a joke *that* is. Yes, indeed, Christian apologists have all the facts, evidence, and heartfelt testimony lined up to show how *other* faiths are wrong. But don't you dare hold Christianity to the same standards! You might make some Tough Problems stand out in bold relief.

The Great See-Through Faith

Christian apologists and practitioners huff and puff defending their various brands of belief, demonstrating petty territoriality so exquisitely. But they merit a resounding *WTF* when they pretend that their dogmas are immune to falsification.

For many lay people there is perhaps weary acceptance of Bible fluff, e.g. virgin birth, healing blindness with spit and mud (John 9:6) and voice-activated resurrections (John 9:43), but these are not really at the heart of faith. When the goodness of God is thrown into question by brutal realities of life on planet Earth, that's something else again. As Barbara Tuchman has said, "Dogma is loosed from its moorings." Stephen Fry was asked what he would say to God, if indeed God exists and meets him at the Pearly Gates. We see that Fry is ready for a confrontation with the Almighty: "Brain cancer in children—what is *that* about?" How many Christians have asked exactly the same thing?

That's part of Tough Problem One. It, and the nine others we've covered, is devastating to Christianity.

———

Problem I: God is perfect love, topped off with omnipotence and omniscience, and he is aware of everything that happens in this world. Not even your innermost thoughts escape his notice. Yet the horrors of evil and suffering on this planet aren't his fault: God gets a free pass. Yes, he's in change, and we must give him credit and praise for everything good that happens, but we can't blame him for anything—certainly not for all the bad stuff that happens. And we are obliged to accept all the excuses that theologians, priests and preachers invent to deflect suspicion that God isn't all he's cracked up to be.

Problem II: God communicates to humans through prayer, visions, meditations, revelations, and intense human emotions. But, strangely enough, these channels work only for people who already believe in him. For outsiders, those who would welcome confirmation that God exists and wants to talk to the human species, there has never been a clear, unambiguous message from the divine realm that everyone can agree on. Never mind that religious people themselves have never been able to agree on what God has communicated. Yet we are asked to believe that visions, meditations, revelations and such really have God behind them—and that the sincerity of believers guarantees them all.

Problem III: God has given his perfect message for humanity in book form, but he had to keep adding installments, first the Hebrew Bible (Old Testament), then the New Testament, followed by the Qu'ran and finally the Book of Mormon. But Jews, Christians, Muslims, and Mormons can't agree on which installment is the purest form of God's word. In fact, they commonly reject the other installments, and have come to blows to defend their sacred books. And they pile on tons of slick excuses to explain away the countless errors, contradictions and moral horrors in these books.

Problem IV: Theologians have been speculating and guessing about God forever, but precious little consistency has been achieved in what they work out God to be and what he expects–and what he's like. Prayer and worship are commonly added to the mix–but wait, how can it be than a supremely good, all-powerful, all-knowing God has to hear prayers to find out what's going on and determine what to do? Why would God crave praise and worship, and welcome subservience? All of the "wonderful" attributes of God claimed by believers add up to a big mess. And theologians have been hard at work for centuries to explain away the contradictions, inconsistencies, absurdities, and blatant silliness.

Problem V: The portraits of "the one true God" offered by Judaism, Christianity, Islam, and Mormonism differ substantially, and in some cases, radically. So which God is it? Who has corned the truth? Has *anyone* cornered the truth? Christians cannot retreat to the safe-haven of the superior Christian option, because there are now more than 31,000 different brands of Christianity: No one agrees on who's right about God. Yet people are confident that the version of the faith that they were born into–or that they shopped around for–is the right faith, and that it will not end up on the scrap heap of history, as have all other religions that have lost popular appeal.

Problem VI: Even a casual reading of the four gospels shows that they fail the test of history. The fantasy and fairy tale aspects predominate, and many different portraits of Jesus can be constructed, depending on which verses you pick and choose. It's especially problematic to penetrate theology and folklore to discern what the original words of Jesus might have been. After a century and a half of intense Jesus scholarship, experts remain stumped: Who was Jesus and what did he say? Yet, as a gesture of respect, congregations rise to their feet to hear the gospels read aloud in church, and people are confident that *they* know what Jesus would do.

Problem VII: Resurrection is a concept borrowed from pagan antiquity, rooted ultimately in the deep craving of humans for rescue from death. Resurrection folklore was grafted onto the story of Jesus, with no precedent whatever based on the Old Testament. The gospel stories of Jesus' resurrection are clumsy and contradictory, and end with the lie that the body of Jesus floated away to heaven, out of sight through the clouds. The party line of the church is that this particular resurrection, defying all reason and logic, provides the magic to guarantee that those who believe in it will be granted eternal life: this is a regression to the age-old gimmick, "Hey, wanna get out of dying?"

Problem VIII: From primitive eras of the human experience, sacrificing the blood of animals–offering their lives upon the altars–was a way to appease the anger of gods or simply to get on their good sides. This degrading religion was practiced at the time of Jesus in the Jerusalem Temple, and the grotesque theology behind it found safe harbor in the New Testament belief that God was no longer content with animal sacrifice. He had decreed that a human sacrifice, his own son, was now the only fit offering. Astonishingly, Christians are not fazed by this barbarity, but welcome and celebrate it.

Problem IX: Even if all the overblown theology about Jesus is devalued and discounted–maybe we can just chuck all the stuff about virgin birth, son of god, and resurrection–people are determined to overcompensate for the loss and rush to affirm that Jesus was a supremely good human being, a magnificent preacher who set the moral compass for humanity. Yet the gospels do *not* bear this out: They display

Jesus as a deeply flawed character who recommended hatred of family and whose expectations about a soon-to-dawn Kingdom of God were delusional. He doesn't get a high rating for many of his moral teachings. His reputation is based on highly selective recitations of texts, yet he is proclaimed the Prince of Peace, the Son of God.

Problem X: Paul's letters ended up as a major chunk of the New Testament and he is the hero of the Book of Acts. After Jesus, he is the most prominent star in the Christian firmament, and his stature has been affirmed by Christian fawning for two millennia. Yet he was wrong about almost everything. He never met Jesus and had no interest whatever in what the Galilean preacher had said and done. Jesus did not return in his lifetime as Paul assured everyone; Paul's teachings about marriage are a joke; he urged that all government leaders have been appointed by God; and he preached obsessively about a magic formula—"just believe in the Risen Christ"—to win a seat in heaven.

Why Don't Christians See Through It?

One of the iconic images of American religious life is that of the preacher shaking hands with parishioners as they leave church. Traditionally he (sometimes *she*) has preached from an elevated pulpit: The ordained pastor—a specialist in spiritual matters, supposedly—has given the word from on high. Religion has thrived on the concept of *authority*, and worship is the practice of channeling the grand source of authority.

Why can't there be an alternative iconic image? We might all be better off if the preacher welcomed the parishioners as they *enter* the church, giving them this advisory:

- Please question everything I say, because I am a paid propagandist.
- Get on your iPhones during the sermon and fact check my statements. We've installed WiFi to make it easy for you to do that.
- Listen carefully to the words in the creeds, liturgies and hymns; ask yourself if they make sense. Even if they can't all be understood literally, do they at least *make sense*?

Of course this alternate image will never be put into practice, because that's not the way religion works. Maybe the preacher even sees through what he's saying and is scared to death that parishioners will notice the flaws as well. Hence the plea of priests and preachers, who have their turfs and livelihoods to protect, has always been: *Just have faith*, muster the faith that can move mountains (as Jesus mindlessly urged), which, of course, is meant to discourage critical thinking. The more something doesn't make sense, the more faith is pushed as the solution, the antidote. This approach has been the primary derailer of the honest evaluation of religious claims and the preserver of faith.

As well as the alternate image of the preacher encouraging suspicions and doubt, we might suggest as well that the liturgy be revised: For each of the Ten Tough Problems, there could be five weeks of biblical reading that demonstrate it. During this time, the embarrassing Bible texts would be cherry picked for reading aloud, instead of the feel-good texts that everyone loves. We would throw in quotes from secular thinkers and Bible scholars who don't sugarcoat things. So that's five weeks of readings for each of the Ten Tough Problems–50 weeks of revised liturgy–with two weeks left over to hear guest sermons by devout Muslim and Jewish theists who can explain how Christianity has it all wrong. What a liturgical year that would be!

But of course it won't happen because church services push the party line. The church has never been on the quest for truth–it already *owns* the truth–and it's gotten its nose bloodied when serious thinkers and scientists have shown when it is just plain wrong.

That's never lessened the church's confidence that it nailed the truth long ago. Its truth has been sealed against inquiry and criticism. Within the walls of the fortress or the cushioned megachurches, tampering with doctrine and dogma *just isn't done*. The crimes of heresy and blasphemy were invented to punish and humiliate those who are too curious and ask too many questions.

Religion is rampant on the planet, and the well-nigh universal willingness to forsake due diligence regarding religious claims doesn't speak well for the human condition or the human capacity to grapple with irrationality. John Loftus has written so eloquently and so abundantly about the failure of devout people to apply the *Outsider Test of Faith*. You may have a bunch of reasons to reject other faiths–you willingly flush away other versions of monotheism, other versions of Christianity–but if you applied those same standards to your *own* faith, why shouldn't it be flushed as well?

But there may be an even greater outside test than this, one that we would most certainly fail. If there are higher intelligences looking down on us–on the human species, that is–how would we rate? And I mean *real* higher intelligences, not deities imagined in heavenly realms.

There is a very real heavenly realm, of course, as revealed by optical and radio telescopes. It is far more interesting and invested with possibility than the heaven that has emerged from overheated religious imaginations. We suspect that there may be real minds "out there." They are the objects of our curiosity, far more so than the supposed Mind of God.

Our Reputation in the Galaxy

A Thought Experiment

There must the thousands of advanced civilizations sprinkled throughout our Milky Way Galaxy, right? Those who grew up watching *Star Trek* or *Star Wars* have no trouble whatever assuming that the Cosmos is teeming with civilizations that would make us look like amateurs. How could it not be? There are hundreds of billions of stars in our galaxy, each with dozens of planets. Just do the numbers. After all, Percival Lowell and H.G. Wells imagined another clever race of beings right here in our own Solar System.

Our galaxy alone has at least a hundred billion stars, and probably just as many other Solar Systems. And our galaxy is just one tiny neighborhood of the Cosmos. The next time you have a clear view of the night sky, take a look at the Big Dipper, especially the "cup" of the dipper. With binoculars, you might see a few sparkling stars. But with a mammoth telescope, it's a far different story, and we are very privileged to live in the Age of Mammoth Telescopes. We have been allowed to glimpse wonders *for first time* in the history of our species. In December 1995 the Hubble Deep Field Survey moved humanity closer to an appreciation of the scope of the Cosmos. In a patch of sky even smaller than the "cup" of the Big Dipper, astronomers counted a *million* galaxies.

The hard truth, however, is that we don't *know* that there are other civilizations. So far, it is human imagination alone that has supplied all the details about aliens and exotic travel routes among the stars.

Among serious scientists and science fiction writers as well, there has been a lot of speculation. Could we actually be alone? *Are* we alone?

The SETI Program (the **S**earch for **E**xtra**t**errestrial **I**ntelligence) has been scanning the heavens for decades, looking and listening for signals that could not have been generated by natural phenomena. We're looking for real, live signal-senders. But so far: zero, zip. This lack of any hint of alien communication is called the Fermi Paradox, named after physicist Enrico Fermi, who was one of the first to pose the question, "Where is everybody?"

One of the first real stabs at figuring the odds of having cosmic neighbors was proposed in 1961 by astronomer Frank Drake. The Drake Equation is a good thought experiment, designed to help calculate how many other "thinking worlds" there could be, but there are too many missing numbers to make it work for the foreseeable future. For example, one of the first numbers in the Drake Equation is: How many stars have planetary systems? Thanks to the Kepler Spacecraft, we've actually made a lot of progress on that number in recent years, and it would appear that planets are a byproduct of star formation. So there must be gazillions of them.

The major imponderable that follows is this: How many solar systems have planets that could harbor life? We're still stumped there as well. There's just so little data to fill in the variables of the famous Drake Equation for determining that number.

$$N = R \cdot f_p \cdot N_e \cdot f_l \cdot f_i \cdot f_c \cdot L$$

N   The number of civilizations in our galaxy with which communication might be possible (i.e. which are on our current past light cone).

R   The average rate of star formation in our galaxy.

f_p The fraction of those stars that have planets.

N_e The average number of planets that can potentially support life per star that has planets.

f_l The fraction of planets that could support life that actually develop life at some point.

f_i The fraction of planets with life that actually go on to develop intelligent life (civilizations).

f_c The fraction of civilizations that develop a technology that releases detectable signs of their existence into space.

L   The length of time for which such civilizations release detectable signals into space.[6]

Of course, life could have arisen on countless planets, but perhaps, in the vast majority of cases, it might be life only on the microbial level. These would be mute neighbors. As one SETI specialist once remarked, it would not be all that satisfying to discover that most other life in the Cosmos is the equivalent of pond scum. There could be billions of life-bearing planets with nothing thriving above the microbial level for millions of eons. That was the case on Earth, after all. What we'd love to find are creatures we could talk to and compare notes with (hypothetically, even if we detected some, since the delays are huge even for radio transmissions.)

So we hold out hope that life could have evolved to produce creatures with major brains, capable of language and discovery. How many of those are there? That is another number in the Drake Equation. In our case, humans plodded along for perhaps 200,000 years before technology was achieved, at the level of science as we know it today. It is only within the last couple of centuries that humans figured out photography, spectrography, radio, flight, space travel, the nature of the atom.

But how long do civilizations that achieve these technologies *survive*? It's possible that very curious creatures elsewhere also have discovered the secret of the atom. Do most civilizations learn to live with that knowledge over the long haul, or do they blow themselves up? How many advanced civilizations manage to stay alive?

The jury is still out on the fate of the Earth, by the way.[7] We had a very close call with nuclear Armageddon in the 1960s, and we are by no means out of the woods. Humans are fond of warfare, and one of the first things we did after the discovery of nuclear energy was build atomic bombs and drop two of them on civilian populations. We "had our reasons," of course, but these actions don't speak well for our sensibilities as a species, or our ultimate survivability. We have made it for 70 years since then without a repeat, but the nuclear arsenals remain massive, in the hands of governments guided by suspicions, hatreds and—in too many cases—religious fervor. Terrorists may soon have the bomb as well. Is it realistic to assume that humans will be able to live an appreciable time after we gained knowledge of the atom?

Hence the final figure on the Drake Equation is this: the number of years that civilizations survive after they've learned to send out signals to alert the galaxy, "We're here!" Very few may survive to receive a reply. We may be more alone than we imagine, certainly more alone than science fiction enthusiasts like to admit.

But we do hope that there are lots of thinking creatures "out there." And if we could get a dialogue going somehow, certainly one of the topics on the table ought to be *theology*. We might get laughed at, but since the topic looms so large in the human psyche, we could hardly pretend it isn't one of humanity's major preoccupations. Way back when I was in seminary, when I wrote that cheeky essay "On the Improbability of God" (described in the Prologue), I argued that theologians have a lot of nerve making confident statements about God. We've not heard the opinions of other thinkers who may have been pondering the Cosmos far, far longer than we have.

Would Our Near Neighbors Even Chat Us Up?

The Andromeda Galaxy is about 2.5 million light years away, which means if we ever detect a signal from there–a signal clearly generated by thinkers, with messages we could somehow decipher–it would be disheartening. The Andromeda civilization that sent the signals 2.5 million years ago would probably be long gone, and our reply would take 2.5 million years to get back.

So let's look for neighbors closer to home, in our own galaxy. The Milky Way has a diameter of about 100,000 light years, so even that is too daunting. Our Sun, at the heart of our solar system, is located in the Sagittarius Arm of the galaxy, one of the major arms of the majestic spiral as seen from above. All of the millions of stars in this arm move along in their orbits of the galactic center, each orbit taking about 225 million years. (The Sun is not fixed in space, anymore than Earth is.) But how many stars are actually close to our Sun, "close" in astronomical terms? The nearest star to us is 4.5 lights years away.[8]

Imagine that our Sun is at the center of an imaginary bubble stretching 500 light years in all directions (1,000 light years in diameter). By some estimates there could be 2-3 million stars in that bubble. If we go with the lower number, and guess (or hope) that even one in a thousand of those stars have planets with space-faring civilizations–think *Star Trek* or *Stars Wars*–we could have 200 neighbors "in the bubble" who have been contemplating the Cosmos, at a sophisticated level of science, aeons longer than we have been. *These* are the tutors I want.[9]

I would gladly sign up for their Cosmology 101 courses. We need input from thinkers who have broken *their* isolation in the Cosmos, who have found a way to compare notes with others in their galactic neighborhood, who have been probing and analyzing the "moment of creation"–figuring the physics, doing the math–hundreds of times longer that we have. The thinkers we want to hear have moved well beyond the levels of naiveté and ignorance that hobble human thought, realizing that figuring out creation is not a *spiritual* matter. The theologians who, in the absence of evidence-based epistemology, have subjected us to babbling and chattering about gods for millennia, should not write another word, should offer no more speculations, until we've had this chat with our neighbors. Dead silence from the seminaries for a few hundred years would be a welcome relief.

We know that alien civilizations within a hundred light years or so of Earth could already be picking up our broadcast signals; reruns of *I Love Lucy* and a billions other artifacts of human culture are streaming outward. But we could be aiming a few SOS's to potential neighbors in our space bubble: a clear and urgent appeal that *we need help figuring this out.*

Frankly–and this truly is the bottom line–all of the "Our Father who art in heaven" chants are worthless, until we've heard from other thinkers in the Cosmos. We want to hear some news from a few awesome intellects elsewhere in our space bubble, those with huge head starts. We might be told, "Yes, these are the experiments we've done, the tests we have applied, and Yes, there is a god, and Yes, this is how it functions." *Then*, and *only* then, will we be getting somewhere.

But would these awesome intellects want to talk with *us*? Of course, a lot depends on what these older civilizations might be like. Would they be interested in conversation or conquest? For the purposes of this thought experiment, however, let's assume that they are benevolent, and truly want to get to know us.

Maybe they've achieved a level of intelligence to take a galactic census, assembling an almanac of the millions of planets scattered across the light years. At some point, perhaps a million years ago, or 50,000, our planet was tagged for monitoring. Life was discovered thriving on our pale blue dot, and they're curious about how it turned out on this planet. So there's a file on us.

Could there be some truth in the H.G. Wells novel? "We know now that in the early years of the twentieth century this world was being watched closely by intelligences greater than man's." Would they come calling?

The Martians Were Sorry They Came Here

The great plot twist in *War of the Worlds* was that the Martians invaders proved to be no match for earthly microbes. They could easily smash people and infrastructures, but they succumbed to disease. This also happens to be the major plot flaw of the novel, because aliens who are smart enough to have mastered planet-hopping would have worked out that microbes on other planets could be deadly. So get your shots first—invent the shots, actually—or stay away.

Are there other reasons, besides our microbes, that space travelers from afar would not come calling on Planet Earth? Perhaps they know too much about us. If they've been monitoring our nightly news broadcasts and watching our movies (R-rated for frontal nudity and curse words, but not for guns and bloodshed), they would realize our capacity for stupidity, and would know for sure if they landed here they'd get shot, notwithstanding the romanticized ending of *Close Encounters of the Third Kind*.

If we have been "watched by intelligences greater than ours" for a few millennia, it would be clear that evolution on this planet dealt us a bad hand: Humans are an incurably violent species. Territoriality and savagery have been wired into our brains.

It takes a lot of socialization for us to be able to get along. Perhaps sticks and stones were our first weapons, followed quickly by the slingshot, and human ingenuity has been applied with fervor to the improvement of weaponry ever since. And we can't get enough of war; we specialize in killing one another for territory, economic advantage, ideology, and religions.

What's next on the list of human failings? I don't think it's just atheist bias to argue that, surely, the human obsession with religion—as we practice it—would be off-putting to creatures with better brains. Since we know zero about alien geniuses, it would be presumptuous to assume that they are atheists, but we can suspect that one of their critiques would be that, here on Earth, we have bungled religion *horribly* and put it to the worst possible uses. We know that ourselves.

They might be amazed that, isolated as we are in the Cosmos, we insist on specific god-ideas with such fanaticism, and are not bothered by the swarms of contradictions and the lack of verification. We have bungled religion because we *can't get it right*. Wouldn't aliens notice this? Humans have invented so many religions, without much thought about finding evidence to back them up—or settling for "evidence" that fails ordinary standards of logic and common sense. We fight fiercely over the products of speculation and fantasy, and do so with the darkest of motivations.

Nor is it farfetched that alien geniuses would be dumbfounded that humans put so much time and energy into religion, at the expense of so many other pursuits that could improve the human condition. Let's suppose—although, as an atheist I think this a stretch—that other thinkers in the Cosmos, armed with scientific tools unknown to us yet, have pierced the ultimate mystery and discovered a Force that ignited everything.

The odds are overwhelming that the Force will bear no resemblance whatever to gods imagined in ancient human scriptures. I'm pretty sure our alien superiors would be stumped: Where did mammals on one isolated planet get the idea that the Force craves praise and worship? And that it has a way to detect their inner thoughts? *Prayer* could be considered the silliest religious practice. Praise, worship and prayers directed at gods are the most naïve vestiges of naïve religions that emerged when gods were thought to be close overhead. As Han Solo said in the 2015 *Star Wars: The Force Awakens*, "That's *not* how the Force works!"

This is *bungled religion*, and the roots of Christianity are precisely in the naïve guesses of primitive humans. Why do these Earthlings waste so much of their time on this stuff? Aliens may say, "It's exhausting to watch humans chase foolishness and nonsense—when there are so many better things to do." At least one theologian that I know of, Uta Ranke-Heinemann, has dared to cast thoughts in this direction: "Unbelievers are luckier, since they can spend their time on more useful things."[10]

Tragically, however, we deserve even more demerits: Religion's complicity with violence—all the while bragging about love, peace, and compassion—is its greatest unforgivable sin. It warrants giving Earth a failing grade as a destination for space explorers. Religionists claim that violence is not the whole story, but it is too much of the story."Think of all the good deeds we do" has a hollow ring to it, when we know very well that people can be motivated to do good deeds without gods looking over their shoulders. Haven't we seen that, on balance, religion has done far more damage than good? Christopher Hitchens claimed that religion poisons everything, and we are entitled to wonder if that is an overstatement. However, read Hitchens's book if you protest too much, if you assume that he exaggerates. It's a stunner.[11]

Religion urges certainty. After all, it loses steam if it fails to claim that it has a lock on the One Truth Faith. Certainty breeds arrogance, which in turn feeds an enforcer mentality: our way or else. Unspeakable violence has been the consequence, and the catalogue of Christian brutality to enforce the faith can fill volumes. Shame on it. We can despair about the ghastly reputation that Christianity and others religions have brought to Planet Earth, if there is anyone "out there" keeping tabs on us.

Beings much wiser than we are (let's also assume they're also more benevolent) who monitor worlds that have made the jump to technological sophistication may say, "Leave that little planet alone. Those folks seem unable to get beyond their attachment to gods and their willingness to fight ferociously on their behalf. It's a very sorry addiction. There's not much point in welcoming them to the galactic community. We know that they're not likely to survive much longer."

———

I'll give the last word to the lead character in Dorothy Sayers's mystery novel *Whose Body?*, who speaks a truth that the world should learn to live by."I don't think you ought to read so much theology," said Lord Peter."It has a brutalizing influence."

Notes

1. Photo: Edwin A. Suominen

2. Matt Herndon, "Goodbye, God? My Favorite Theology Professor Became an Atheist. Will I?", mattherndon.net/blog-1.

3. Victor Stenger, "The Folly of Faith: The Incompatibility of Science and Christianity," in John Loftus, ed., *Christianity Is Not Great: How Faith Fails* (Prometheus, 2014), p.64.

4. Photo: NASA.

5. Stenger at pp. 58-59.

6. Copied verbatim from en.wikipedia.org/wiki/Drake_equation, Creative Commons licensed.

7. A book of that title on the consequences of nuclear war remains a classic: Jonathan Schell, *The Fate of the Earth* (Knopf, 1982).

8. Actually a triple-star system. As mentioned in an earlier chapter, it would take the Space Shuttle, travelling 18,500 miles per hour, 160,000 years to get there.

9. Even 200 is highly unlikely–wildly optimistic–but remember, this is a thought experiment.

10. Uta Ranke-Heinemann, *Putting Away Childish Things*, p. 70.

11. Christopher Hitchens, *God Is Not Great*.

Acknowledgements

I cannot guarantee that no believers were harmed during the making of this book, because I do not know the religious beliefs of all of the people whom I wish to thank for being my cheerleaders and critical readers. These are the folks who were equal to the task of pointing out my mistakes or telling me to tone it down; of course, all the errors or misjudgments that remain in this book are my fault alone.

I owe a lot to Aubrey Adrianson, Sylvia Allen, Jane Everhart, Gail Fletcher, Willie Fuchs, Elizabeth Gordon, Luis Granados, Claire Jacobs, Bennett Kremen, Krisula Gosdis Moyer, Tom Rafferty, Rick Raubenheimer, Ruth Robbins, Carolyn Shadle, Larry Shaw, Michael Sweeney, Harry White, and Scott Wilson.

"There's nothing to writing," Red Smith once said."All you do is sit down at a typewriter, open your veins and bleed." The words do trickle out, or–if you're lucky–flow onto the page, and authors commonly view each paragraph as a priceless achievement. It is the editor's role, however, to provide a critical eye and the scissors. It has been my great privilege to work with Ed Suominen of Tellectual Press, who knew where to trim and enhance, and–having escaped from Christianity himself–did not try to dampen my ridicule and sarcasm. He helped sharpen my knife, in fact. Ed is handing to you, dear reader, a better book than I handed to him.

Dr. David Orenstein has been a constant source of encouragement, and it was an honor to be interviewed for his book, *Godless Grace: How Nonbelievers Are Making the World Safer, Richer and Kinder*. David is the founder of The Godless Grace Foundation.

Chris Johnson, photographer and documentary maker, has been a part of a small band of atheists who meet as the Secular Board of Advisors. We get together to offer encouragement and brainstorming, to set short and long-term goals on our various projects for the atheist cause. I have appreciated his input and suggestions, and we all should appreciate his phenomenal work and tireless efforts. He wrote the stunning large-format book, *A Better Life: 100 Atheists Speak Out on Joy & Meaning in a World Without God*, and created the accompanying video. These days Chris travels the world to show the film.

Michael Trollan is the founder of the Secular Board of Advisors, and invited me to be one of the original members. His advice and guidance over the years have been invaluable; he is one of the most precise thinkers I have ever come across. He created the website SecularAction.org to enable anyone, anywhere, to get involved, and is the incoming president of The Secular Coalition for America. Michael has helped in so many ways, including the creation of this book's website, TenToughProblems.com. I have never seen Michael in a bad mood, and he merits his reputation for being a hell of a nice guy.

Finally: My husband, David Pandozzi, has endured the many hours that I've had to hunker down alone at my laptop, in so many locations, to write. But he has also pulled me back to our shared life to get us out for walks, movies and Broadway theatre–his passion. Many years ago he introduced me to Paris, and our love affair with that city has enriched our lives immeasurably.

Further Reading

Other titles available from Tellectual Press

Now that you've finished David Madison's *Ten Tough Problems*, here are some other titles you may wish to consider from Tellectual Press (**tellectual.com**):

For more about Jesus' failings that Dr. Madison covers in Tough Problem IX, see a book he cites: Dr. Robert M. Price's **Blaming Jesus for Jehovah**. There, having his loins girt with a lifelong regard for rational truth, wearing the breastplate of former fundamentalism and the helmet of biblical scholarship, Dr. Price does some bomb squad investigation around the deadly and hidden charge lurking under the moral foundations of Christianity.

In **Evolving out of Eden**, Dr. Price and co-author Edwin A. Suominen delve further into nature's "reign of terror" that David touches on in Tough Problem Chapter I. They criticize John Haught's airy theology (see David's Tough Problem II), as well as the Bible's lack of revelation about anything scientifically useful (Tough Problem III). Writing with the combination of high criticism and low humor that fans have come to love from Dr. Price, they survey the apologetic landscape and offer a frank reckoning of evolution's significance for Christian belief. Religion originally provided the explanation for everything, they say in the book's concluding chapter, but now *it* is what requires so much explaining from its frustrated adherents.

In his Tough Problem VI, David shows why we should be skeptical about the gospels' claims of a Historical Jesus. That is a skepticism shared, indeed championed, by Dr. Price, who also applies it to another biblical figure in **Moses and Minimalism**. The saga of Moses the Lawgiver, Price says, is a mighty oak that has grown strong and thick through the centuries from an acorn of information found in the first five books of the Bible. But even the biblical Moses was the product of earlier stories, assembled by an unnamed, undated compiler.

For a bit of Bible-based fiction, check out Murray Sheehan's beautiful literary novel on the Garden of Eden story, **Eden**, originally published in 1928. It's a great retelling of the Genesis human-origins story, wonderfully written and still very engaging to read nearly a century later. The Tellectual Press reprint includes an Introduction by Dr. Price and Edwin A. Suominen.

———

Each of these titles is available from Tellectual Press in both print and e-book format.

Index

55658283R00203

Made in the USA
Lexington, KY
29 September 2016